Oyayubi kara Romance

...Touch

HEY...
TELL ME AGAIN, WHERE ARE WE IN THE STORY?
What?!
WE JUST ARRIVED AT THE MASSAGE SCHOOL!!
Please don't forget!!
READ VOL. 4 IN ORDER TO REVIEW THE STORY!

Vol. 5

Story & Art by Izumi Tsubaki

The Magic Touch
Oyayubi kara Romance

Story and Characters Introduction

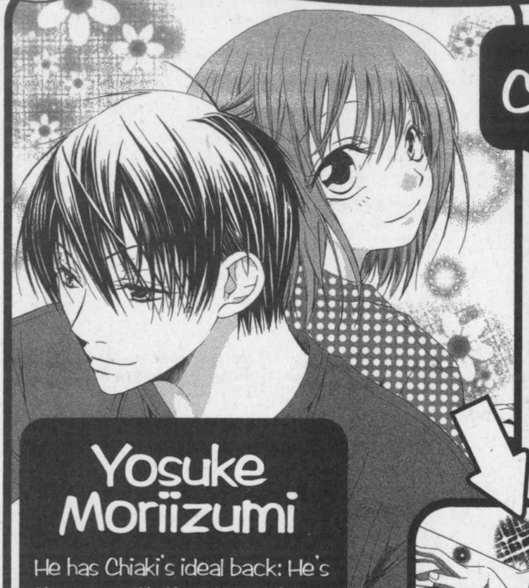

Chiaki Togu

The main character of this story. She's a first-year student in Futouka Academy's Massage Research Club and a rising star in the club.☆ She has an incredible passion and a great talent for massage! But she's normally quiet.

Yosuke Moriizumi

He has Chiaki's ideal back: He's the guy with the stiffest body at Futouka Academy. He's a popular boy with lots of experience with girls. But has Chiaki captured his heart?!

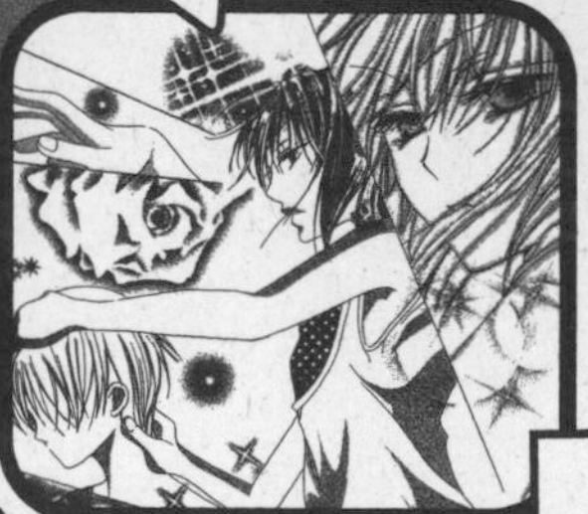

She suddenly changes when she becomes absorbed in massage!

Tsubo

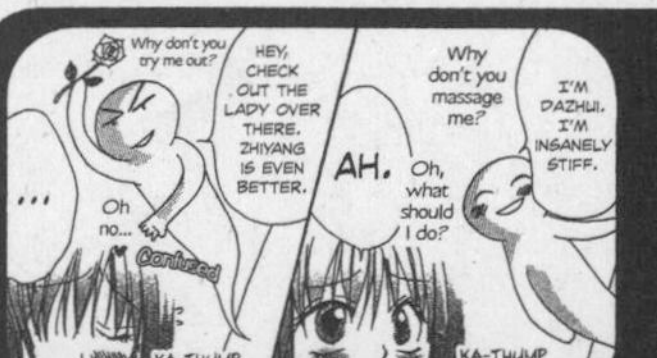
I'M DAZHUI. I'M INSANELY STIFF.
Why don't you massage me?
AH.
Oh, what should I do?
KA-THUMP KA-THUMP
HEY, CHECK OUT THE LADY OVER THERE. ZHIYANG IS EVEN BETTER.
Why don't you try me out?
Oh no...
...
Confused
KA-THUMP KA-THUMP

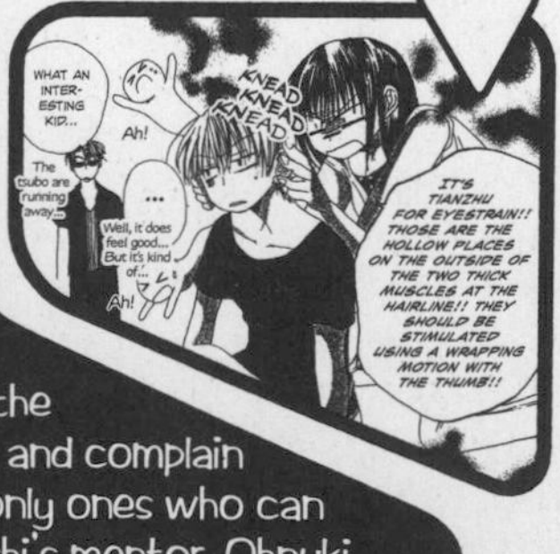
IT'S TIANZHU FOR EYESTRAIN!! THOSE ARE THE HOLLOW PLACES ON THE OUTSIDE OF THE TWO THICK MUSCLES AT THE HAIRLINE!! THEY SHOULD BE STIMULATED USING A WRAPPING MOTION WITH THE THUMB!!
KNEAD KNEAD KNEAD
Ah!
...
Well, it does feel good... But it's kind of...
Ah!
WHAT AN INTERESTING KID...
The tsubo are running away...

And furthermore...

Creatures (?!) that can be seen (maybe) by people who love massage the most. They come out from the tsubo and complain that "it's stiff here."♥ For now, the only ones who can see them are Chiaki, Takeshi and Takeshi's mentor, Ohnuki.

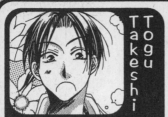

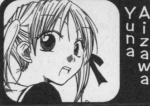

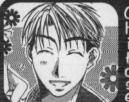

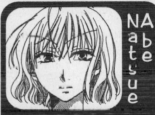

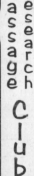

★ Futouka Academy Massage Research Club ★

Aizawa Yuna

Chiaki's friend. She is very competent at massage. She has feelings for Togu Senpai!

Togu Takeshi

Chiaki's brother, who's a year older. He's living with his mentor right now as an apprentice. He's a master at gal games.

Abe Natsue

She's the treasurer for the Massage Research Club. She has a nice body, but she's ruthless when money is involved.

Harumi Chitose

He's the manager of the Massage Research Club. He's normally carefree. His family seems to be rich.

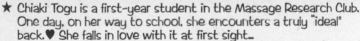

♥ The Story So Far ♥

★ Chiaki Togu is a first-year student in the Massage Research Club. One day, on her way to school, she encounters a truly "ideal" back.♥ She falls in love with it at first sight...

★ When searching for the stiffest back at her school, the person Chiaki finds is Yosuke Moriizumi, the most popular boy at school. In response to Chiaki's pleas to "let me massage your back," he sets one condition: Chiaki must make him fall in love with her!

★ Despite many events and misunderstandings, the two start going out. They make progress, but things are sometimes awkward between Yosuke, a player who has broken many hearts, and Chiaki, who is extremely shy when she's not involved in massage.

★ Chiaki, Yosuke, and Takeshi are invited to visit the massage school run by Takeshi's mentor, Ohnuki. What awaits the three inside the splendid-looking school?!

CONTENTS

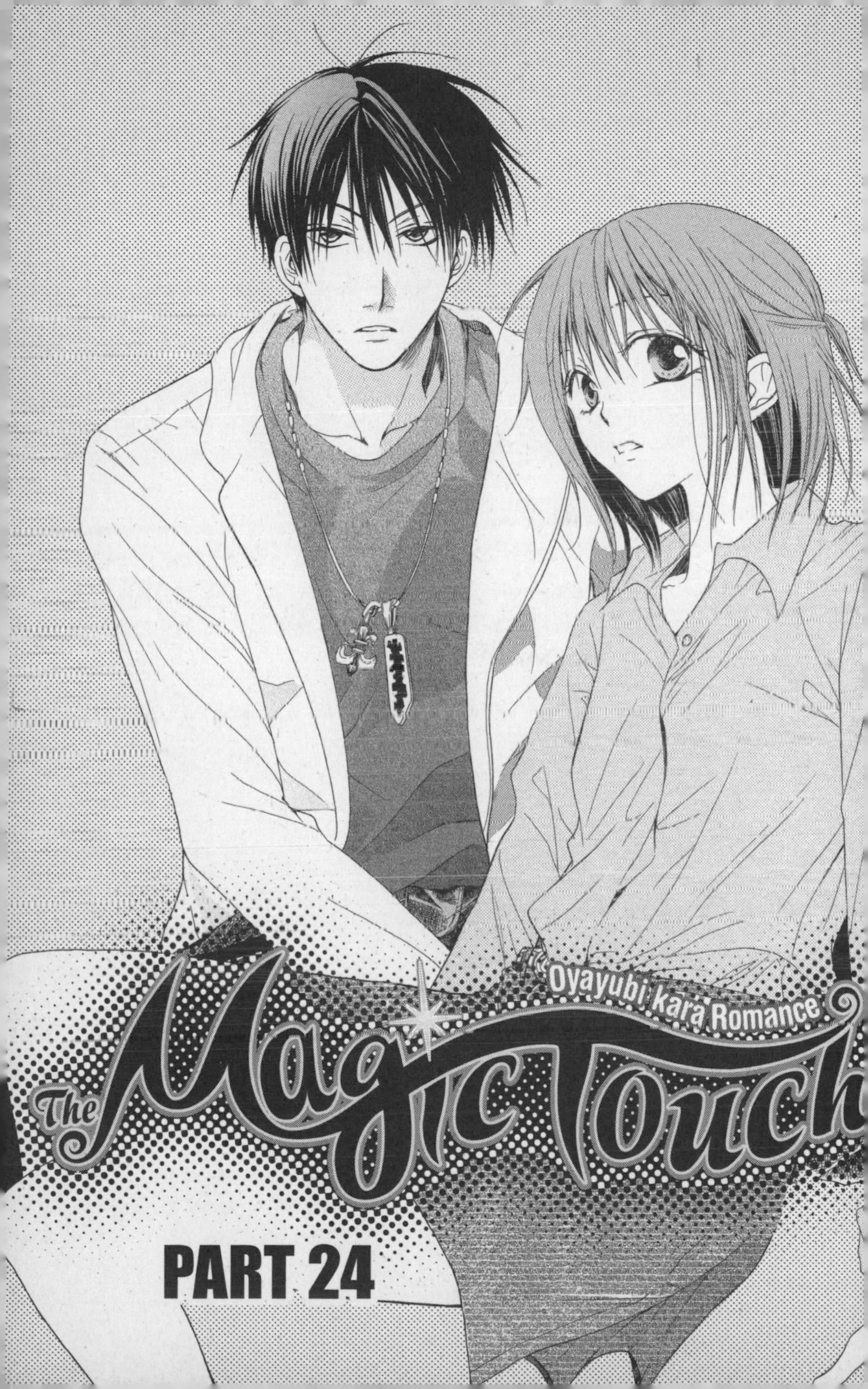
The Magic Touch
Oyayubi kara Romance
PART 24

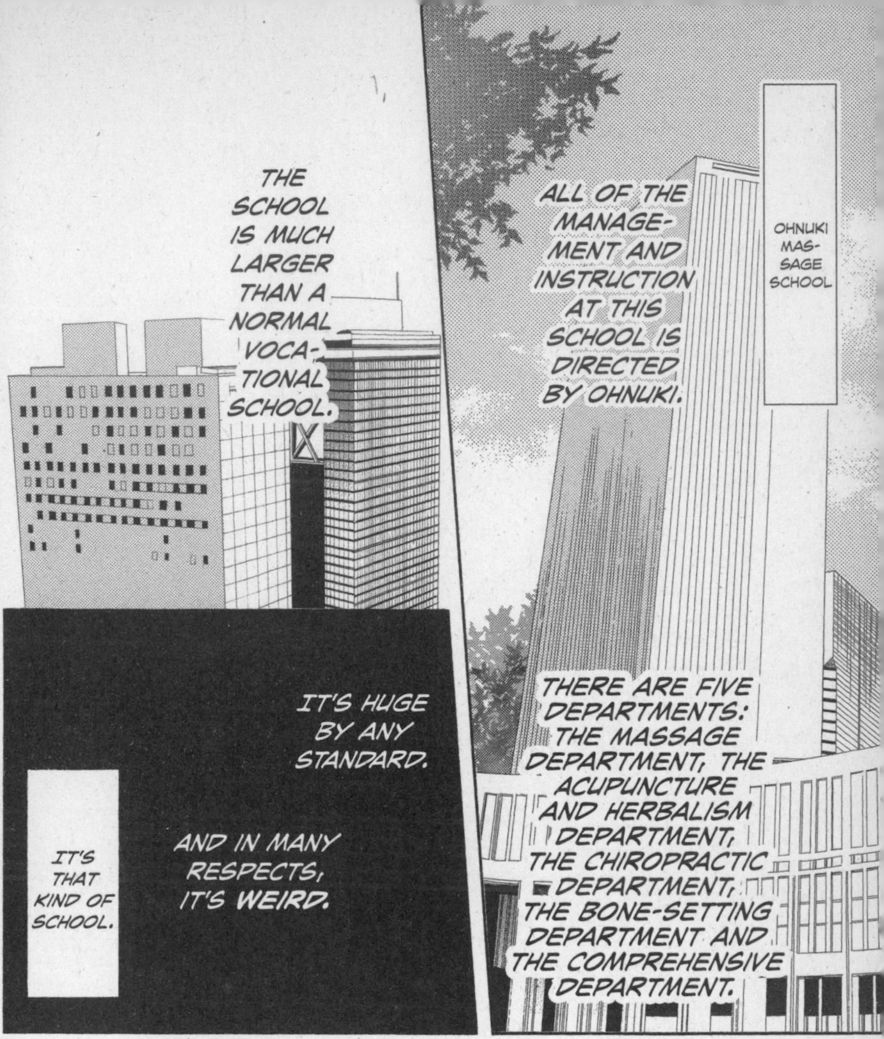
OHNUKI MASSAGE SCHOOL
ALL OF THE MANAGEMENT AND INSTRUCTION AT THIS SCHOOL IS DIRECTED BY OHNUKI.
THERE ARE FIVE DEPARTMENTS: THE MASSAGE DEPARTMENT, THE ACUPUNCTURE AND HERBALISM DEPARTMENT, THE CHIROPRACTIC DEPARTMENT, THE BONE-SETTING DEPARTMENT AND THE COMPREHENSIVE DEPARTMENT.
THE SCHOOL IS MUCH LARGER THAN A NORMAL VOCATIONAL SCHOOL.
IT'S HUGE BY ANY STANDARD.
AND IN MANY RESPECTS, IT'S **WEIRD**.
IT'S THAT KIND OF SCHOOL.

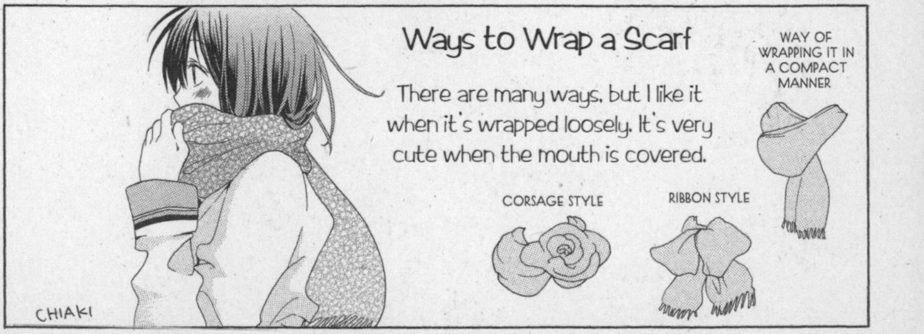
Ways to Wrap a Scarf
There are many ways, but I like it when it's wrapped loosely. It's very cute when the mouth is covered.
WAY OF WRAPPING IT IN A COMPACT MANNER
CORSAGE STYLE
RIBBON STYLE
CHIAKI

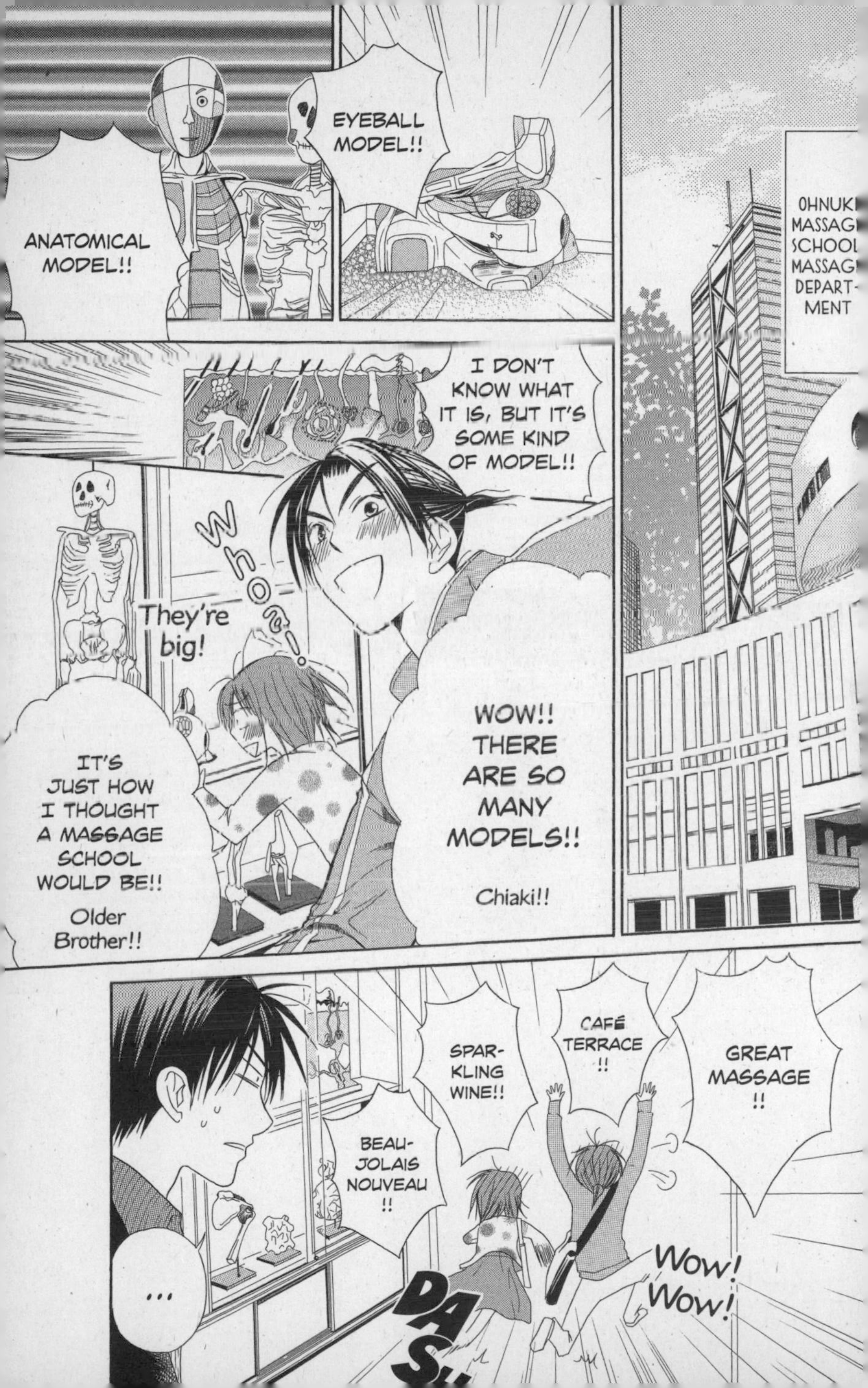
OHNUKI MASSAG SCHOOL MASSAG DEPART-MENT
EYEBALL MODEL!!
ANATOMICAL MODEL!!
I DON'T KNOW WHAT IT IS, BUT IT'S SOME KIND OF MODEL!!
WOW!! THERE ARE SO MANY MODELS!!
Chiaki!!
Whoa!!
They're big!
IT'S JUST HOW I THOUGHT A MASSAGE SCHOOL WOULD BE!!
Older Brother!!
GREAT MASSAGE !!
CAFÉ TERRACE !!
SPAR-KLING WINE!!
BEAU-JOLAIS NOUVEAU !!
Wow! Wow!
DASH
...

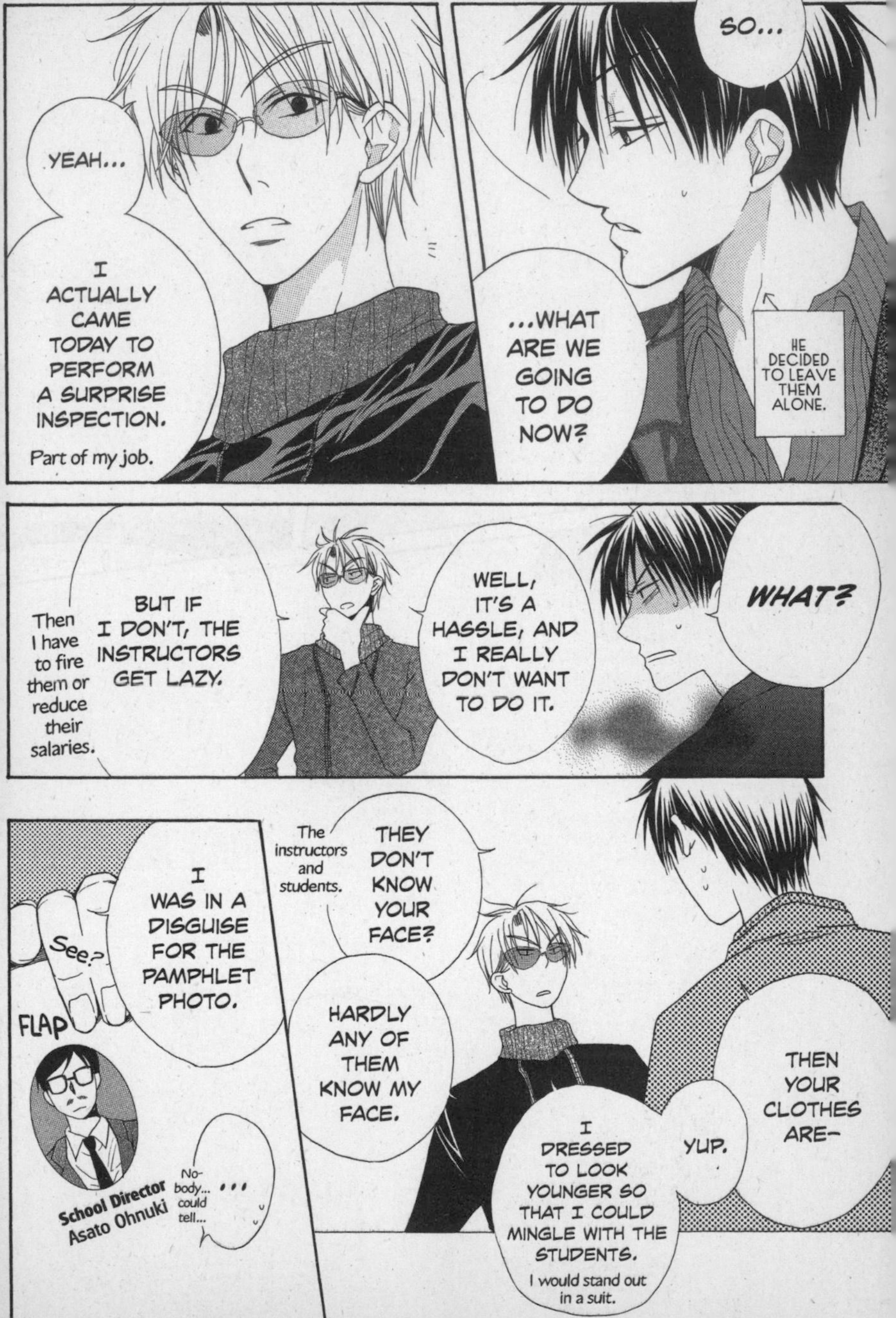
SO...
...WHAT ARE WE GOING TO DO NOW?
HE DECIDED TO LEAVE THEM ALONE.
YEAH...
I ACTUALLY CAME TODAY TO PERFORM A SURPRISE INSPECTION.
Part of my job.
WHAT?
WELL, IT'S A HASSLE, AND I REALLY DON'T WANT TO DO IT.
BUT IF I DON'T, THE INSTRUCTORS GET LAZY.
Then I have to fire them or reduce their salaries.
THEN YOUR CLOTHES ARE–
YUP.
I DRESSED TO LOOK YOUNGER SO THAT I COULD MINGLE WITH THE STUDENTS.
I would stand out in a suit.
THEY DON'T KNOW YOUR FACE?
The instructors and students.
HARDLY ANY OF THEM KNOW MY FACE.
I WAS IN A DISGUISE FOR THE PAMPHLET PHOTO.
See?
FLAP
School Director Asato Ohnuki
...
Nobody... could tell...

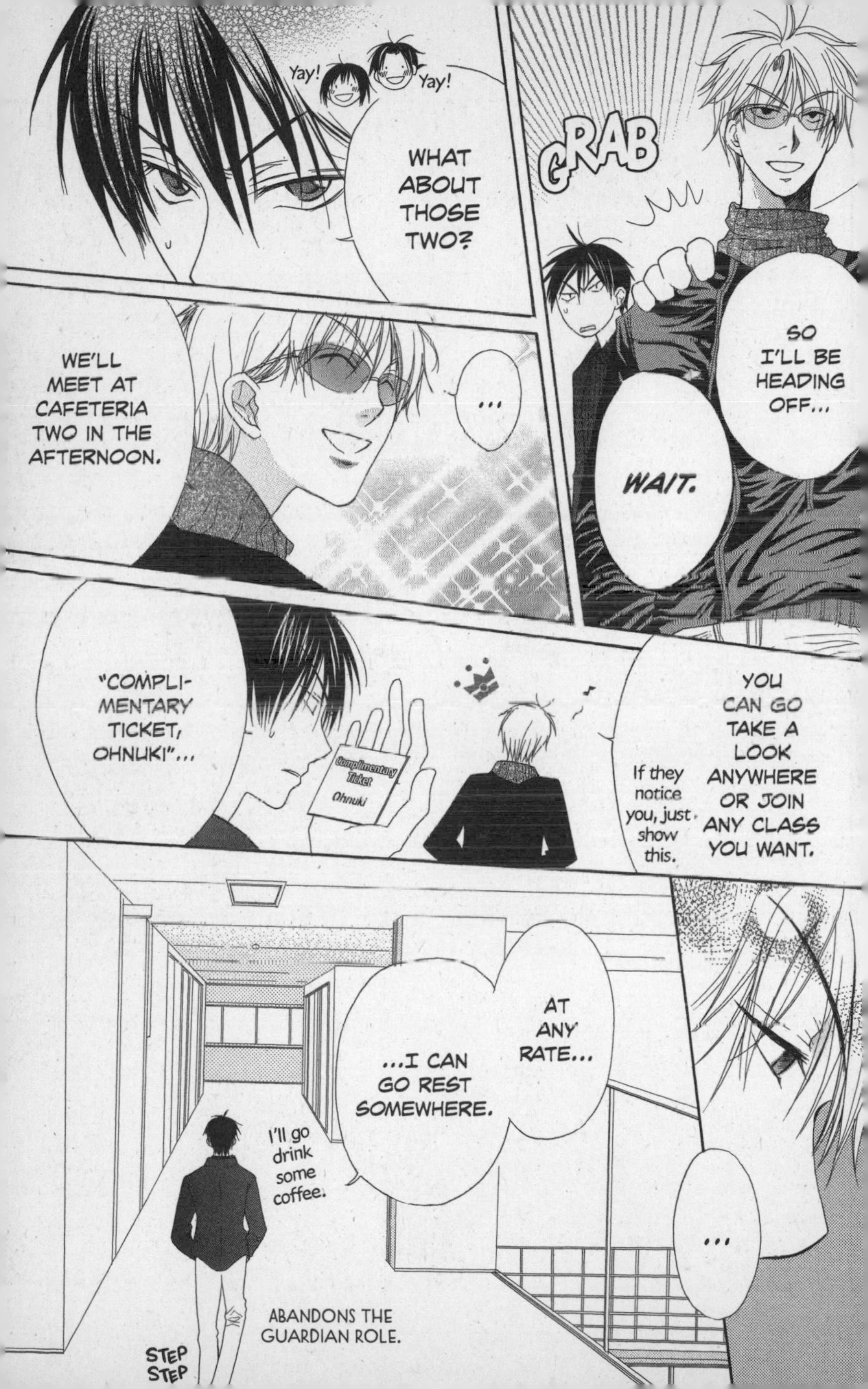
GRAB
SO I'LL BE HEADING OFF...
WAIT.
Yay!
Yay!
WHAT ABOUT THOSE TWO?
...
WE'LL MEET AT CAFETERIA TWO IN THE AFTERNOON.
YOU CAN GO TAKE A LOOK ANYWHERE OR JOIN ANY CLASS YOU WANT.
If they notice you, just show this.
Complimentary Ticket
Ohnuki
"COMPLIMENTARY TICKET, OHNUKI"...
...
AT ANY RATE...
...I CAN GO REST SOMEWHERE.
I'll go drink some coffee.
ABANDONS THE GUARDIAN ROLE.
STEP
STEP

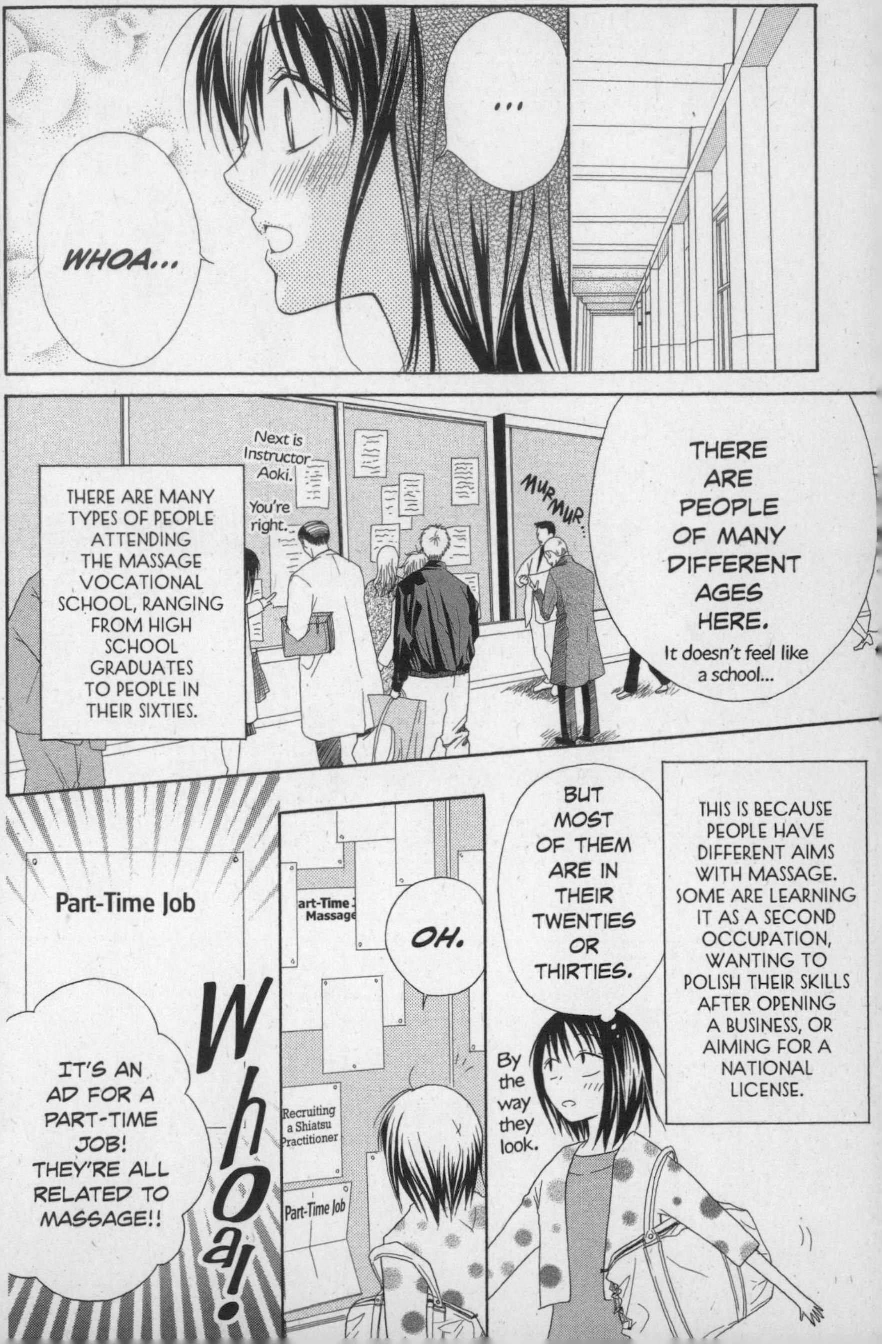
...
WHOA...
THERE ARE PEOPLE OF MANY DIFFERENT AGES HERE.
It doesn't feel like a school...
MURMUR...
Next is Instructor Aoki.
You're right.
THERE ARE MANY TYPES OF PEOPLE ATTENDING THE MASSAGE VOCATIONAL SCHOOL, RANGING FROM HIGH SCHOOL GRADUATES TO PEOPLE IN THEIR SIXTIES.
THIS IS BECAUSE PEOPLE HAVE DIFFERENT AIMS WITH MASSAGE. SOME ARE LEARNING IT AS A SECOND OCCUPATION, WANTING TO POLISH THEIR SKILLS AFTER OPENING A BUSINESS, OR AIMING FOR A NATIONAL LICENSE.
BUT MOST OF THEM ARE IN THEIR TWENTIES OR THIRTIES.
By the way they look.
OH.
Recruiting a Shiatsu Practitioner
Part-Time Job
Whoa!
IT'S AN AD FOR A PART-TIME JOB! THEY'RE ALL RELATED TO MASSAGE!!
Part-Time Job

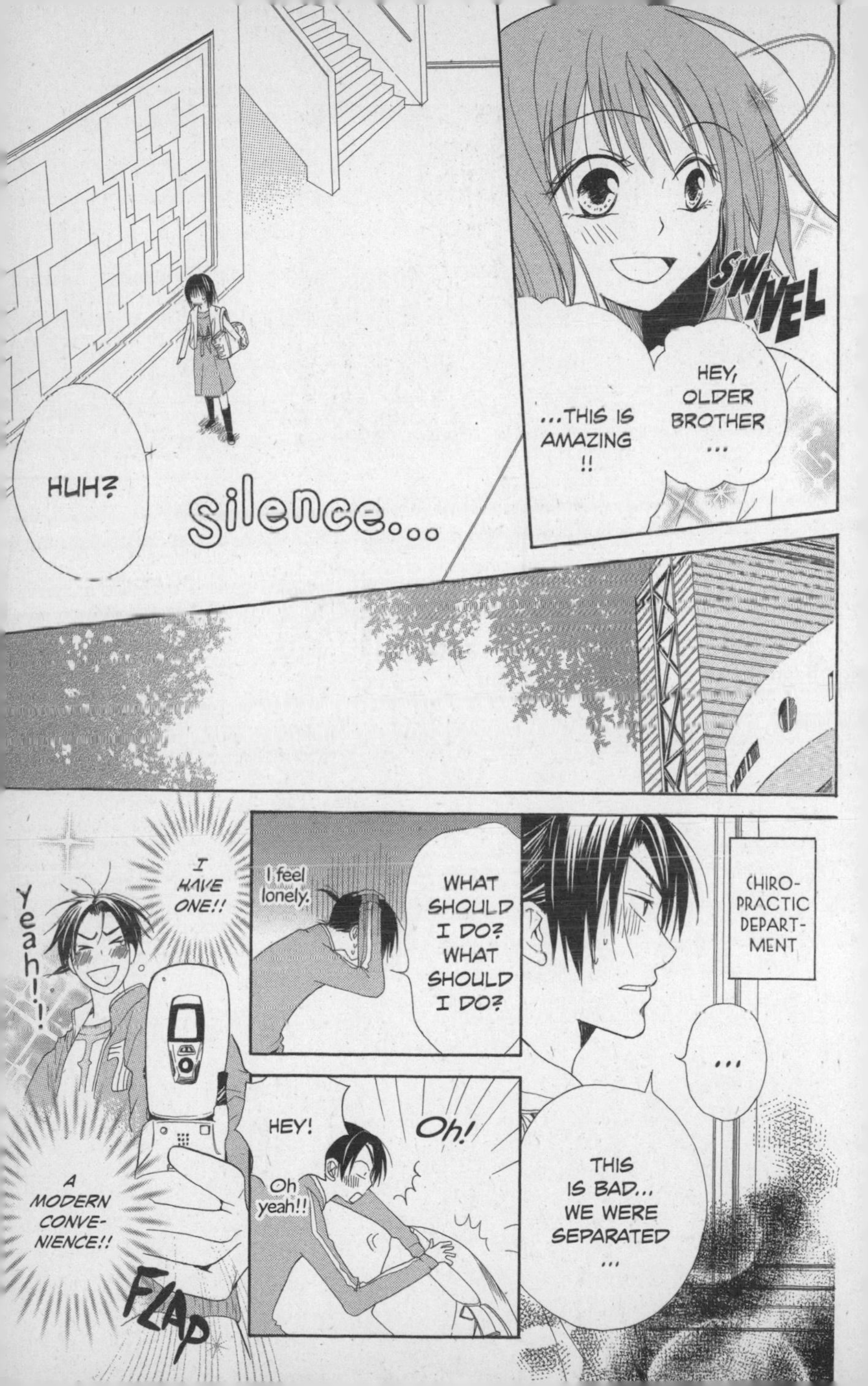
HEY, OLDER BROTHER...
SWIVEL
...THIS IS AMAZING!!
silence...
HUH?
CHIRO-PRACTIC DEPART-MENT
...
THIS IS BAD... WE WERE SEPARATED...
WHAT SHOULD I DO? WHAT SHOULD I DO?
I feel lonely.
Oh!
HEY!
Oh yeah!!
I HAVE ONE!!
Yeah!!
A MODERN CONVE-NIENCE!!
FLAP

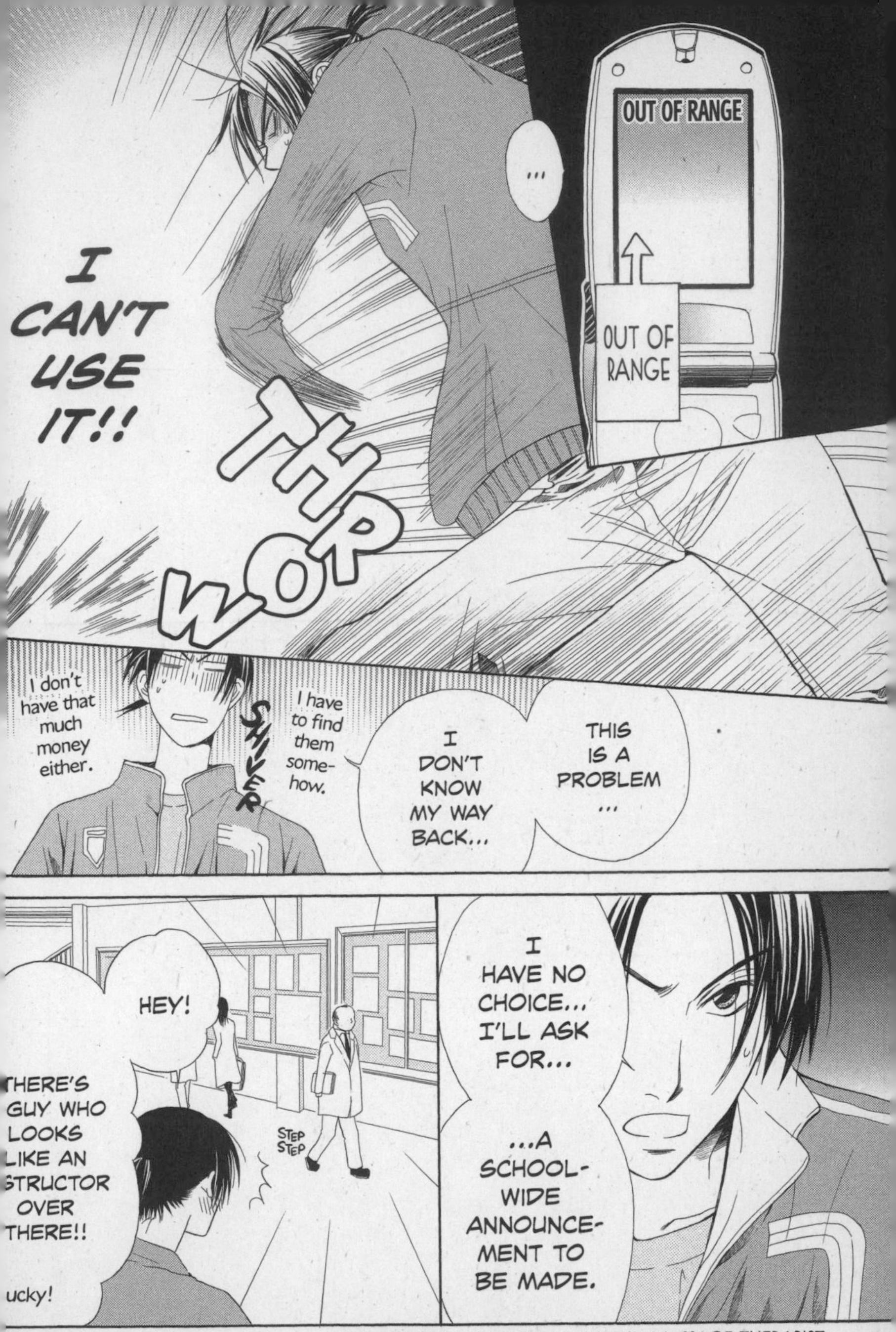
OUT OF RANGE
OUT OF RANGE
...
I CAN'T USE IT!!
THROW
THIS IS A PROBLEM ...
I DON'T KNOW MY WAY BACK...
I have to find them some-how.
SHIVER
I don't have that much money either.
I HAVE NO CHOICE... I'LL ASK FOR...
...A SCHOOL-WIDE ANNOUNCE-MENT TO BE MADE.
HEY!
THERE'S GUY WHO LOOKS LIKE AN STRUCTOR OVER THERE!!
ucky!
STEP STEP

* IN ORDER TO BECOME A SHIATSU MASSAGE THERAPIST, YOU HAVE TO PASS THE SHIATSU MASSEUR EXAM, AND THEN REGISTER WITH THE JAPANESE MINISTER OF HEALTH, LABOR AND WELFARE IN ORDER TO GET A LICENSE.

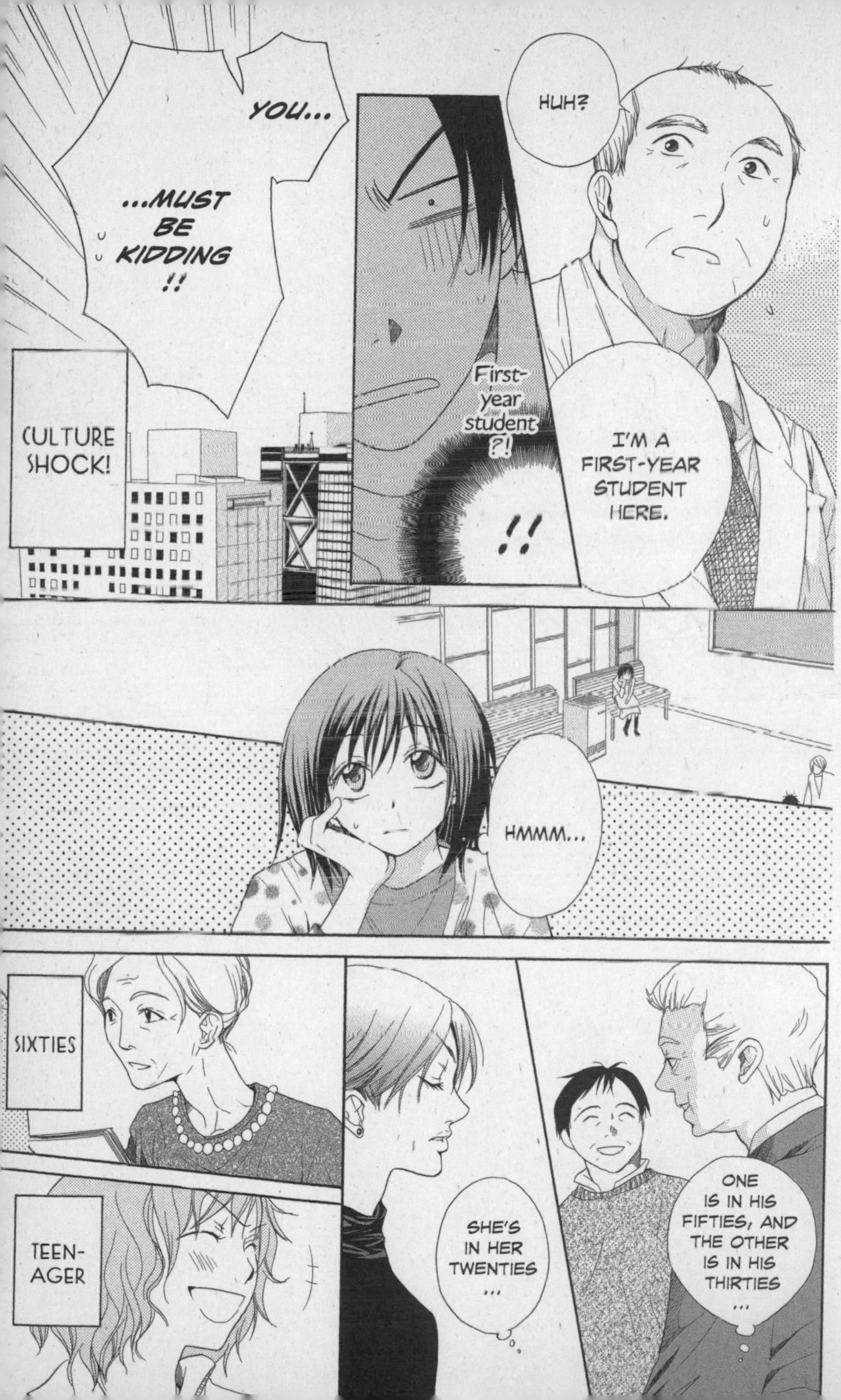
HUH?
I'M A FIRST-YEAR STUDENT HERE.
First-year student?!
!!
YOU...
...MUST BE KIDDING!!
CULTURE SHOCK!
HMMM...
ONE IS IN HIS FIFTIES, AND THE OTHER IS IN HIS THIRTIES...
SHE'S IN HER TWENTIES...
SIXTIES
TEEN-AGER

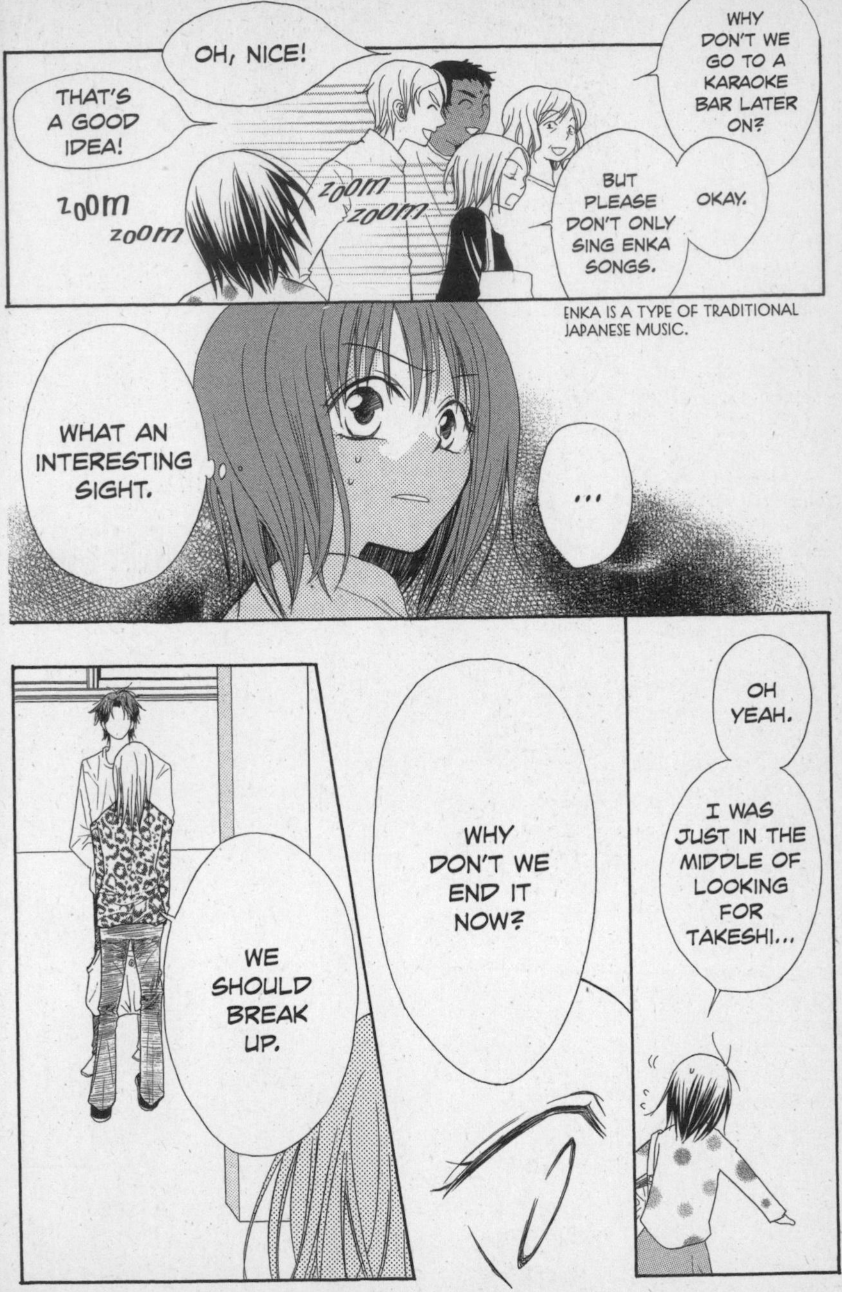
WHY DON'T WE GO TO A KARAOKE BAR LATER ON?
OKAY.
BUT PLEASE DON'T ONLY SING ENKA SONGS.
OH, NICE!
THAT'S A GOOD IDEA!
ZOOM ZOOM
ZOOM ZOOM
ENKA IS A TYPE OF TRADITIONAL JAPANESE MUSIC.
...
WHAT AN INTERESTING SIGHT.
OH YEAH.
I WAS JUST IN THE MIDDLE OF LOOKING FOR TAKESHI...
WHY DON'T WE END IT NOW?
WE SHOULD BREAK UP.

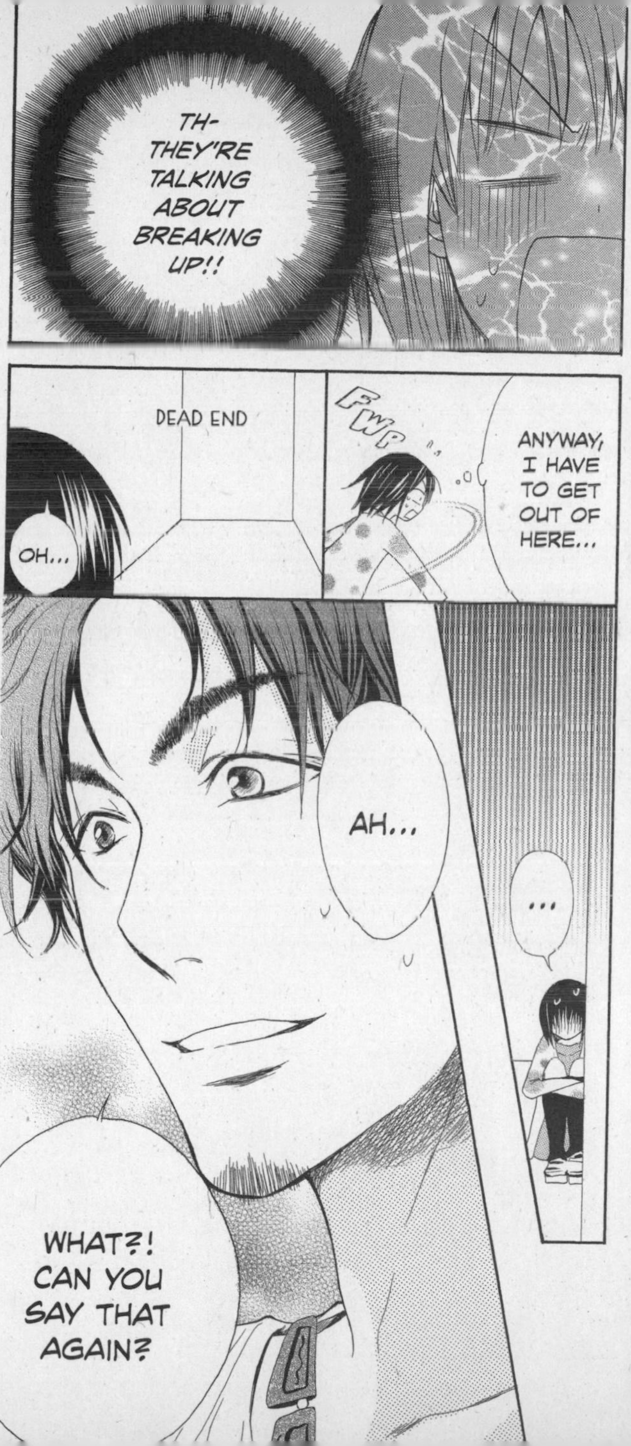
TH- THEY'RE TALKING ABOUT BREAKING UP!!
FWP
ANYWAY, I HAVE TO GET OUT OF HERE...
DEAD END
OH...
...
AH...
WHAT?! CAN YOU SAY THAT AGAIN?

It's Volume 5!

Nice to see you again—or nice to meet you for the first time. This is Izumi Tsubaki. This is the first release of my comic book in eight months. I was surprised that a good deal of time passed by.

The cover of volume 5 is the mentor and his merry friends. It's no longer a "Chiaki and XXXX Series"...

Let me see... This volume covers the Massage School series. This is based on a work of fiction. Every part of the story is not an original creation, and I have appropriated lots of things. I hope the readers enjoy this series as a manga.

If you want to learn more about a real massage school, please contact a professional school directly. (Lots of schools have programs allowing you to visit the classes.) See you later...

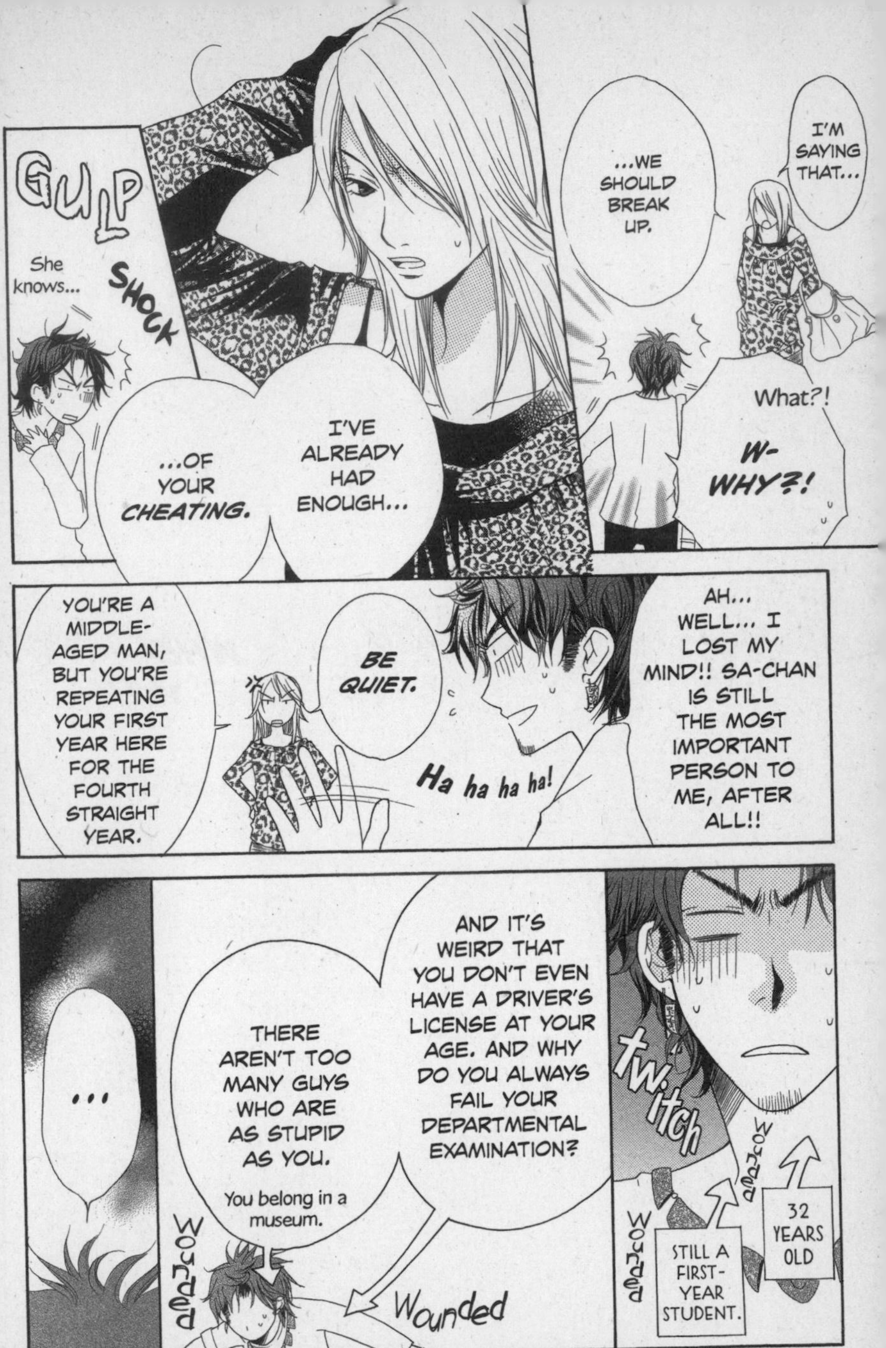

I'M SAYING THAT...
...WE SHOULD BREAK UP.
What?!
W-WHY?!
I'VE ALREADY HAD ENOUGH...
...OF YOUR CHEATING.
GULP
SHOCK
She knows...
AH... WELL... I LOST MY MIND!! SA-CHAN IS STILL THE MOST IMPORTANT PERSON TO ME, AFTER ALL!!
Ha ha ha ha!
BE QUIET.
YOU'RE A MIDDLE-AGED MAN, BUT YOU'RE REPEATING YOUR FIRST YEAR HERE FOR THE FOURTH STRAIGHT YEAR.
twitch
32 YEARS OLD
Wounded
STILL A FIRST-YEAR STUDENT.
Wounded
AND IT'S WEIRD THAT YOU DON'T EVEN HAVE A DRIVER'S LICENSE AT YOUR AGE. AND WHY DO YOU ALWAYS FAIL YOUR DEPARTMENTAL EXAMINATION?
THERE AREN'T TOO MANY GUYS WHO ARE AS STUPID AS YOU.
You belong in a museum.
Wounded
Wounded
...

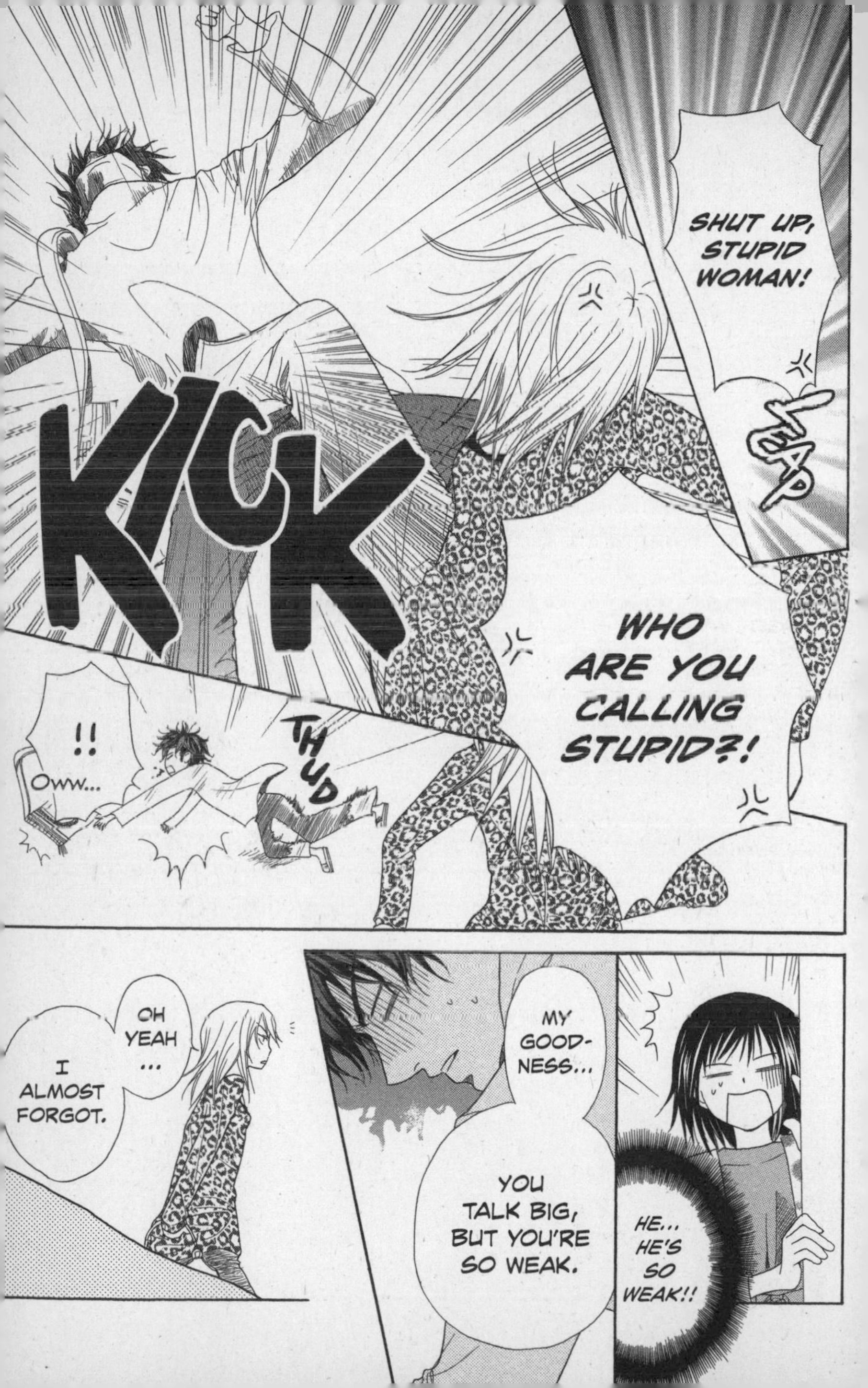
SHUT UP, STUPID WOMAN!
LEAP
KICK
WHO ARE YOU CALLING STUPID?!
THUD
!!
Oww...
HE... HE'S SO WEAK!!
MY GOODNESS...
YOU TALK BIG, BUT YOU'RE SO WEAK.
OH YEAH ...
I ALMOST FORGOT.

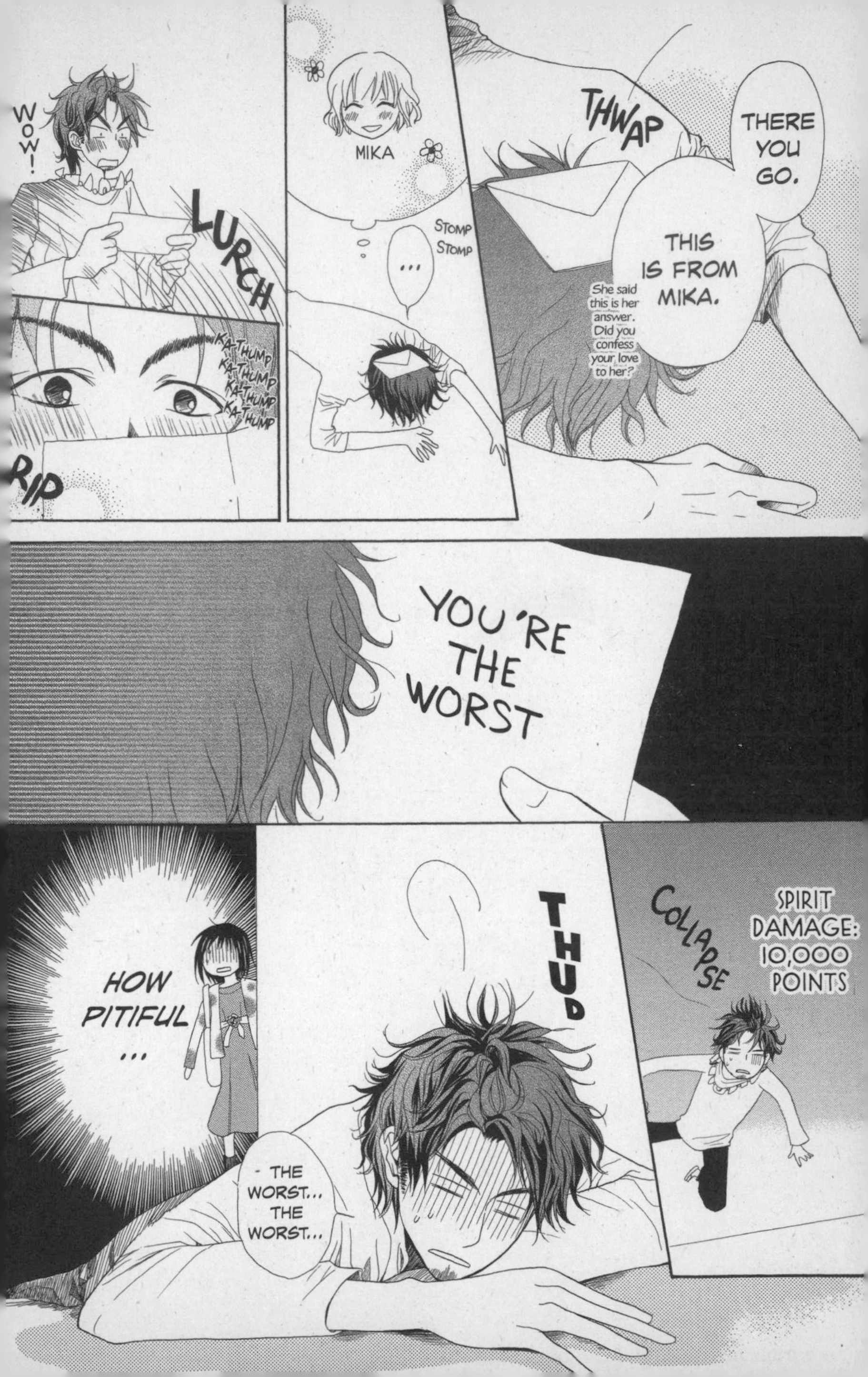
THWAP
THERE YOU GO.
THIS IS FROM MIKA.
She said this is her answer. Did you confess your love to her?
MIKA
STOMP STOMP
...
WOW!
LURCH
KA-THUMP KA-THUMP KA-THUMP KA-THUMP
RIP
YOU'RE THE WORST
SPIRIT DAMAGE: 10,000 POINTS
COLLAPSE
THUD
THE WORST... THE WORST...
HOW PITIFUL ...

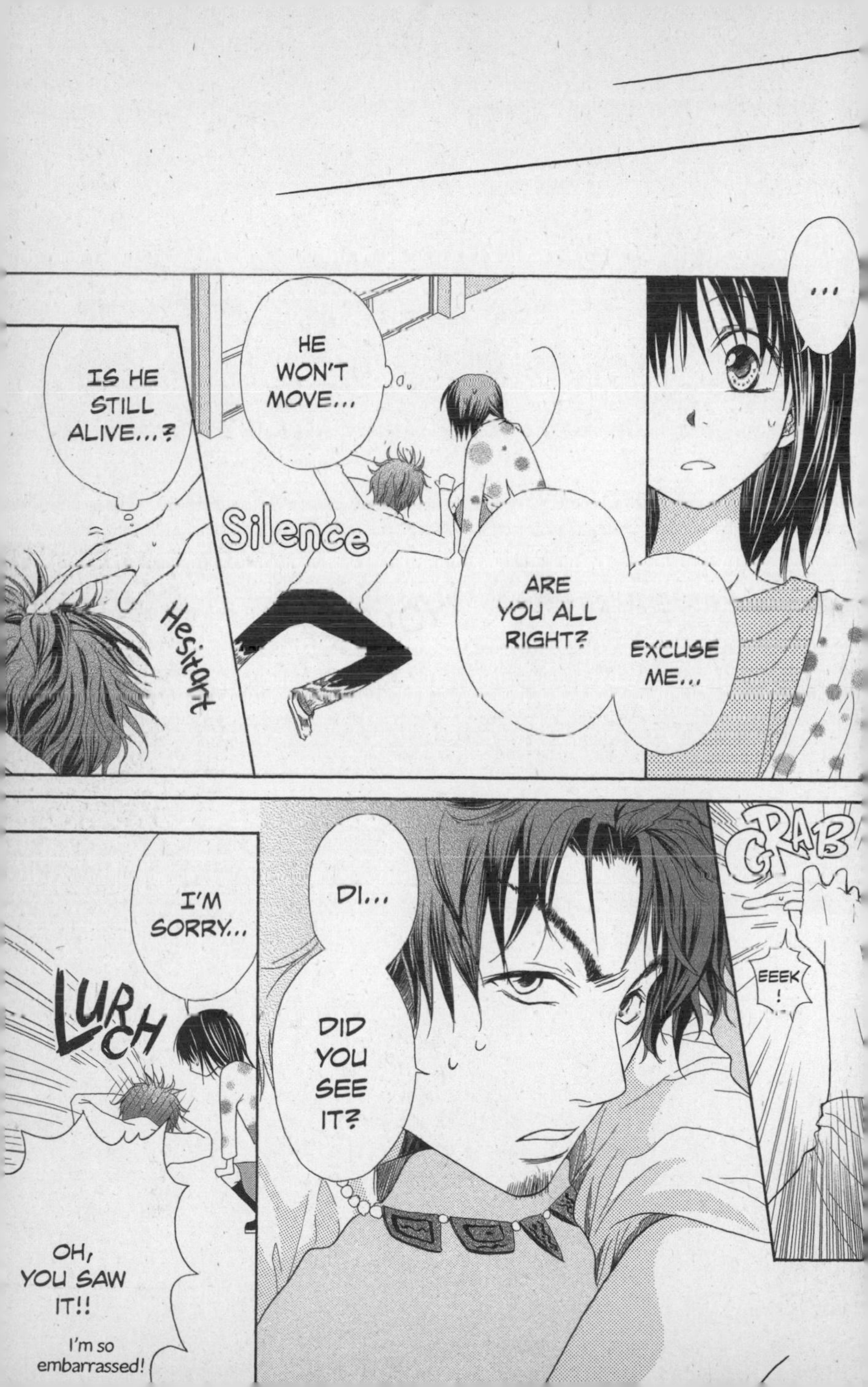
...
EXCUSE ME...
ARE YOU ALL RIGHT?
HE WON'T MOVE...
Silence
IS HE STILL ALIVE...?
Hesitant
GRAB
EEEK!
DI...
DID YOU SEE IT?
I'M SORRY...
LURCH
OH, YOU SAW IT!!
I'm so embarrassed!

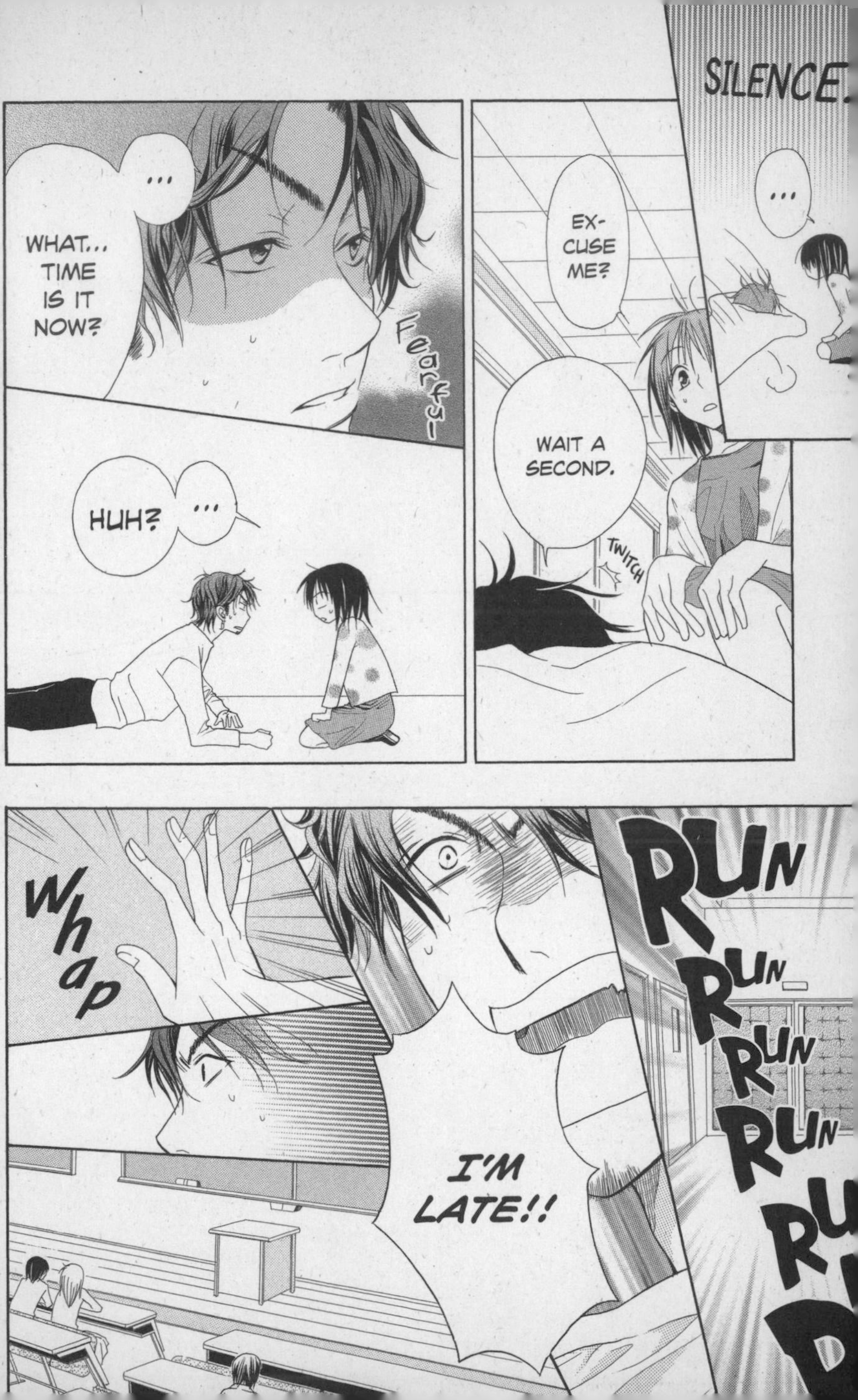
SILENCE...
...
EX-CUSE ME?
WAIT A SECOND.
TWITCH
...
WHAT... TIME IS IT NOW?
Fearful
...
HUH?
RUN RUN RUN RUN RUN RU
Whap
I'M LATE!!

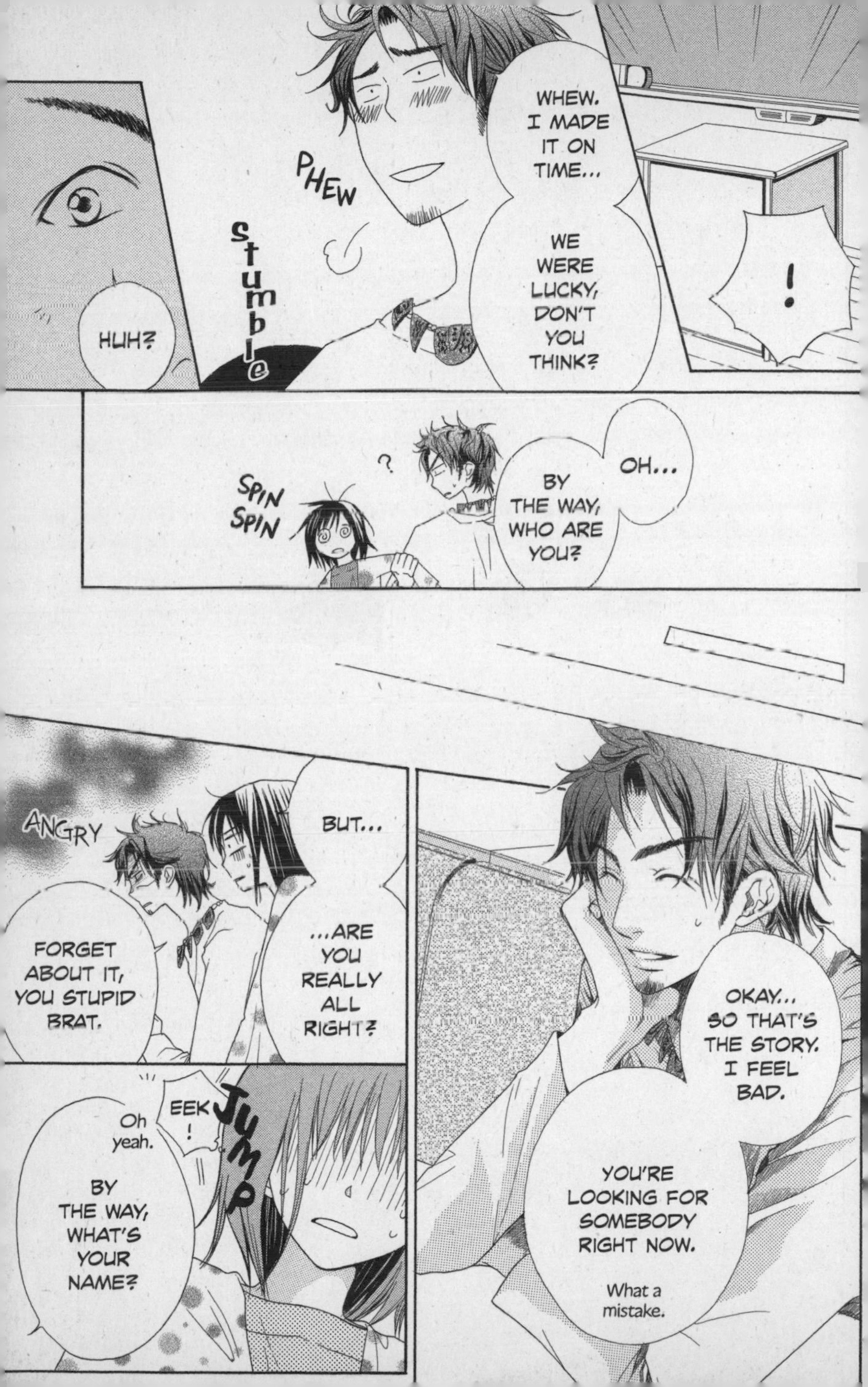
!
PHEW
WHEW. I MADE IT ON TIME...
WE WERE LUCKY, DON'T YOU THINK?
stumble
HUH?
OH...
BY THE WAY, WHO ARE YOU?
SPIN SPIN
OKAY... SO THAT'S THE STORY. I FEEL BAD.
YOU'RE LOOKING FOR SOMEBODY RIGHT NOW.
What a mistake.
BUT...
...ARE YOU REALLY ALL RIGHT?
ANGRY
FORGET ABOUT IT, YOU STUPID BRAT.
JUMP
EEK!
Oh yeah.
BY THE WAY, WHAT'S YOUR NAME?

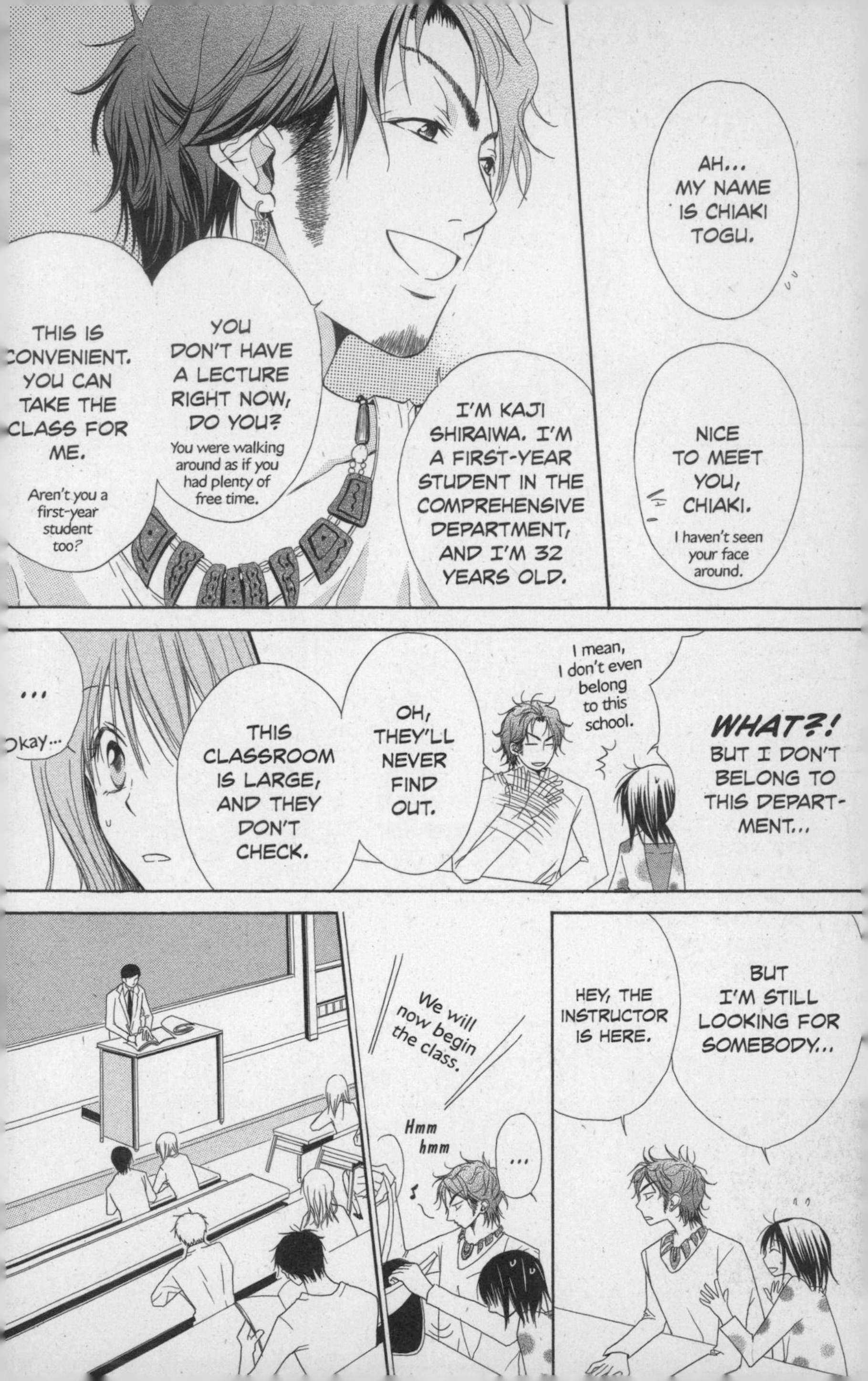
AH... MY NAME IS CHIAKI TOGU.
NICE TO MEET YOU, CHIAKI.
I haven't seen your face around.
I'M KAJI SHIRAIWA. I'M A FIRST-YEAR STUDENT IN THE COMPREHENSIVE DEPARTMENT, AND I'M 32 YEARS OLD.
YOU DON'T HAVE A LECTURE RIGHT NOW, DO YOU?
You were walking around as if you had plenty of free time.
THIS IS CONVENIENT. YOU CAN TAKE THE CLASS FOR ME.
Aren't you a first-year student too?
WHAT?! BUT I DON'T BELONG TO THIS DEPART-MENT...
I mean, I don't even belong to this school.
OH, THEY'LL NEVER FIND OUT.
THIS CLASSROOM IS LARGE, AND THEY DON'T CHECK.
...
Okay...
BUT I'M STILL LOOKING FOR SOMEBODY...
HEY, THE INSTRUCTOR IS HERE.
...
Hmm hmm
We will now begin the class.

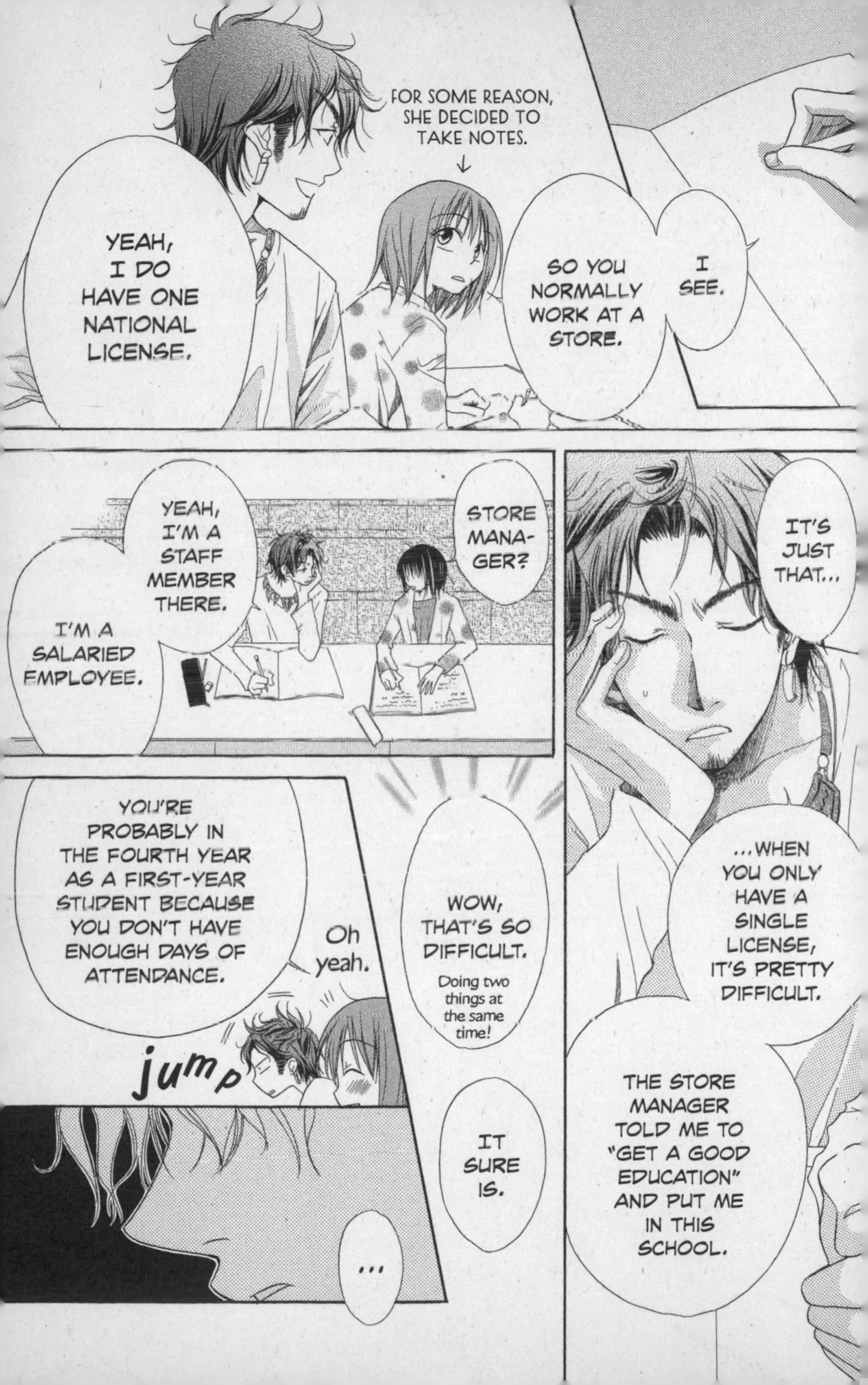
I SEE.
SO YOU NORMALLY WORK AT A STORE.
FOR SOME REASON, SHE DECIDED TO TAKE NOTES.
YEAH, I DO HAVE ONE NATIONAL LICENSE.
IT'S JUST THAT...
...WHEN YOU ONLY HAVE A SINGLE LICENSE, IT'S PRETTY DIFFICULT.
THE STORE MANAGER TOLD ME TO "GET A GOOD EDUCATION" AND PUT ME IN THIS SCHOOL.
STORE MANAGER?
YEAH, I'M A STAFF MEMBER THERE.
I'M A SALARIED EMPLOYEE.
WOW, THAT'S SO DIFFICULT.
Doing two things at the same time!
YOU'RE PROBABLY IN THE FOURTH YEAR AS A FIRST-YEAR STUDENT BECAUSE YOU DON'T HAVE ENOUGH DAYS OF ATTENDANCE.
Oh yeah.
jump
IT SURE IS.
...

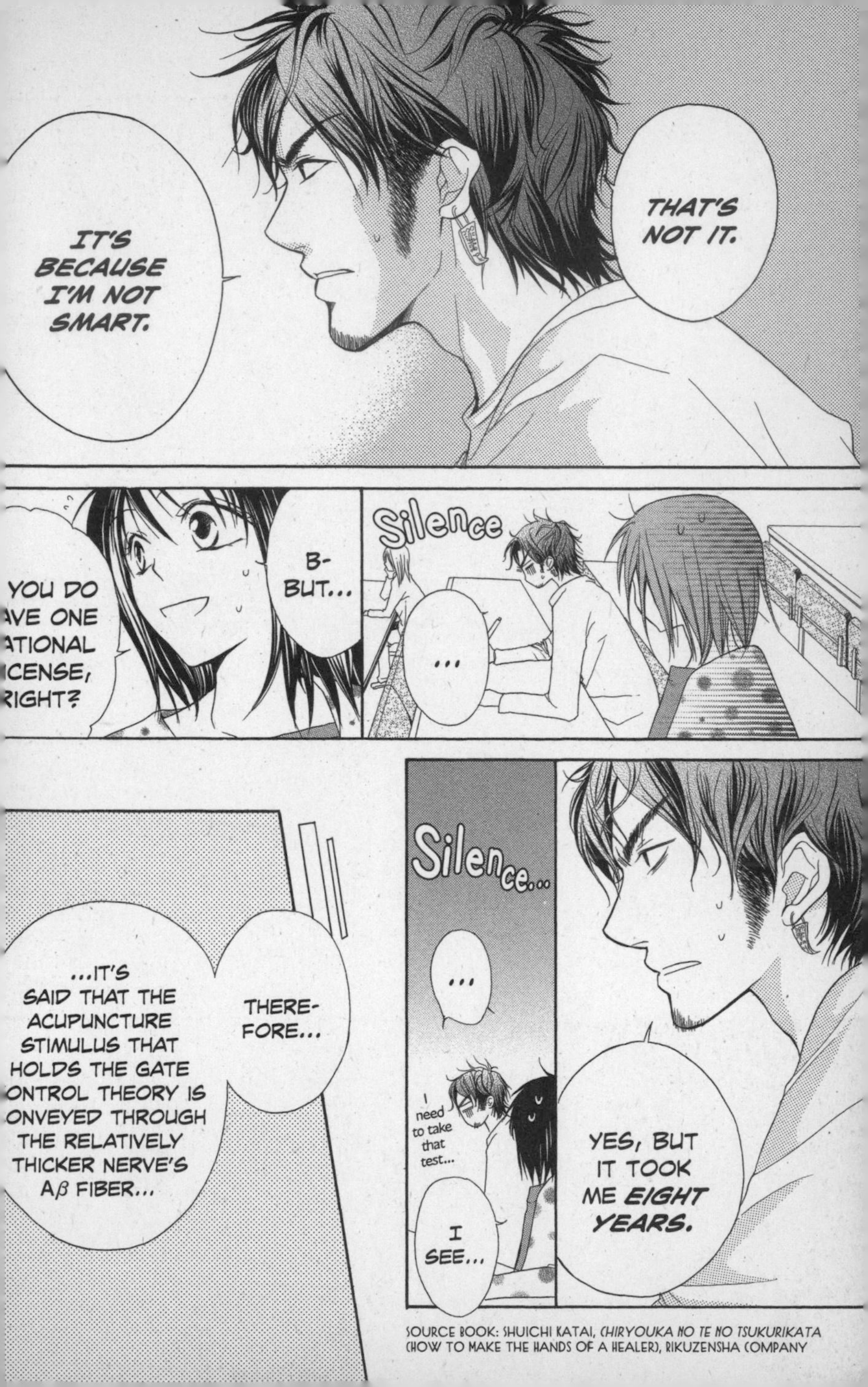

THAT'S NOT IT.
IT'S BECAUSE I'M NOT SMART.
Silence
...
B-BUT...
YOU DO
AVE ONE
ATIONAL
ICENSE,
RIGHT?
YES, BUT IT TOOK ME EIGHT YEARS.
Silence...
...
I need to take that test...
I SEE...
THERE-FORE...
...IT'S SAID THAT THE ACUPUNCTURE STIMULUS THAT HOLDS THE GATE
ONTROL THEORY IS
ONVEYED THROUGH
THE RELATIVELY THICKER NERVE'S Aβ FIBER...

SOURCE BOOK: SHUICHI KATAI, CHIRYOUKA NO TE NO TSUKURIKATA (HOW TO MAKE THE HANDS OF A HEALER), RIKUZENSHA COMPANY

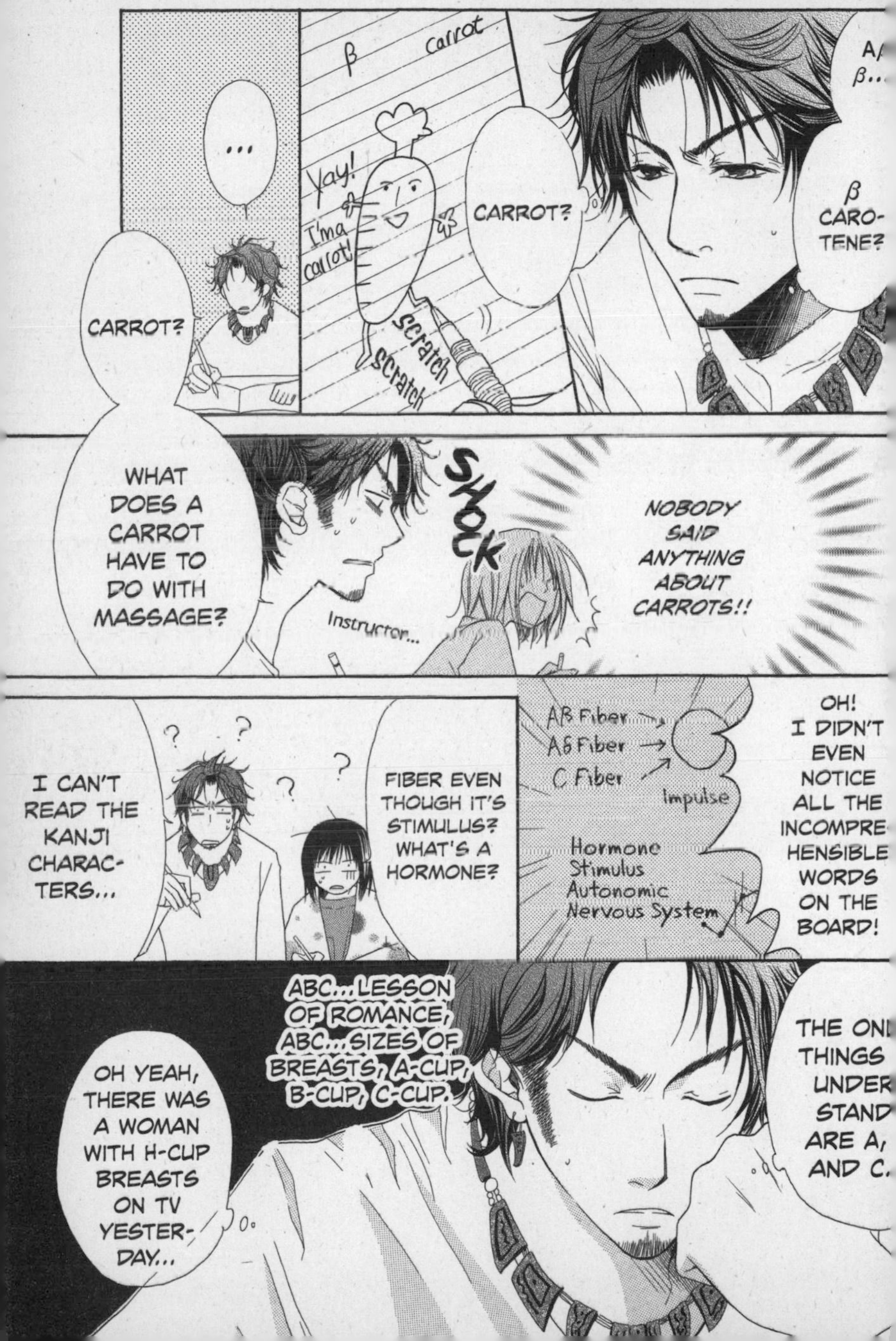
A/ β...
β CARO- TENE?
CARROT?
β carrot
Yay! I'm a carrot!
scratch scratch
...
CARROT?
NOBODY SAID ANYTHING ABOUT CARROTS!!
SHOCK
Instructor...
WHAT DOES A CARROT HAVE TO DO WITH MASSAGE?
OH! I DIDN'T EVEN NOTICE ALL THE INCOMPRE- HENSIBLE WORDS ON THE BOARD!
Aβ Fiber
Aδ Fiber
C Fiber
Impulse
Hormone Stimulus Autonomic Nervous System
FIBER EVEN THOUGH IT'S STIMULUS? WHAT'S A HORMONE?
I CAN'T READ THE KANJI CHARAC- TERS...
THE ON THINGS UNDER STAND ARE A, AND C.
ABC...LESSON OF ROMANCE, ABC...SIZES OF BREASTS, A-CUP, B-CUP, C-CUP.
OH YEAH, THERE WAS A WOMAN WITH H-CUP BREASTS ON TV YESTER- DAY...

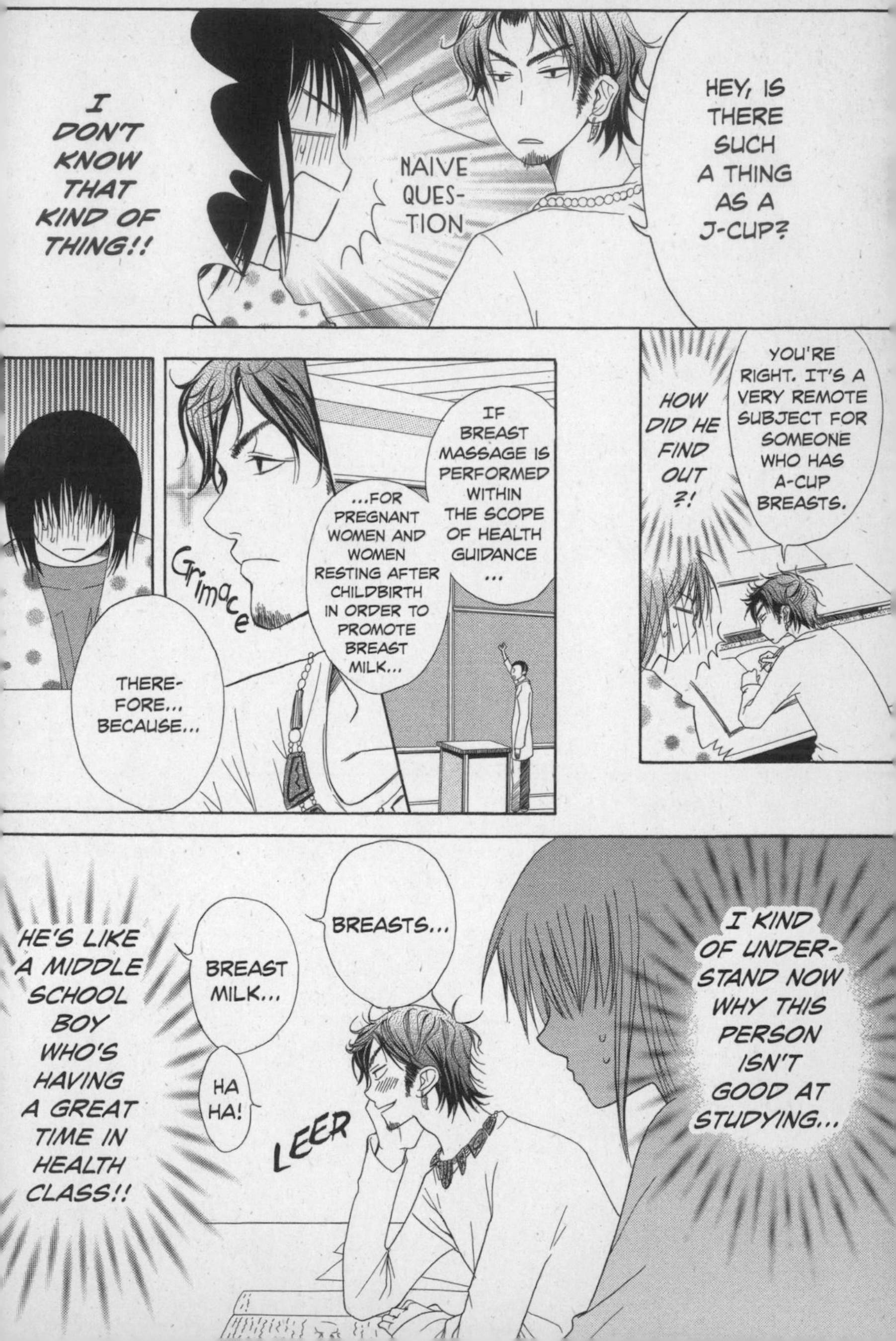
HEY, IS THERE SUCH A THING AS A J-CUP?
NAIVE QUES-TION
I DON'T KNOW THAT KIND OF THING!!
YOU'RE RIGHT. IT'S A VERY REMOTE SUBJECT FOR SOMEONE WHO HAS A-CUP BREASTS.
HOW DID HE FIND OUT?!
IF BREAST MASSAGE IS PERFORMED WITHIN THE SCOPE OF HEALTH GUIDANCE...
...FOR PREGNANT WOMEN AND WOMEN RESTING AFTER CHILDBIRTH IN ORDER TO PROMOTE BREAST MILK...
Grimace
THERE-FORE... BECAUSE...
I KIND OF UNDER-STAND NOW WHY THIS PERSON ISN'T GOOD AT STUDYING...
BREASTS...
BREAST MILK...
HA HA!
LEER
HE'S LIKE A MIDDLE SCHOOL BOY WHO'S HAVING A GREAT TIME IN HEALTH CLASS!!

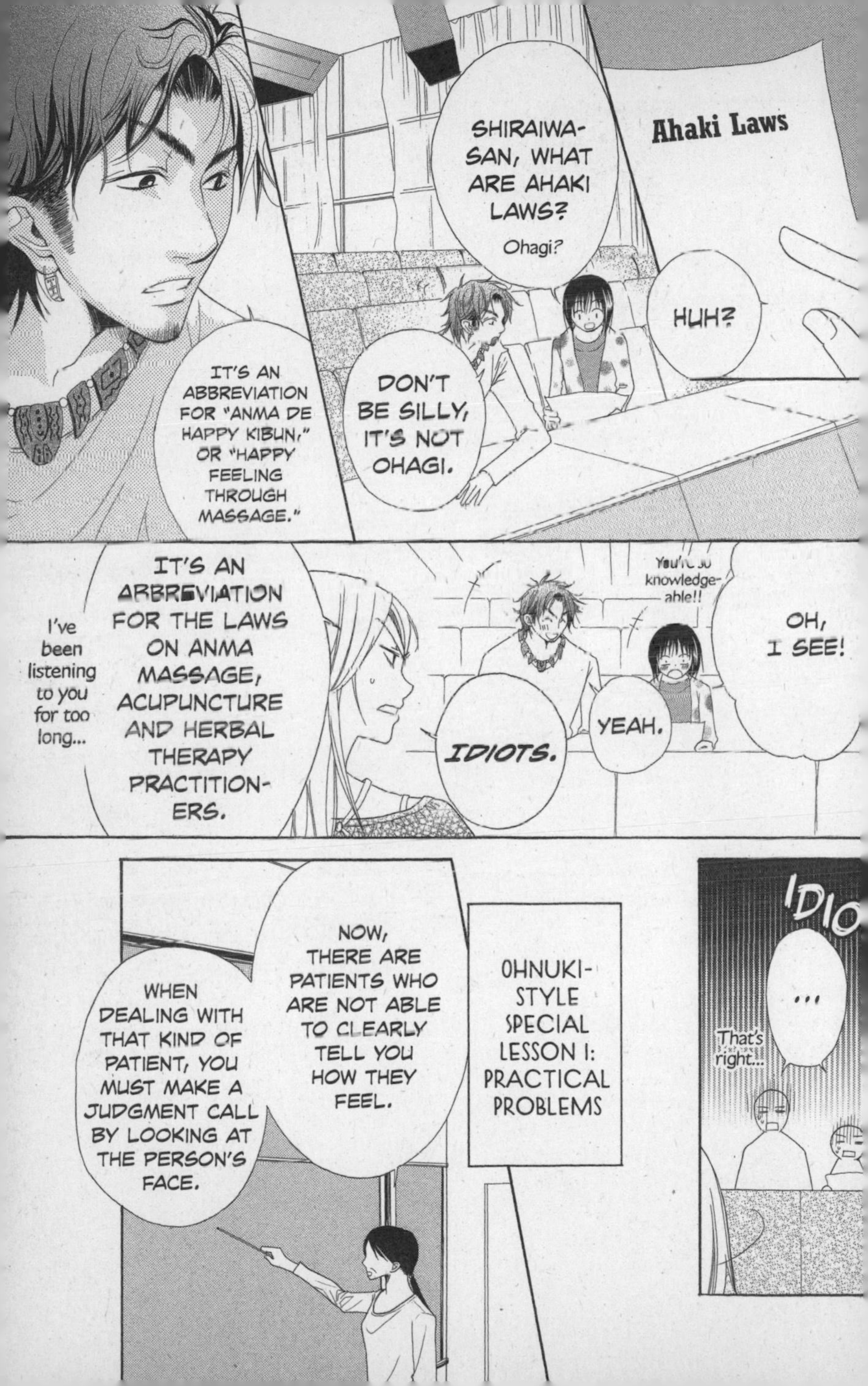
Ahaki Laws
SHIRAIWA-SAN, WHAT ARE AHAKI LAWS?
Ohagi?
HUH?
DON'T BE SILLY, IT'S NOT OHAGI.
IT'S AN ABBREVIATION FOR "ANMA DE HAPPY KIBUN," OR "HAPPY FEELING THROUGH MASSAGE."
OH, I SEE!
You're so knowledge-able!!
YEAH.
IDIOTS.
IT'S AN ABBREVIATION FOR THE LAWS ON ANMA MASSAGE, ACUPUNCTURE AND HERBAL THERAPY PRACTITION-ERS.
I've been listening to you for too long...
IDIO
...
That's right...
OHNUKI-STYLE SPECIAL LESSON 1: PRACTICAL PROBLEMS
NOW, THERE ARE PATIENTS WHO ARE NOT ABLE TO CLEARLY TELL YOU HOW THEY FEEL.
WHEN DEALING WITH THAT KIND OF PATIENT, YOU MUST MAKE A JUDGMENT CALL BY LOOKING AT THE PERSON'S FACE.

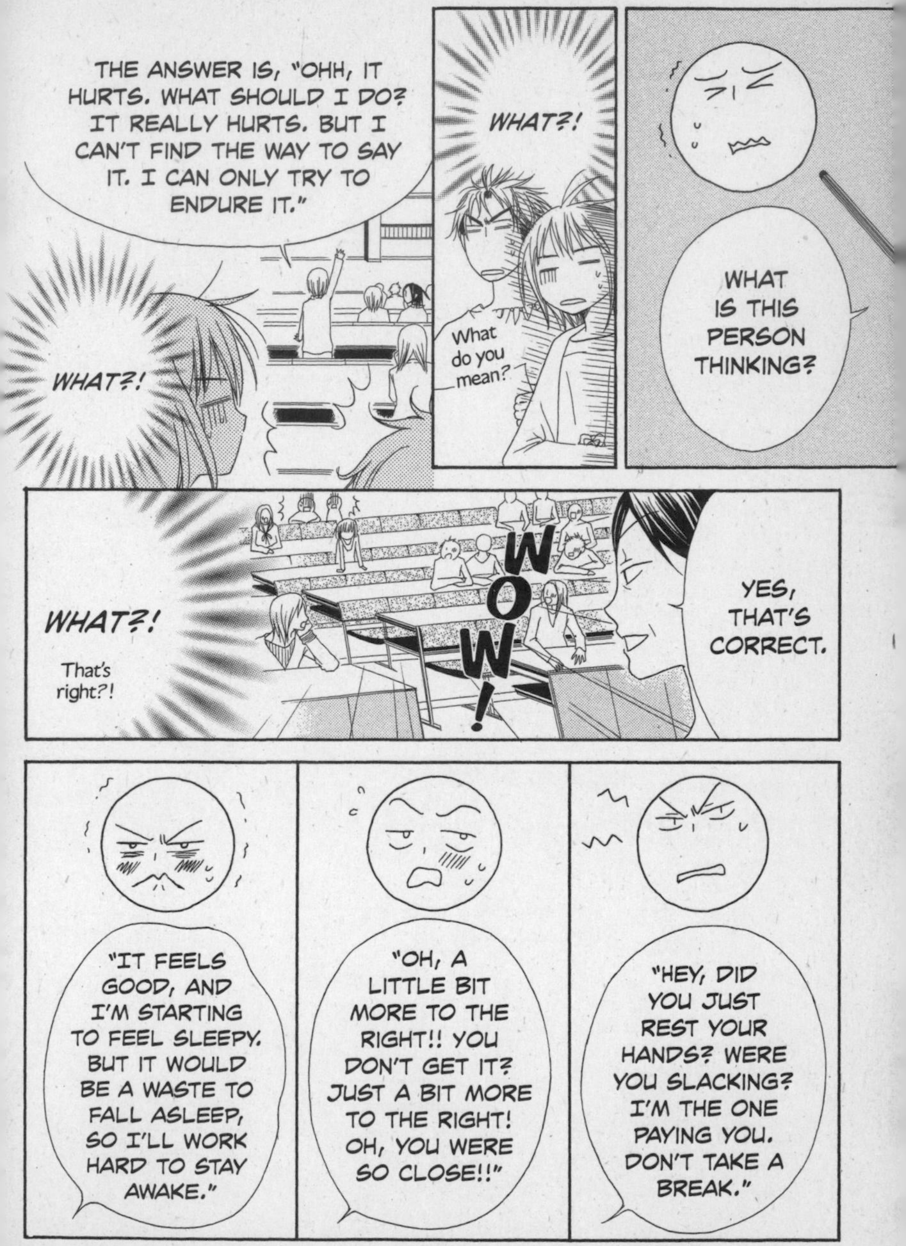
WHAT IS THIS PERSON THINKING?
WHAT?!
What do you mean?
THE ANSWER IS, "OHH, IT HURTS. WHAT SHOULD I DO? IT REALLY HURTS. BUT I CAN'T FIND THE WAY TO SAY IT. I CAN ONLY TRY TO ENDURE IT."
WHAT?!
YES, THAT'S CORRECT.
WOW!
WHAT?!
That's right?!
"HEY, DID YOU JUST REST YOUR HANDS? WERE YOU SLACKING? I'M THE ONE PAYING YOU. DON'T TAKE A BREAK."
"OH, A LITTLE BIT MORE TO THE RIGHT!! YOU DON'T GET IT? JUST A BIT MORE TO THE RIGHT! OH, YOU WERE SO CLOSE!!"
"IT FEELS GOOD, AND I'M STARTING TO FEEL SLEEPY. BUT IT WOULD BE A WASTE TO FALL ASLEEP, SO I'LL WORK HARD TO STAY AWAKE."

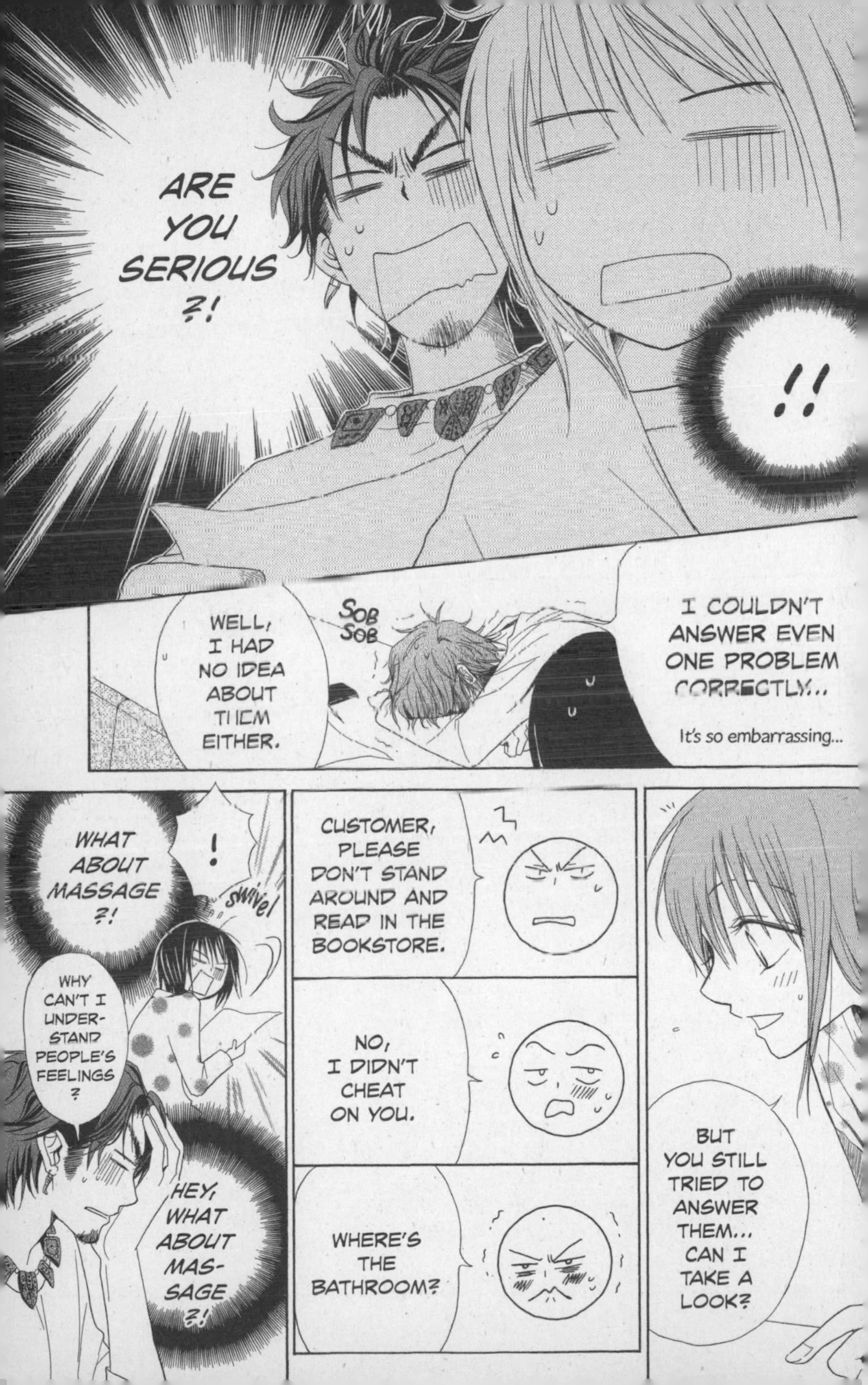
ARE YOU SERIOUS?!
!!
I COULDN'T ANSWER EVEN ONE PROBLEM CORRECTLY...
It's so embarrassing...
SOB SOB
WELL, I HAD NO IDEA ABOUT THEM EITHER.
BUT YOU STILL TRIED TO ANSWER THEM... CAN I TAKE A LOOK?
CUSTOMER, PLEASE DON'T STAND AROUND AND READ IN THE BOOKSTORE.
NO, I DIDN'T CHEAT ON YOU.
WHERE'S THE BATHROOM?
WHAT ABOUT MASSAGE?!
!
swivel
WHY CAN'T I UNDER-STAND PEOPLE'S FEELINGS?
HEY, WHAT ABOUT MAS-SAGE?!

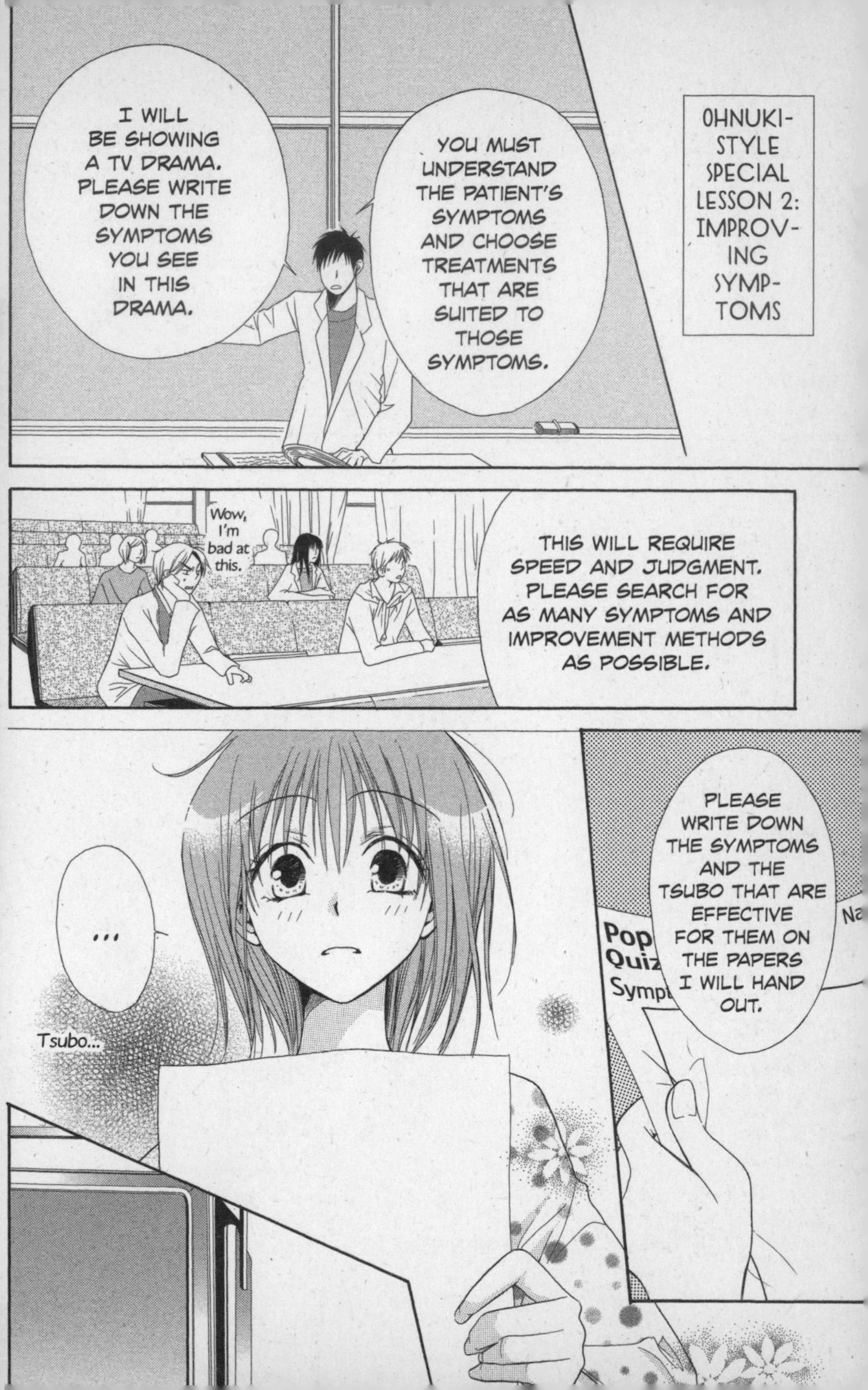
OHNUKI-STYLE SPECIAL LESSON 2: IMPROVING SYMPTOMS
YOU MUST UNDERSTAND THE PATIENT'S SYMPTOMS AND CHOOSE TREATMENTS THAT ARE SUITED TO THOSE SYMPTOMS.
I WILL BE SHOWING A TV DRAMA. PLEASE WRITE DOWN THE SYMPTOMS YOU SEE IN THIS DRAMA.
THIS WILL REQUIRE SPEED AND JUDGMENT. PLEASE SEARCH FOR AS MANY SYMPTOMS AND IMPROVEMENT METHODS AS POSSIBLE.
Wow, I'm bad at this.
PLEASE WRITE DOWN THE SYMPTOMS AND THE TSUBO THAT ARE EFFECTIVE FOR THEM ON THE PAPERS I WILL HAND OUT.
Pop Quiz
...
Tsubo...

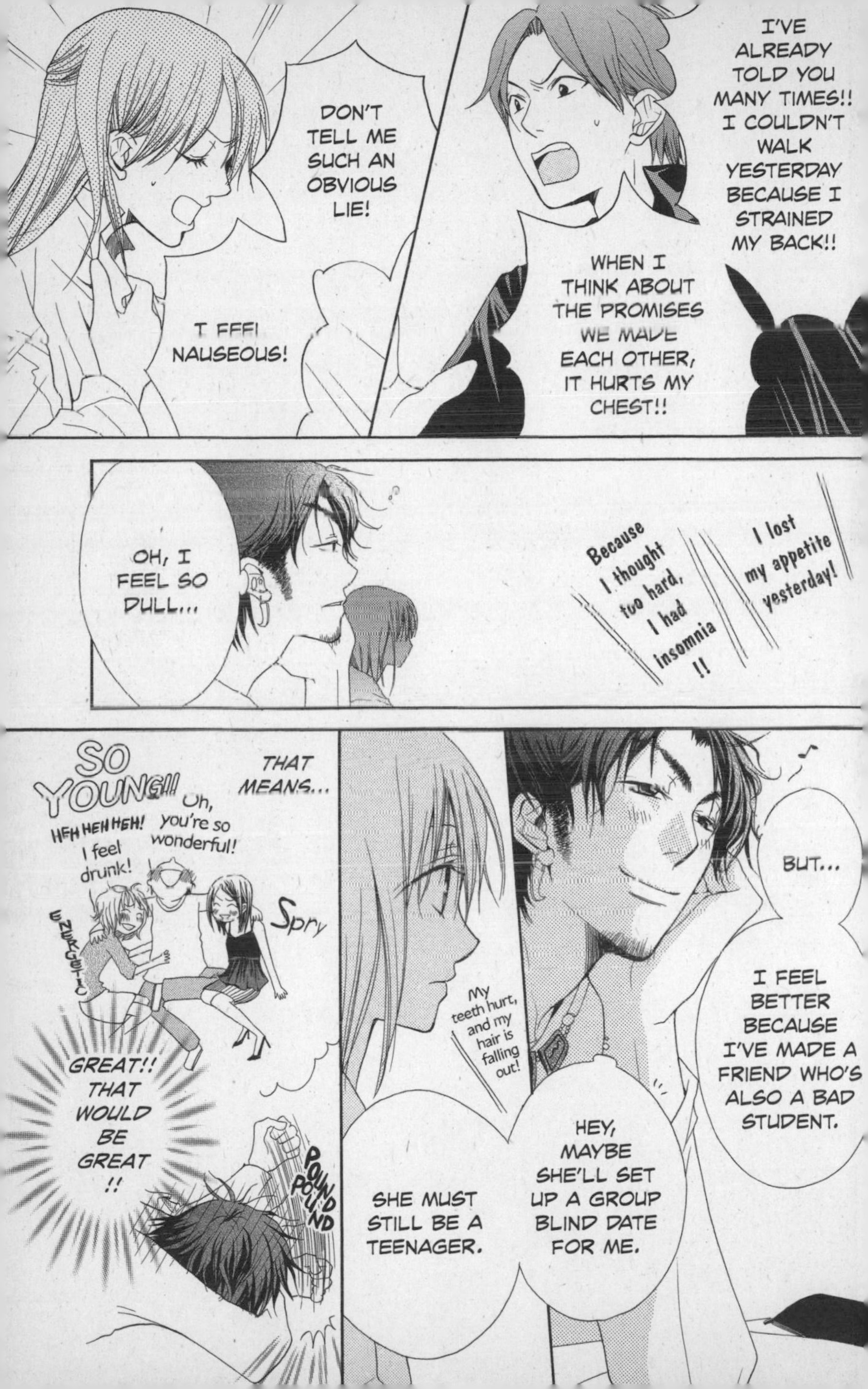
I'VE ALREADY TOLD YOU MANY TIMES!! I COULDN'T WALK YESTERDAY BECAUSE I STRAINED MY BACK!!
WHEN I THINK ABOUT THE PROMISES WE MADE EACH OTHER, IT HURTS MY CHEST!!
DON'T TELL ME SUCH AN OBVIOUS LIE!
I FEEL NAUSEOUS!
I lost my appetite yesterday!
Because I thought too hard, I had insomnia !!
OH, I FEEL SO DULL...
BUT...
I FEEL BETTER BECAUSE I'VE MADE A FRIEND WHO'S ALSO A BAD STUDENT.
HEY, MAYBE SHE'LL SET UP A GROUP BLIND DATE FOR ME.
SHE MUST STILL BE A TEENAGER.
My teeth hurt, and my hair is falling out!
THAT MEANS...
SO YOUNG!!
Oh, you're so wonderful!
HEH HEH HEH! I feel drunk!
ENERGETIC
Spry
GREAT!! THAT WOULD BE GREAT !!
POUND POUND

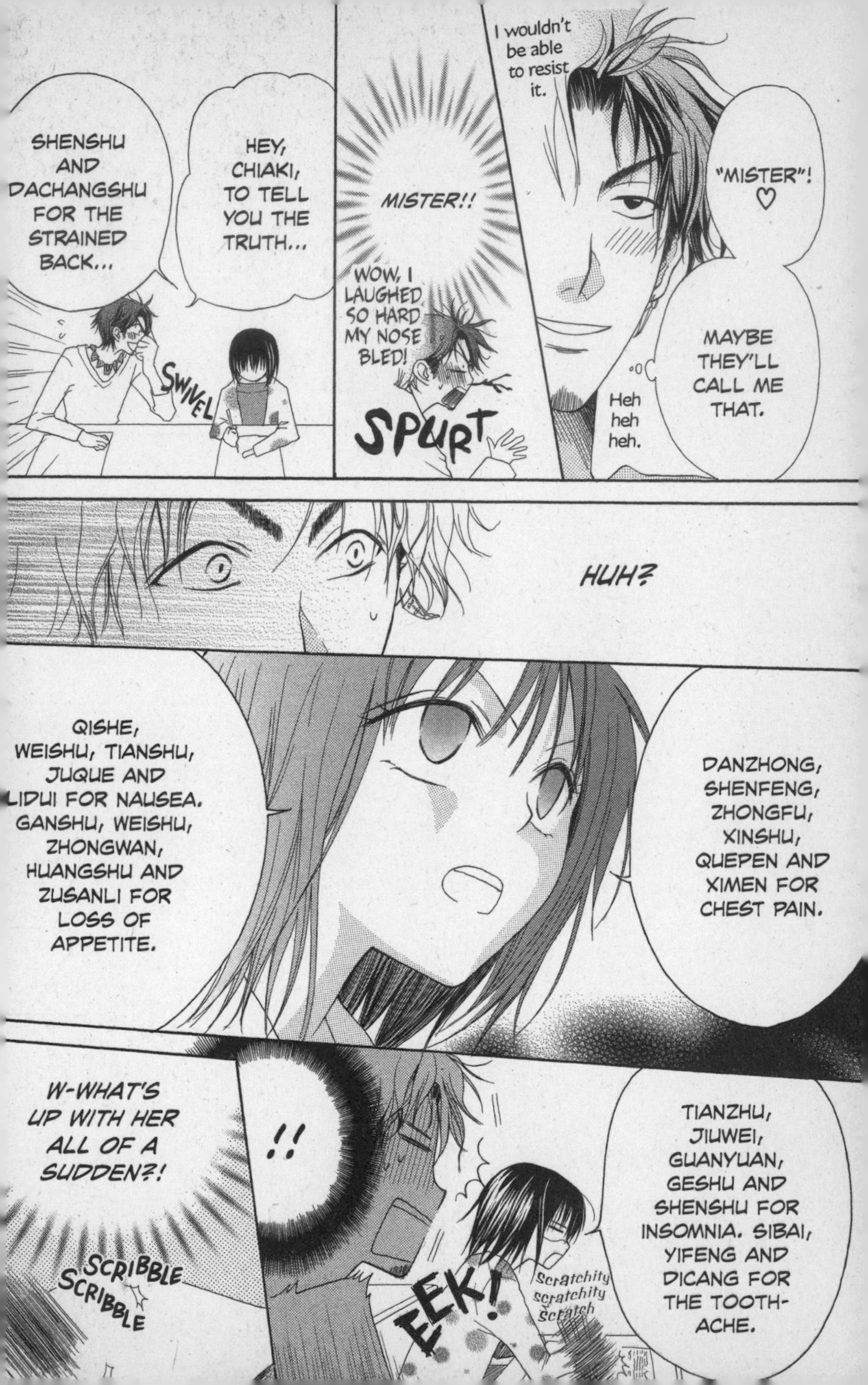
I wouldn't be able to resist it.
"MISTER"! ♡
MAYBE THEY'LL CALL ME THAT.
Heh heh heh.
MISTER!!
WOW, I LAUGHED SO HARD MY NOSE BLED!
SPURT
HEY, CHIAKI, TO TELL YOU THE TRUTH...
SHENSHU AND DACHANGSHU FOR THE STRAINED BACK...
SWIVEL
HUH?
DANZHONG, SHENFENG, ZHONGFU, XINSHU, QUEPEN AND XIMEN FOR CHEST PAIN.
QISHE, WEISHU, TIANSHU, JUQUE AND LIDUI FOR NAUSEA. GANSHU, WEISHU, ZHONGWAN, HUANGSHU AND ZUSANLI FOR LOSS OF APPETITE.
TIANZHU, JIUWEI, GUANYUAN, GESHU AND SHENSHU FOR INSOMNIA. SIBAI, YIFENG AND DICANG FOR THE TOOTH-ACHE.
Scratchity scratchity scratch
EEK!
!!
W-WHAT'S UP WITH HER ALL OF A SUDDEN?!
SCRIBBLE SCRIBBLE

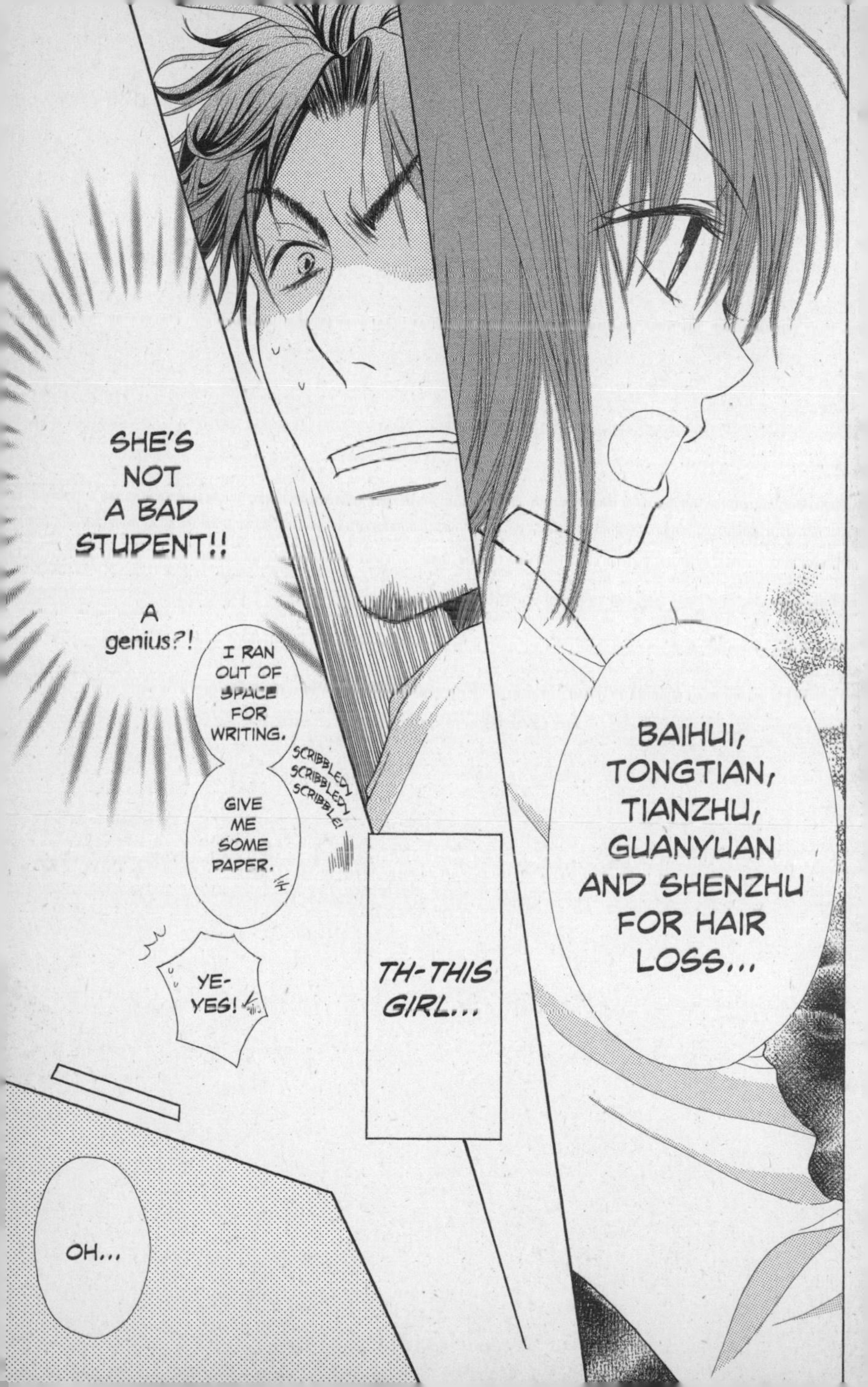
BAIHUI, TONGTIAN, TIANZHU, GUANYUAN AND SHENZHU FOR HAIR LOSS...
TH-THIS GIRL...
SHE'S NOT A BAD STUDENT!!
A genius?!
I RAN OUT OF SPACE FOR WRITING.
SCRIBBLEDY SCRIBBLEDY SCRIBBLE!
GIVE ME SOME PAPER.
YE-YES!
OH...

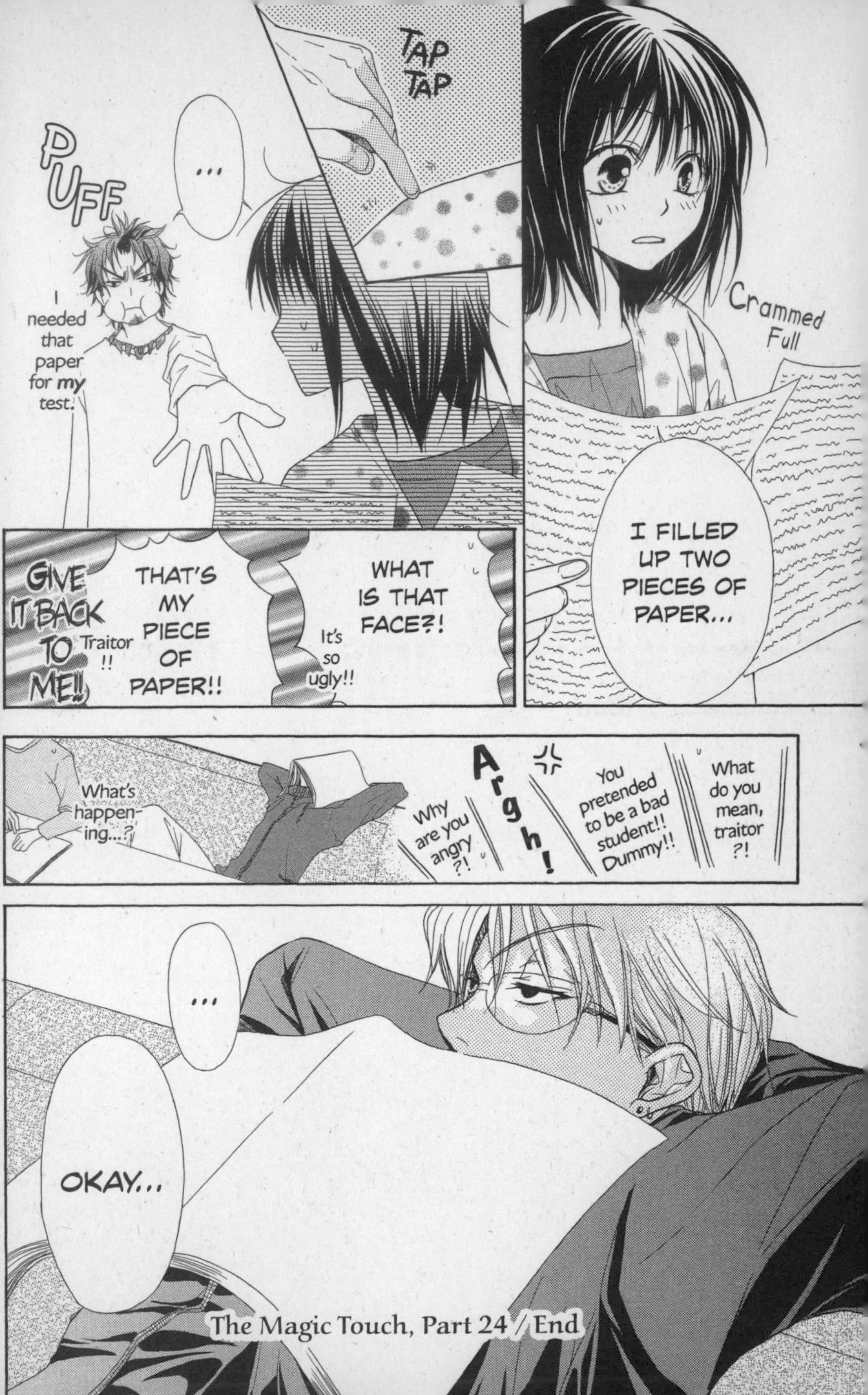
Crammed Full
I FILLED UP TWO PIECES OF PAPER...
TAP TAP
...
PUFF
I needed that paper for my test.
WHAT IS THAT FACE?!
It's so ugly!!
THAT'S MY PIECE OF PAPER!!
GIVE IT BACK TO ME!!
Traitor!!
What do you mean, traitor?!
You pretended to be a bad student!! Dummy!!
Argh!
Why are you angry?!
What's happening...?
...
OKAY...
The Magic Touch, Part 24 / End

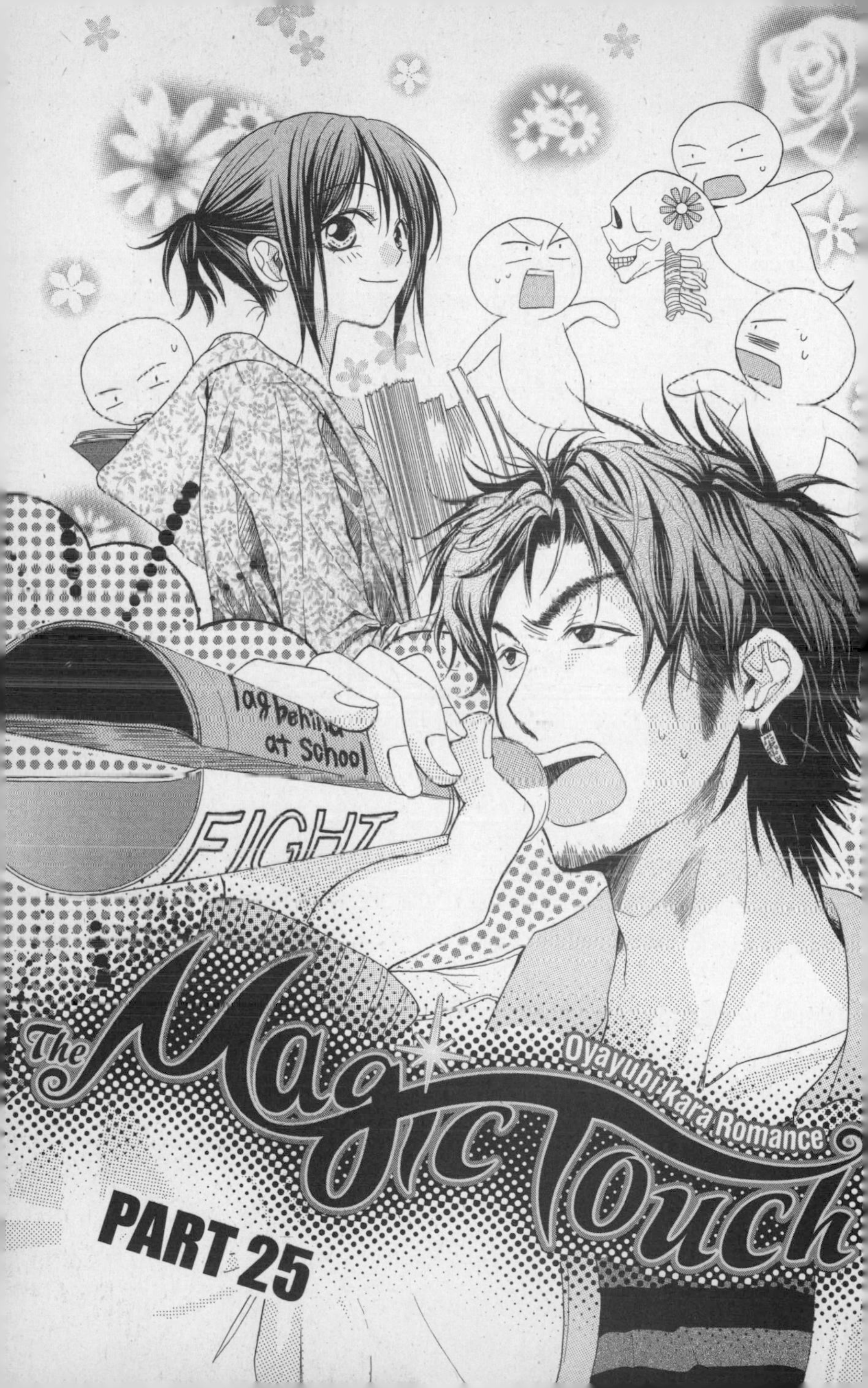
lag behind at school
FIGHT
The Magic Touch
Oyayubi Kara Romance
PART 25

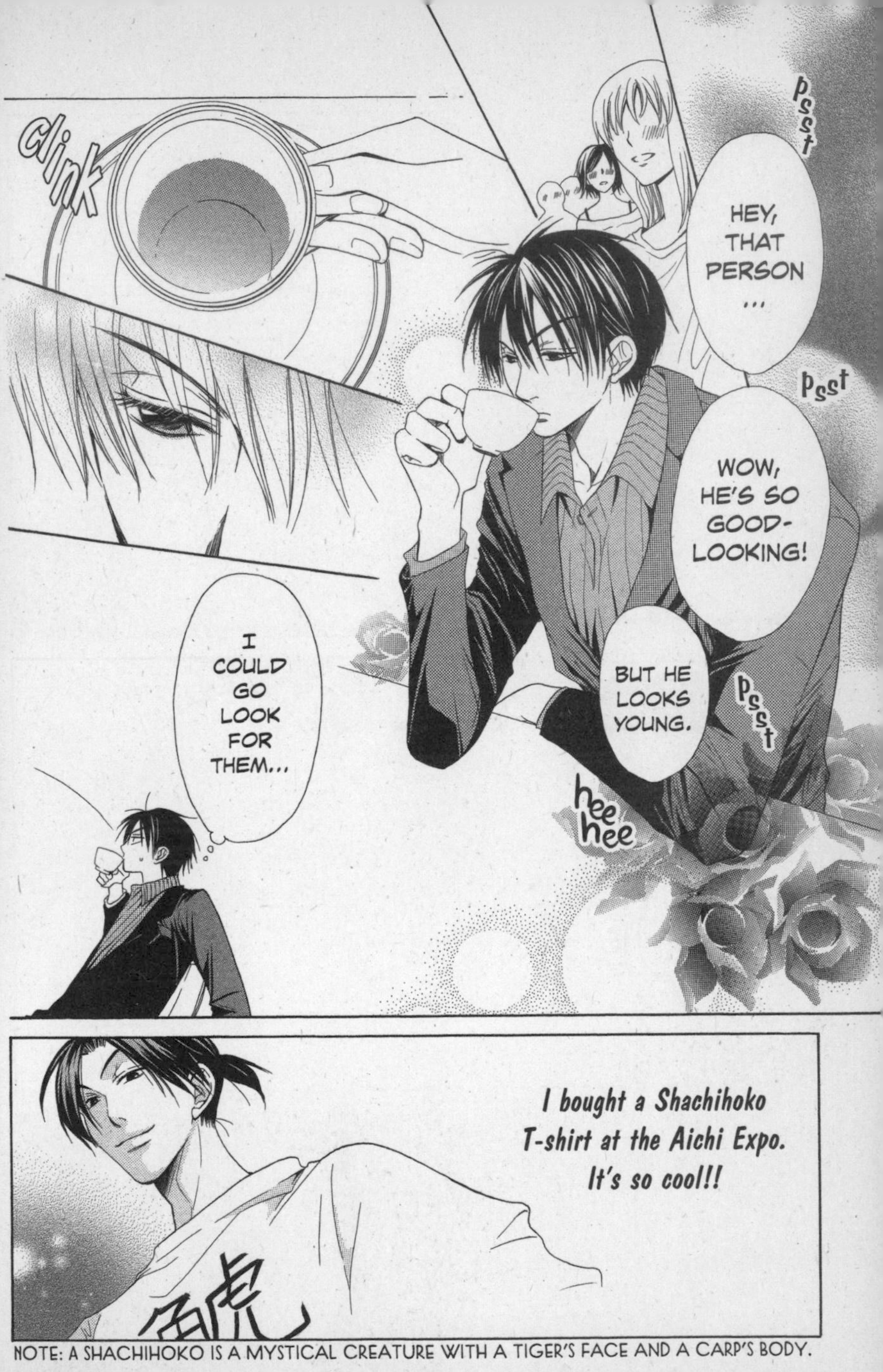
psst
HEY, THAT PERSON ...
psst
WOW, HE'S SO GOOD-LOOKING!
BUT HE LOOKS YOUNG.
psst
hee hee
clink
I COULD GO LOOK FOR THEM...
I bought a Shachihoko T-shirt at the Aichi Expo. It's so cool!!
NOTE: A SHACHIHOKO IS A MYSTICAL CREATURE WITH A TIGER'S FACE AND A CARP'S BODY.

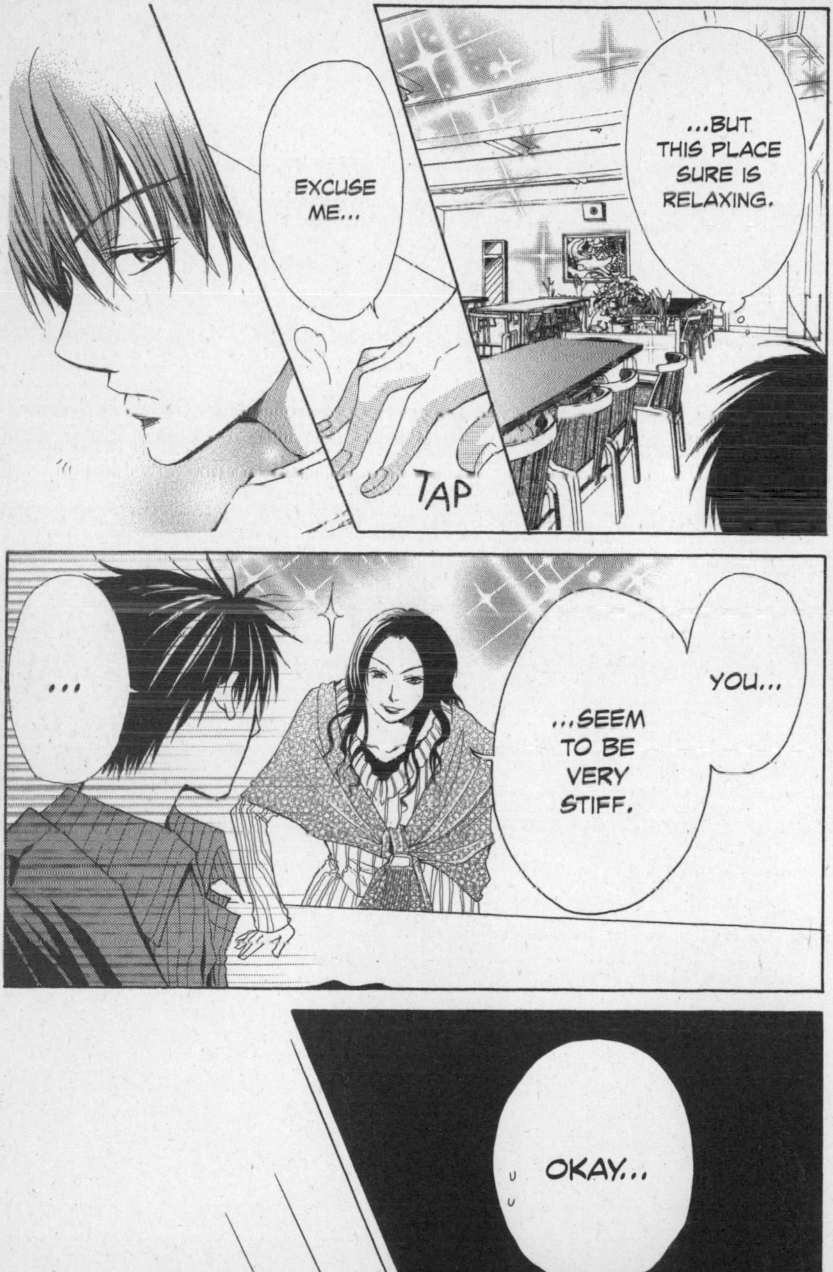
...BUT THIS PLACE SURE IS RELAXING.
EXCUSE ME...
TAP
YOU...
...SEEM TO BE VERY STIFF.
...
OKAY...

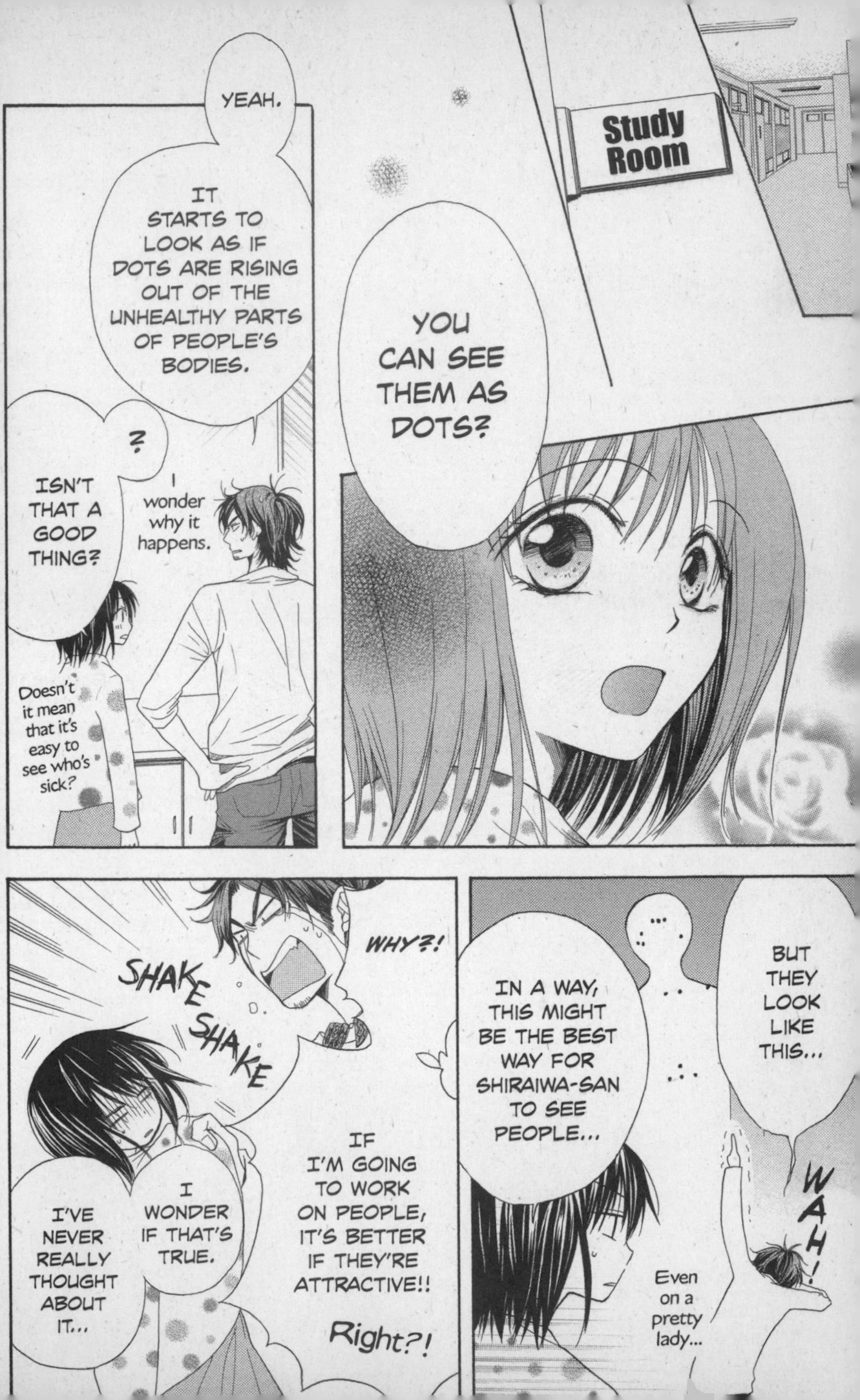
Study Room
YOU CAN SEE THEM AS DOTS?
YEAH.
IT STARTS TO LOOK AS IF DOTS ARE RISING OUT OF THE UNHEALTHY PARTS OF PEOPLE'S BODIES.
?
I wonder why it happens.
ISN'T THAT A GOOD THING?
Doesn't it mean that it's easy to see who's sick?
BUT THEY LOOK LIKE THIS...
WAH!
Even on a pretty lady...
...
IN A WAY, THIS MIGHT BE THE BEST WAY FOR SHIRAIWA-SAN TO SEE PEOPLE...
WHY?!
SHAKE SHAKE
IF I'M GOING TO WORK ON PEOPLE, IT'S BETTER IF THEY'RE ATTRACTIVE!!
Right?!
I WONDER IF THAT'S TRUE.
I'VE NEVER REALLY THOUGHT ABOUT IT...

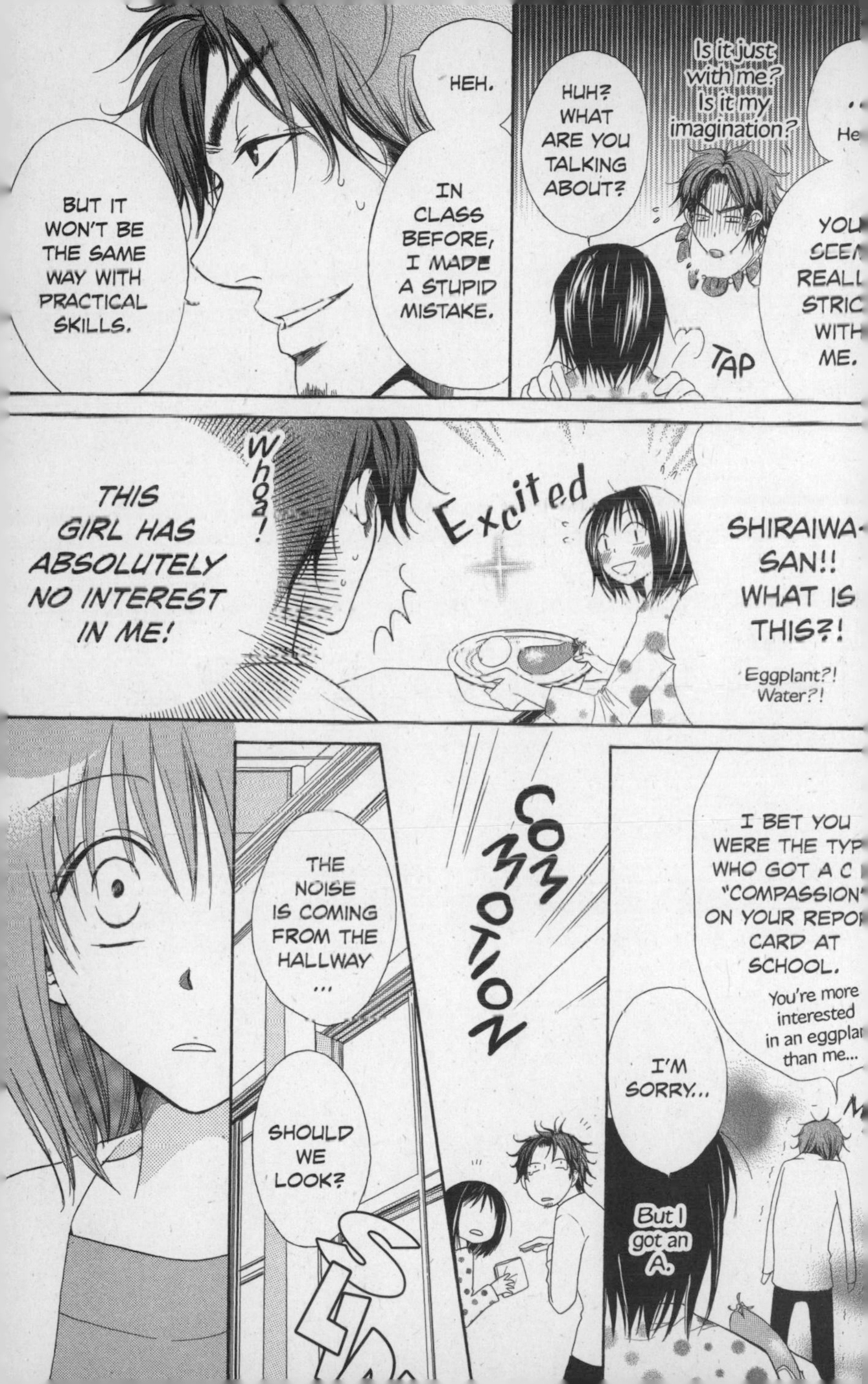
...
He
Is it just with me? Is it my imagination?
YOU SCEM REALL STRIC WITH ME.
HUH? WHAT ARE YOU TALKING ABOUT?
TAP
HEH.
IN CLASS BEFORE, I MADE A STUPID MISTAKE.
BUT IT WON'T BE THE SAME WAY WITH PRACTICAL SKILLS.
SHIRAIWA-SAN!! WHAT IS THIS?!
Eggplant?! Water?!
Excited
Whoa!
THIS GIRL HAS ABSOLUTELY NO INTEREST IN ME!
I BET YOU WERE THE TYP WHO GOT A C "COMPASSION" ON YOUR REPOI CARD AT SCHOOL.
You're more interested in an eggplai than me...
I'M SORRY...
But I got an A.
COMMOTION
THE NOISE IS COMING FROM THE HALLWAY...
SHOULD WE LOOK?

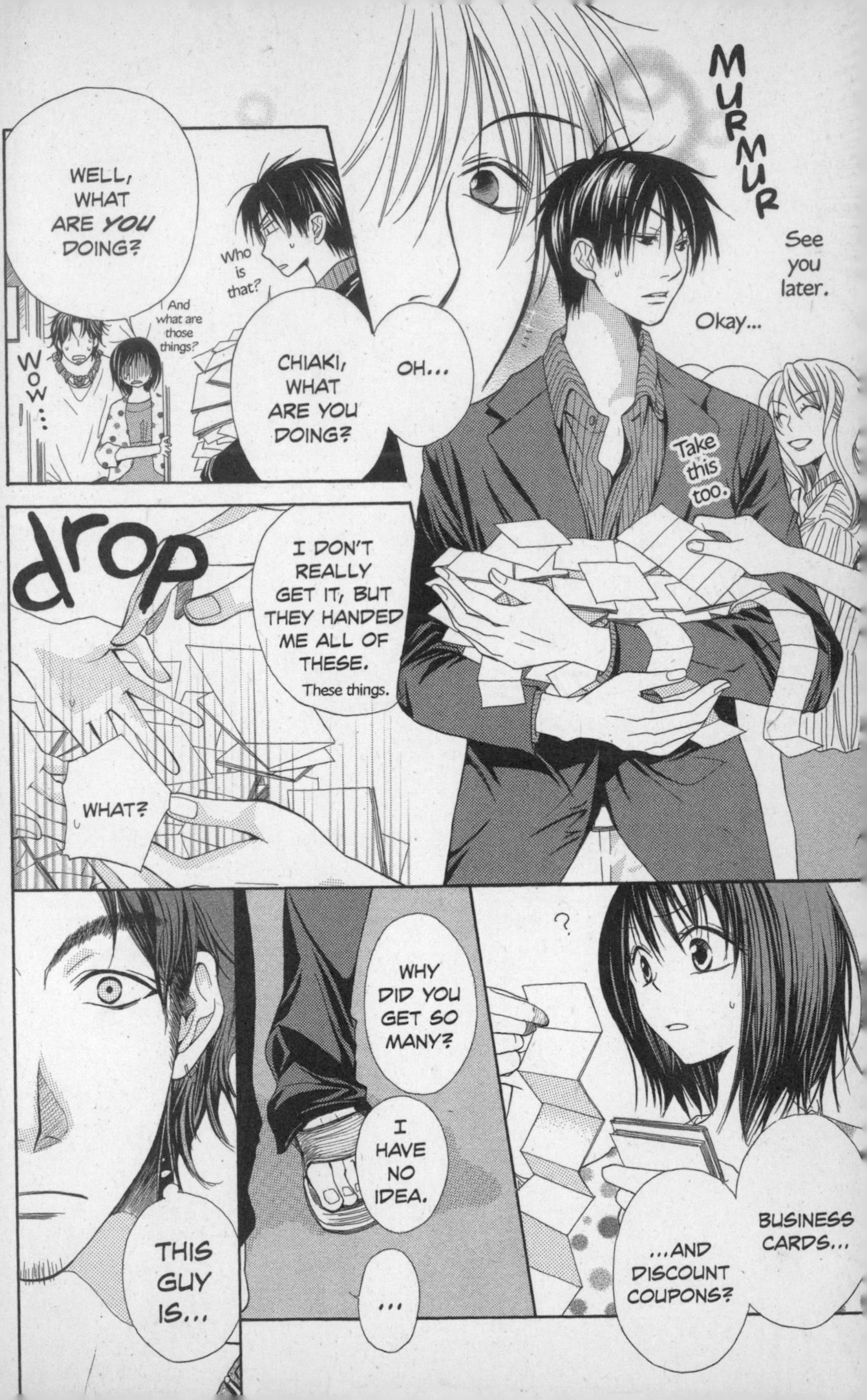
MURMUR
See you later.
Okay...
Take this too.
OH...
CHIAKI, WHAT ARE YOU DOING?
Who is that?
And what are those things?
WELL, WHAT ARE *YOU* DOING?
WOW...
I DON'T REALLY GET IT, BUT THEY HANDED ME ALL OF THESE.
These things.
drop
WHAT?
?
BUSINESS CARDS...
...AND DISCOUNT COUPONS?
WHY DID YOU GET SO MANY?
I HAVE NO IDEA.
...
THIS GUY IS...

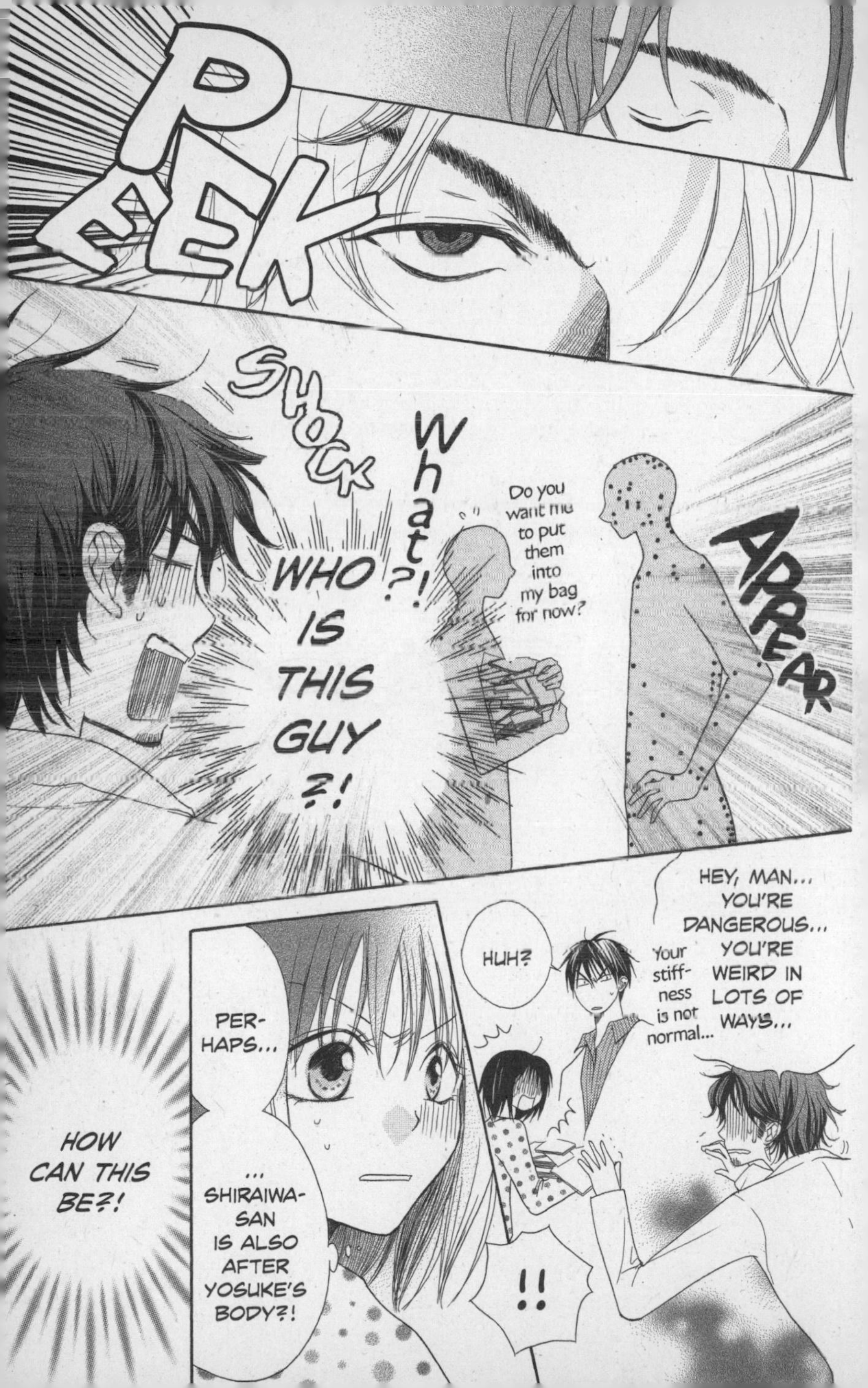
PEEK
APPEAR
Do you want me to put them into my bag for now?
What?!
SHOCK
WHO IS THIS GUY?!
HEY, MAN... YOU'RE DANGEROUS... YOU'RE WEIRD IN LOTS OF WAYS...
Your stiffness is not normal...
HUH?
!!
PERHAPS...
...SHIRAIWA-SAN IS ALSO AFTER YOSUKE'S BODY?!
HOW CAN THIS BE?!

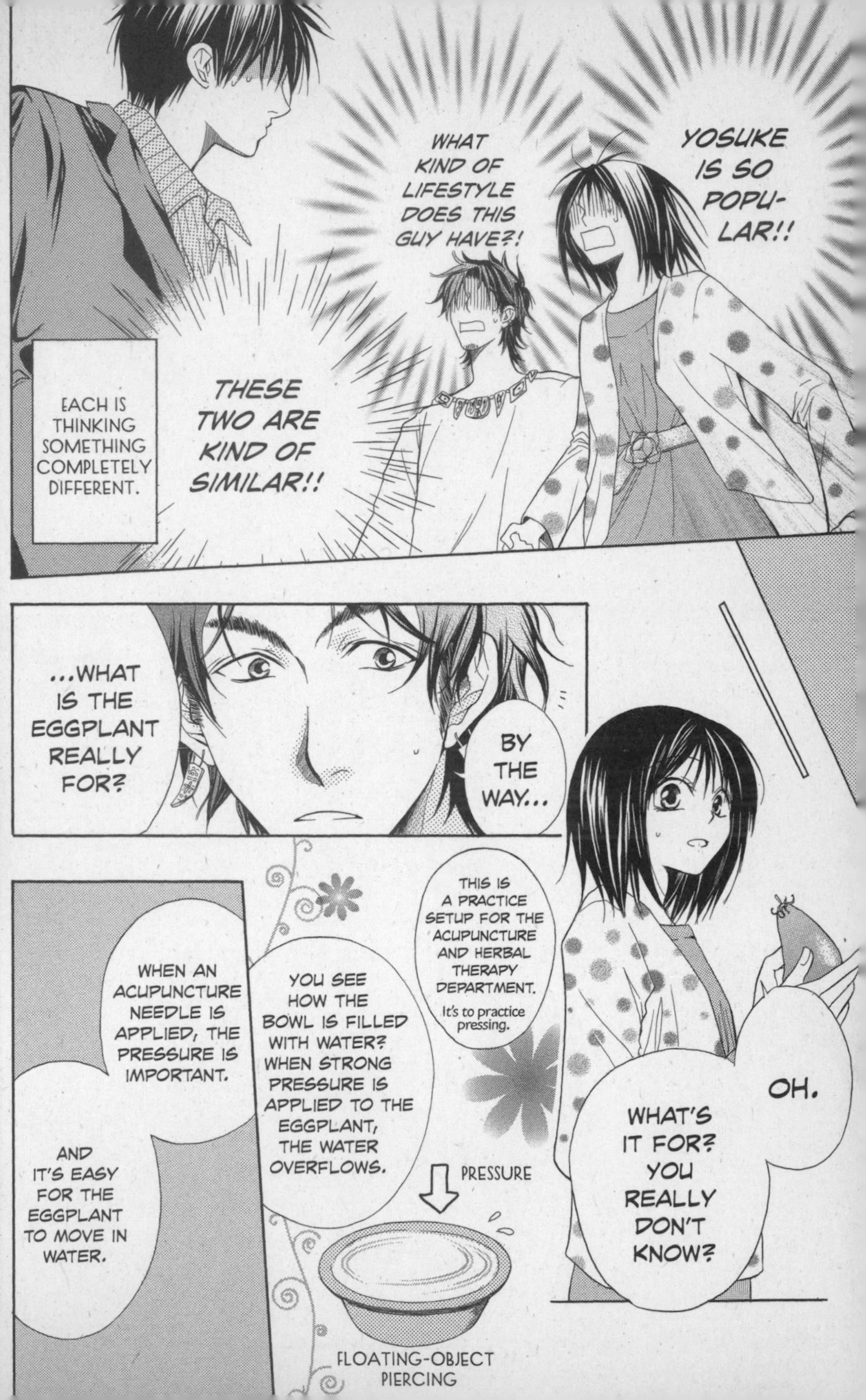
YOSUKE IS SO POPU-LAR!!
WHAT KIND OF LIFESTYLE DOES THIS GUY HAVE?!
THESE TWO ARE KIND OF SIMILAR!!
EACH IS THINKING SOMETHING COMPLETELY DIFFERENT.
BY THE WAY...
...WHAT IS THE EGGPLANT REALLY FOR?
OH.
WHAT'S IT FOR? YOU REALLY DON'T KNOW?
THIS IS A PRACTICE SETUP FOR THE ACUPUNCTURE AND HERBAL THERAPY DEPARTMENT.
It's to practice pressing.
YOU SEE HOW THE BOWL IS FILLED WITH WATER? WHEN STRONG PRESSURE IS APPLIED TO THE EGGPLANT, THE WATER OVERFLOWS.
PRESSURE
FLOATING-OBJECT PIERCING
WHEN AN ACUPUNCTURE NEEDLE IS APPLIED, THE PRESSURE IS IMPORTANT.
AND IT'S EASY FOR THE EGGPLANT TO MOVE IN WATER.

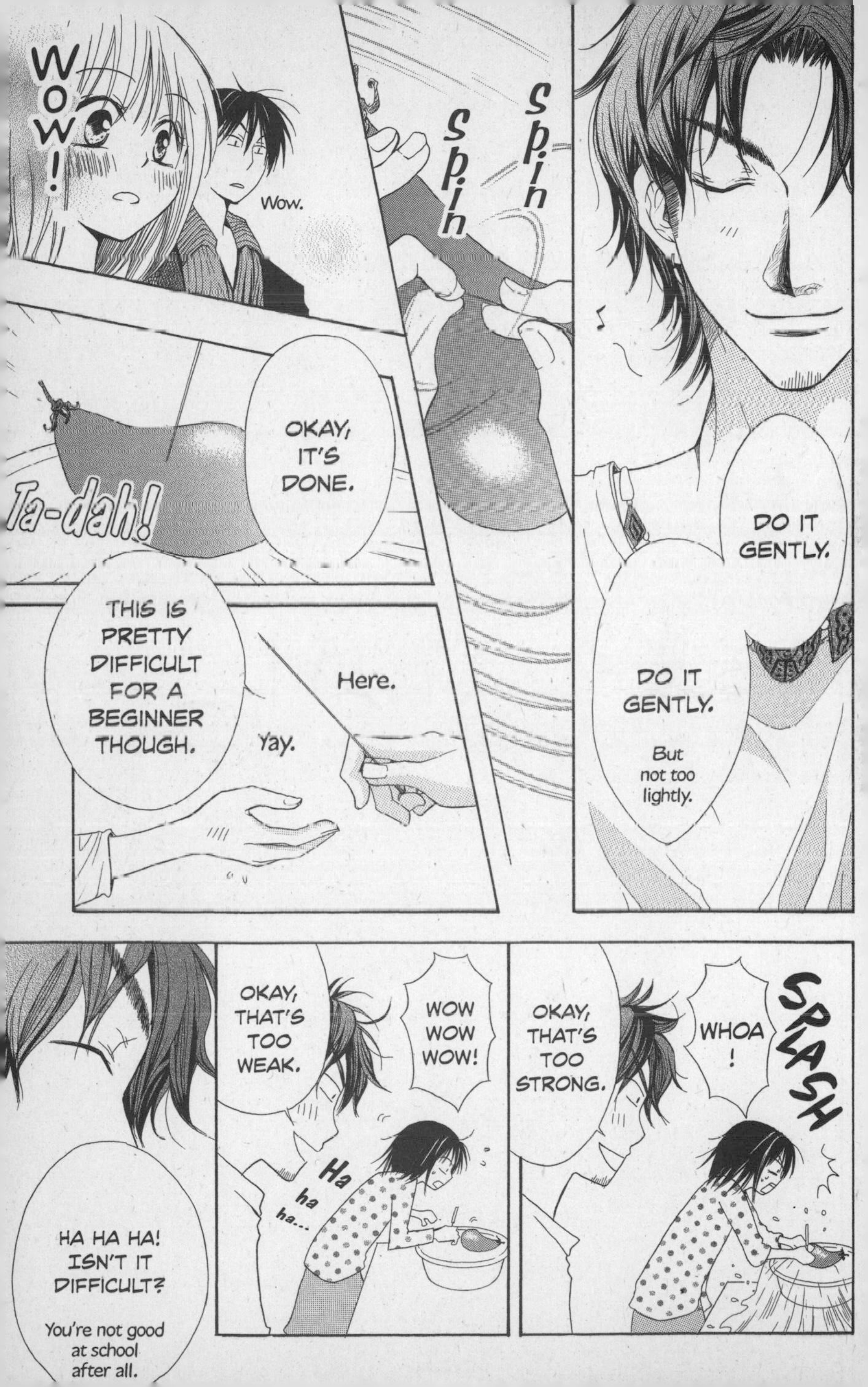
DO IT GENTLY.
DO IT GENTLY.
But not too lightly.
Spin
Spin
WOW!
Wow.
OKAY, IT'S DONE.
Ta-dah!
THIS IS PRETTY DIFFICULT FOR A BEGINNER THOUGH.
Here.
Yay.
SPLASH
WHOA!
OKAY, THAT'S TOO STRONG.
WOW WOW WOW!
OKAY, THAT'S TOO WEAK.
Ha ha ha...
HA HA HA! ISN'T IT DIFFICULT?
You're not good at school after all.

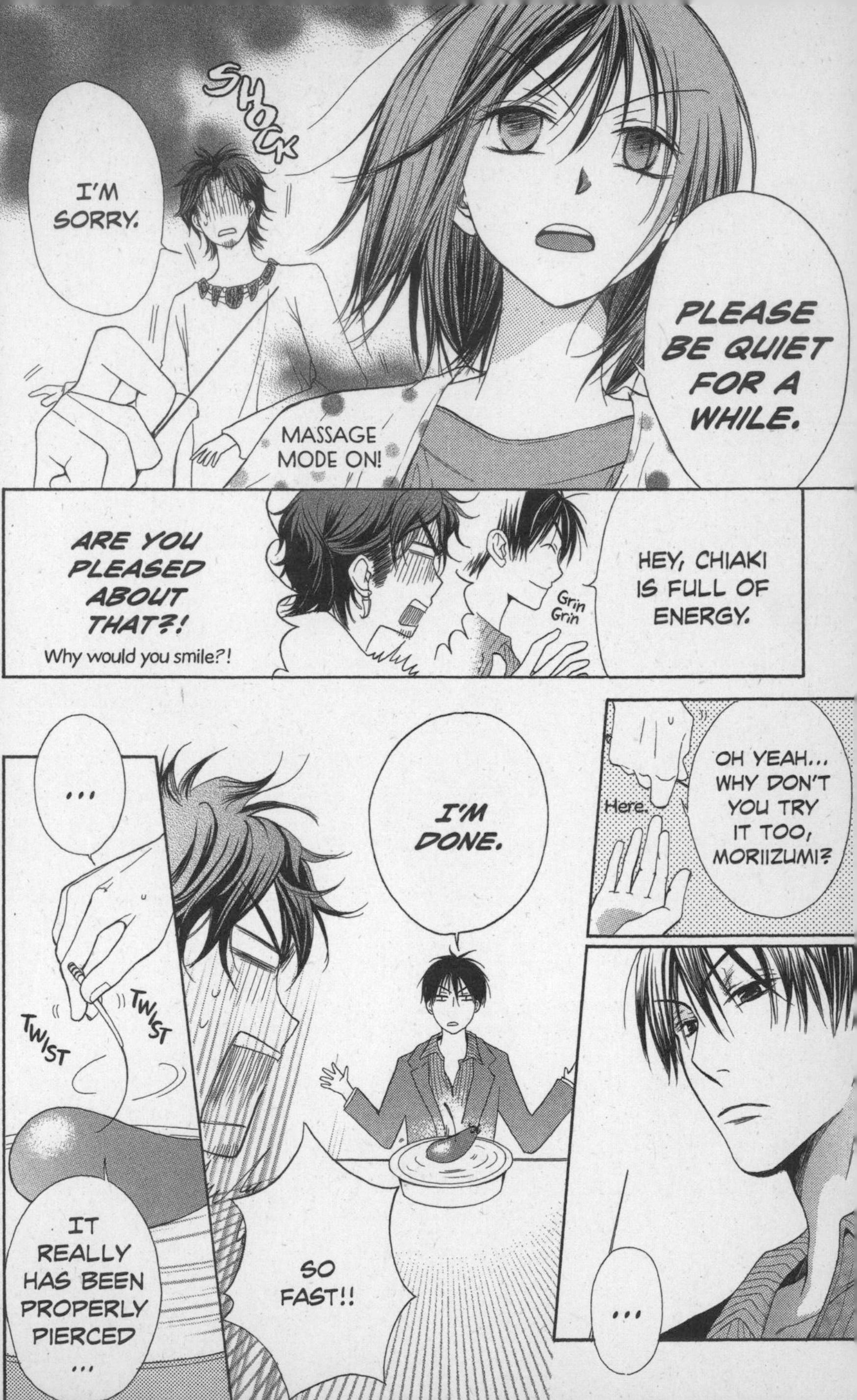
PLEASE BE QUIET FOR A WHILE.
SHOCK
I'M SORRY.
MASSAGE MODE ON!
HEY, CHIAKI IS FULL OF ENERGY.
Grin Grin
ARE YOU PLEASED ABOUT THAT?!
Why would you smile?!
OH YEAH... WHY DON'T YOU TRY IT TOO, MORIIZUMI?
Here.
...
I'M DONE.
SO FAST!!
...
TWIST
TWIST
IT REALLY HAS BEEN PROPERLY PIERCED...

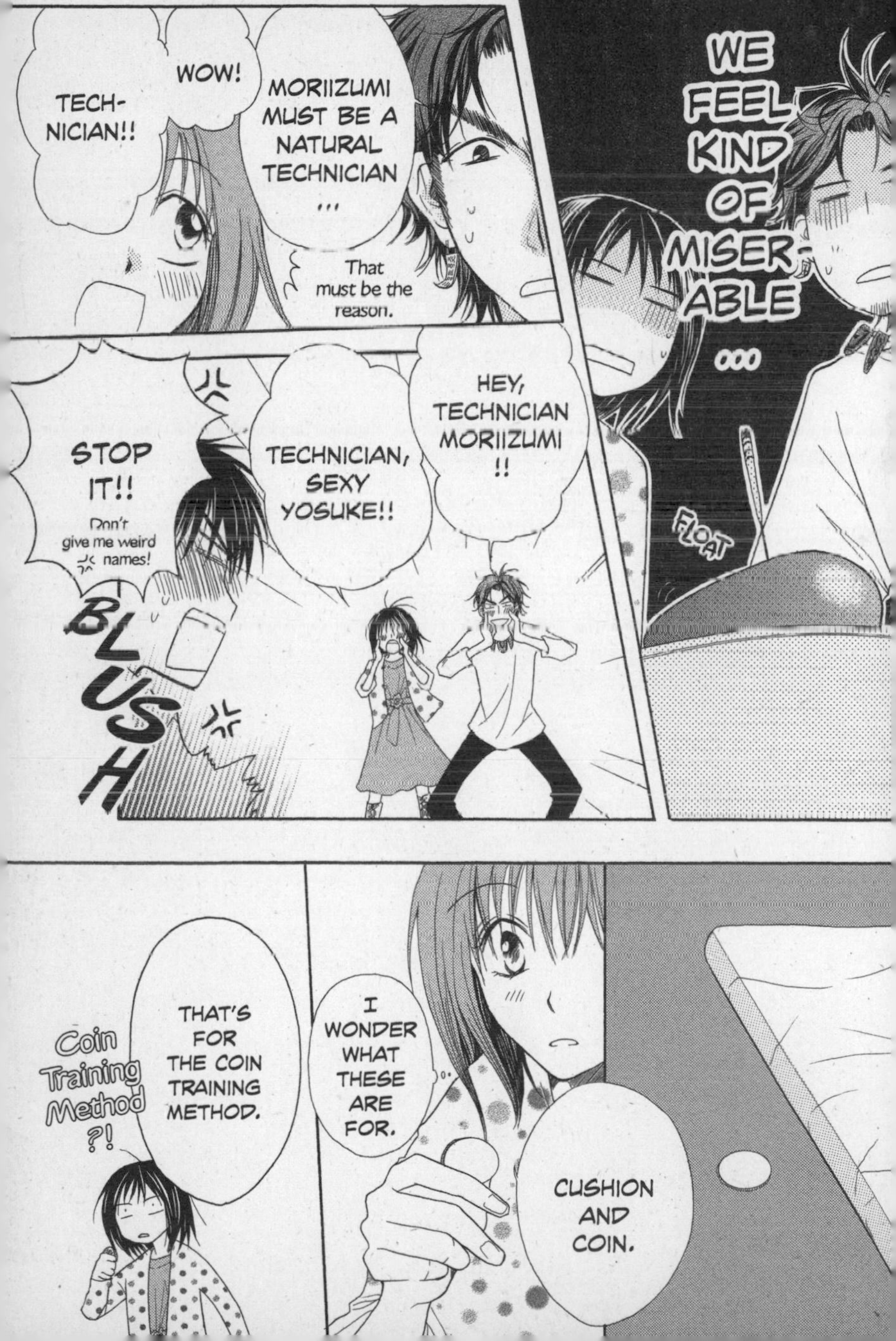
WE FEEL KIND OF MISER-ABLE ...
FLOAT
MORIIZUMI MUST BE A NATURAL TECHNICIAN ...
That must be the reason.
WOW!
TECH-NICIAN!!
HEY, TECHNICIAN MORIIZUMI !!
TECHNICIAN, SEXY YOSUKE!!
STOP IT!!
Don't give me weird names!
BLUSH
CUSHION AND COIN.
I WONDER WHAT THESE ARE FOR.
THAT'S FOR THE COIN TRAINING METHOD.
Coin Training Method ?!

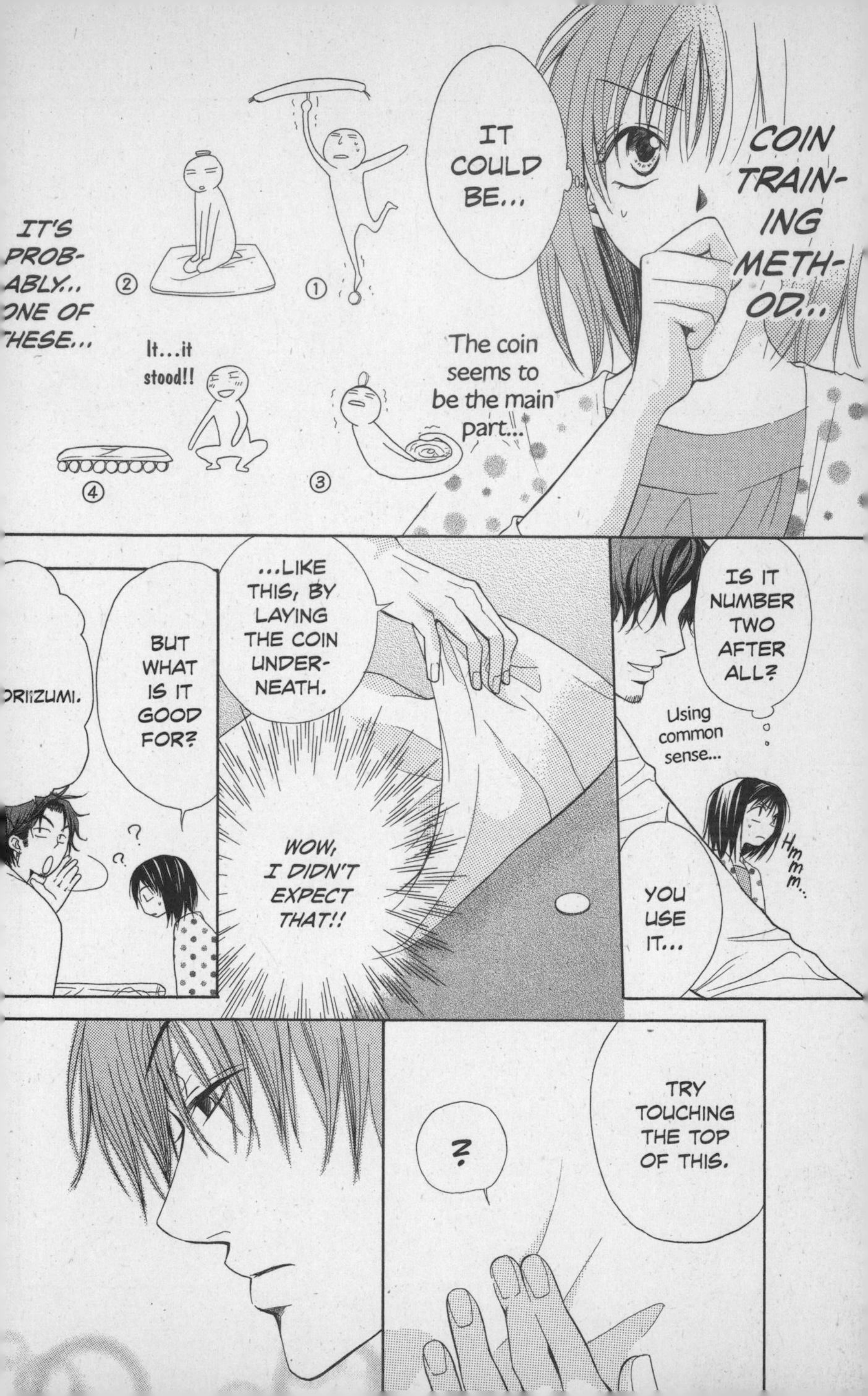
COIN TRAINING METHOD...
IT COULD BE...
The coin seems to be the main part...
IT'S PROBABLY... ONE OF THESE...
①
②
It...it stood!!
③
④
IS IT NUMBER TWO AFTER ALL?
Using common sense...
Hmmm...
YOU USE IT...
...LIKE THIS, BY LAYING THE COIN UNDERNEATH.
WOW, I DIDN'T EXPECT THAT!!
BUT WHAT IS IT GOOD FOR?
RIIZUMI.
TRY TOUCHING THE TOP OF THIS.
?

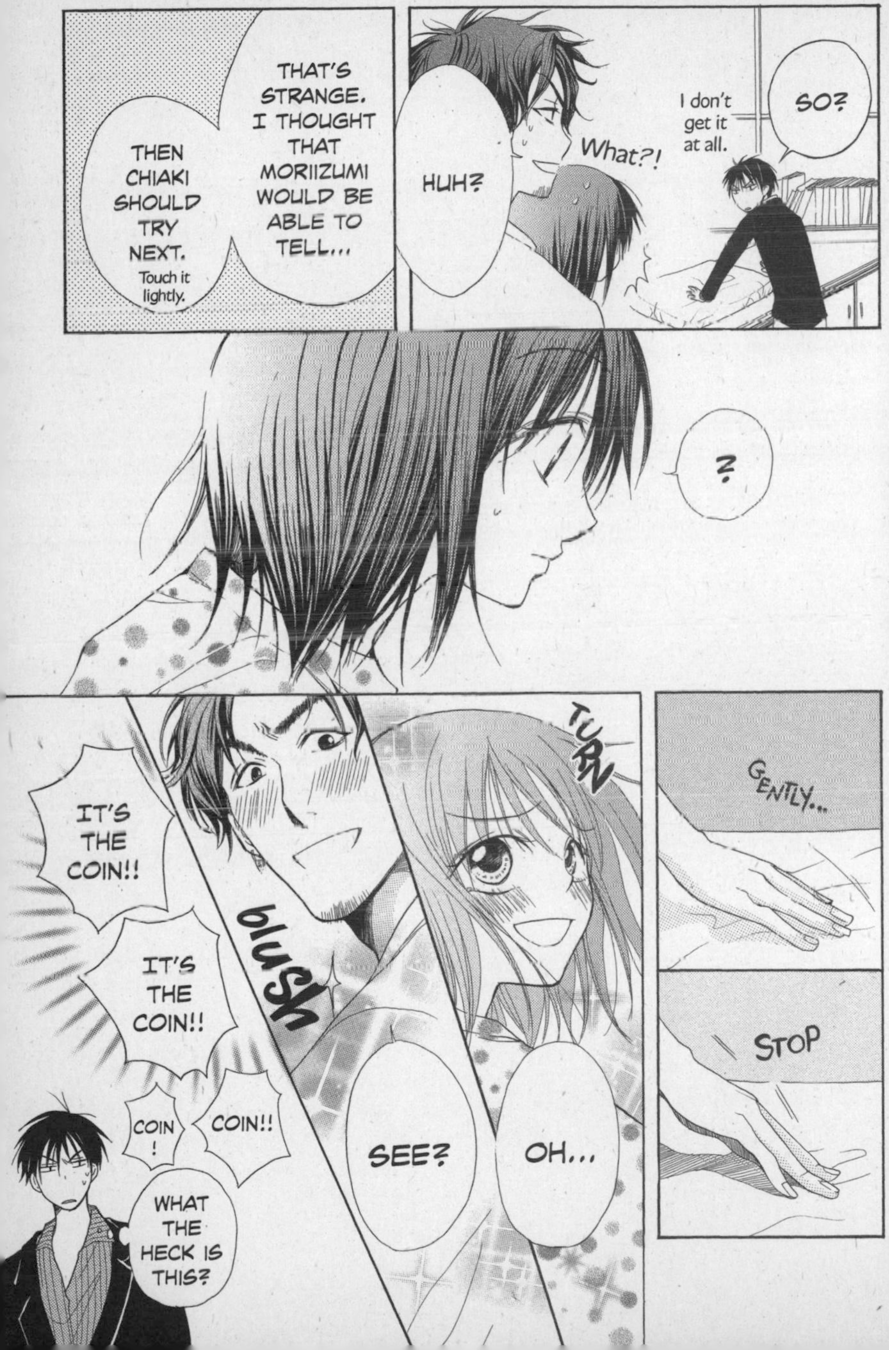
SO?
I don't get it at all.
What?!
HUH?
THAT'S STRANGE. I THOUGHT THAT MORIIZUMI WOULD BE ABLE TO TELL...
THEN CHIAKI SHOULD TRY NEXT.
Touch it lightly.
?
GENTLY...
STOP
TURN
blush
OH...
SEE?
IT'S THE COIN!!
IT'S THE COIN!!
COIN!!
COIN!
WHAT THE HECK IS THIS?

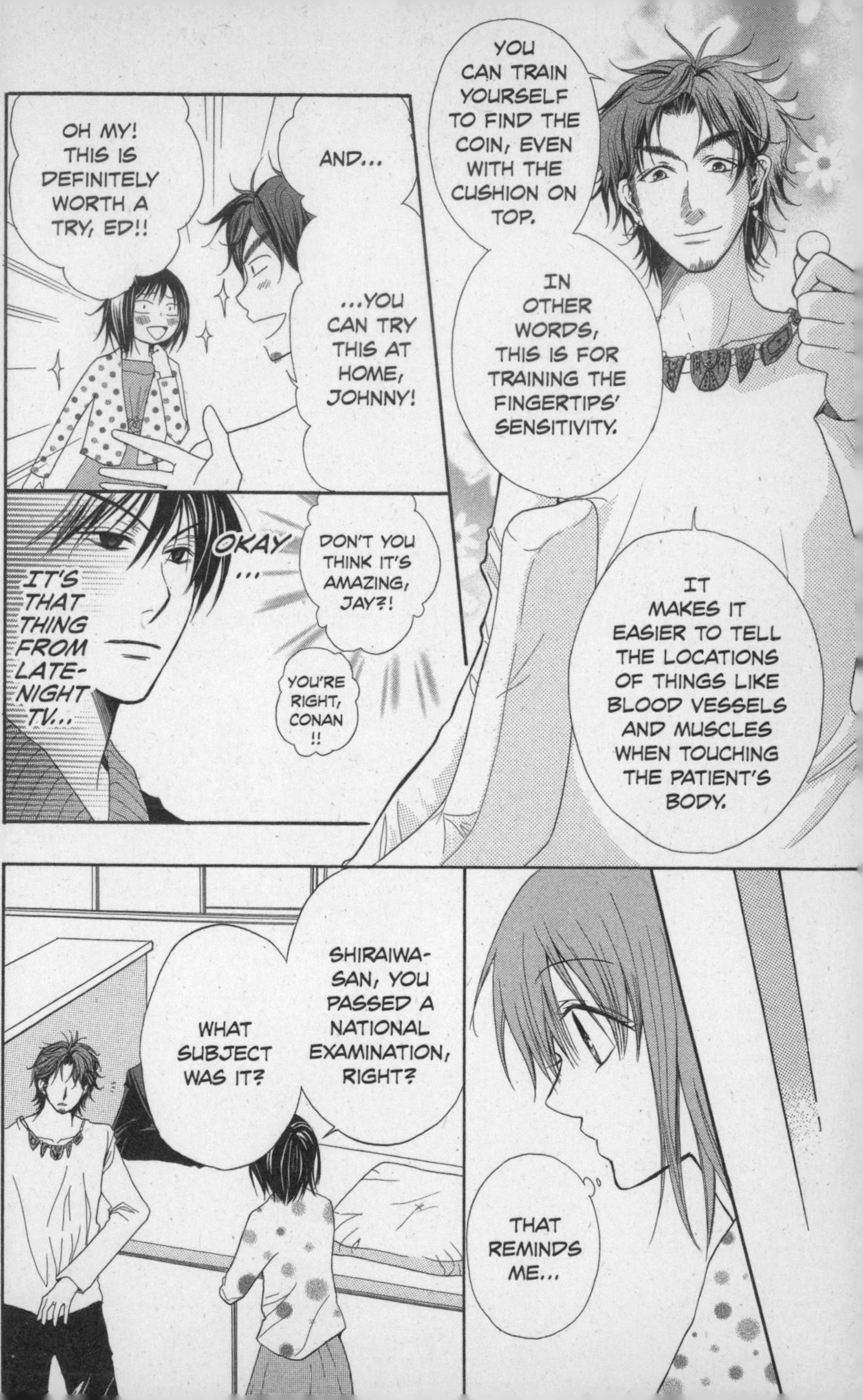
YOU CAN TRAIN YOURSELF TO FIND THE COIN, EVEN WITH THE CUSHION ON TOP.
IN OTHER WORDS, THIS IS FOR TRAINING THE FINGERTIPS' SENSITIVITY.
IT MAKES IT EASIER TO TELL THE LOCATIONS OF THINGS LIKE BLOOD VESSELS AND MUSCLES WHEN TOUCHING THE PATIENT'S BODY.
AND...
...YOU CAN TRY THIS AT HOME, JOHNNY!
OH MY! THIS IS DEFINITELY WORTH A TRY, ED!!
DON'T YOU THINK IT'S AMAZING, JAY?!
YOU'RE RIGHT, CONAN!!
OKAY...
IT'S THAT THING FROM LATE-NIGHT TV...
THAT REMINDS ME...
SHIRAIWA-SAN, YOU PASSED A NATIONAL EXAMINATION, RIGHT?
WHAT SUBJECT WAS IT?

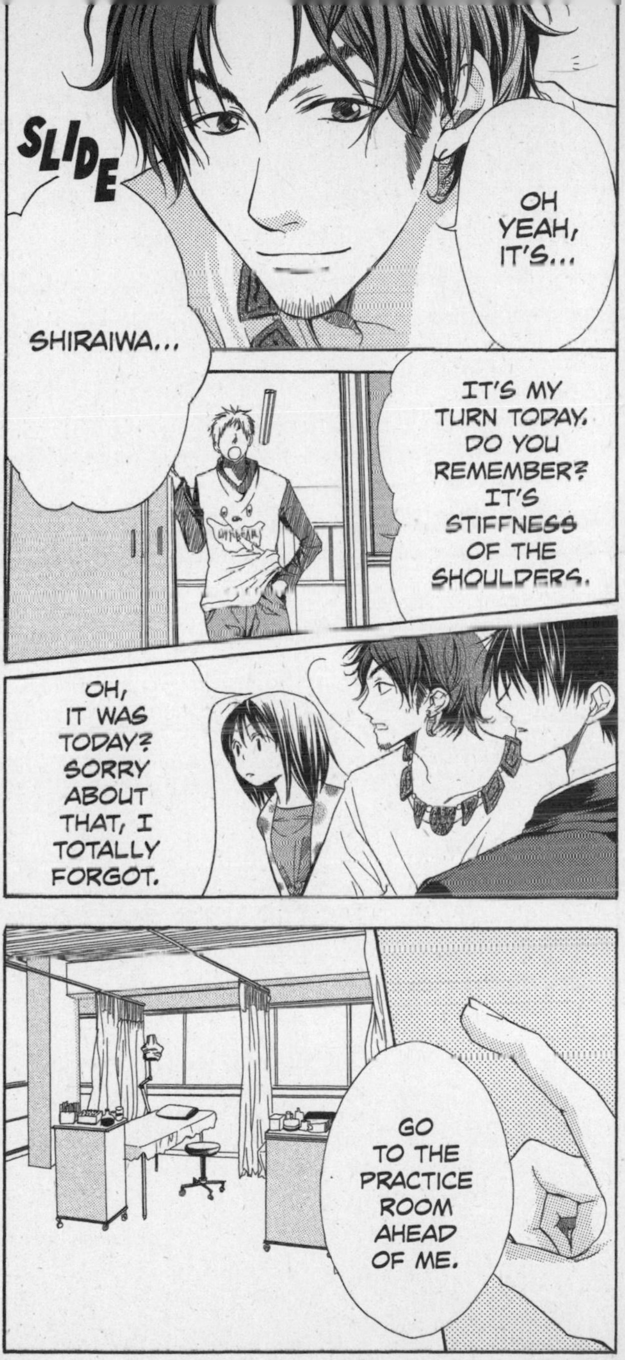
OH YEAH, IT'S...
SLIDE
SHIRAIWA...
IT'S MY TURN TODAY. DO YOU REMEMBER? IT'S STIFFNESS OF THE SHOULDERS.
OH, IT WAS TODAY? SORRY ABOUT THAT, I TOTALLY FORGOT.
GO TO THE PRACTICE ROOM AHEAD OF ME.

I Went to a Massage School

FOR AN INTRODUCTORY SESSION.

I went undercover, mixing in with the students applying there. The textbooks looked very difficult.

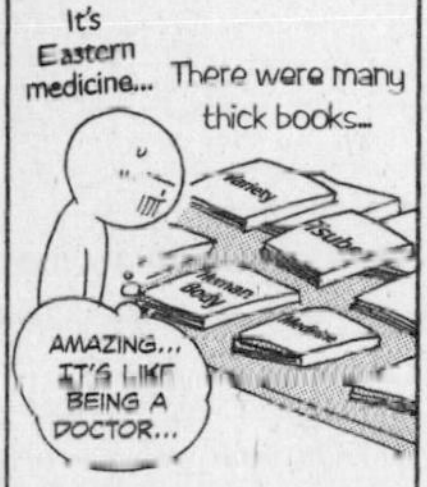
It's Eastern medicine...
There were many thick books...
AMAZING... IT'S LIKE BEING A DOCTOR...

There was a young high school student among the people taking the exam!!

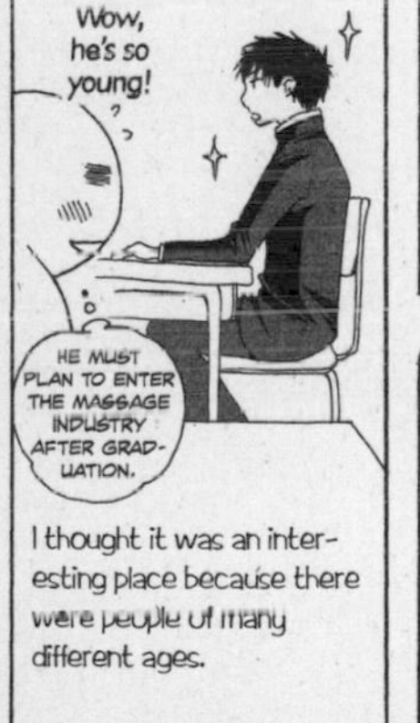
Wow, he's so young!
HE MUST PLAN TO ENTER THE MASSAGE INDUSTRY AFTER GRADUATION.

I thought it was an interesting place because there were people of many different ages.

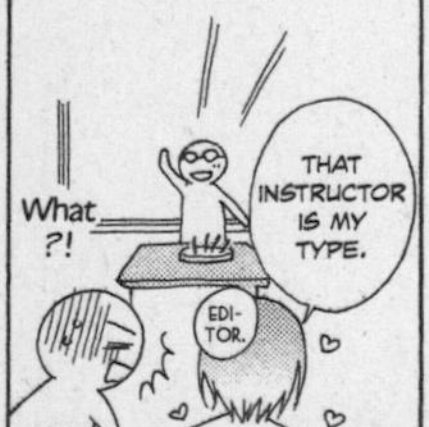
What?!
THAT INSTRUCTOR IS MY TYPE.
EDITOR.

The instructor was young.

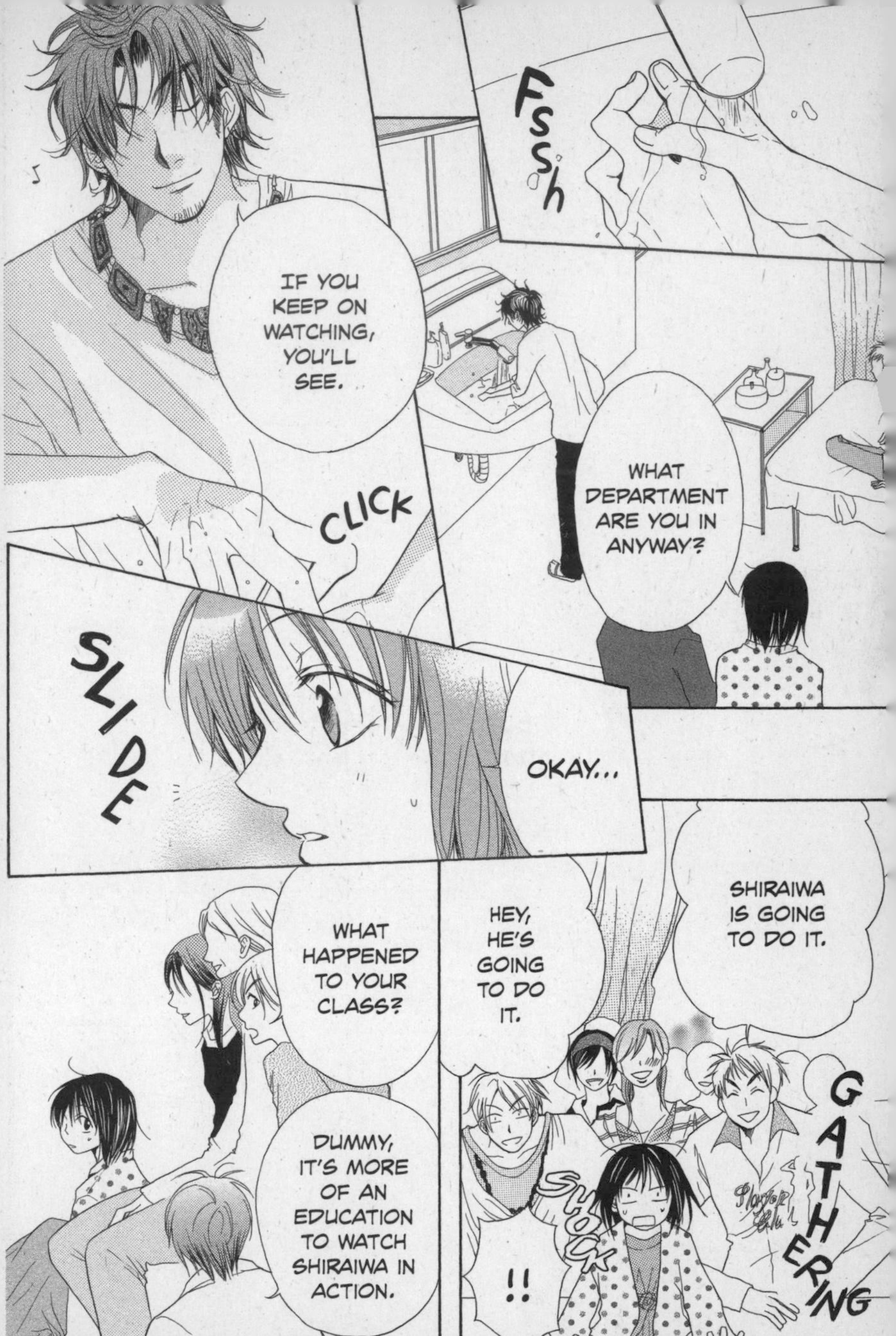
Fssh
IF YOU KEEP ON WATCHING, YOU'LL SEE.
CLICK
WHAT DEPARTMENT ARE YOU IN ANYWAY?
SLIDE
OKAY...
SHIRAIWA IS GOING TO DO IT.
HEY, HE'S GOING TO DO IT.
GATHERING
SHOCK
!!
WHAT HAPPENED TO YOUR CLASS?
DUMMY, IT'S MORE OF AN EDUCATION TO WATCH SHIRAIWA IN ACTION.

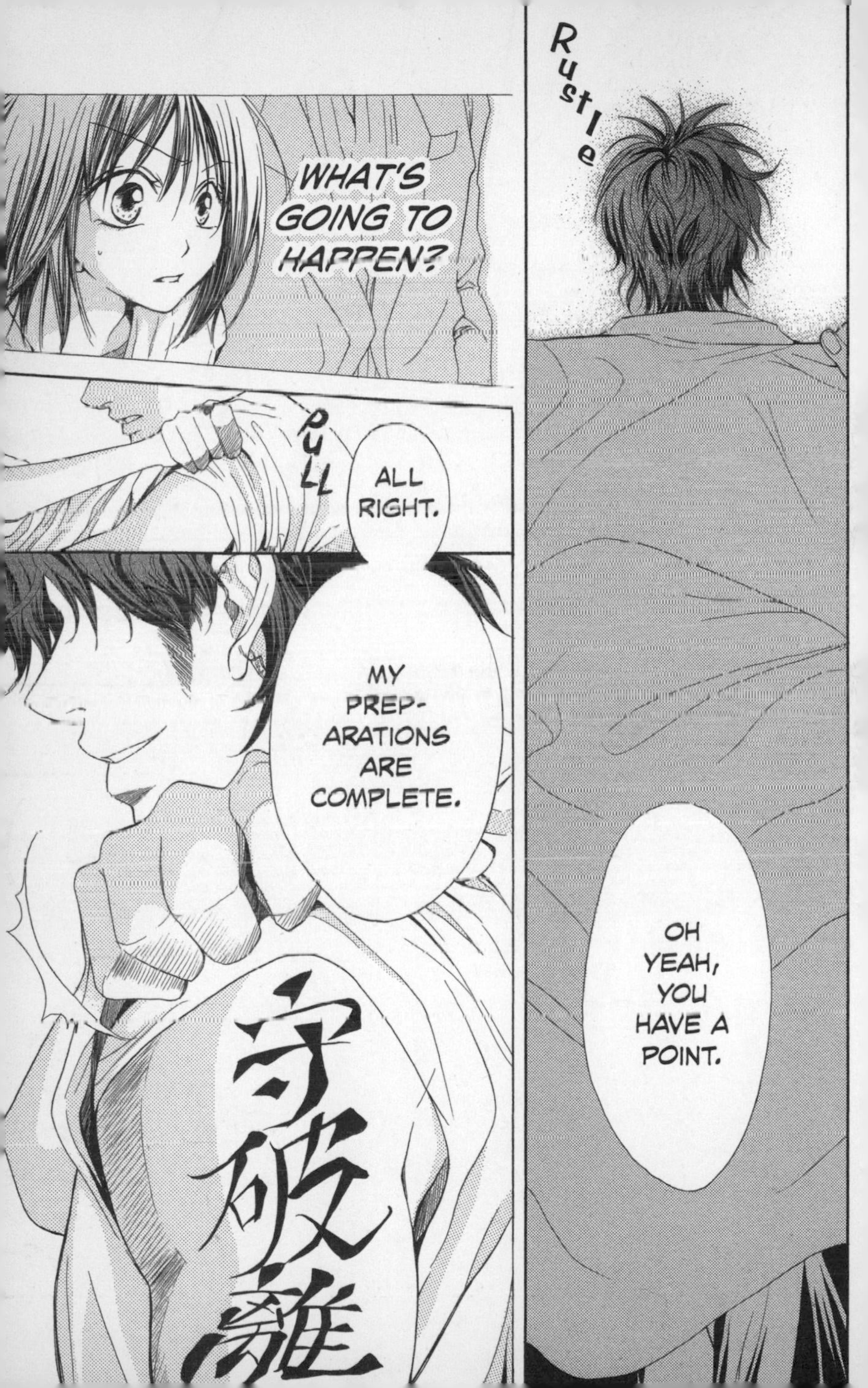
Rustle
OH YEAH, YOU HAVE A POINT.
WHAT'S GOING TO HAPPEN?
PULL
ALL RIGHT.
MY PREP-ARATIONS ARE COMPLETE.
守破離

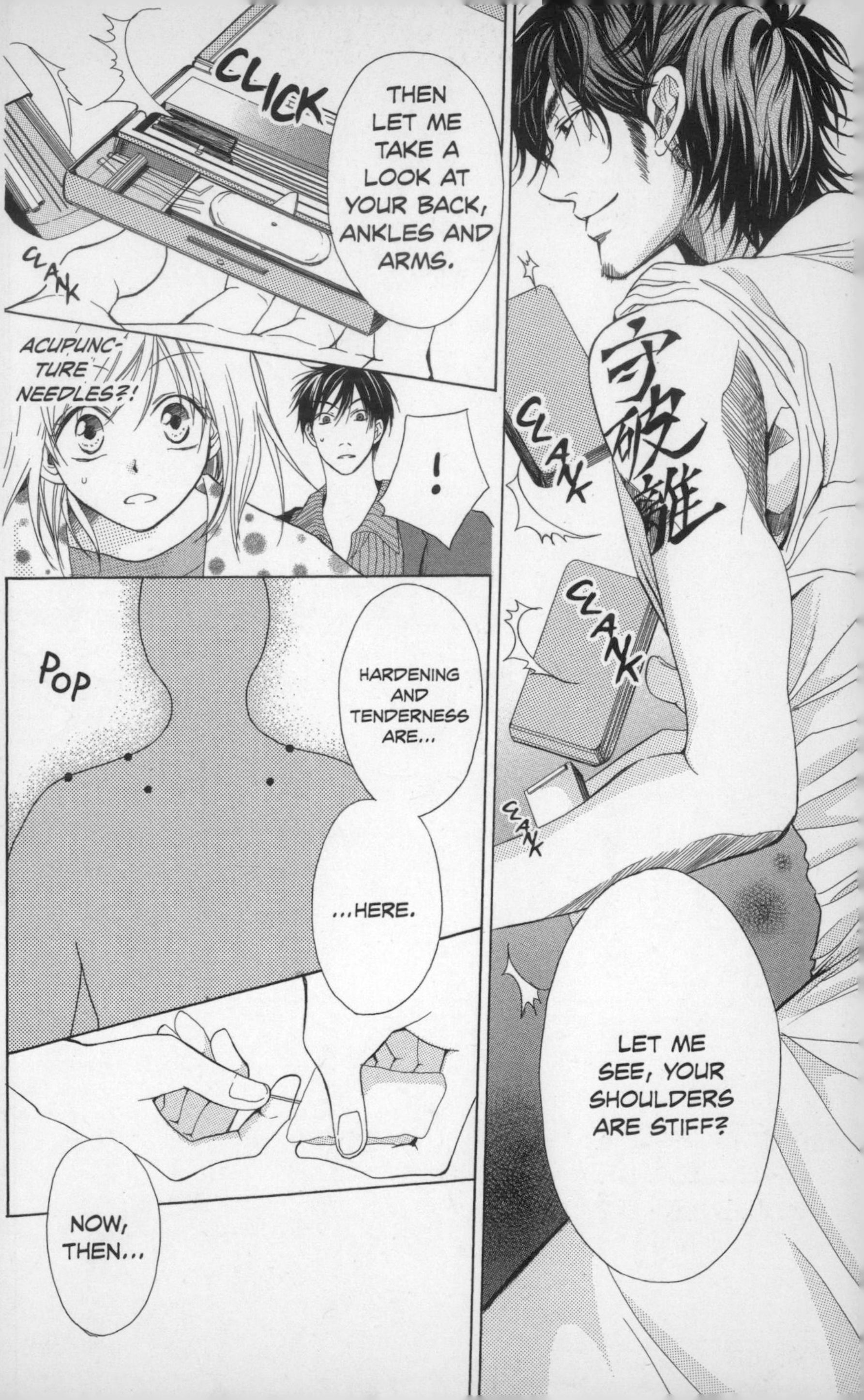
守破離
CLANK
CLANK
CLANK
LET ME SEE, YOUR SHOULDERS ARE STIFF?
CLICK
THEN LET ME TAKE A LOOK AT YOUR BACK, ANKLES AND ARMS.
CLANK
!
ACUPUNCTURE NEEDLES?!
HARDENING AND TENDERNESS ARE...
...HERE.
POP
NOW, THEN...

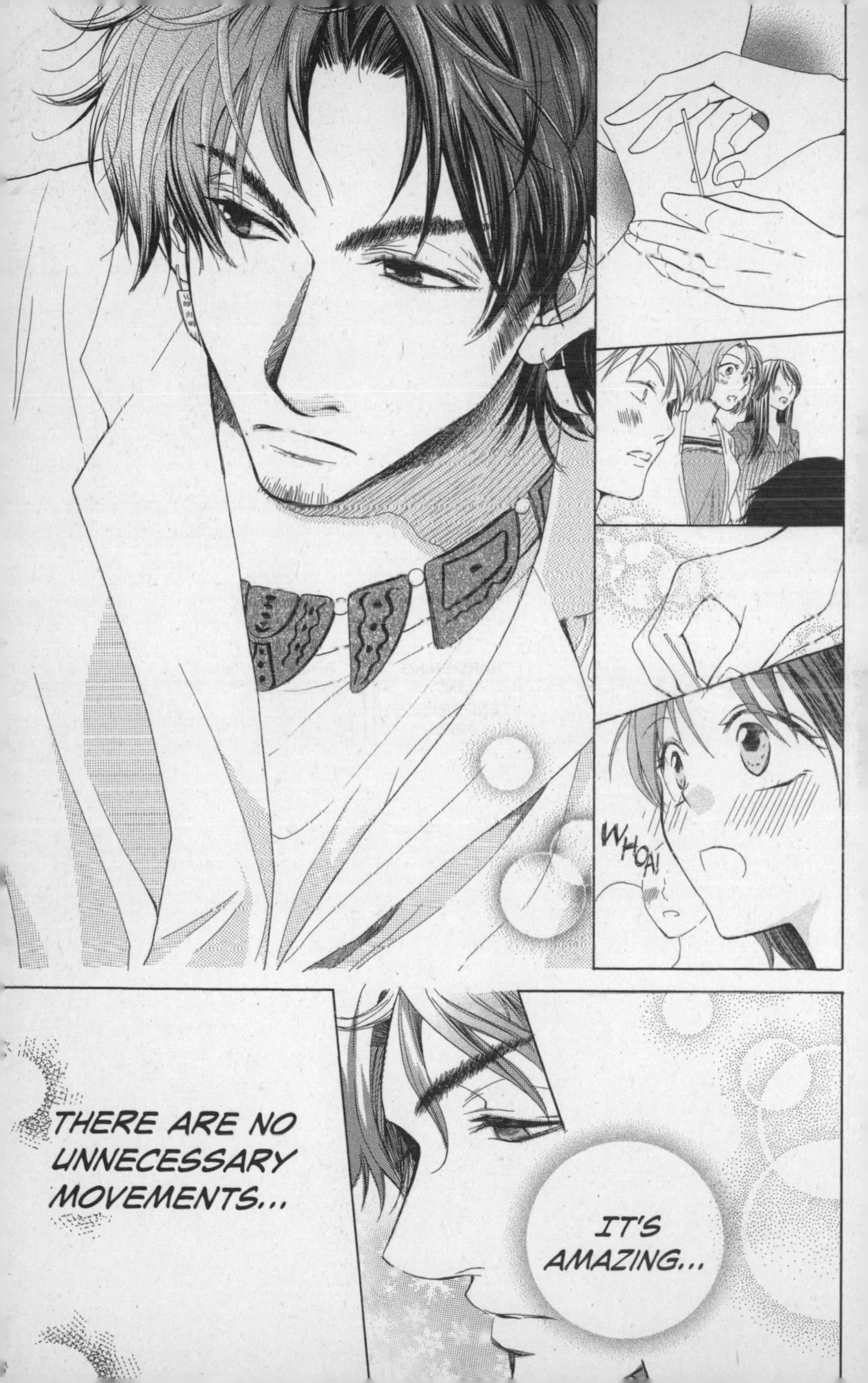
WHOA!
THERE ARE NO UNNECESSARY MOVEMENTS...
IT'S AMAZING...

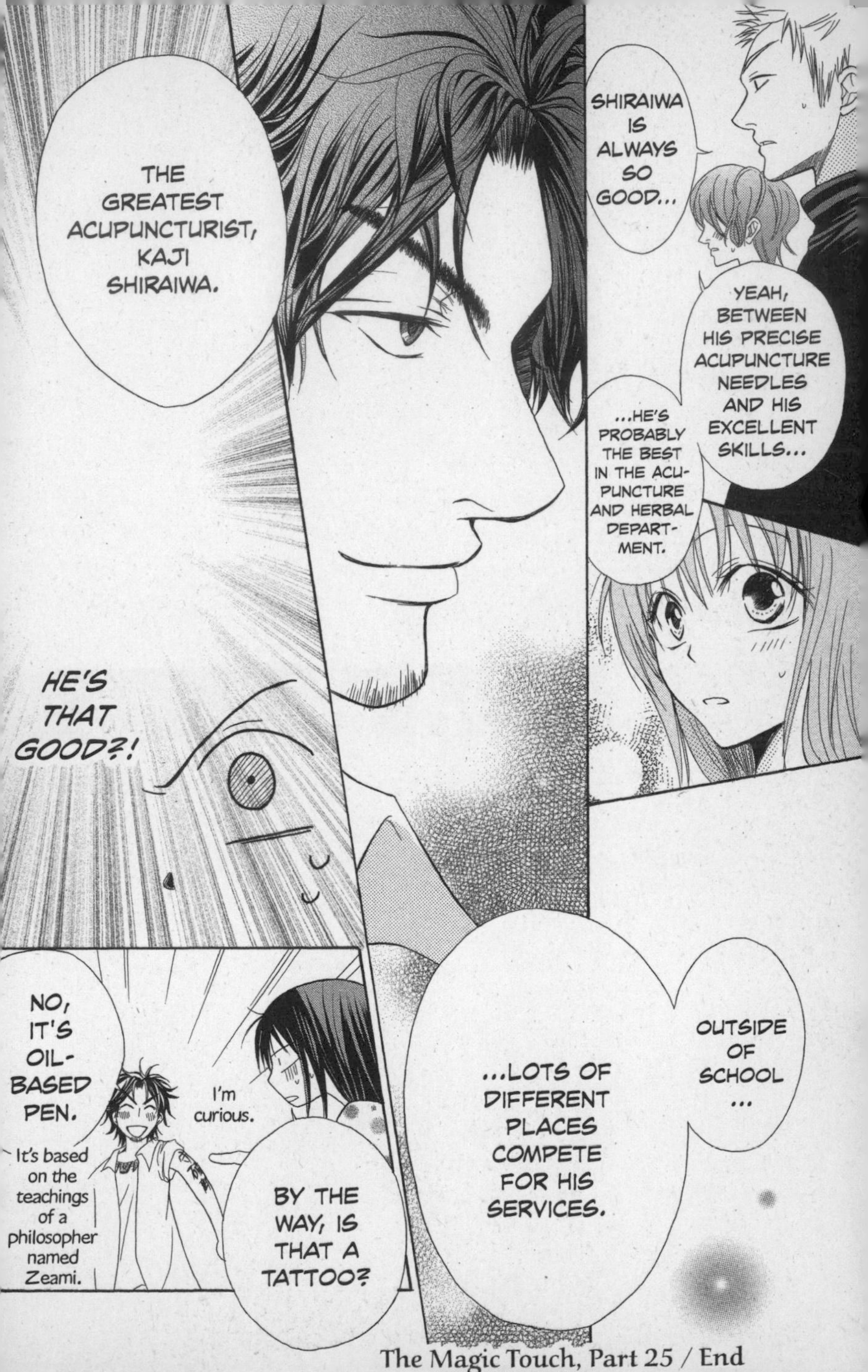
SHIRAIWA IS ALWAYS SO GOOD...
YEAH, BETWEEN HIS PRECISE ACUPUNCTURE NEEDLES AND HIS EXCELLENT SKILLS...
...HE'S PROBABLY THE BEST IN THE ACU-PUNCTURE AND HERBAL DEPART-MENT.
THE GREATEST ACUPUNCTURIST, KAJI SHIRAIWA.
HE'S THAT GOOD?!
OUTSIDE OF SCHOOL...
...LOTS OF DIFFERENT PLACES COMPETE FOR HIS SERVICES.
BY THE WAY, IS THAT A TATTOO?
I'm curious.
NO, IT'S OIL-BASED PEN.
It's based on the teachings of a philosopher named Zeami.

The Magic Touch, Part 25 / End

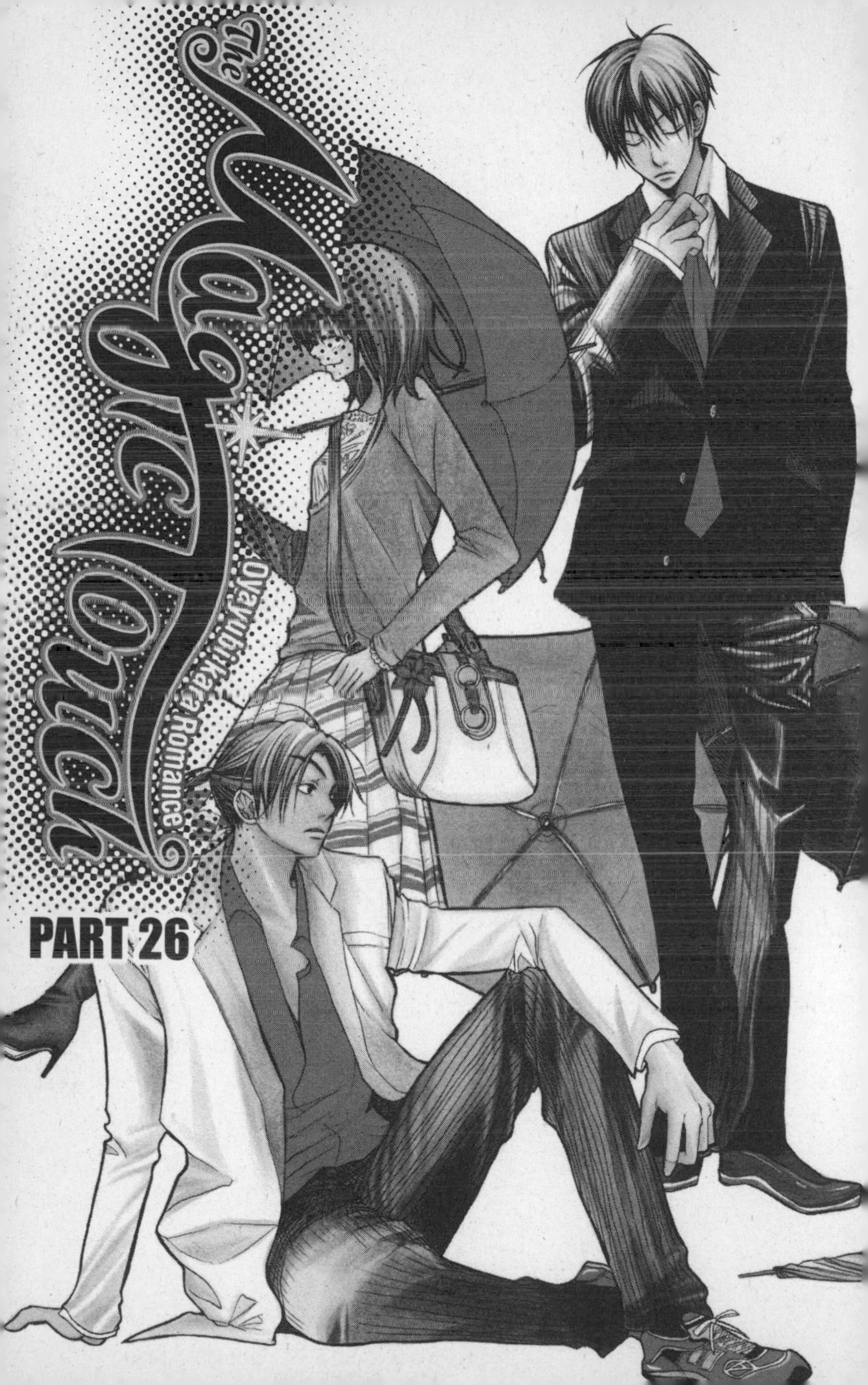
The Magic Touch
Oyayubi kara Romance
PART 26

SENPAI AND ME 1

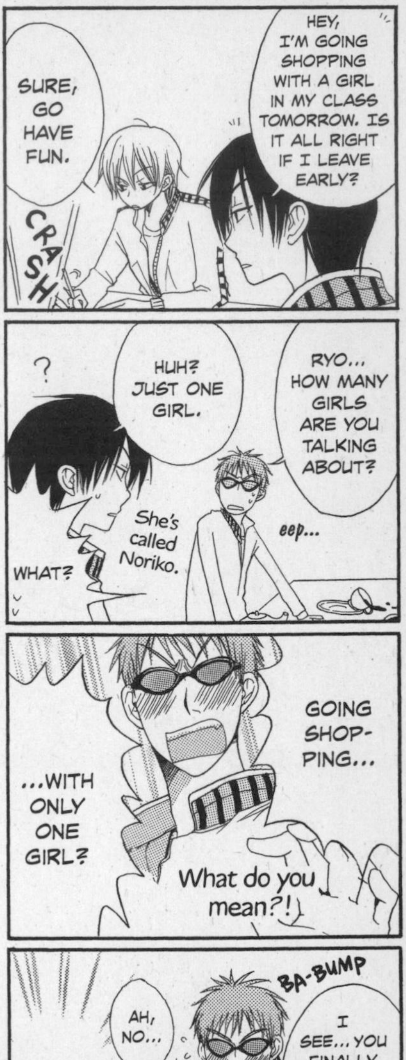
HEY, I'M GOING SHOPPING WITH A GIRL IN MY CLASS TOMORROW. IS IT ALL RIGHT IF I LEAVE EARLY?
SURE, GO HAVE FUN.
CRASH
RYO... HOW MANY GIRLS ARE YOU TALKING ABOUT?
eep...
HUH? JUST ONE GIRL.
She's called Noriko.
?
WHAT?
GOING SHOP-PING...
What do you mean?!
...WITH ONLY ONE GIRL?
BA-BUMP
I SEE... YOU FINALLY HAVE A GIRLFRIEND! THAT'S GREAT, RYO!
You're such an adult!!
?
AH, NO...
HE'S SO...!!

MIHIME IS VERY FORGETFUL.

SENPAI AND ME 2

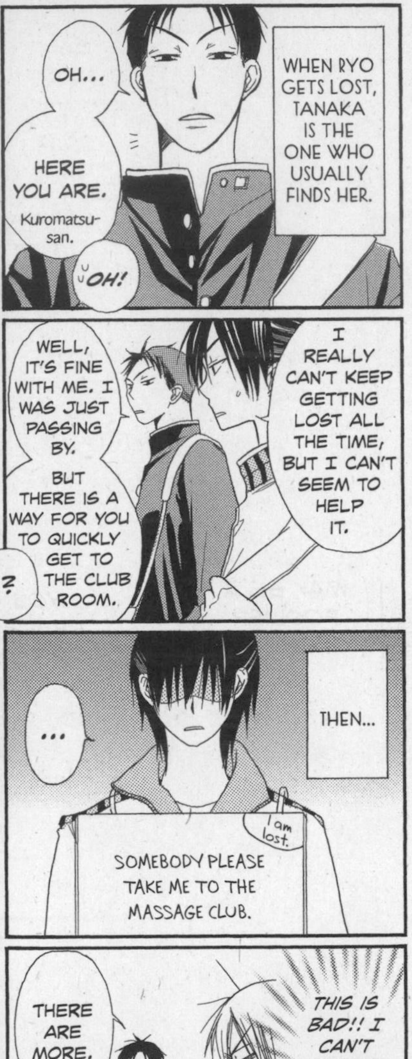
WHEN RYO GETS LOST, TANAKA IS THE ONE WHO USUALLY FINDS HER.
OH...
HERE YOU ARE.
Kuromatsu-san.
OH!
I REALLY CAN'T KEEP GETTING LOST ALL THE TIME, BUT I CAN'T SEEM TO HELP IT.
WELL, IT'S FINE WITH ME. I WAS JUST PASSING BY.
BUT THERE IS A WAY FOR YOU TO QUICKLY GET TO THE CLUB ROOM.
?
THEN...
I am lost.
SOMEBODY PLEASE TAKE ME TO THE MASSAGE CLUB.
...
THIS IS BAD!! I CAN'T OBJECT BECAUSE I CAN'T TELL IF HE'S BEING SERIOUS!!
Which is it?!
Somebody please take me to the train station.
THERE ARE MORE.
WHICH IS IT?!

↑ THE WANDERING HAND.

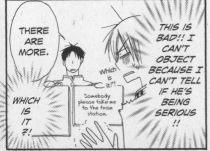

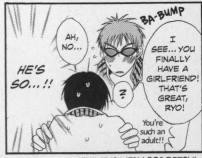

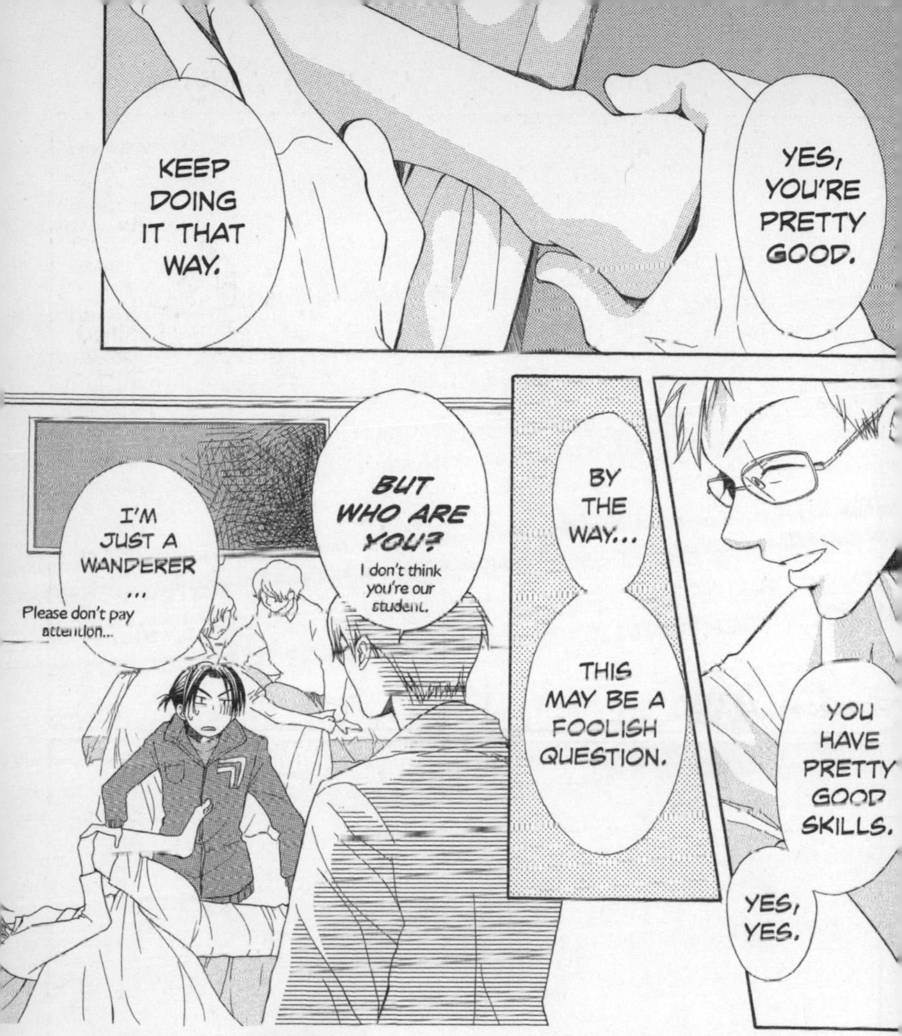
YES, YOU'RE PRETTY GOOD.
KEEP DOING IT THAT WAY.
YOU HAVE PRETTY GOOD SKILLS.
YES, YES.
BY THE WAY...
THIS MAY BE A FOOLISH QUESTION.
BUT WHO ARE YOU?
I don't think you're our student.
I'M JUST A WANDERER...
Please don't pay attention...

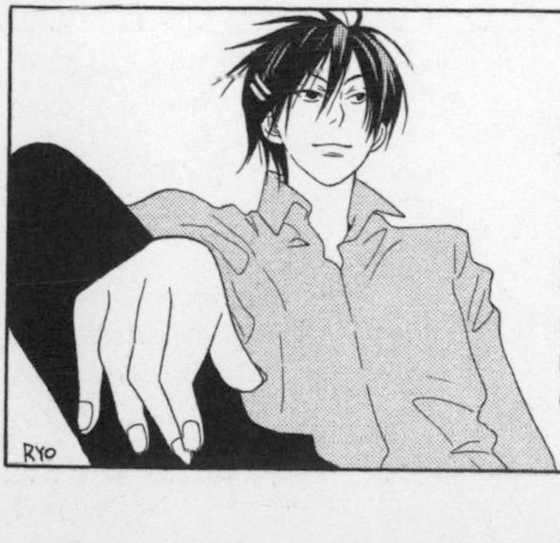
RYO

What *Shuhari* Means...

Koji's tattoo refers to the three steps to becoming independent after starting to study a subject. First, you firmly follow your mentor's teachings—"shu." Next, you break those rules and reform them to your own style—"ha." Ultimately, you aim to complete that style and go away from the mentor—"ri." That is the meaning of the term. It's a teaching that resonates on any path.

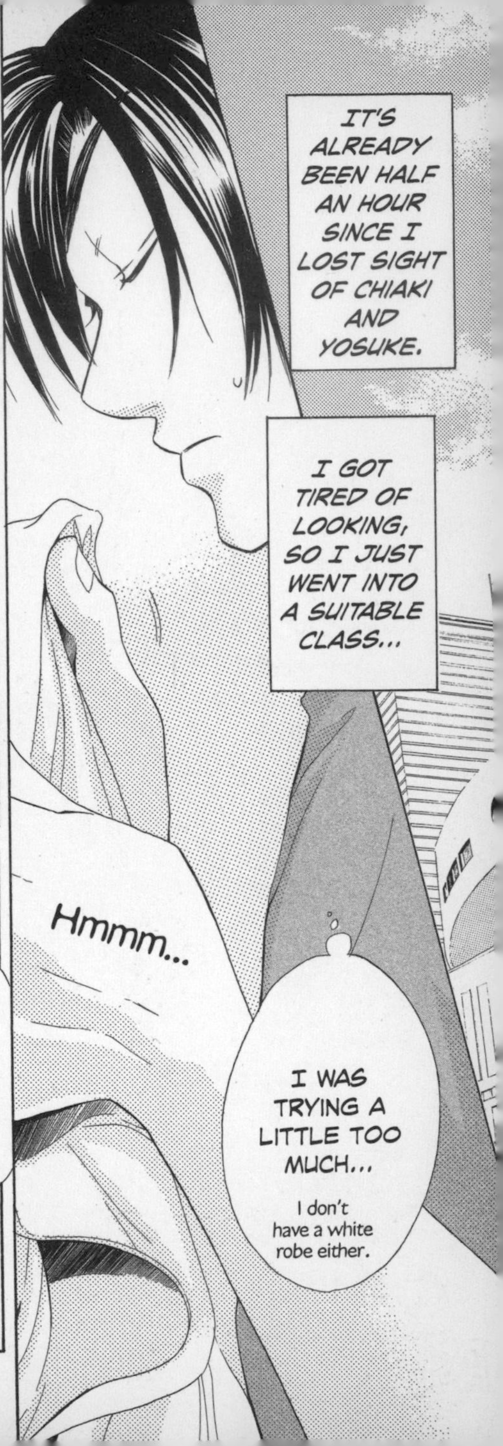
IT'S ALREADY BEEN HALF AN HOUR SINCE I LOST SIGHT OF CHIAKI AND YOSUKE.
I GOT TIRED OF LOOKING, SO I JUST WENT INTO A SUITABLE CLASS...
Hmmm...
I WAS TRYING A LITTLE TOO MUCH...
I don't have a white robe either.

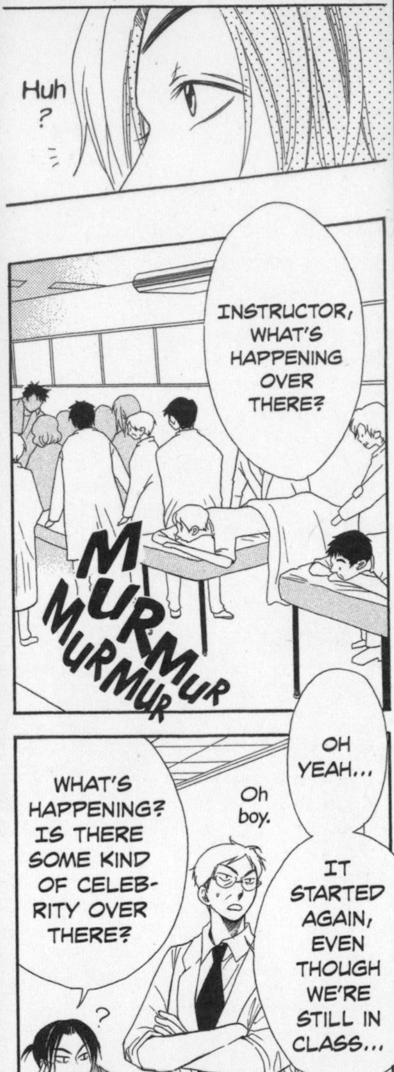
Huh?
INSTRUCTOR, WHAT'S HAPPENING OVER THERE?
MURMUR MURMUR
OH YEAH...
IT STARTED AGAIN, EVEN THOUGH WE'RE STILL IN CLASS...
Oh boy.
WHAT'S HAPPENING? IS THERE SOME KIND OF CELEBRITY OVER THERE?
?
It reminds me of somebody I know.

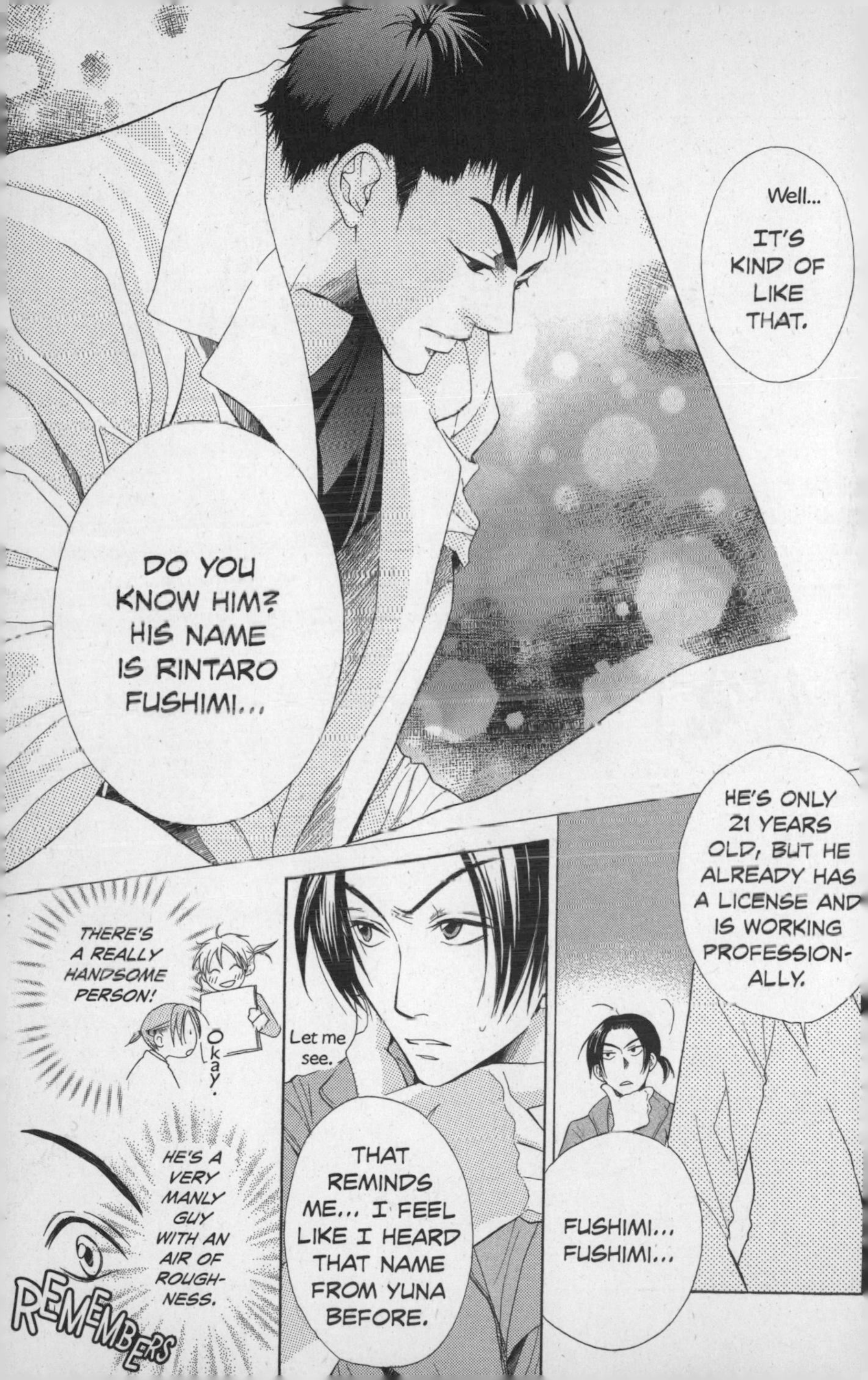
Well... IT'S KIND OF LIKE THAT.
DO YOU KNOW HIM? HIS NAME IS RINTARO FUSHIMI...
HE'S ONLY 21 YEARS OLD, BUT HE ALREADY HAS A LICENSE AND IS WORKING PROFESSION-ALLY.
FUSHIMI... FUSHIMI...
Let me see.
THAT REMINDS ME... I FEEL LIKE I HEARD THAT NAME FROM YUNA BEFORE.
THERE'S A REALLY HANDSOME PERSON!
Okay.
HE'S A VERY MANLY GUY WITH AN AIR OF ROUGH-NESS.
REMEMBERS

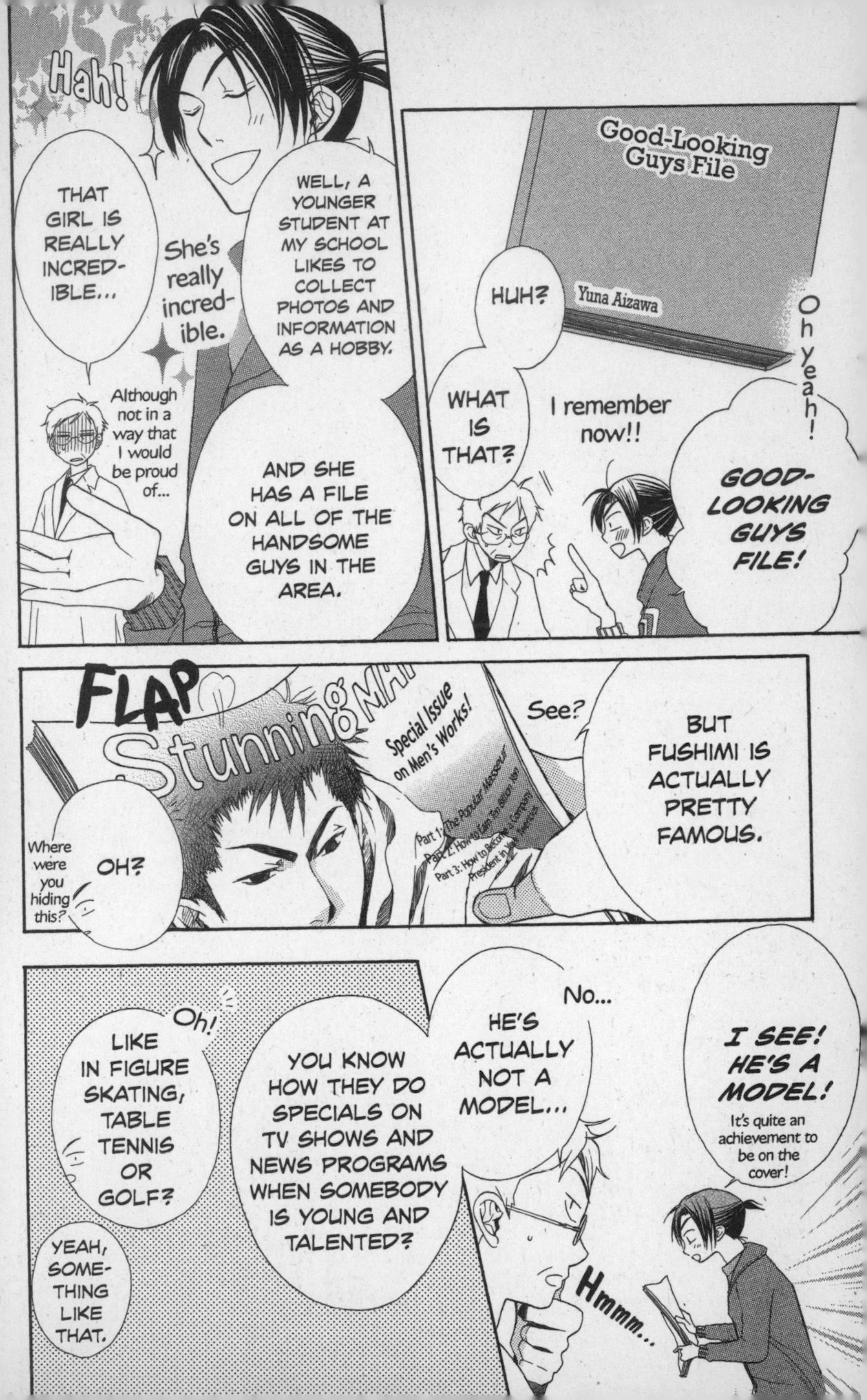
Good-Looking Guys File
Yuna Aizawa
Oh yeah!
GOOD-LOOKING GUYS FILE!
I remember now!!
HUH?
WHAT IS THAT?
Hah!
WELL, A YOUNGER STUDENT AT MY SCHOOL LIKES TO COLLECT PHOTOS AND INFORMATION AS A HOBBY.
AND SHE HAS A FILE ON ALL OF THE HANDSOME GUYS IN THE AREA.
She's really incredible.
THAT GIRL IS REALLY INCREDIBLE...
Although not in a way that I would be proud of...
BUT FUSHIMI IS ACTUALLY PRETTY FAMOUS.
See?
Stunning MAN
Special Issue on Men's Works!
Part 1: The Popular Masseur
FLAP
OH?
Where were you hiding this?
I SEE! HE'S A MODEL!
It's quite an achievement to be on the cover!
No...
HE'S ACTUALLY NOT A MODEL...
Hmmm...
YOU KNOW HOW THEY DO SPECIALS ON TV SHOWS AND NEWS PROGRAMS WHEN SOMEBODY IS YOUNG AND TALENTED?
Oh!
LIKE IN FIGURE SKATING, TABLE TENNIS OR GOLF?
YEAH, SOMETHING LIKE THAT.

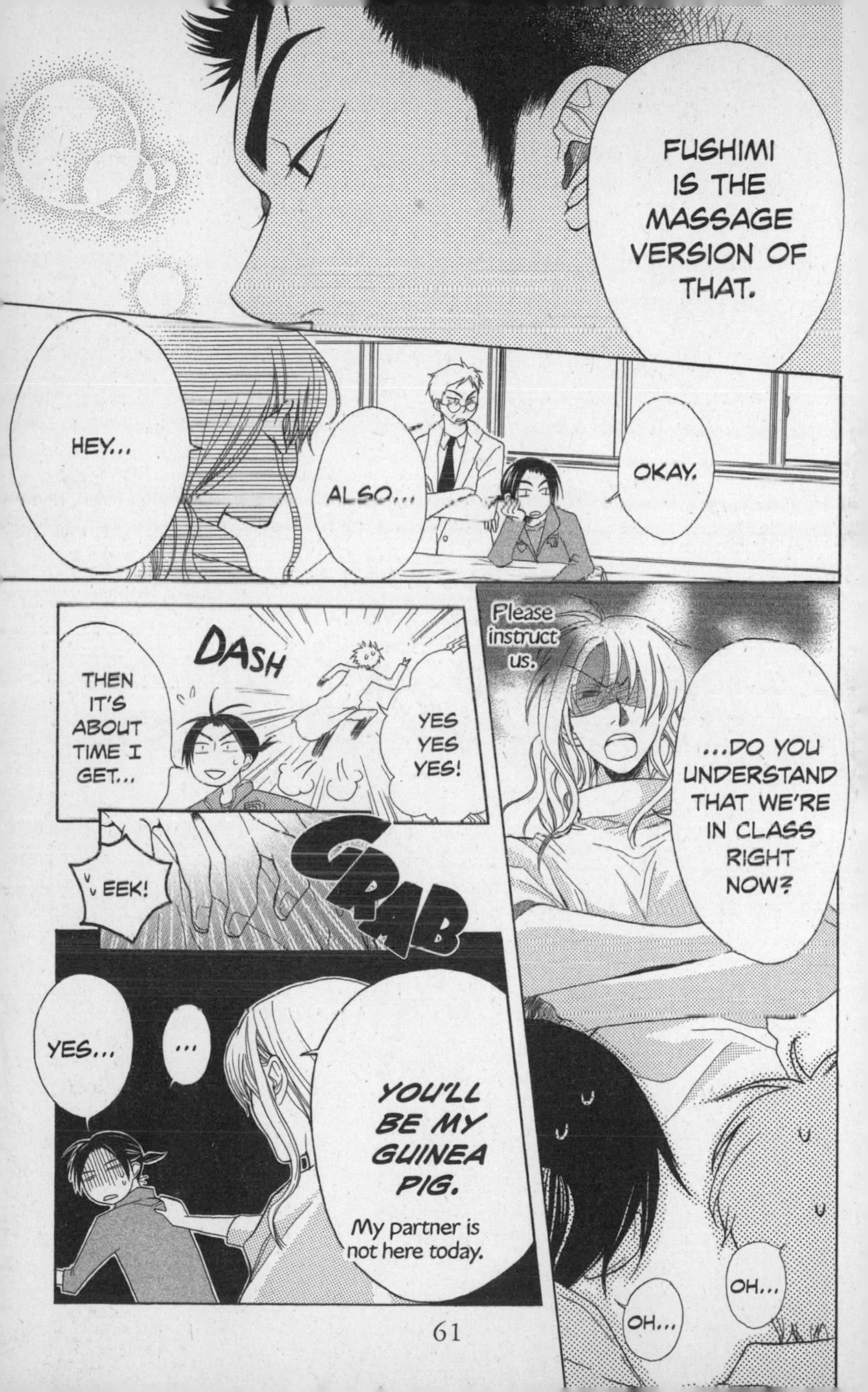
FUSHIMI IS THE MASSAGE VERSION OF THAT.
OKAY.
ALSO...
HEY...
Please instruct us.
...DO YOU UNDERSTAND THAT WE'RE IN CLASS RIGHT NOW?
OH...
OH...
DASH
YES YES YES!
THEN IT'S ABOUT TIME I GET...
GRAB
EEK!
YOU'LL BE MY GUINEA PIG.
My partner is not here today.
...
YES...

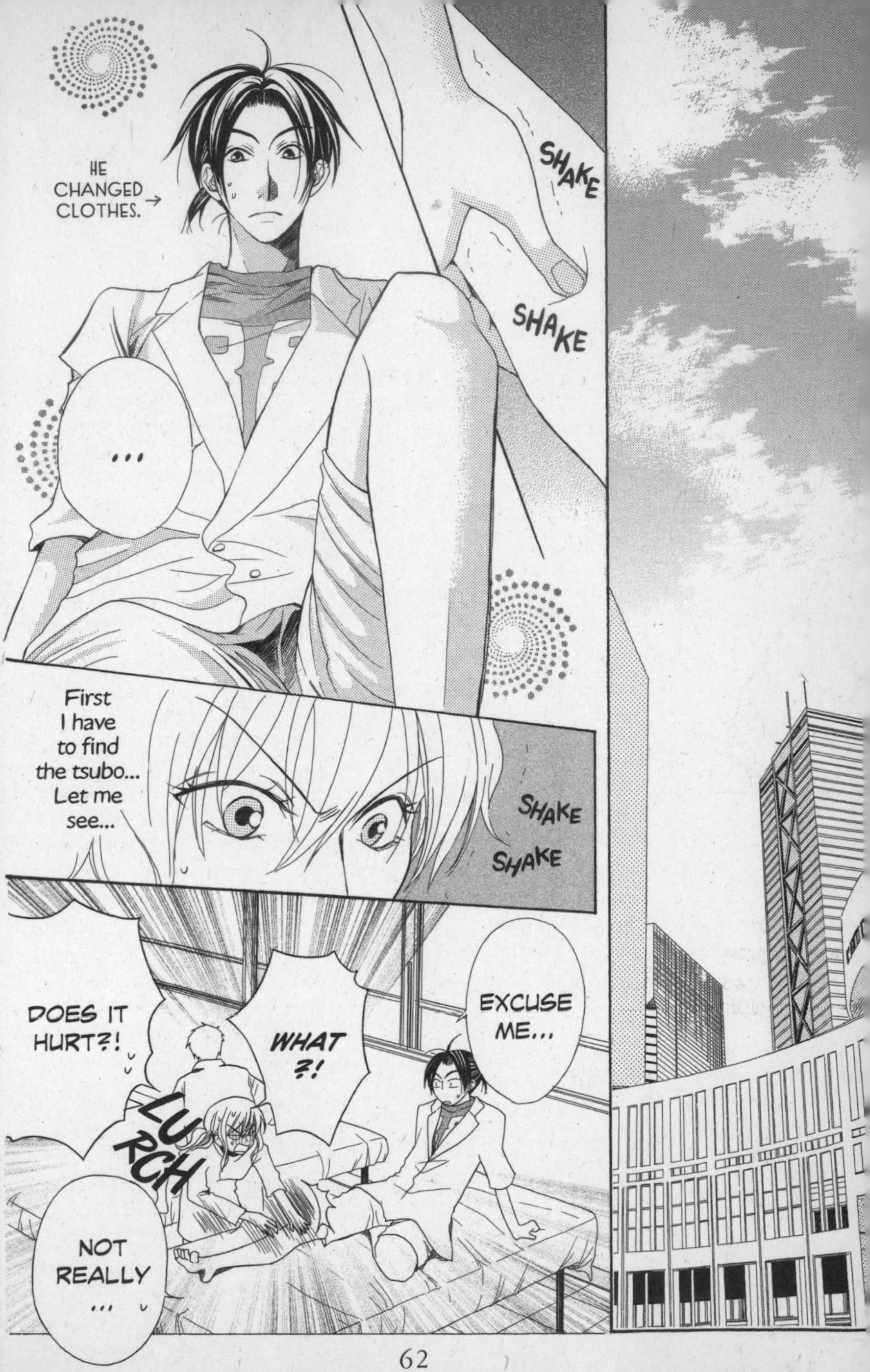
SHAKE
SHAKE
HE CHANGED CLOTHES.
...
SHAKE
SHAKE
First I have to find the tsubo... Let me see...
EXCUSE ME...
WHAT?!
DOES IT HURT?!
LURCH
NOT REALLY...

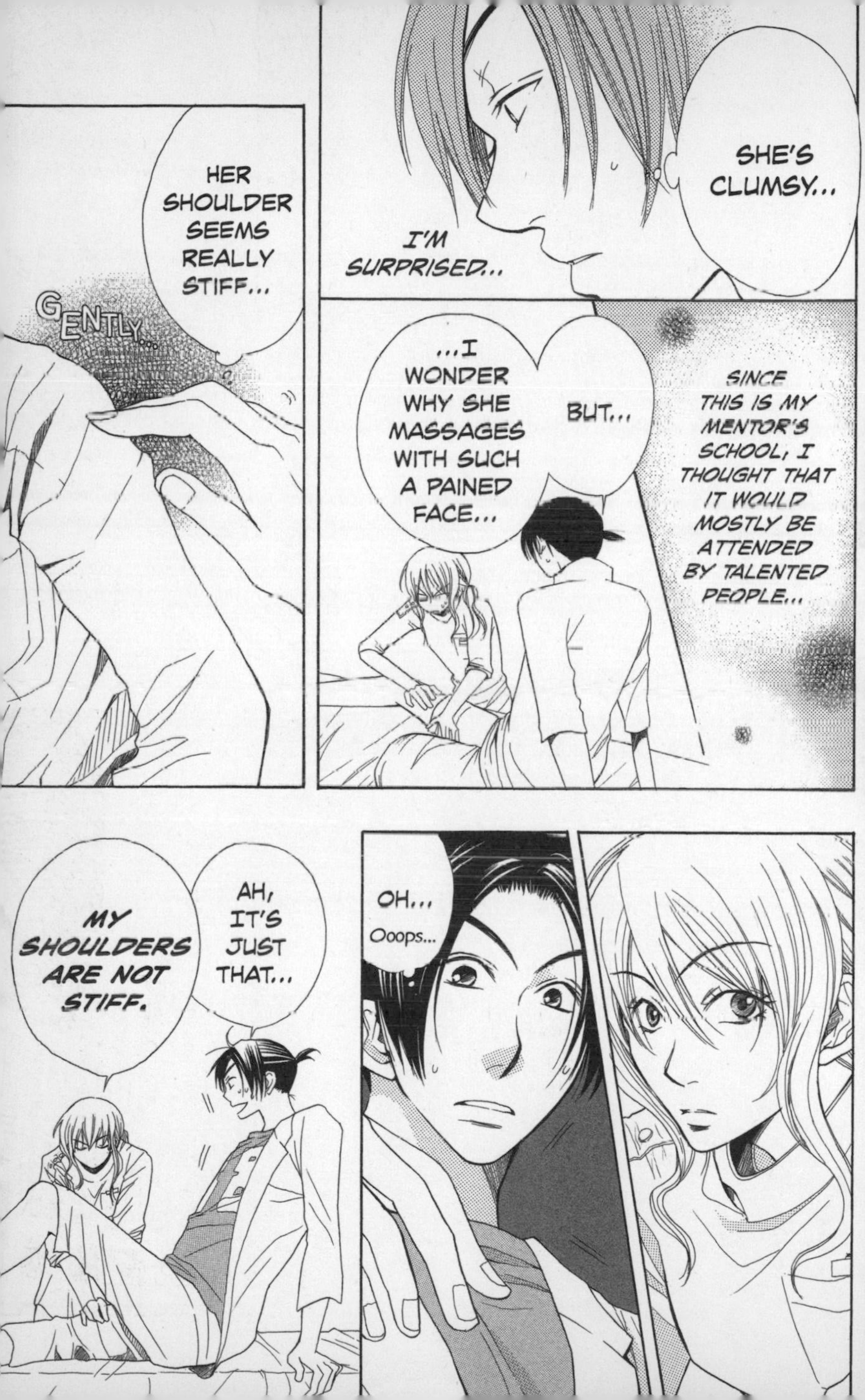
SHE'S CLUMSY...
I'M SURPRISED...
SINCE THIS IS MY MENTOR'S SCHOOL, I THOUGHT THAT IT WOULD MOSTLY BE ATTENDED BY TALENTED PEOPLE...
BUT...
...I WONDER WHY SHE MASSAGES WITH SUCH A PAINED FACE...
HER SHOULDER SEEMS REALLY STIFF...
GENTLY...
OH...
Ooops...
AH, IT'S JUST THAT...
MY SHOULDERS ARE NOT STIFF.

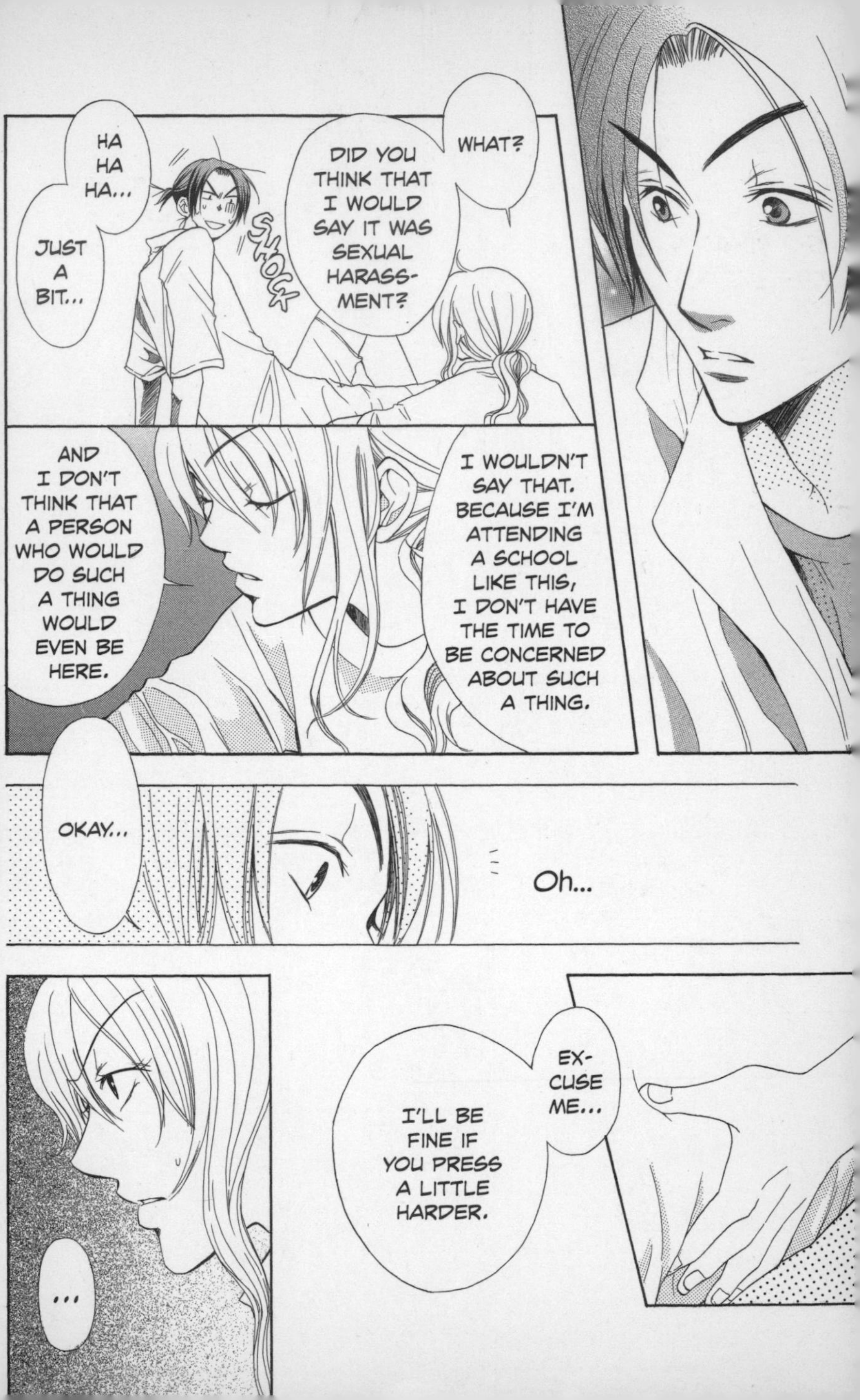
WHAT?
DID YOU THINK THAT I WOULD SAY IT WAS SEXUAL HARASS-MENT?
SHOCK
HA HA HA...
JUST A BIT...
I WOULDN'T SAY THAT. BECAUSE I'M ATTENDING A SCHOOL LIKE THIS, I DON'T HAVE THE TIME TO BE CONCERNED ABOUT SUCH A THING.
AND I DON'T THINK THAT A PERSON WHO WOULD DO SUCH A THING WOULD EVEN BE HERE.
Oh...
OKAY...
EX-CUSE ME...
I'LL BE FINE IF YOU PRESS A LITTLE HARDER.
...

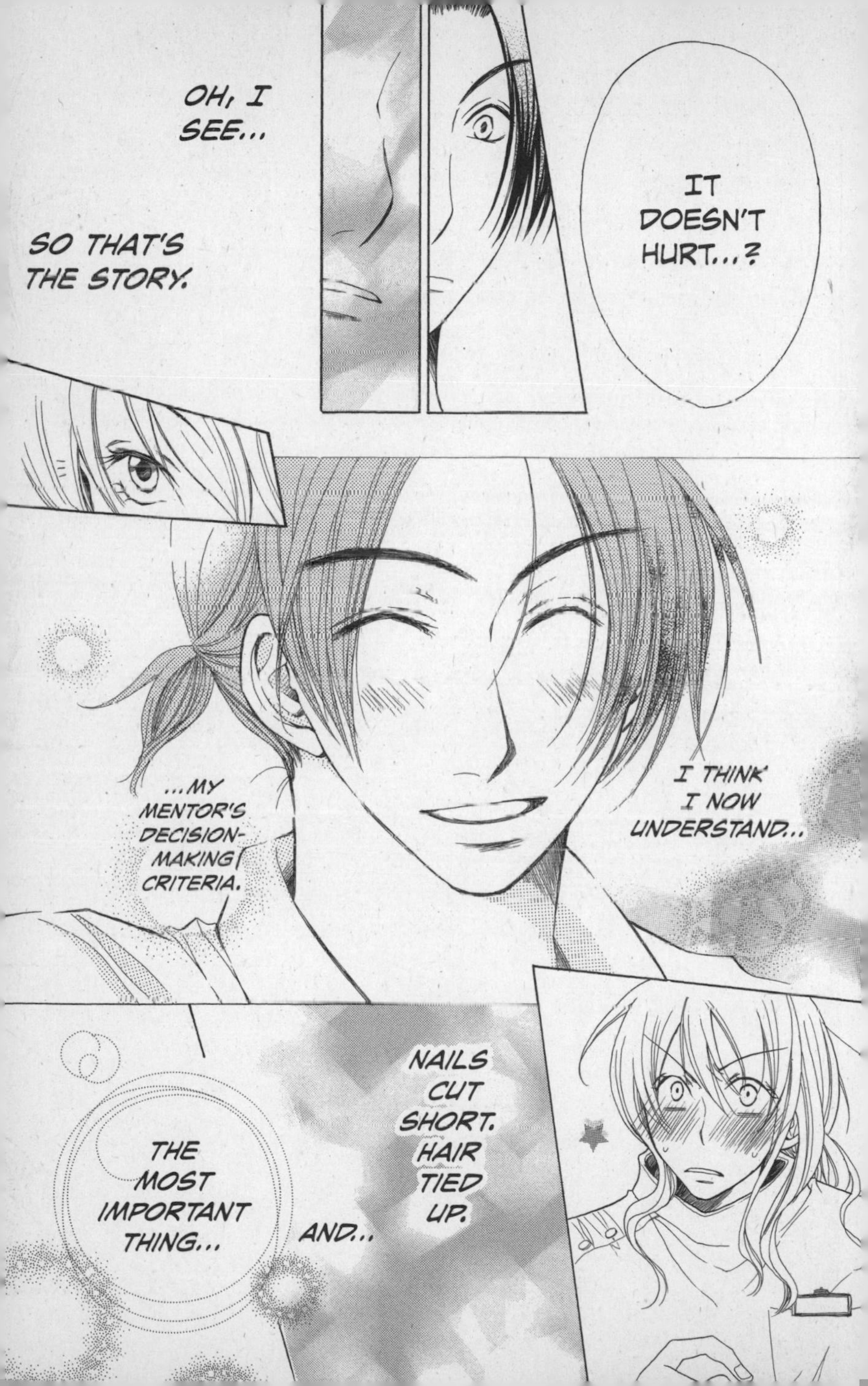
IT DOESN'T HURT...?
OH, I SEE...
SO THAT'S THE STORY.
I THINK I NOW UNDERSTAND...
...MY MENTOR'S DECISION-MAKING CRITERIA.
NAILS CUT SHORT. HAIR TIED UP.
AND...
THE MOST IMPORTANT THING...

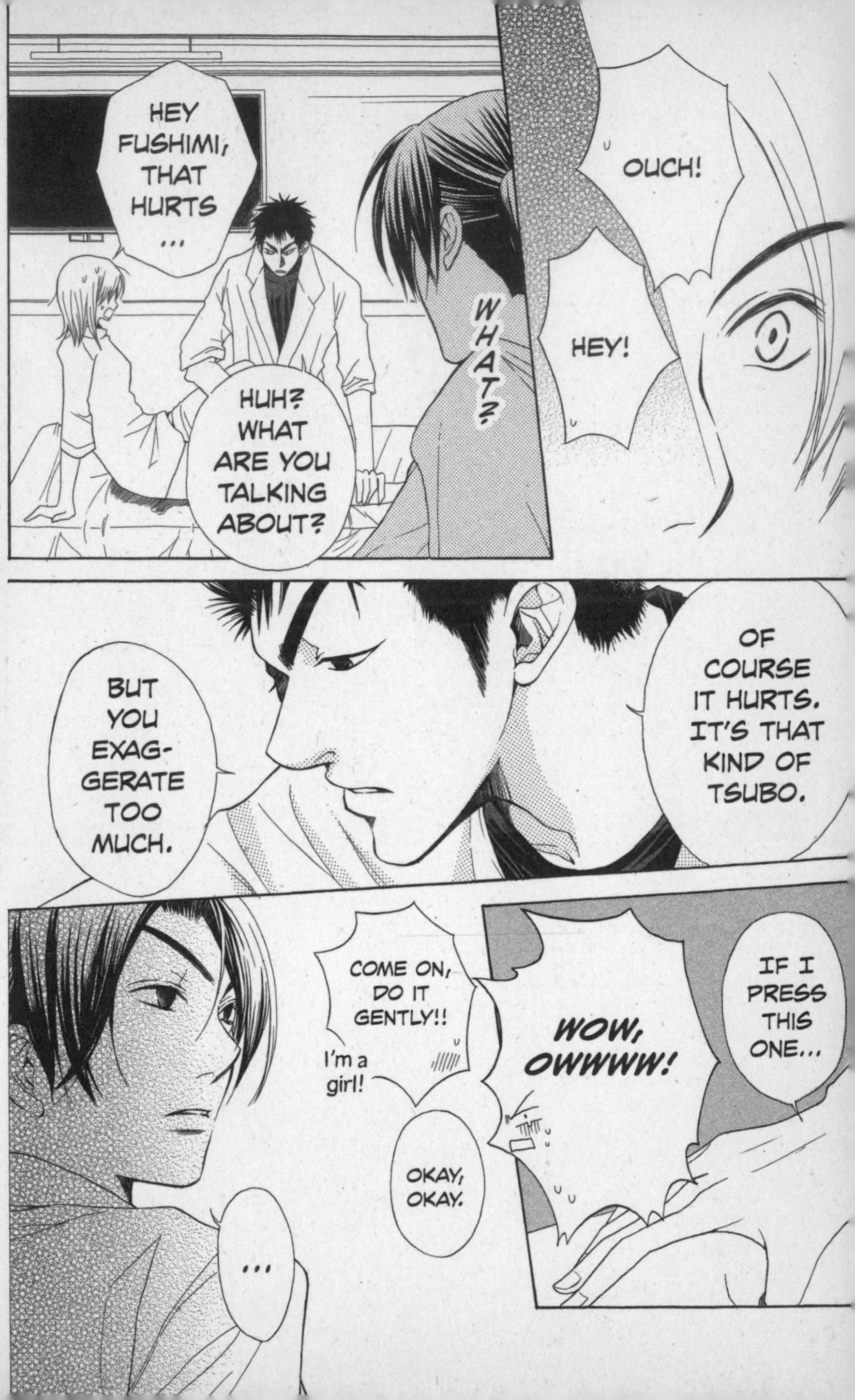
OUCH!
HEY!
HEY FUSHIMI, THAT HURTS ...
WHAT?
HUH? WHAT ARE YOU TALKING ABOUT?
OF COURSE IT HURTS. IT'S THAT KIND OF TSUBO.
BUT YOU EXAG-GERATE TOO MUCH.
IF I PRESS THIS ONE...
WOW, OWWWW!
COME ON, DO IT GENTLY!!
I'm a girl!
OKAY, OKAY.
...

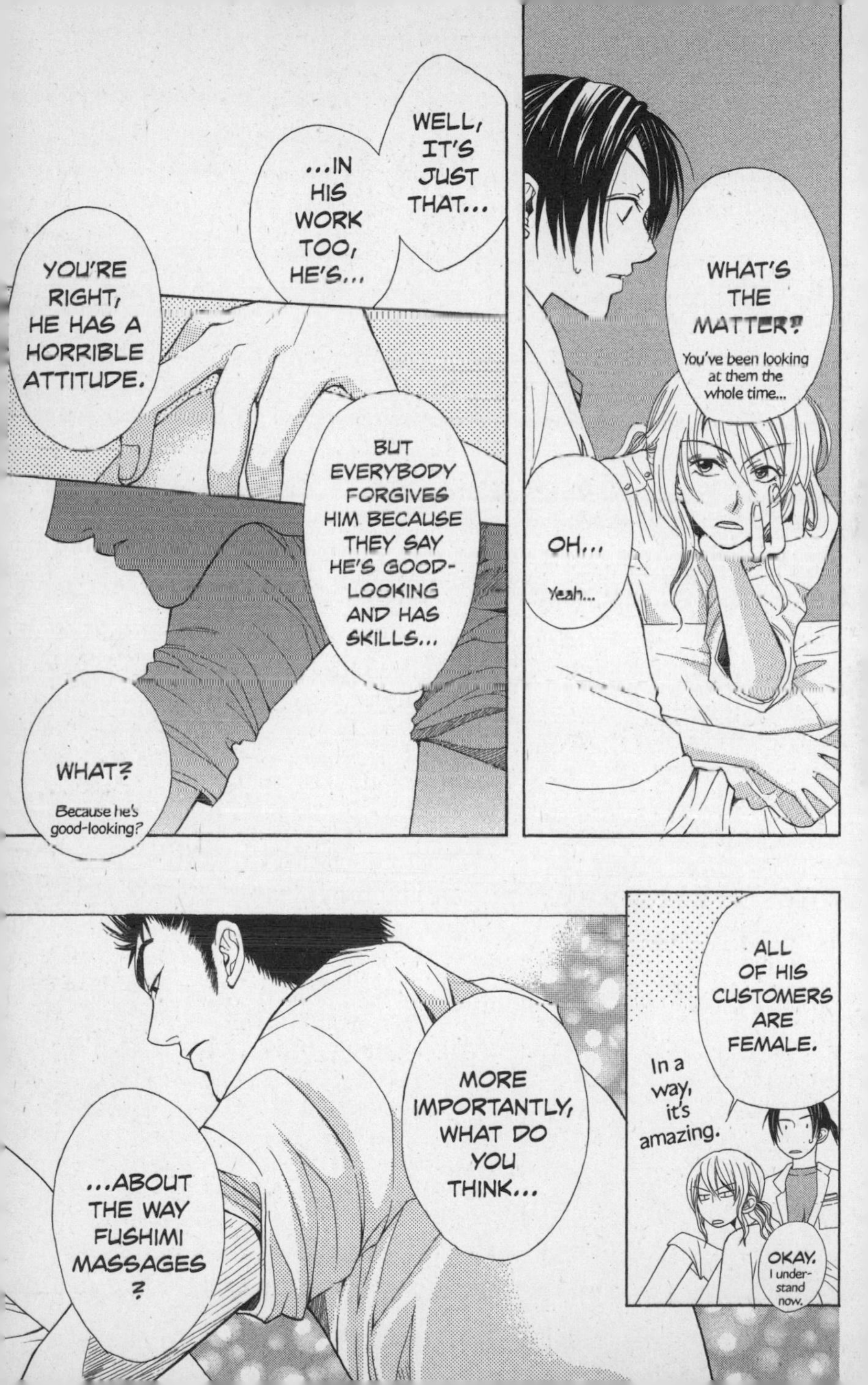
WHAT'S THE MATTER?!
You've been looking at them the whole time...
OH...
Yeah...
WELL, IT'S JUST THAT...
...IN HIS WORK TOO, HE'S...
YOU'RE RIGHT, HE HAS A HORRIBLE ATTITUDE.
BUT EVERYBODY FORGIVES HIM BECAUSE THEY SAY HE'S GOOD-LOOKING AND HAS SKILLS...
WHAT?
Because he's good-looking?
ALL OF HIS CUSTOMERS ARE FEMALE.
In a way, it's amazing.
OKAY.
I understand now.
MORE IMPORTANTLY, WHAT DO YOU THINK...
...ABOUT THE WAY FUSHIMI MASSAGES?

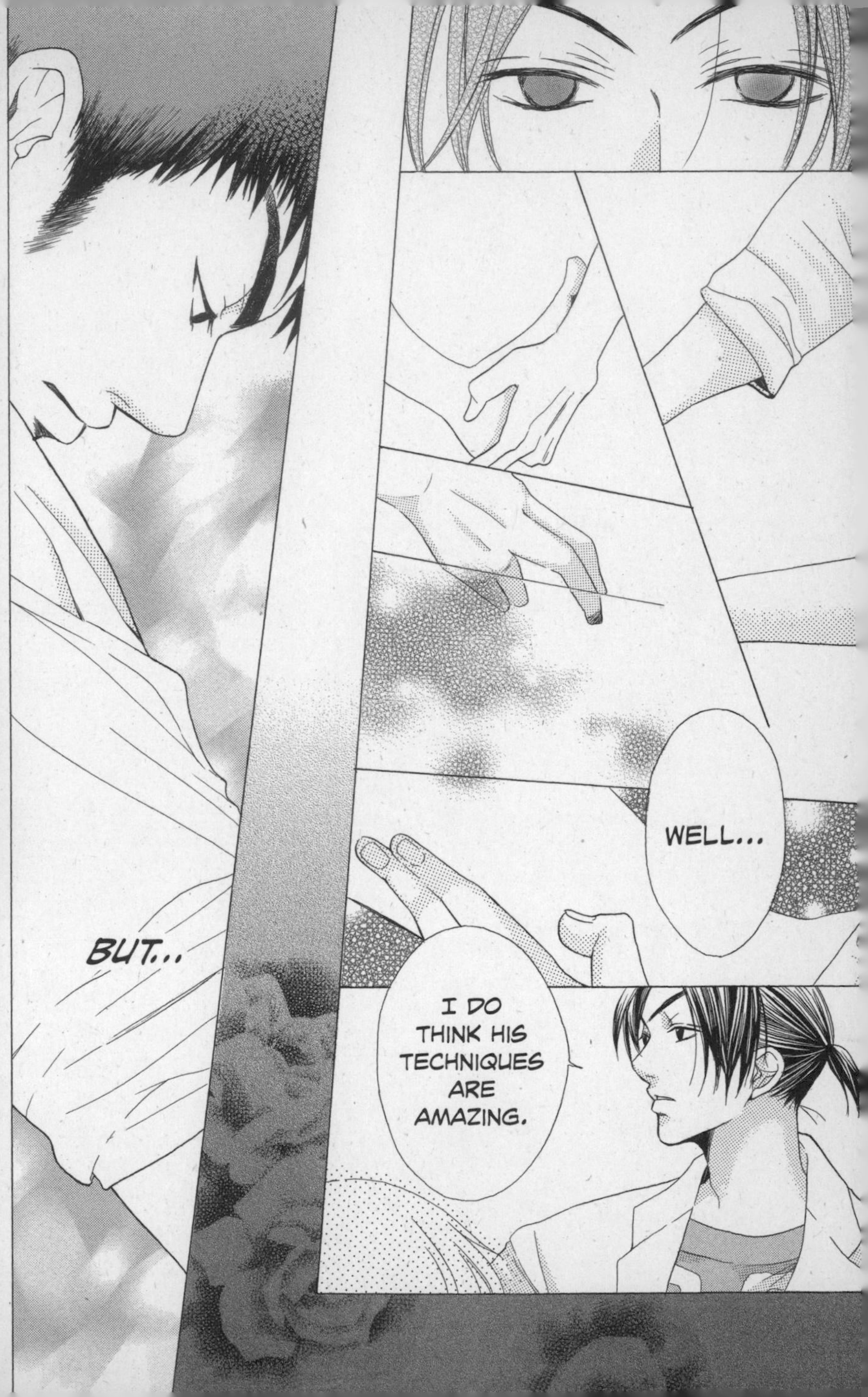
WELL...
I DO THINK HIS TECHNIQUES ARE AMAZING.
BUT...

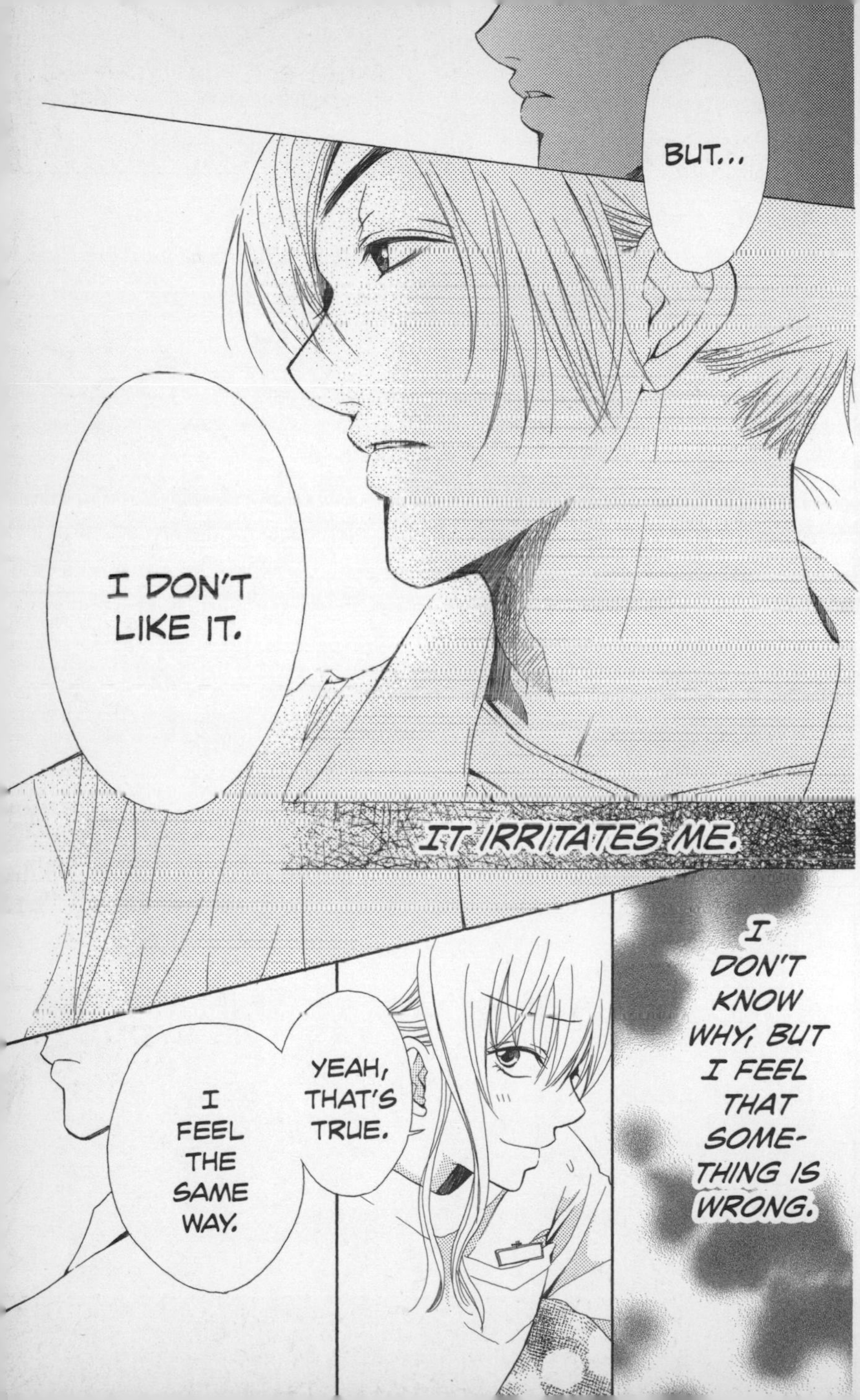
BUT...
I DON'T LIKE IT.
IT IRRITATES ME.
I DON'T KNOW WHY, BUT I FEEL THAT SOME-THING IS WRONG.
YEAH, THAT'S TRUE.
I FEEL THE SAME WAY.

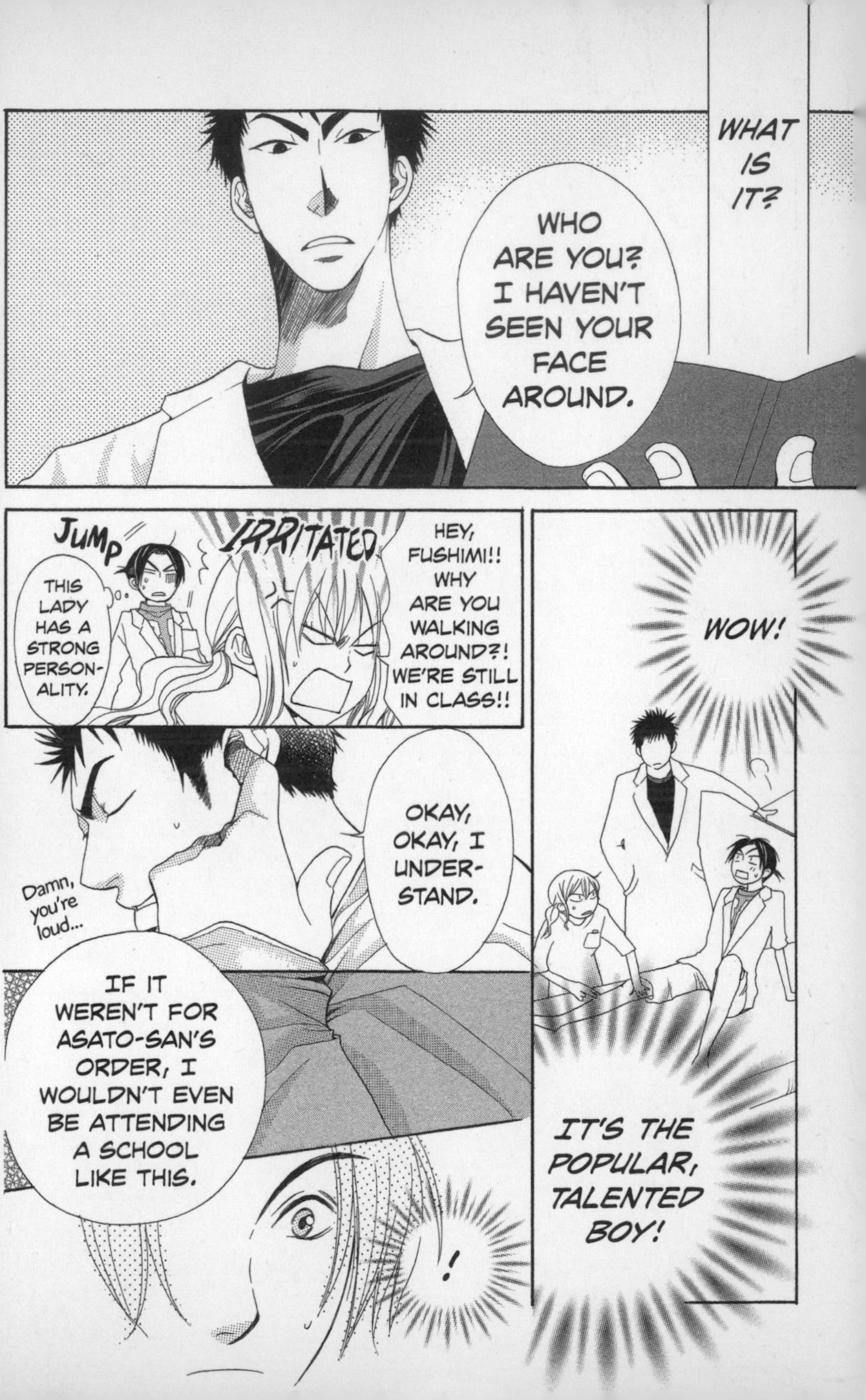
WHAT IS IT?
WHO ARE YOU? I HAVEN'T SEEN YOUR FACE AROUND.
WOW!
IT'S THE POPULAR, TALENTED BOY!
HEY, FUSHIMI!! WHY ARE YOU WALKING AROUND?! WE'RE STILL IN CLASS!!
IRRITATED
JUMP
THIS LADY HAS A STRONG PERSONALITY.
OKAY, OKAY, I UNDERSTAND.
Damn, you're loud...
IF IT WEREN'T FOR ASATO-SAN'S ORDER, I WOULDN'T EVEN BE ATTENDING A SCHOOL LIKE THIS.
!

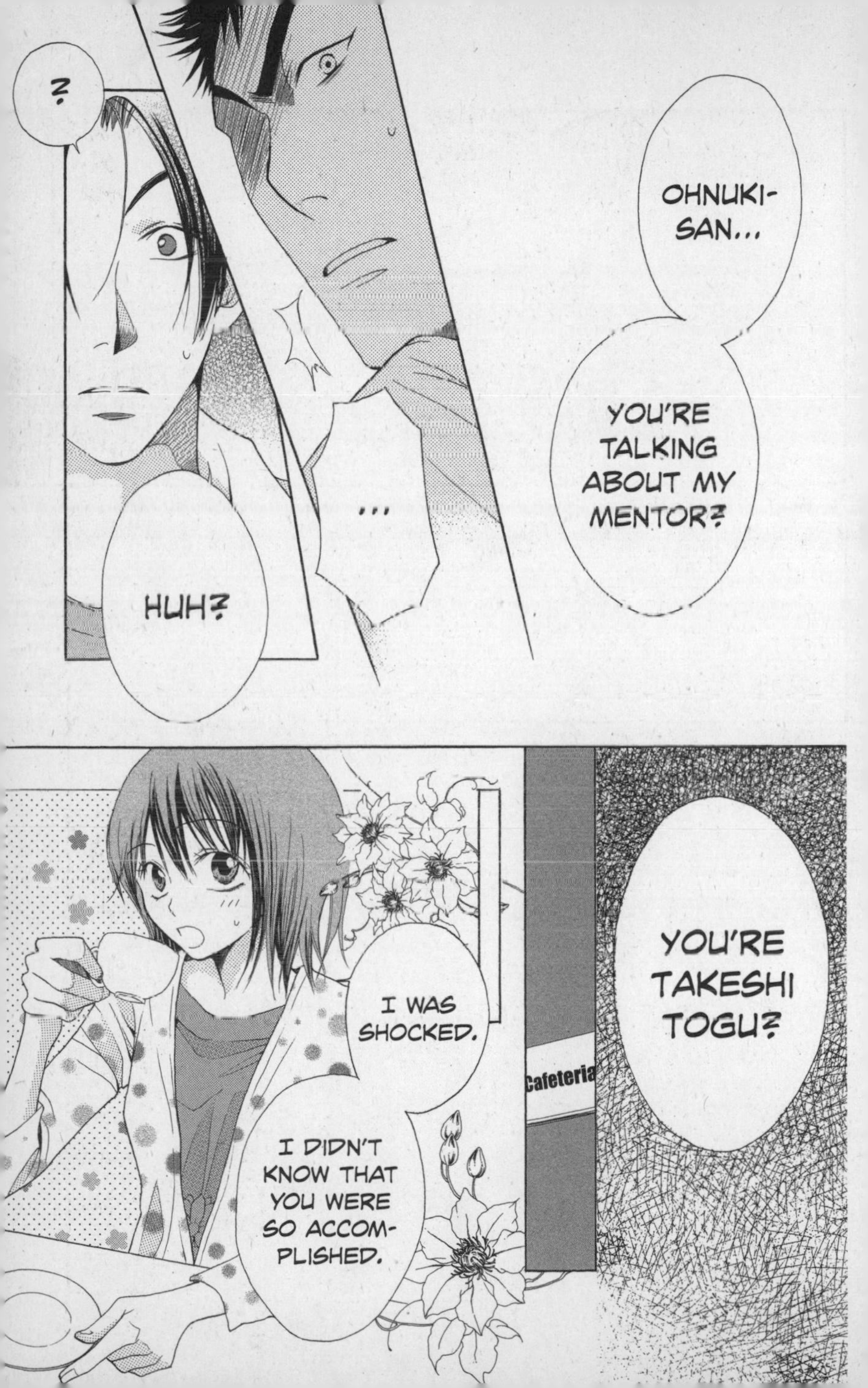
OHNUKI-SAN...
YOU'RE TALKING ABOUT MY MENTOR?
...
?
HUH?
YOU'RE TAKESHI TOGU?
Cafeteria
I WAS SHOCKED.
I DIDN'T KNOW THAT YOU WERE SO ACCOMPLISHED.

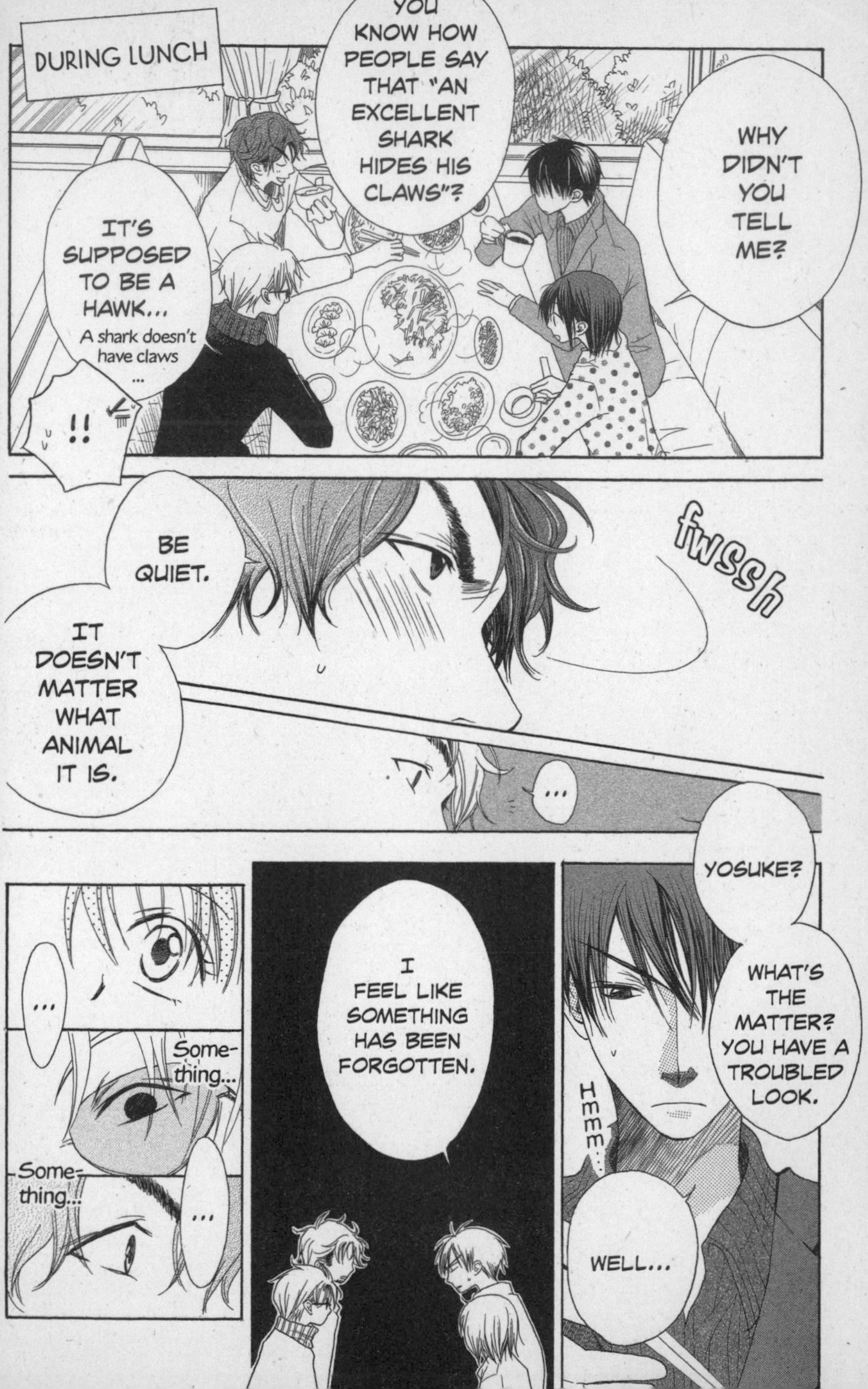
DURING LUNCH
YOU KNOW HOW PEOPLE SAY THAT "AN EXCELLENT SHARK HIDES HIS CLAWS"?
WHY DIDN'T YOU TELL ME?
IT'S SUPPOSED TO BE A HAWK...
A shark doesn't have claws ...
!!
fwssh
BE QUIET.
IT DOESN'T MATTER WHAT ANIMAL IT IS.
...
YOSUKE?
WHAT'S THE MATTER? YOU HAVE A TROUBLED LOOK.
Hmmm...
WELL...
I FEEL LIKE SOMETHING HAS BEEN FORGOTTEN.
...
Some-thing...
Some-thing...
...

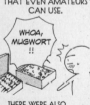

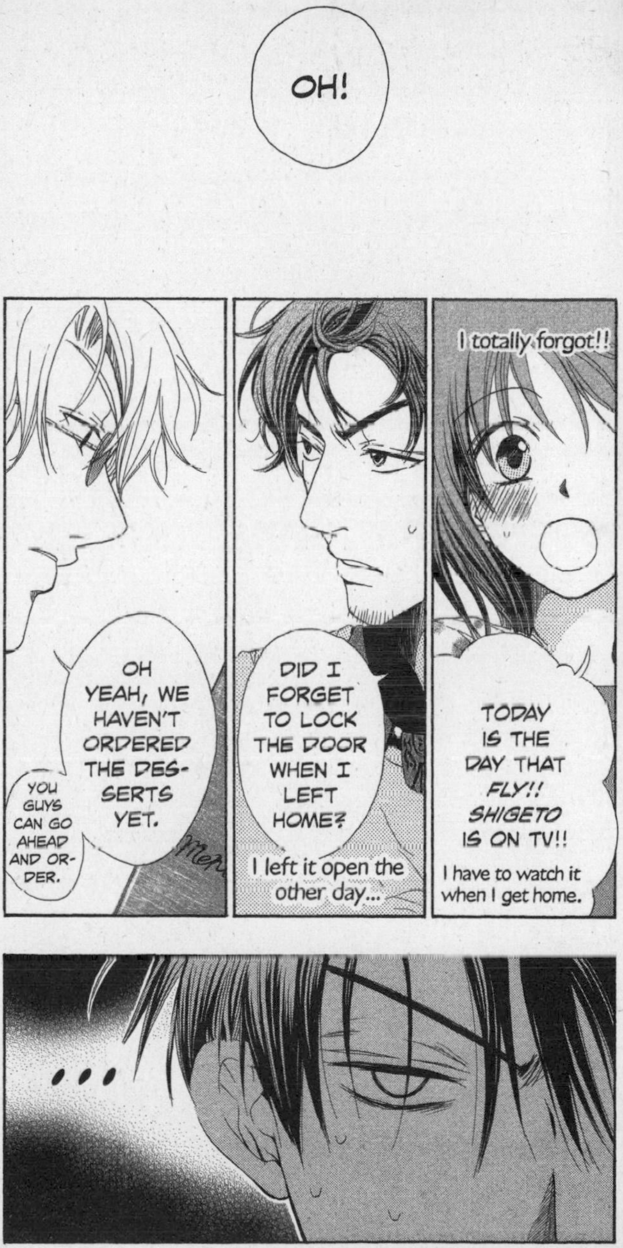
OH!
I totally forgot!!
TODAY IS THE DAY THAT FLY!! SHIGETO IS ON TV!!
I have to watch it when I get home.
DID I FORGET TO LOCK THE DOOR WHEN I LEFT HOME?
I left it open the other day...
OH YEAH, WE HAVEN'T ORDERED THE DES-SERTS YET.
YOU GUYS CAN GO AHEAD AND OR-DER.
...

It's Not Expensive to Get a Massage!

For young people who think that massage is expensive, I recommend school festivals at professional schools.
★You receive a very good massage either free or for only ¥100.

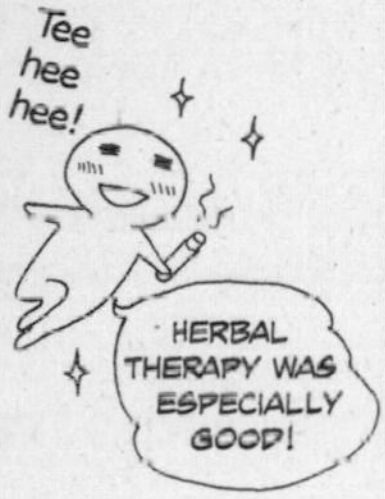
Tee hee hee!
HERBAL THERAPY WAS ESPECIALLY GOOD!

There were also massage goods being sold.

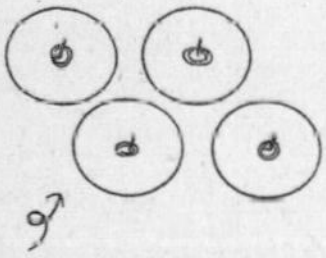

ACUPUNCTURE NEEDLES THAT EVEN AMATEURS CAN USE.

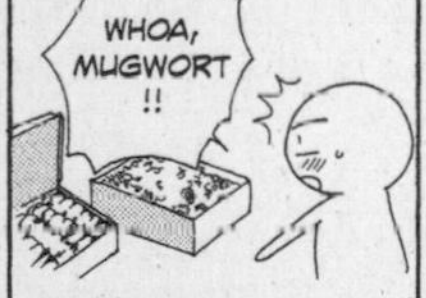
WHOA, MUGWORT !!

THERE WERE ALSO MANY GOODS FOR HERBAL THERAPY.

IT WAS IMPRESSIVE. THERE WAS ALSO A PRESENTATION THAT WAS EASY TO UNDERSTAND...

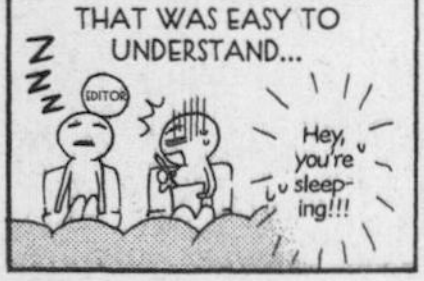
ZZZ
EDITOR
Hey, you're sleep-ing!!!

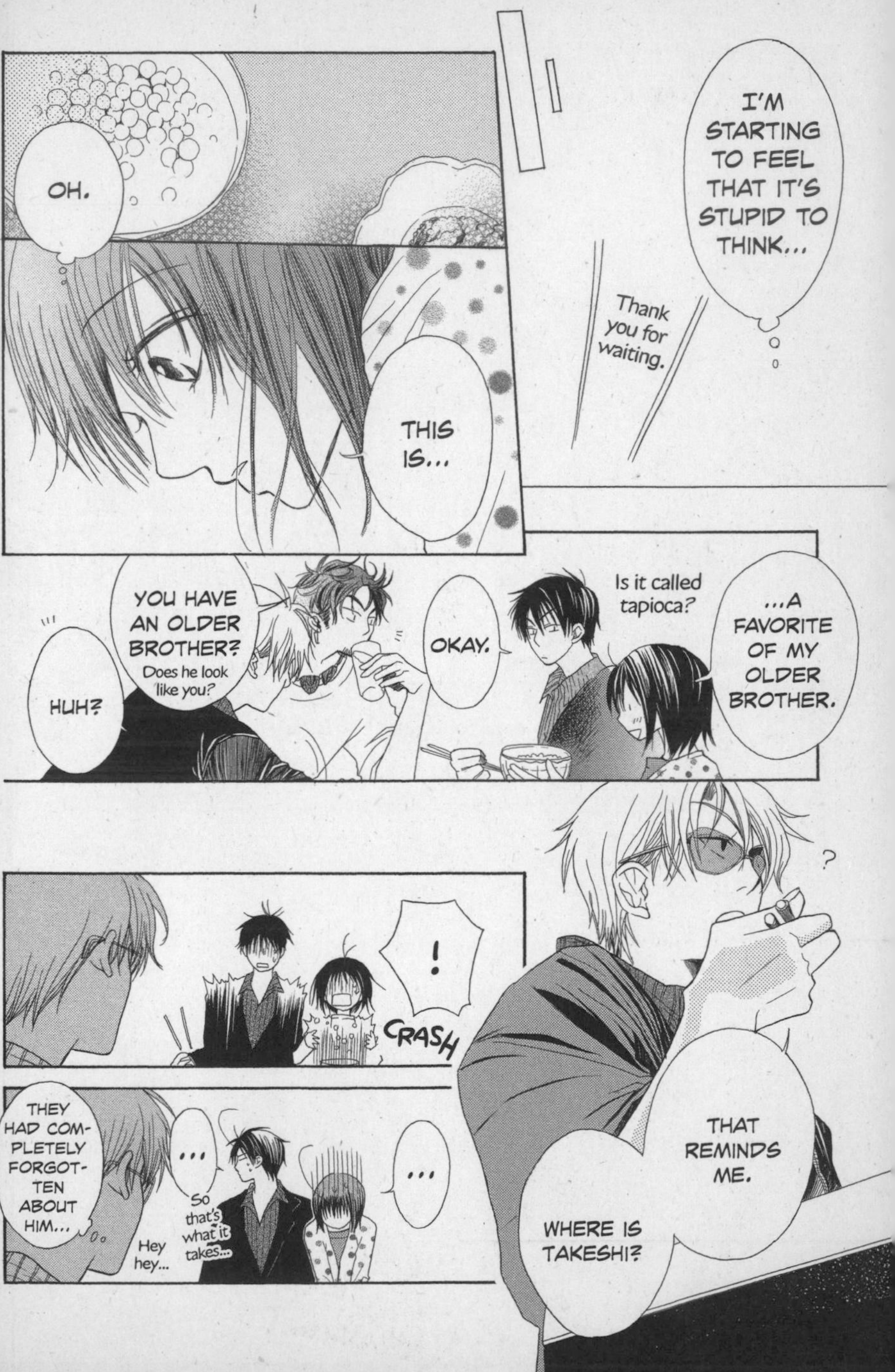
I'M STARTING TO FEEL THAT IT'S STUPID TO THINK...
Thank you for waiting.
OH.
THIS IS...
...A FAVORITE OF MY OLDER BROTHER.
Is it called tapioca?
OKAY.
YOU HAVE AN OLDER BROTHER?
Does he look like you?
HUH?
?
THAT REMINDS ME.
WHERE IS TAKESHI?
!
CRASH
...
...
So that's what it takes...
Hey hey...
THEY HAD COM-PLETELY FORGOT-TEN ABOUT HIM...

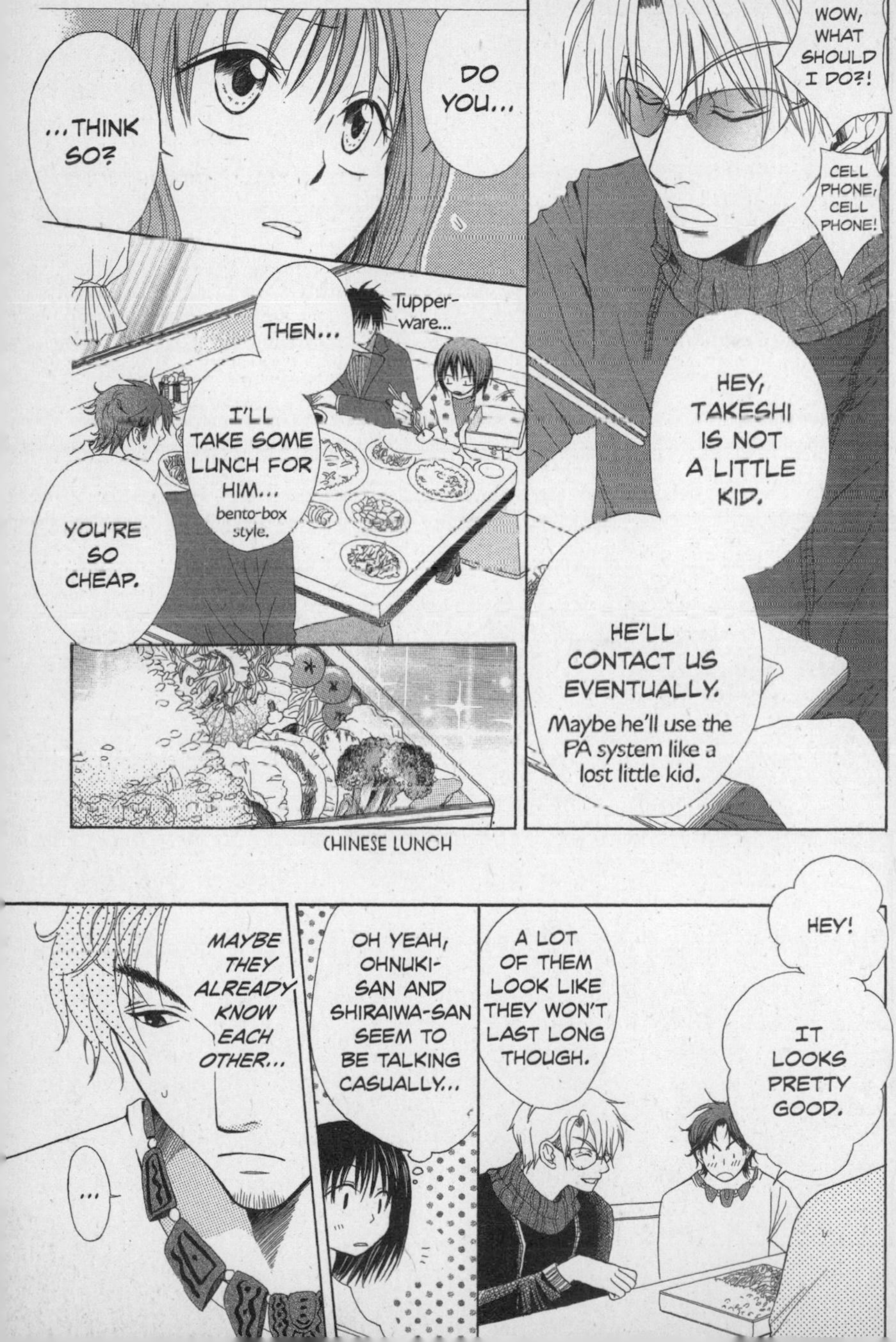
WOW, WHAT SHOULD I DO?!
CELL PHONE, CELL PHONE!
HEY, TAKESHI IS NOT A LITTLE KID.
HE'LL CONTACT US EVENTUALLY.
Maybe he'll use the PA system like a lost little kid.
DO YOU...
...THINK SO?
THEN...
Tupper-ware...
I'LL TAKE SOME LUNCH FOR HIM...
bento-box style.
YOU'RE SO CHEAP.
CHINESE LUNCH
HEY!
IT LOOKS PRETTY GOOD.
A LOT OF THEM LOOK LIKE THEY WON'T LAST LONG THOUGH.
OH YEAH, OHNUKI-SAN AND SHIRAIWA-SAN SEEM TO BE TALKING CASUALLY...
MAYBE THEY ALREADY KNOW EACH OTHER...
...

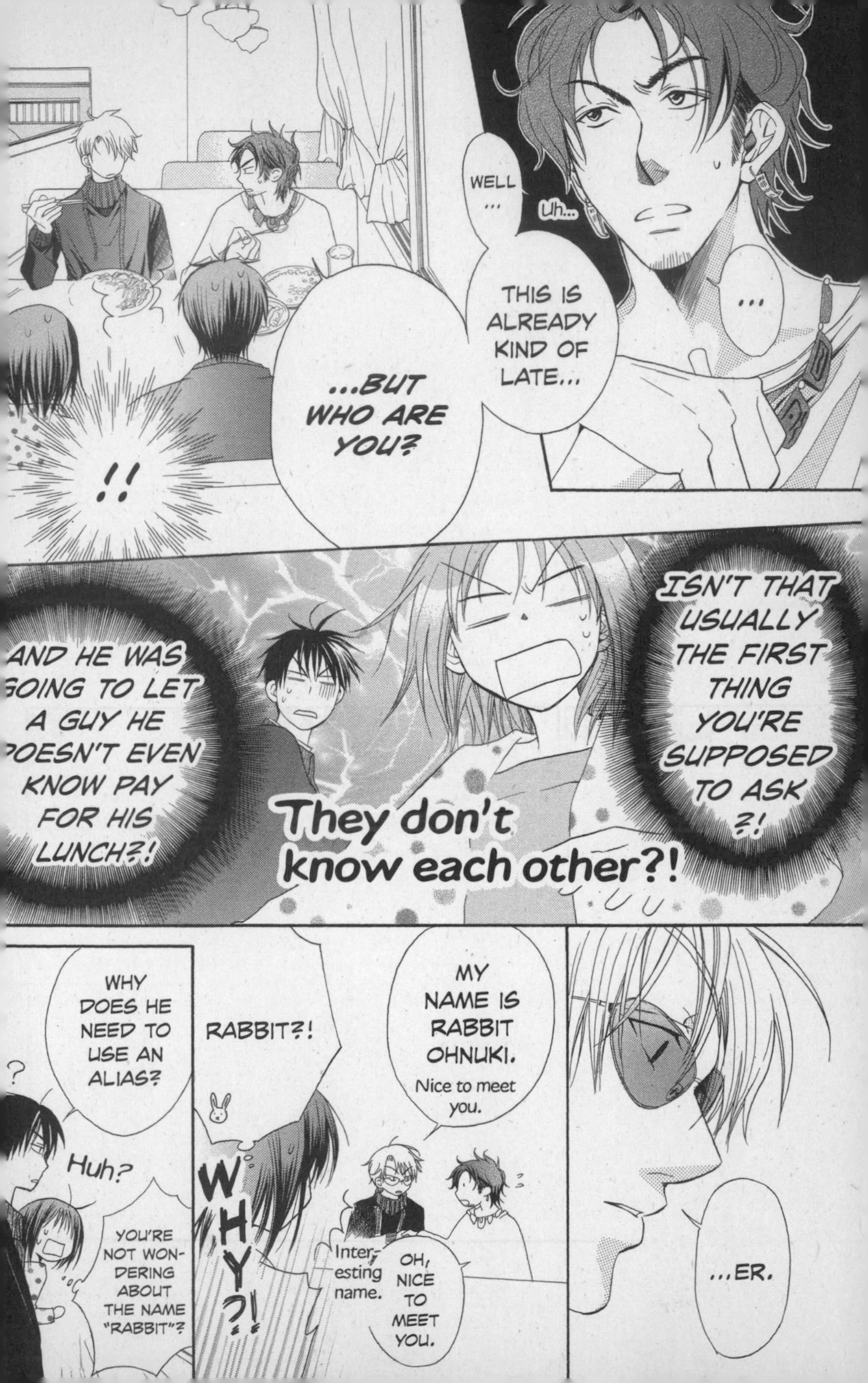
...
WELL ...
Uh...
THIS IS ALREADY KIND OF LATE...
...BUT WHO ARE YOU?
!!
ISN'T THAT USUALLY THE FIRST THING YOU'RE SUPPOSED TO ASK?!
They don't know each other?!
AND HE WAS GOING TO LET A GUY HE DOESN'T EVEN KNOW PAY FOR HIS LUNCH?!
...ER.
MY NAME IS RABBIT OHNUKI.
Nice to meet you.
RABBIT?!
WHY?!
Inter-esting name.
OH, NICE TO MEET YOU.
WHY DOES HE NEED TO USE AN ALIAS?
?
Huh?
YOU'RE NOT WON-DERING ABOUT THE NAME "RABBIT"?

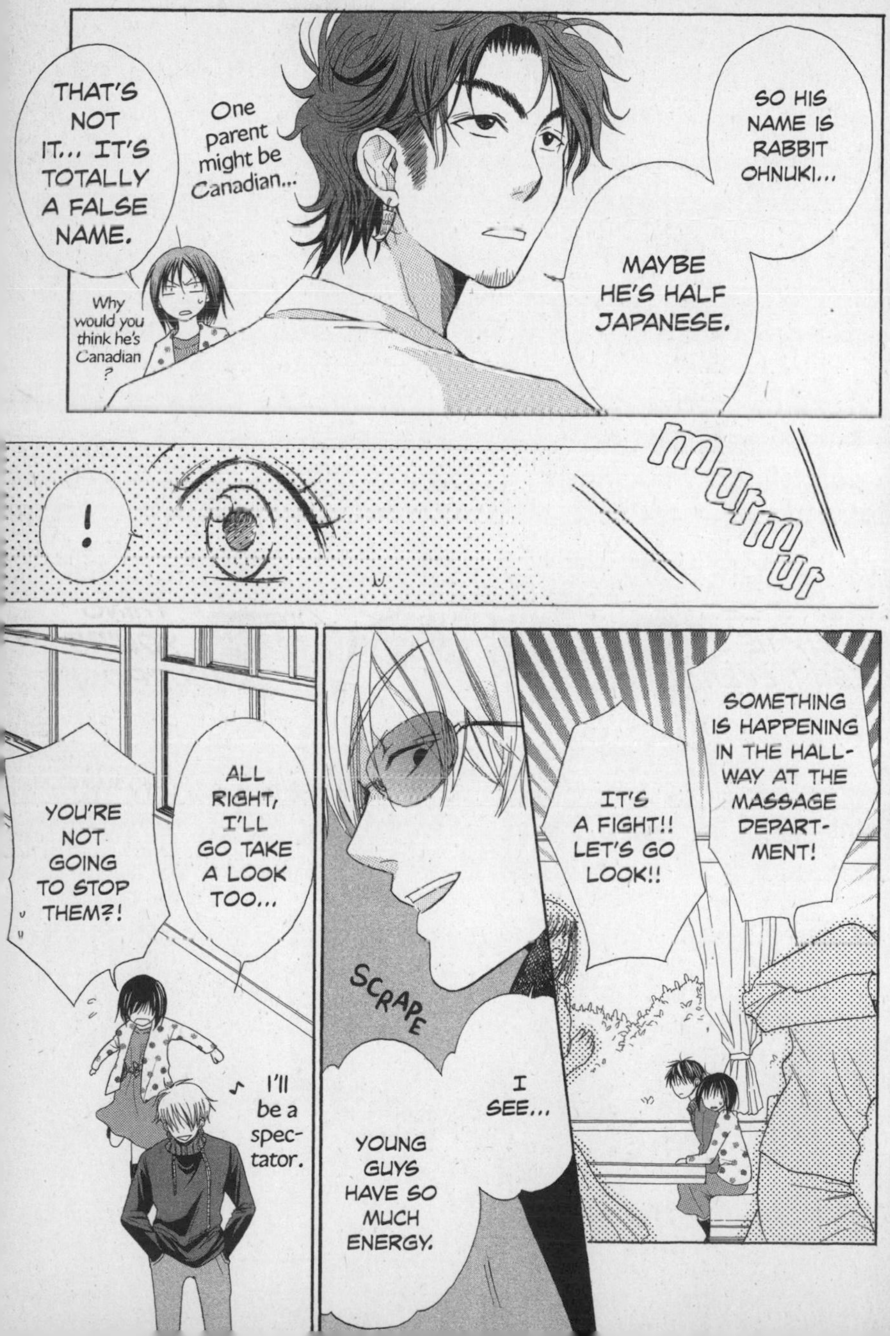
SO HIS NAME IS RABBIT OHNUKI...
MAYBE HE'S HALF JAPANESE.
One parent might be Canadian...
THAT'S NOT IT... IT'S TOTALLY A FALSE NAME.
Why would you think he's Canadian?
murmur
!
SOMETHING IS HAPPENING IN THE HALLWAY AT THE MASSAGE DEPARTMENT!
IT'S A FIGHT!! LET'S GO LOOK!!
SCRAPE
I SEE...
YOUNG GUYS HAVE SO MUCH ENERGY.
ALL RIGHT, I'LL GO TAKE A LOOK TOO...
YOU'RE NOT GOING TO STOP THEM?!
I'll be a spectator.

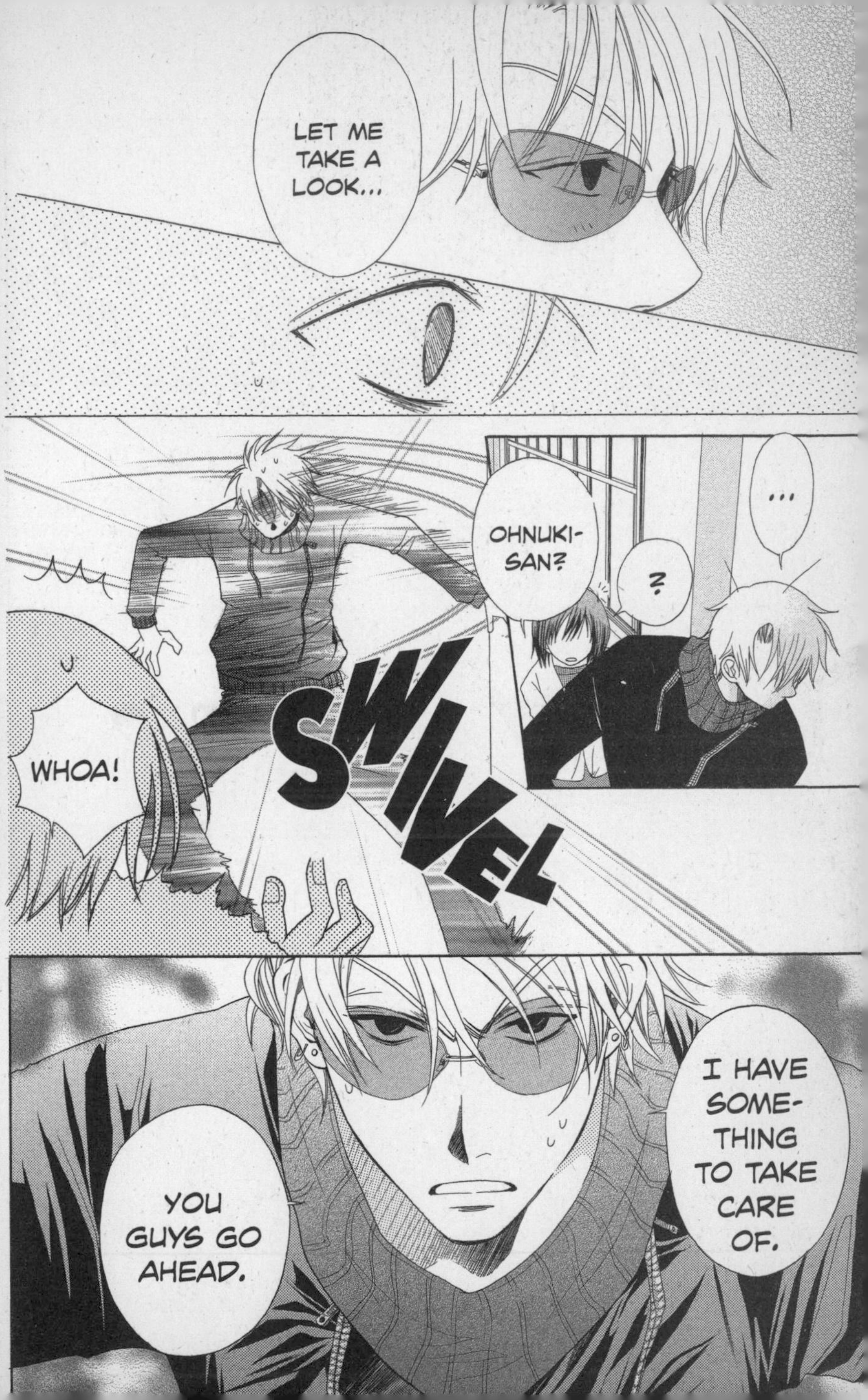
LET ME TAKE A LOOK...
...
OHNUKI-SAN?
?
SWIVEL
WHOA!
I HAVE SOME-THING TO TAKE CARE OF.
YOU GUYS GO AHEAD.

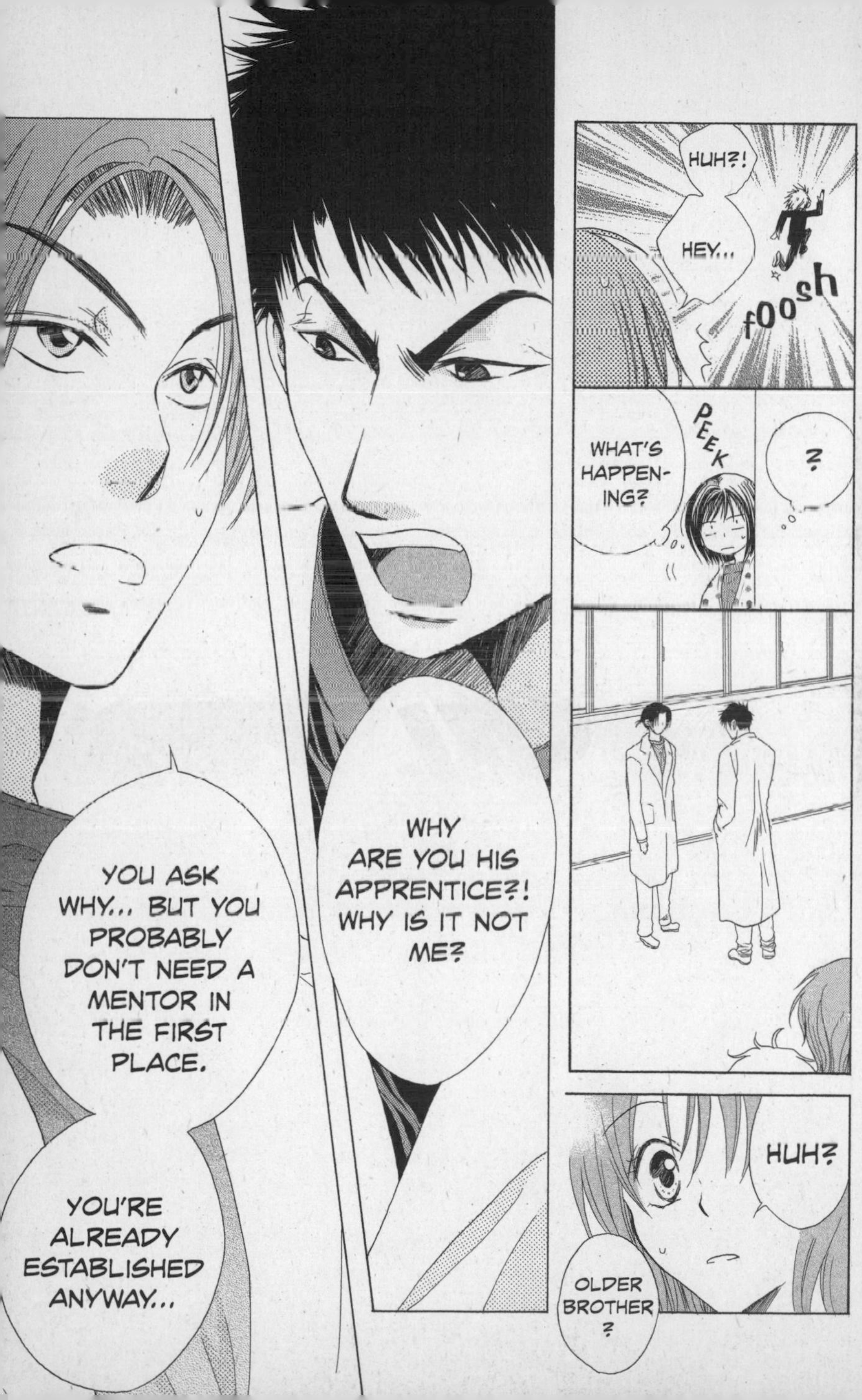
HUH?!
HEY...
foosh
?
PEEK
WHAT'S HAPPENING?
HUH?
OLDER BROTHER?
WHY ARE YOU HIS APPRENTICE?! WHY IS IT NOT ME?
YOU ASK WHY... BUT YOU PROBABLY DON'T NEED A MENTOR IN THE FIRST PLACE.
YOU'RE ALREADY ESTABLISHED ANYWAY...

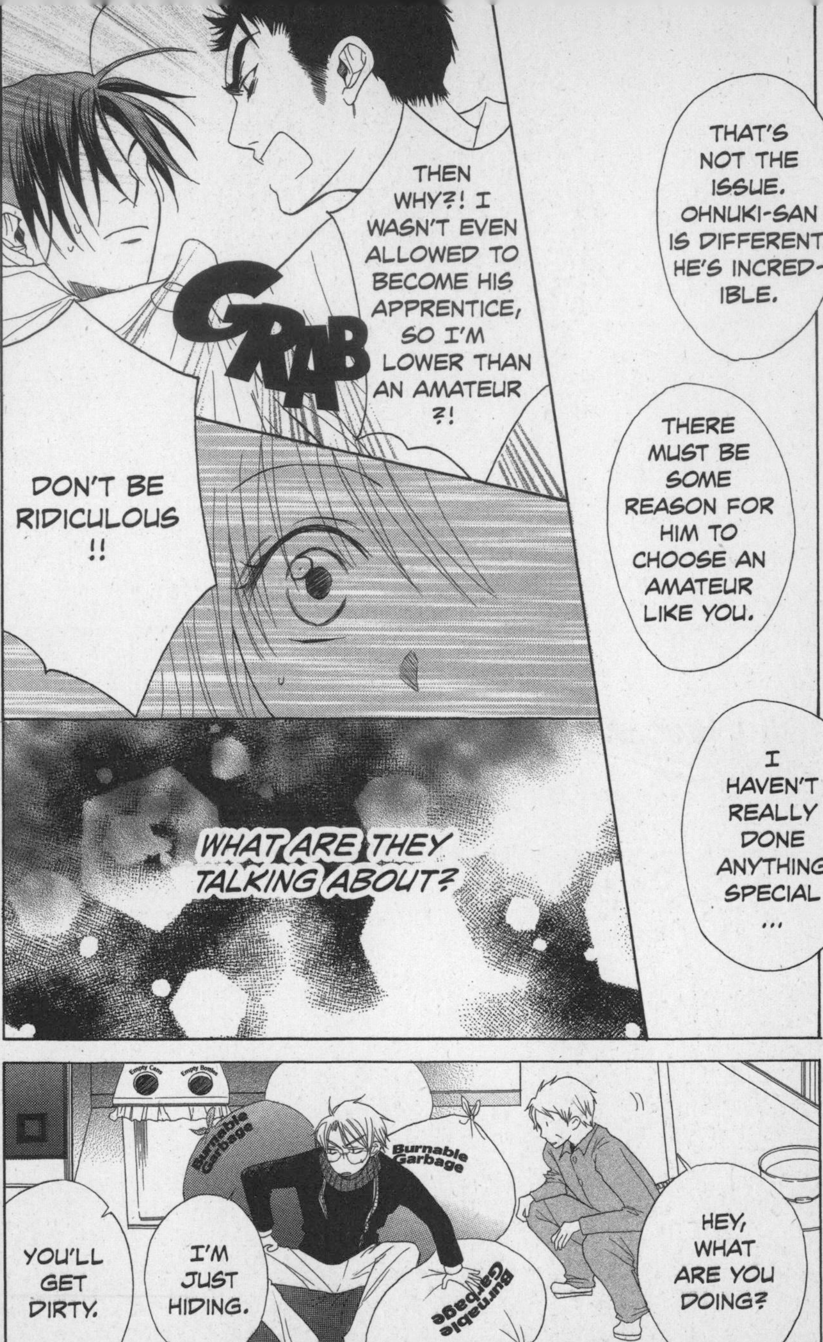
THAT'S NOT THE ISSUE. OHNUKI-SAN IS DIFFERENT. HE'S INCRED-IBLE.
THEN WHY?! I WASN'T EVEN ALLOWED TO BECOME HIS APPRENTICE, SO I'M LOWER THAN AN AMATEUR?!
GRAB
THERE MUST BE SOME REASON FOR HIM TO CHOOSE AN AMATEUR LIKE YOU.
DON'T BE RIDICULOUS!!
I HAVEN'T REALLY DONE ANYTHING SPECIAL...
WHAT ARE THEY TALKING ABOUT?
Empty Cans
Empty Bottles
Burnable Garbage
Burnable Garbage
Burnable Garbage
HEY, WHAT ARE YOU DOING?
I'M JUST HIDING.
YOU'LL GET DIRTY.

The Magic Touch, Part 26 / End

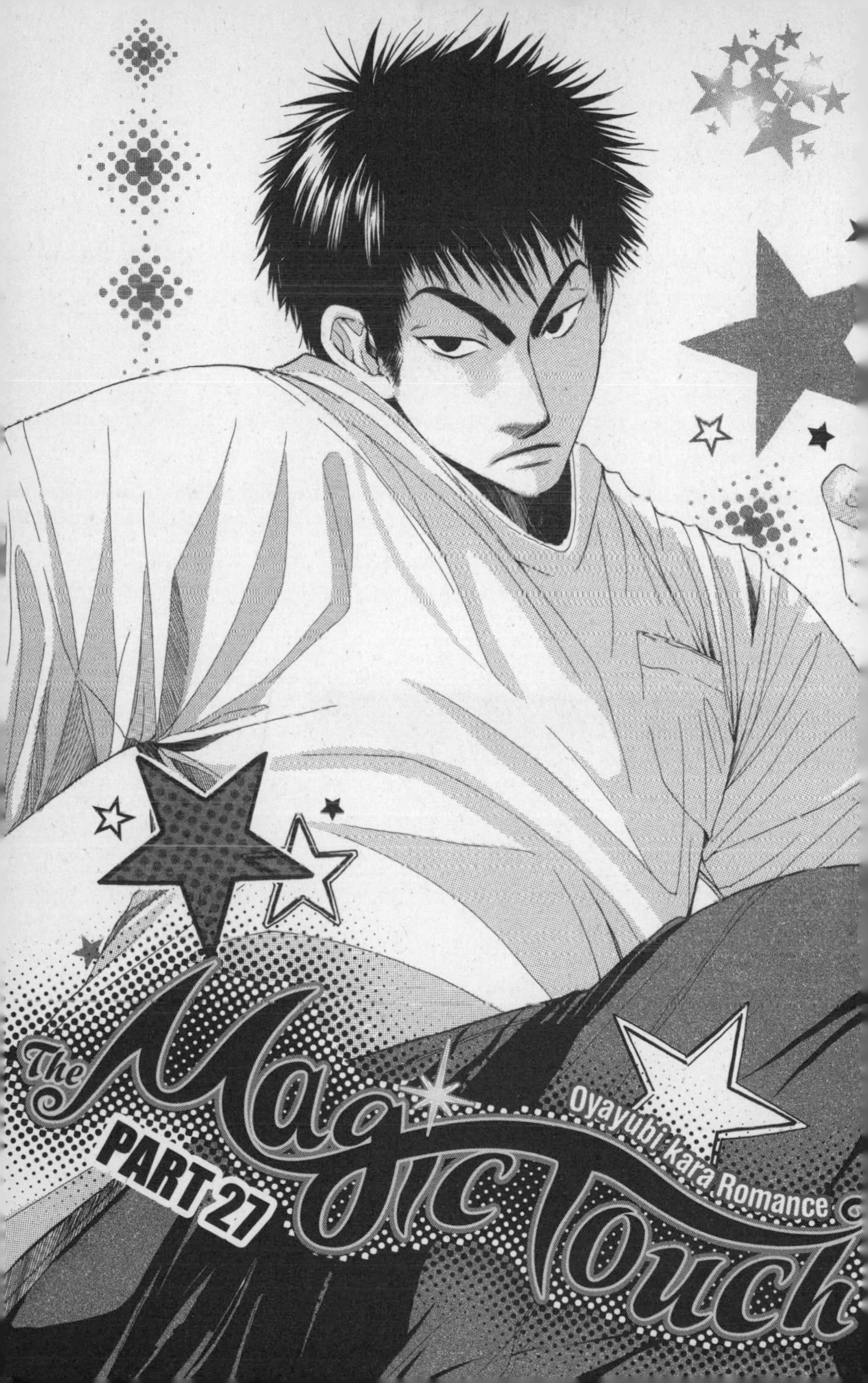
The Magic Touch
PART 27
Oyayubi kara Romance

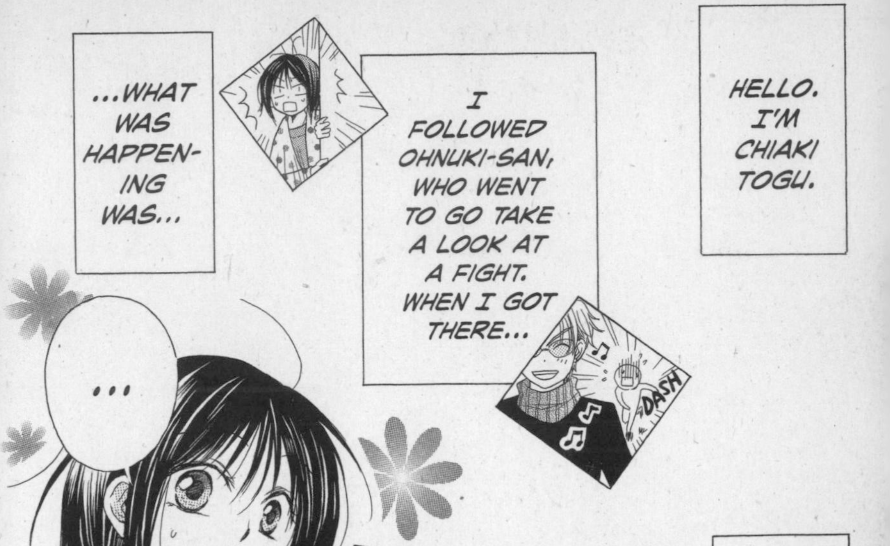
HELLO. I'M CHIAKI TOGU.
I FOLLOWED OHNUKI-SAN, WHO WENT TO GO TAKE A LOOK AT A FIGHT. WHEN I GOT THERE...
DASH
...WHAT WAS HAPPEN-ING WAS...
...
...MY BROTHER HAVING HIS NECK TIGHT-ENED.
UNGH
EEEK!
Creak
HE'S STRANGLING HIM!! MY OLDER BROTHER!

THAT SHOULD CATCH YOU UP THROUGH THE LAST CHAPTER.

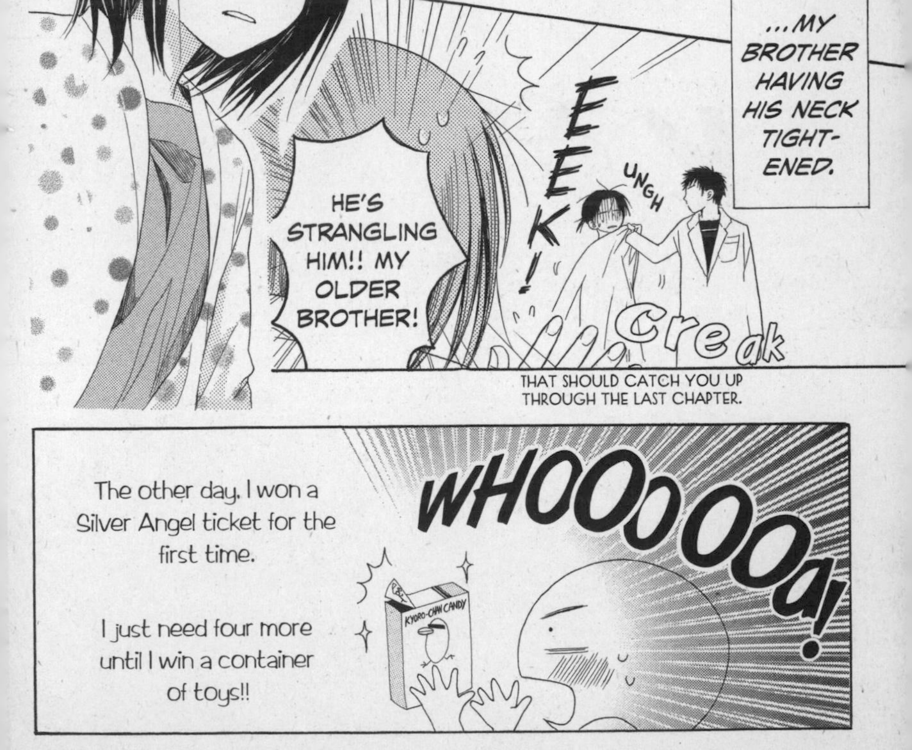
WHOOOOOOa!
KYORO-CHAN CANDY
The other day, I won a Silver Angel ticket for the first time.
I just need four more until I win a container of toys!!

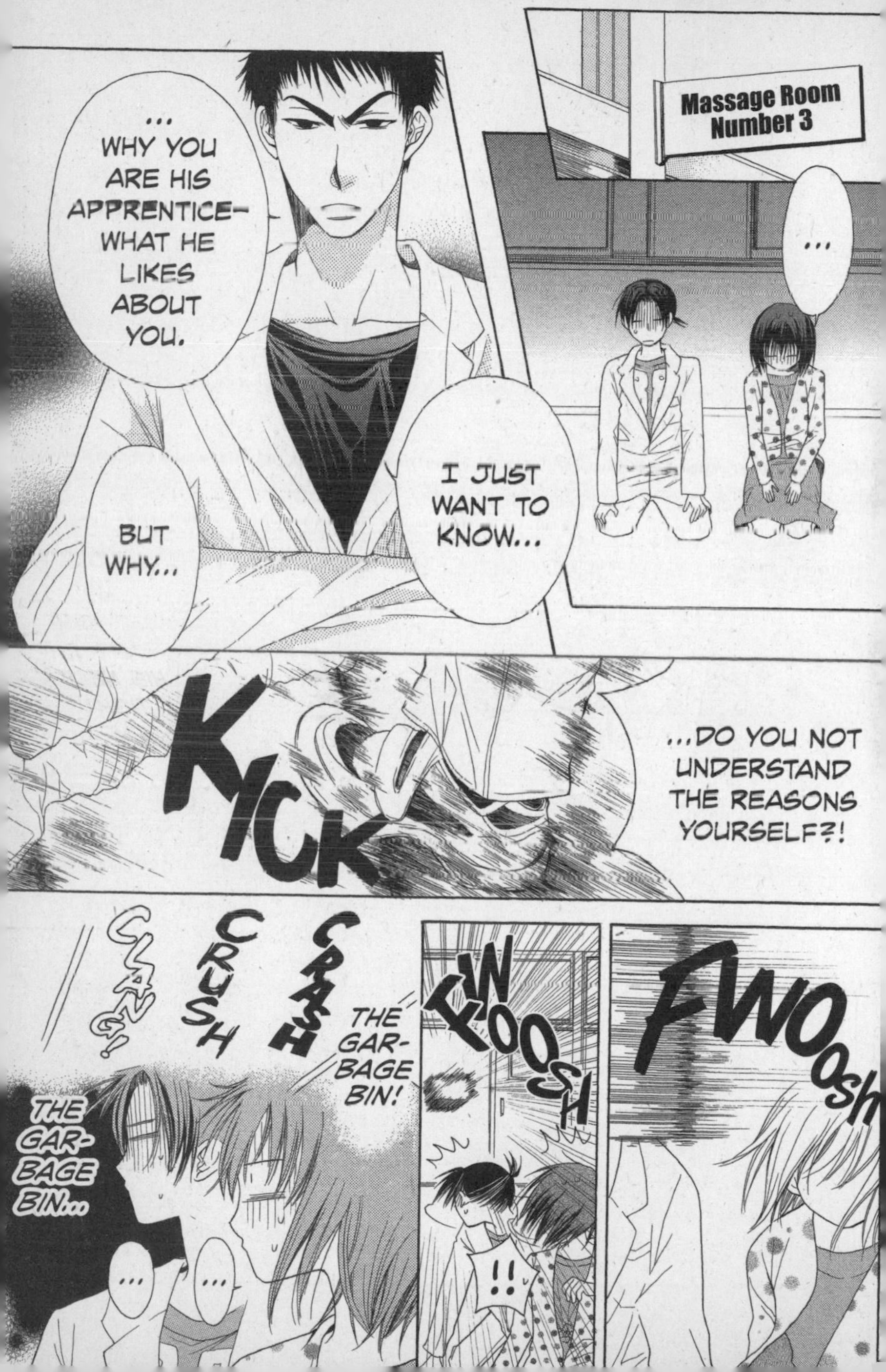
Massage Room Number 3
...
I JUST WANT TO KNOW...
...WHY YOU ARE HIS APPRENTICE—WHAT HE LIKES ABOUT YOU.
BUT WHY...
KICK
...DO YOU NOT UNDERSTAND THE REASONS YOURSELF?!
FWOOSH
FWOOSH
!!
CRASH
CRUSH
CLANG!
THE GAR-BAGE BIN!
THE GAR-BAGE BIN...
...
...

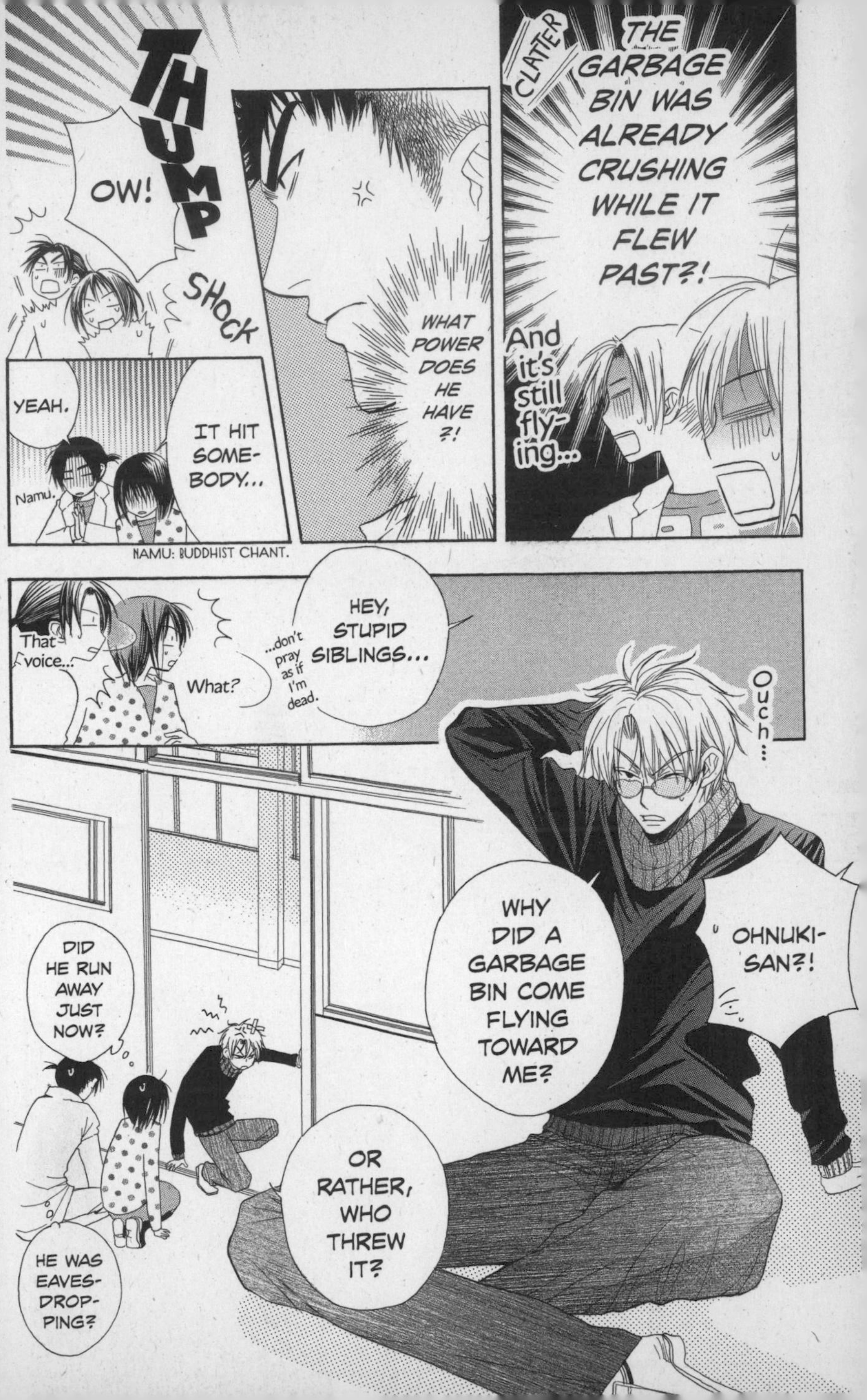
CLATTER
THE GARBAGE BIN WAS ALREADY CRUSHING WHILE IT FLEW PAST?!
And it's still flying...
WHAT POWER DOES HE HAVE?!
THUMP
OW!
SHOCK
IT HIT SOMEBODY...
YEAH.
Namu.
Ouch...
HEY, STUPID SIBLINGS...
...don't pray as if I'm dead.
What?
That voice...
OHNUKI-SAN?!
WHY DID A GARBAGE BIN COME FLYING TOWARD ME?
OR RATHER, WHO THREW IT?
DID HE RUN AWAY JUST NOW?
HE WAS EAVES-DROPPING?
NAMU: BUDDHIST CHANT.

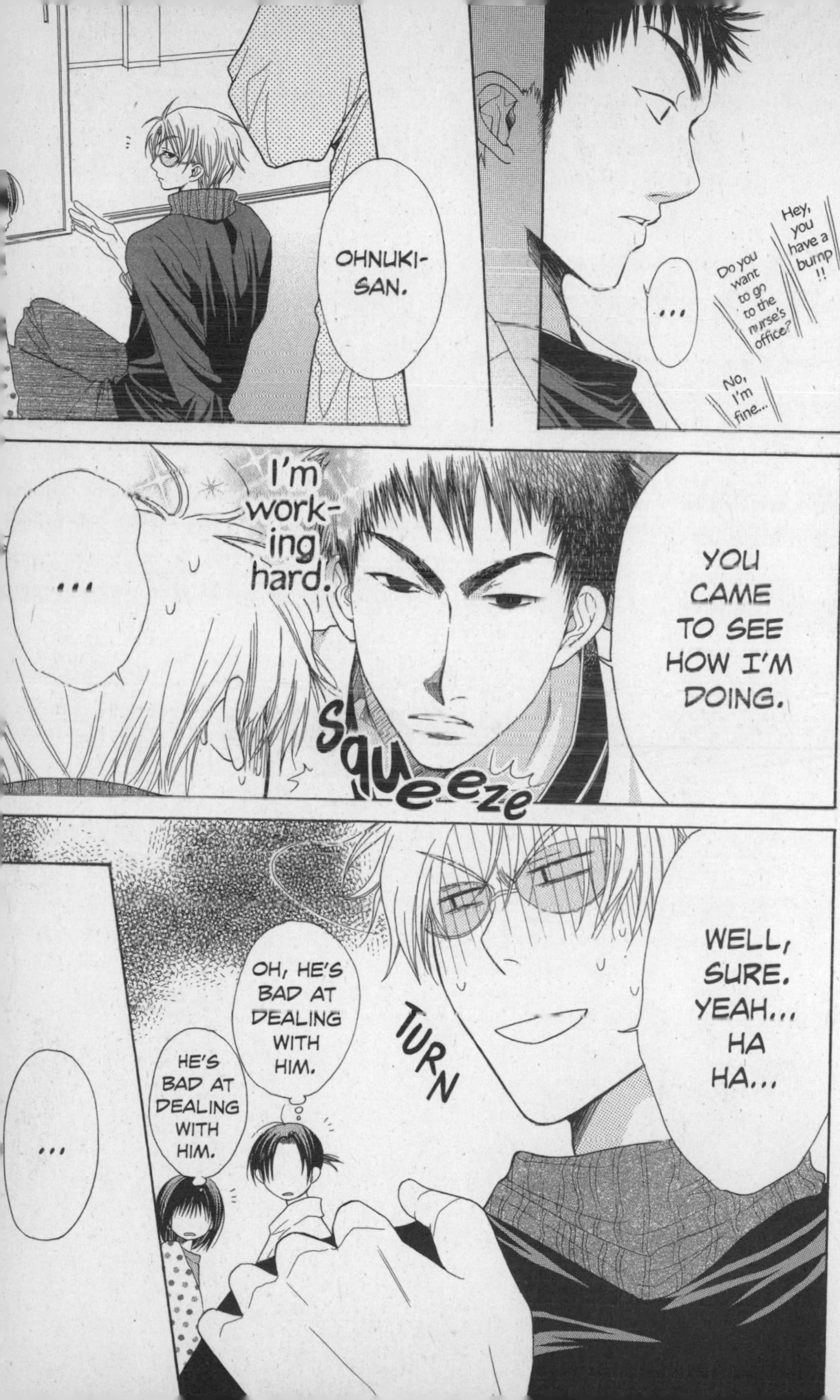
Hey, you have a bump !!
Do you want to go to the nurse's office?
...
No, I'm fine...
OHNUKI-SAN.
YOU CAME TO SEE HOW I'M DOING.
I'm work-ing hard.
Squeeze
...
WELL, SURE. YEAH... HA HA...
TURN
OH, HE'S BAD AT DEALING WITH HIM.
HE'S BAD AT DEALING WITH HIM.
...

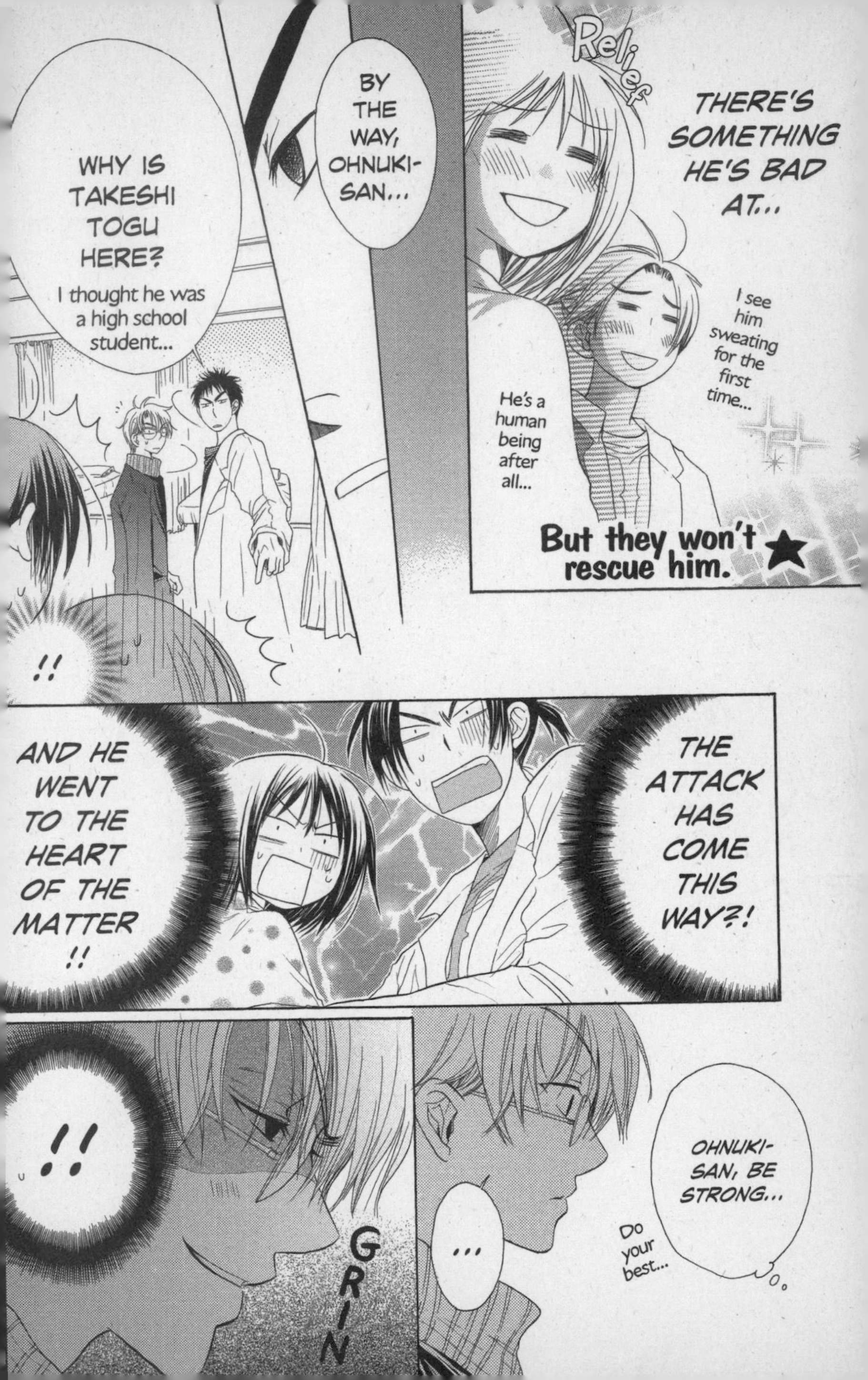
Relief
THERE'S SOMETHING HE'S BAD AT...
I see him sweating for the first time...
He's a human being after all...
But they won't rescue him.
BY THE WAY, OHNUKI-SAN...
WHY IS TAKESHI TOGU HERE?
I thought he was a high school student...
!!
THE ATTACK HAS COME THIS WAY?!
AND HE WENT TO THE HEART OF THE MATTER!!
OHNUKI-SAN, BE STRONG...
Do your best...
...
!!
GRIN

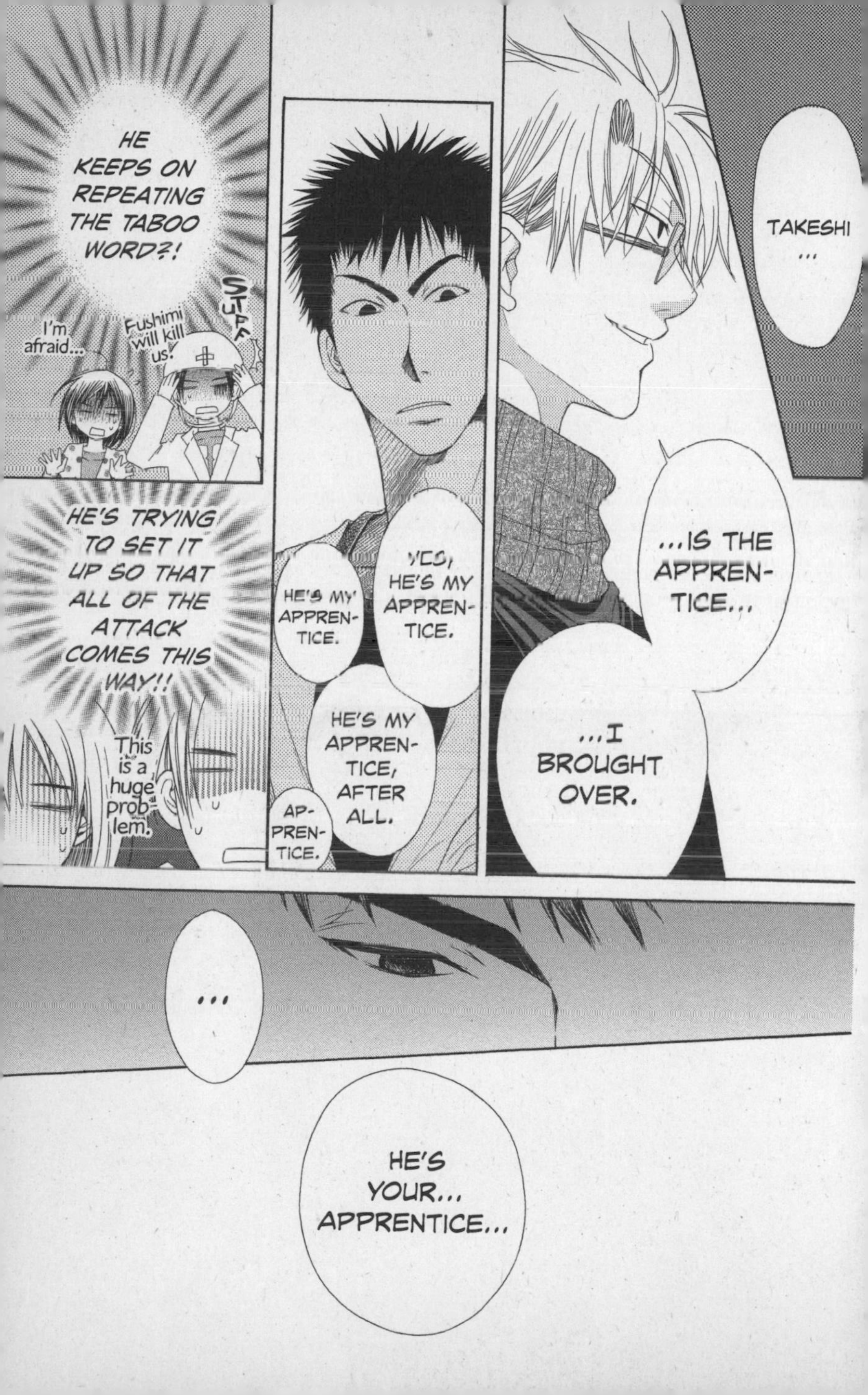
TAKESHI ...
...IS THE APPRENTICE...
...I BROUGHT OVER.
YES, HE'S MY APPRENTICE.
HE'S MY APPRENTICE.
HE'S MY APPRENTICE, AFTER ALL.
APPRENTICE.
HE KEEPS ON REPEATING THE TABOO WORD?!
STUFF
Fushimi will kill us!
I'm afraid...
HE'S TRYING TO SET IT UP SO THAT ALL OF THE ATTACK COMES THIS WAY!!
This is a huge problem.
...
HE'S YOUR... APPRENTICE...

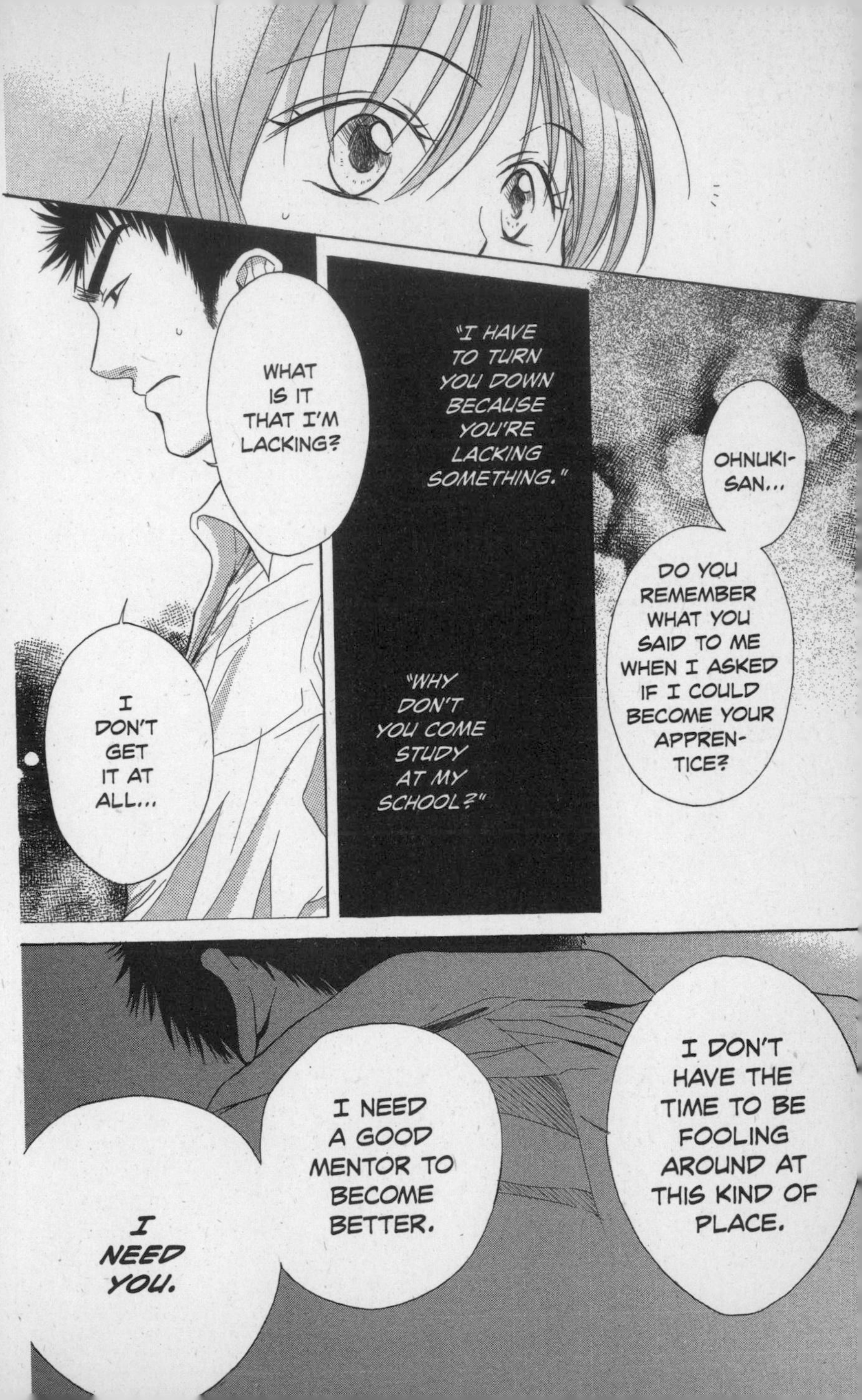
OHNUKI-SAN...
DO YOU REMEMBER WHAT YOU SAID TO ME WHEN I ASKED IF I COULD BECOME YOUR APPREN-TICE?
"I HAVE TO TURN YOU DOWN BECAUSE YOU'RE LACKING SOMETHING."
"WHY DON'T YOU COME STUDY AT MY SCHOOL?"
WHAT IS IT THAT I'M LACKING?
I DON'T GET IT AT ALL...
I DON'T HAVE THE TIME TO BE FOOLING AROUND AT THIS KIND OF PLACE.
I NEED A GOOD MENTOR TO BECOME BETTER.
I NEED YOU.

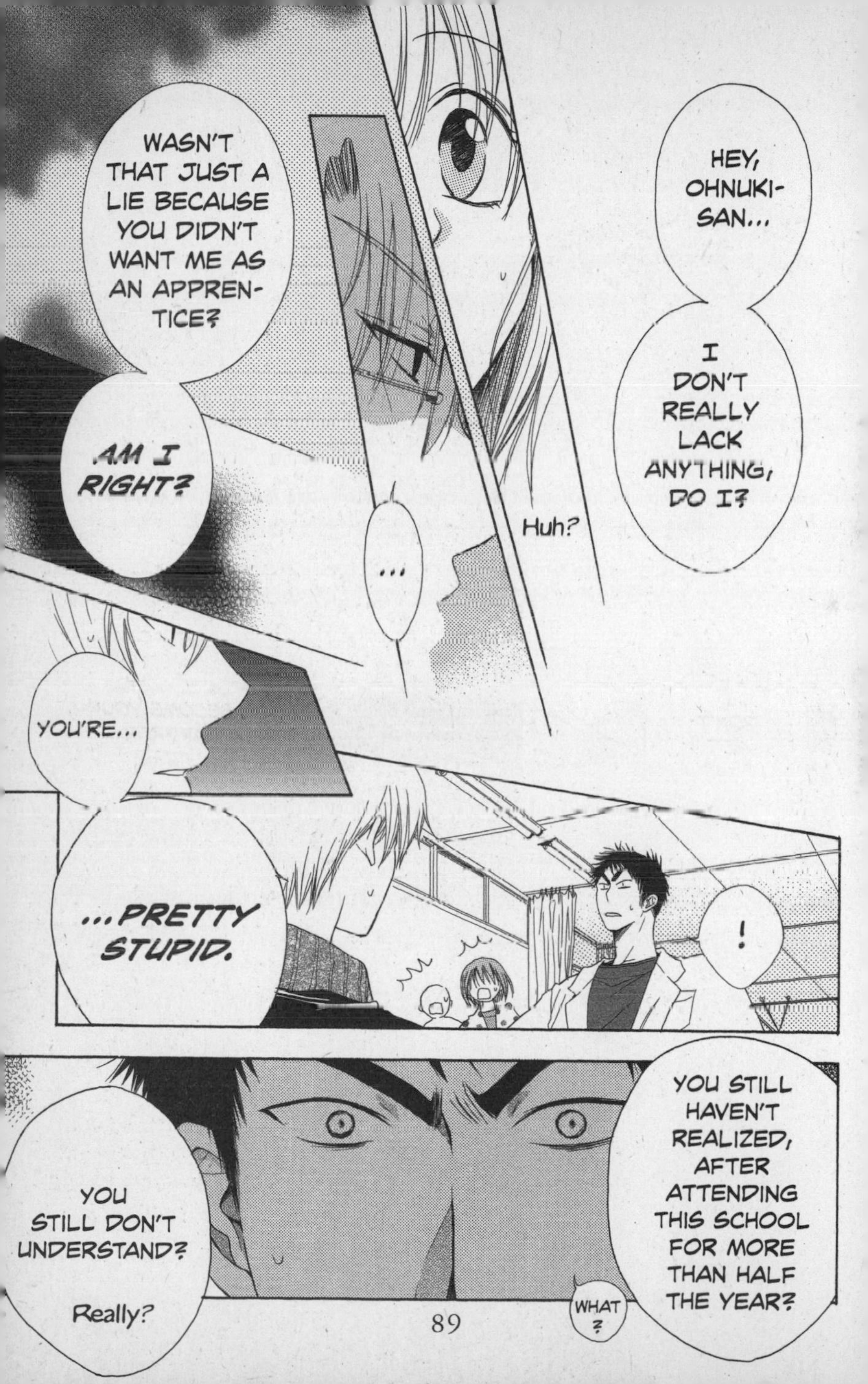
HEY, OHNUKI-SAN...
I DON'T REALLY LACK ANYTHING, DO I?
Huh?
...
WASN'T THAT JUST A LIE BECAUSE YOU DIDN'T WANT ME AS AN APPRENTICE?
AM I RIGHT?
YOU'RE...
...PRETTY STUPID.
!
YOU STILL HAVEN'T REALIZED, AFTER ATTENDING THIS SCHOOL FOR MORE THAN HALF THE YEAR?
WHAT?
YOU STILL DON'T UNDERSTAND?
Really?

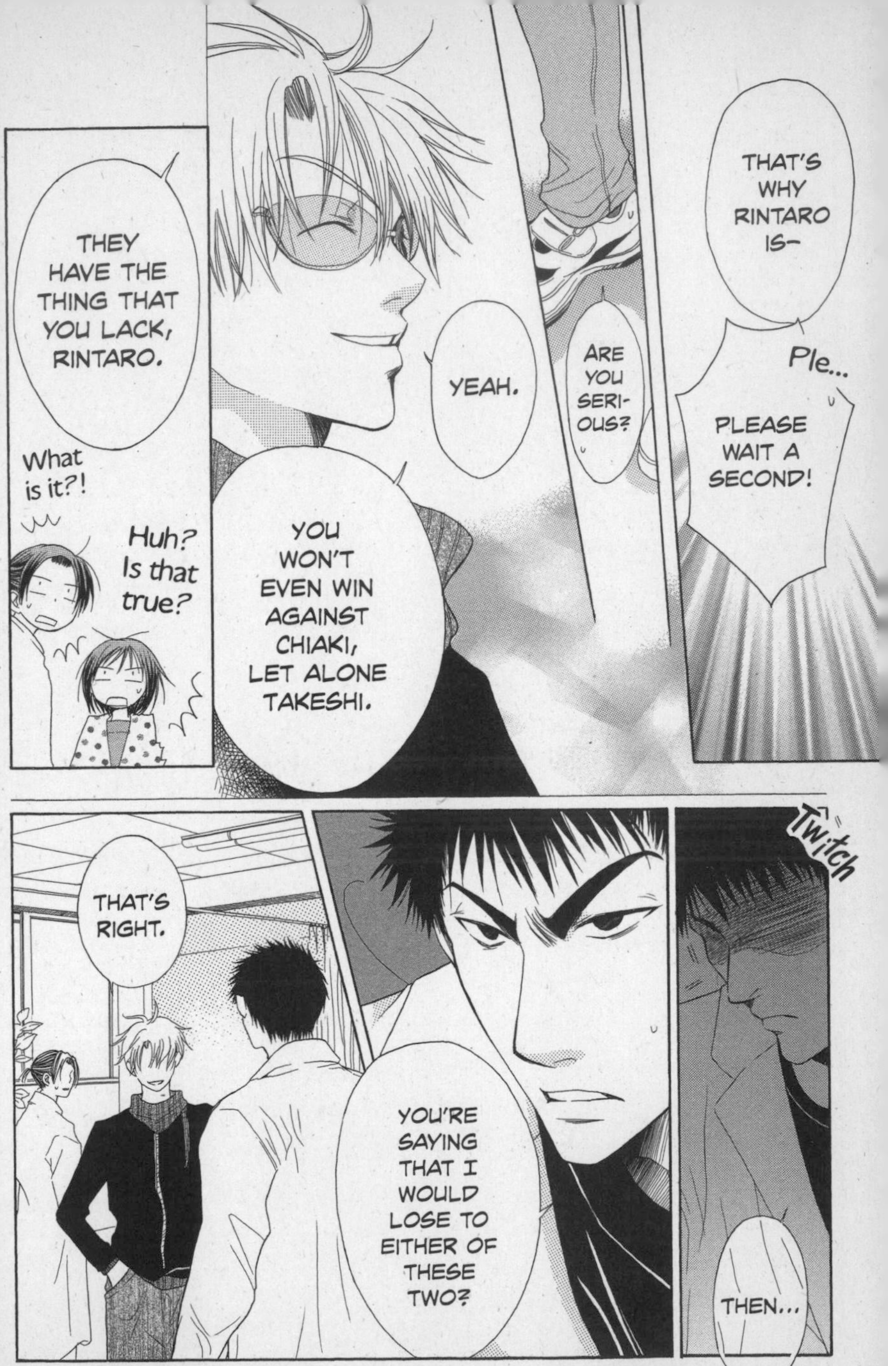
THAT'S WHY RINTARO IS—
Ple...
PLEASE WAIT A SECOND!
ARE YOU SERIOUS?
YEAH.
YOU WON'T EVEN WIN AGAINST CHIAKI, LET ALONE TAKESHI.
THEY HAVE THE THING THAT YOU LACK, RINTARO.
What is it?!
Huh? Is that true?
Twitch
THEN...
YOU'RE SAYING THAT I WOULD LOSE TO EITHER OF THESE TWO?
THAT'S RIGHT.

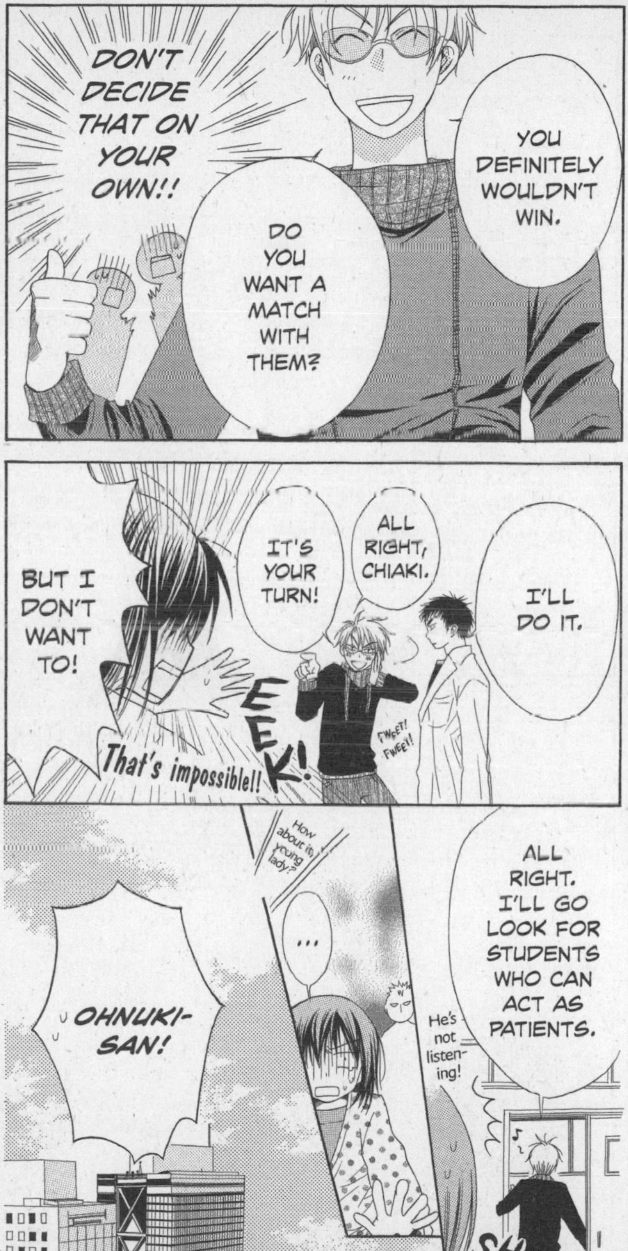
YOU DEFINITELY WOULDN'T WIN.
DO YOU WANT A MATCH WITH THEM?
DON'T DECIDE THAT ON YOUR OWN!!
I'LL DO IT.
ALL RIGHT, CHIAKI.
IT'S YOUR TURN!
FWEET! FWEET!
EEK!
BUT I DON'T WANT TO!
That's impossible!!
ALL RIGHT. I'LL GO LOOK FOR STUDENTS WHO CAN ACT AS PATIENTS.
SHOCK
He's not listening!
How about it, young lady?
...
OHNUKI-SAN!

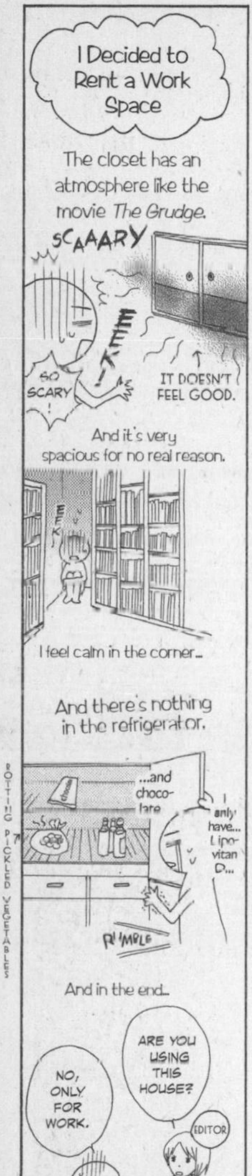
I Decided to Rent a Work Space
The closet has an atmosphere like the movie The Grudge.
SCAAARY
EEEK!
SO SCARY!
IT DOESN'T FEEL GOOD.
And it's very spacious for no real reason.
EEK
I feel calm in the corner...
And there's nothing in the refrigerator.
...and chocolate
I only have... Lipovitan D...
ROTTING PICKLED VEGETABLES
RUMBLE
And in the end...
ARE YOU USING THIS HOUSE?
NO, ONLY FOR WORK.
EDITOR
Thank goodness that it's close to my family's house!!

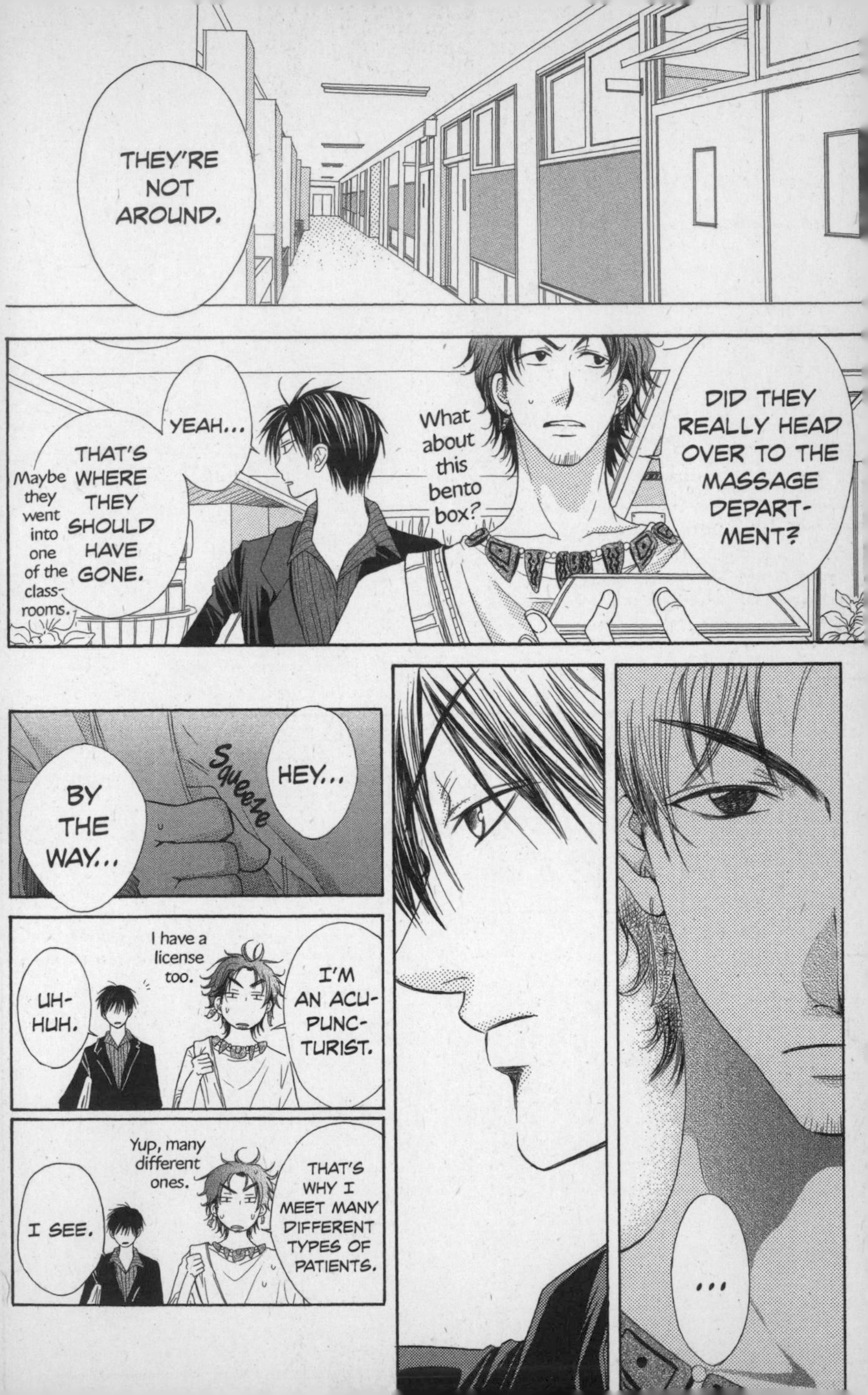
THEY'RE NOT AROUND.
DID THEY REALLY HEAD OVER TO THE MASSAGE DEPART-MENT?
What about this bento box?
YEAH...
THAT'S WHERE THEY SHOULD HAVE GONE.
Maybe they went into one of the class-rooms.
...
HEY...
Squeeze
BY THE WAY...
I'M AN ACU-PUNC-TURIST.
I have a license too.
UH-HUH.
THAT'S WHY I MEET MANY DIFFERENT TYPES OF PATIENTS.
Yup, many different ones.
I SEE.

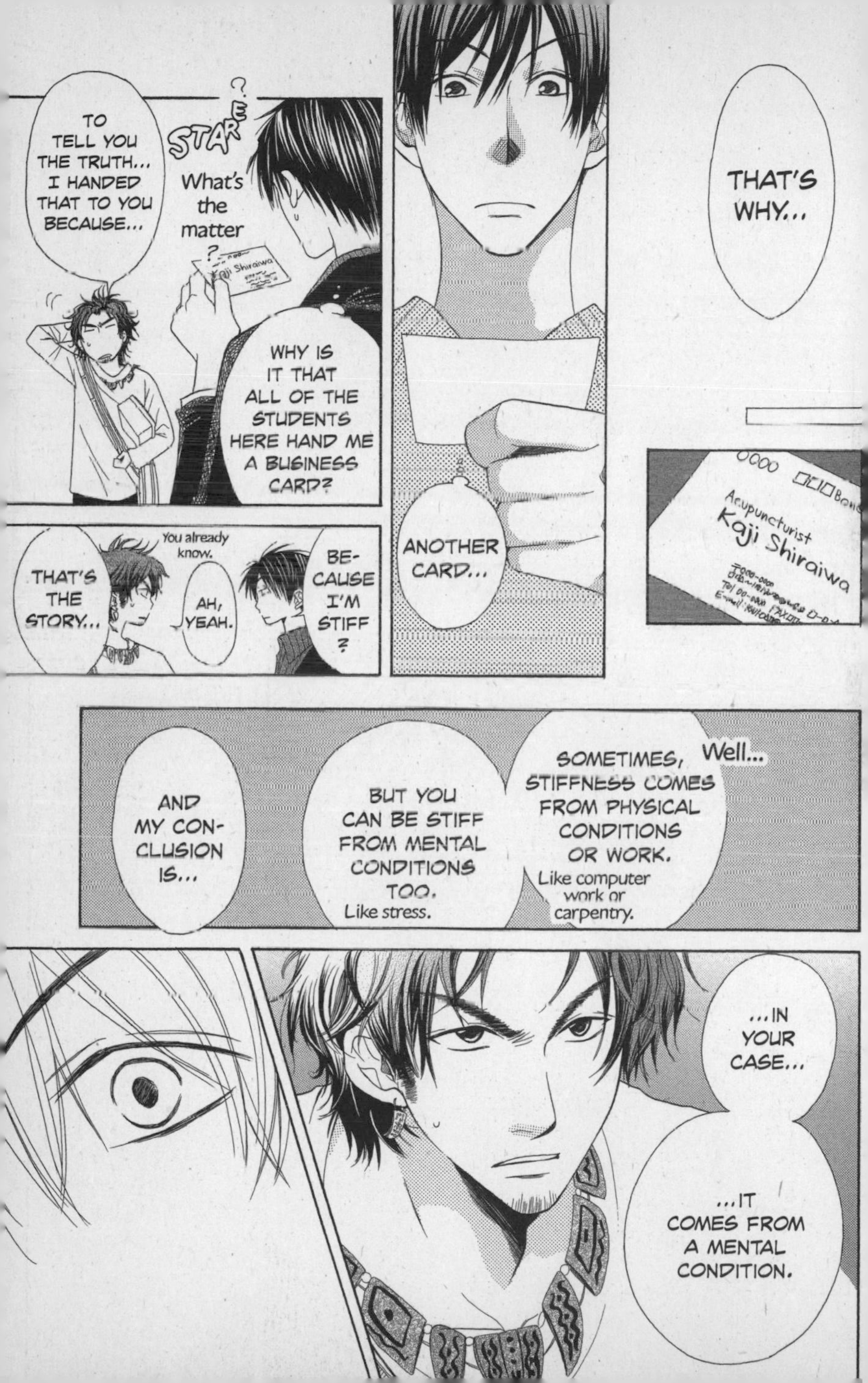

THAT'S WHY...
Acupuncturist
Kaji Shiraiwa
ANOTHER CARD...
WHY IS IT THAT ALL OF THE STUDENTS HERE HAND ME A BUSINESS CARD?
STARE
What's the matter?
Kaji Shiraiwa
TO TELL YOU THE TRUTH... I HANDED THAT TO YOU BECAUSE...
BECAUSE I'M STIFF?
AH, YEAH.
You already know.
THAT'S THE STORY...
SOMETIMES, STIFFNESS COMES FROM PHYSICAL CONDITIONS OR WORK.
Well...
Like computer work or carpentry.
BUT YOU CAN BE STIFF FROM MENTAL CONDITIONS TOO.
Like stress.
AND MY CONCLUSION IS...
...IN YOUR CASE...
...IT COMES FROM A MENTAL CONDITION.

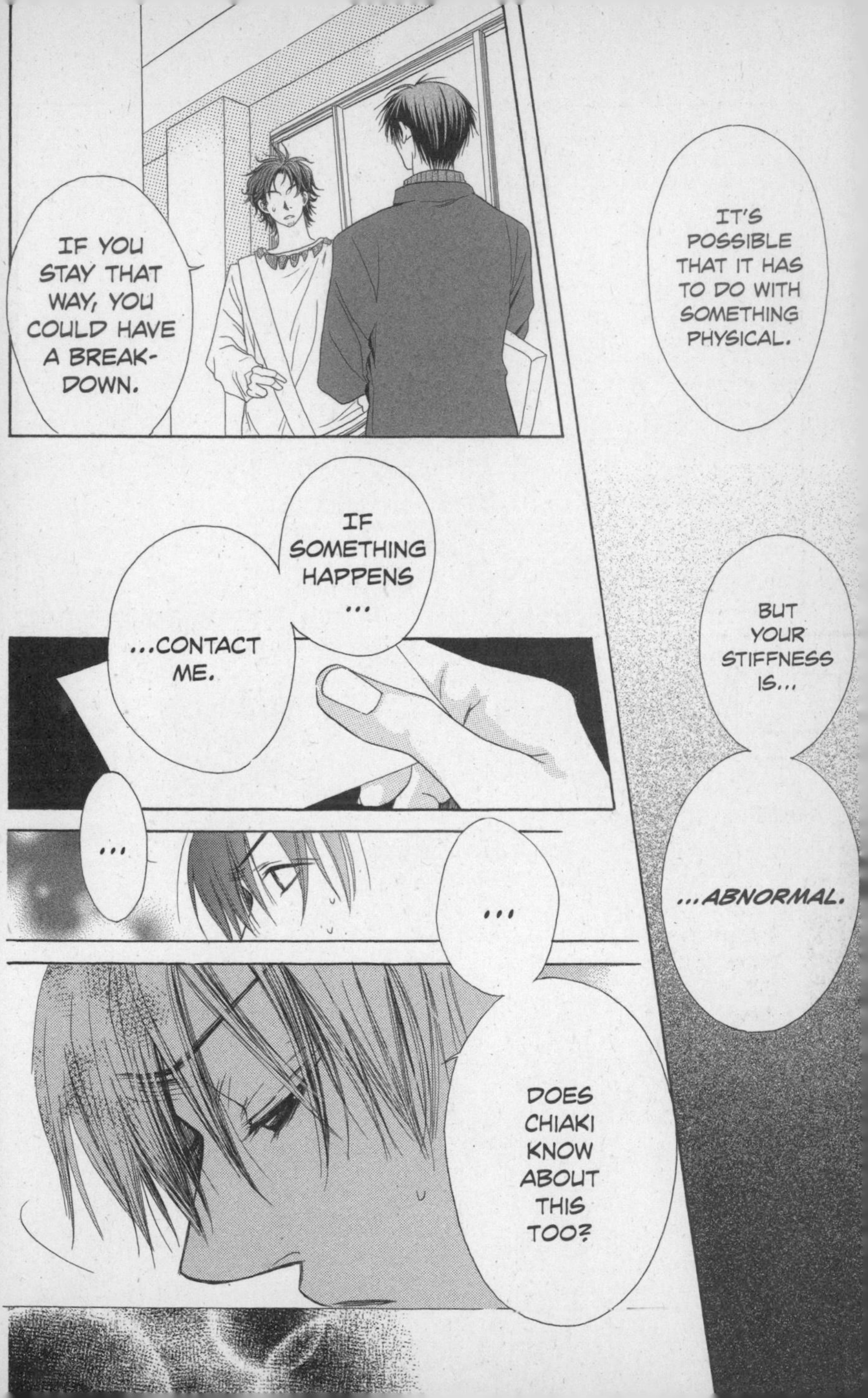
IT'S POSSIBLE THAT IT HAS TO DO WITH SOMETHING PHYSICAL.
BUT YOUR STIFFNESS IS...
...ABNORMAL.
IF YOU STAY THAT WAY, YOU COULD HAVE A BREAK-DOWN.
IF SOMETHING HAPPENS...
...CONTACT ME.
...
...
DOES CHIAKI KNOW ABOUT THIS TOO?

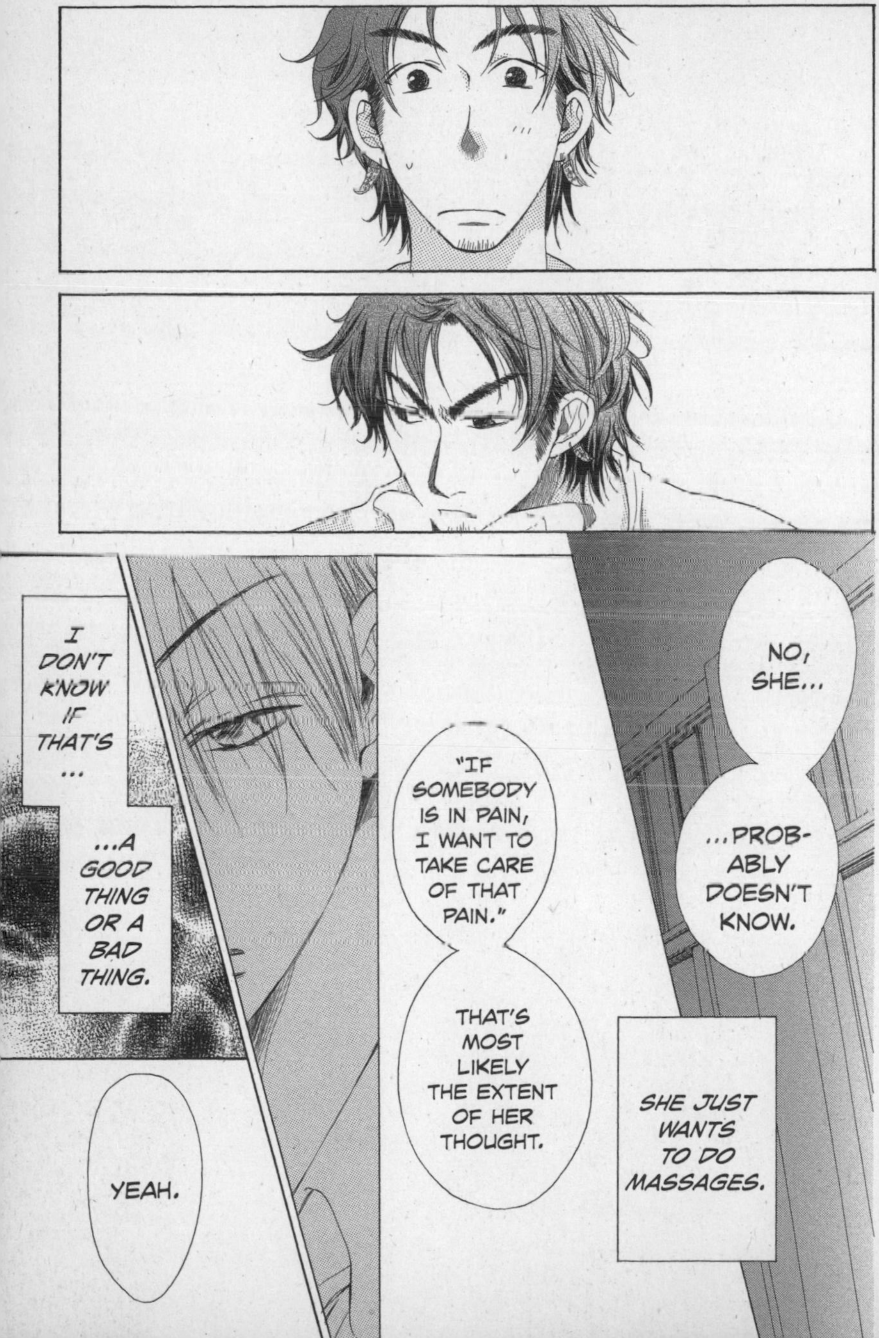
NO, SHE...
...PROBABLY DOESN'T KNOW.
SHE JUST WANTS TO DO MASSAGES.
"IF SOMEBODY IS IN PAIN, I WANT TO TAKE CARE OF THAT PAIN."
THAT'S MOST LIKELY THE EXTENT OF HER THOUGHT.
I DON'T KNOW IF THAT'S...
...A GOOD THING OR A BAD THING.
YEAH.

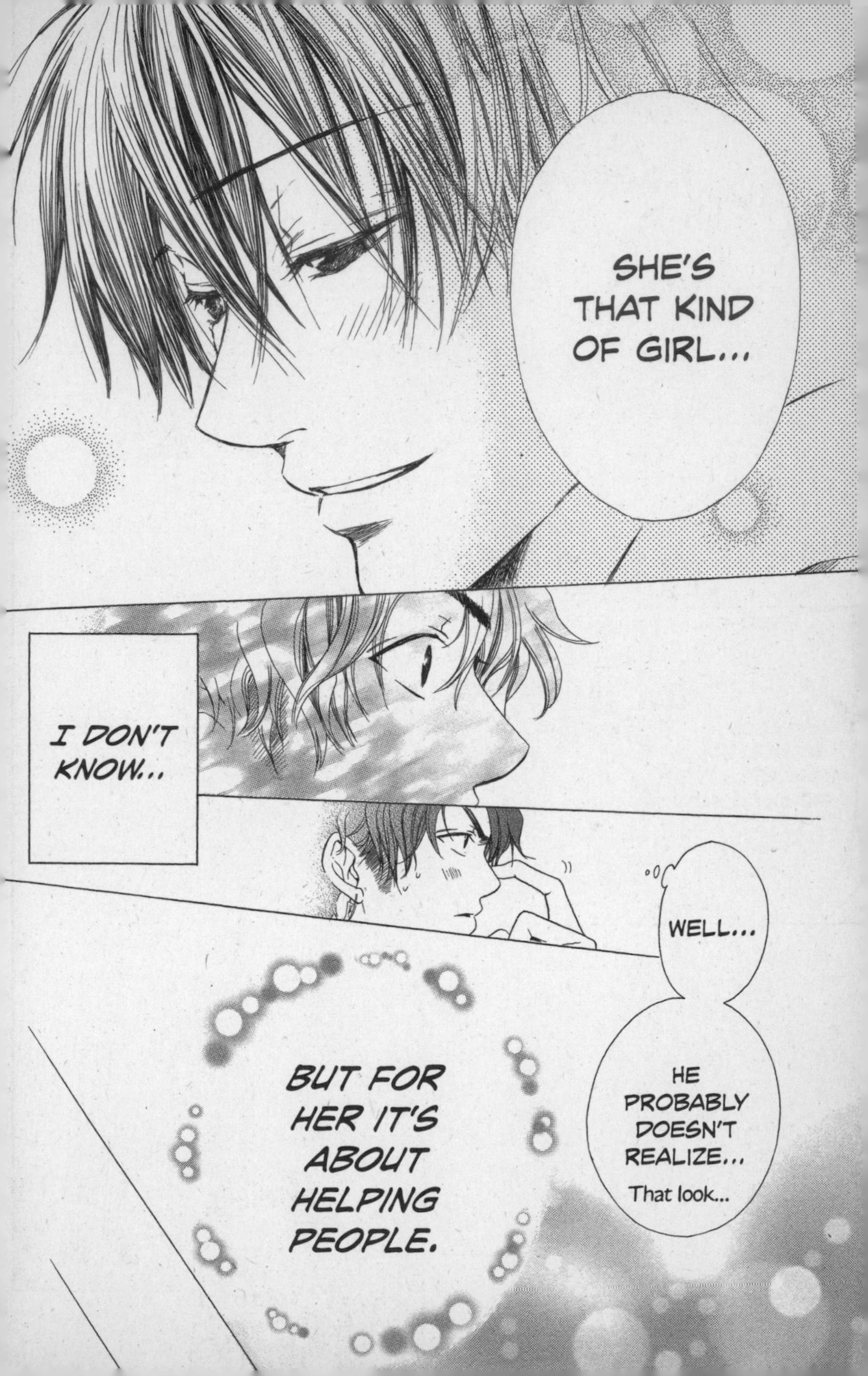
SHE'S THAT KIND OF GIRL...
I DON'T KNOW...
WELL...
HE PROBABLY DOESN'T REALIZE...
That look...
BUT FOR HER IT'S ABOUT HELPING PEOPLE.

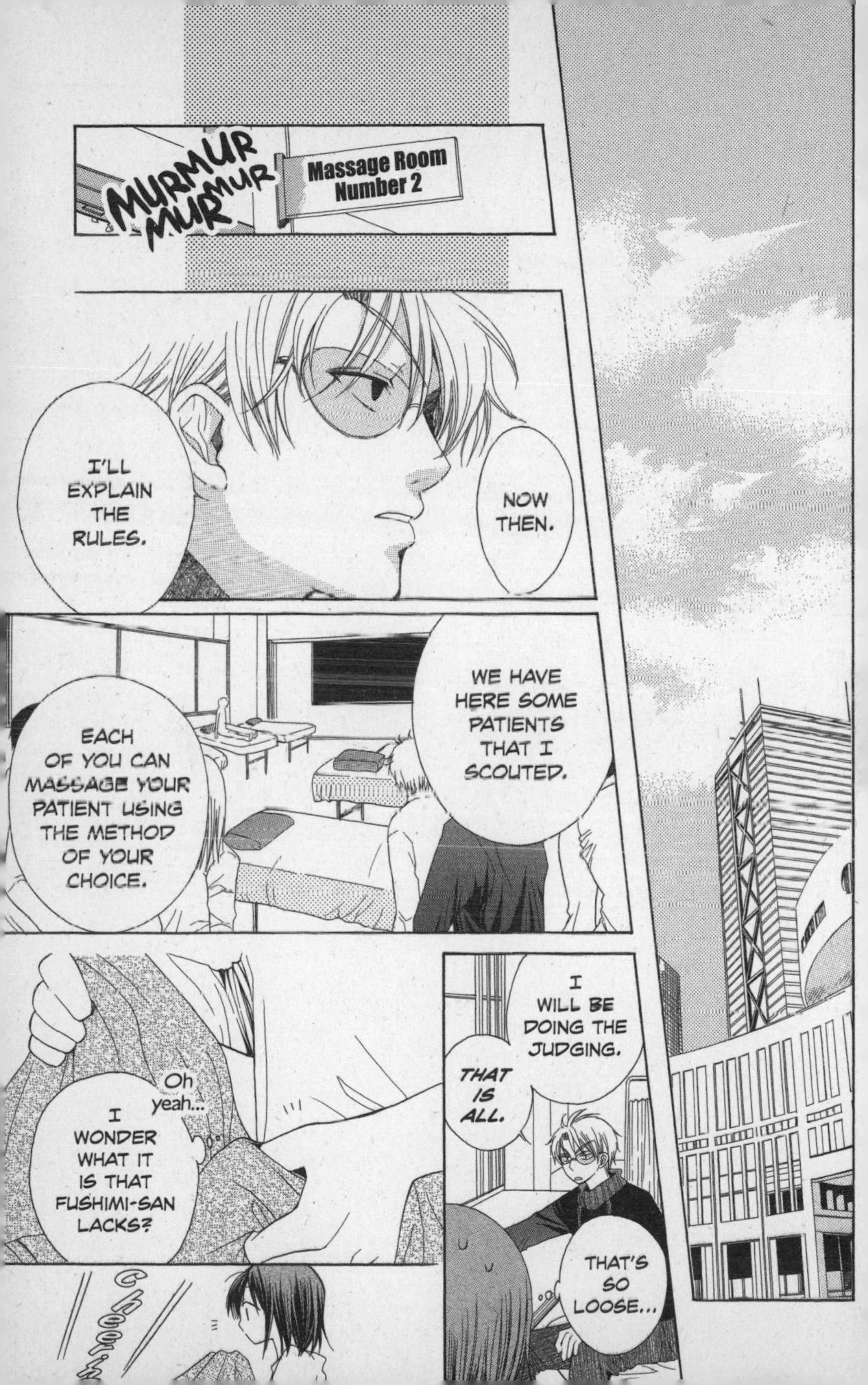
Massage Room Number 2
MURMUR MURMUR MUR
NOW THEN.
I'LL EXPLAIN THE RULES.
WE HAVE HERE SOME PATIENTS THAT I SCOUTED.
EACH OF YOU CAN MASSAGE YOUR PATIENT USING THE METHOD OF YOUR CHOICE.
I WILL BE DOING THE JUDGING.
THAT IS ALL.
THAT'S SO LOOSE...
Oh yeah...
I WONDER WHAT IT IS THAT FUSHIMI-SAN LACKS?

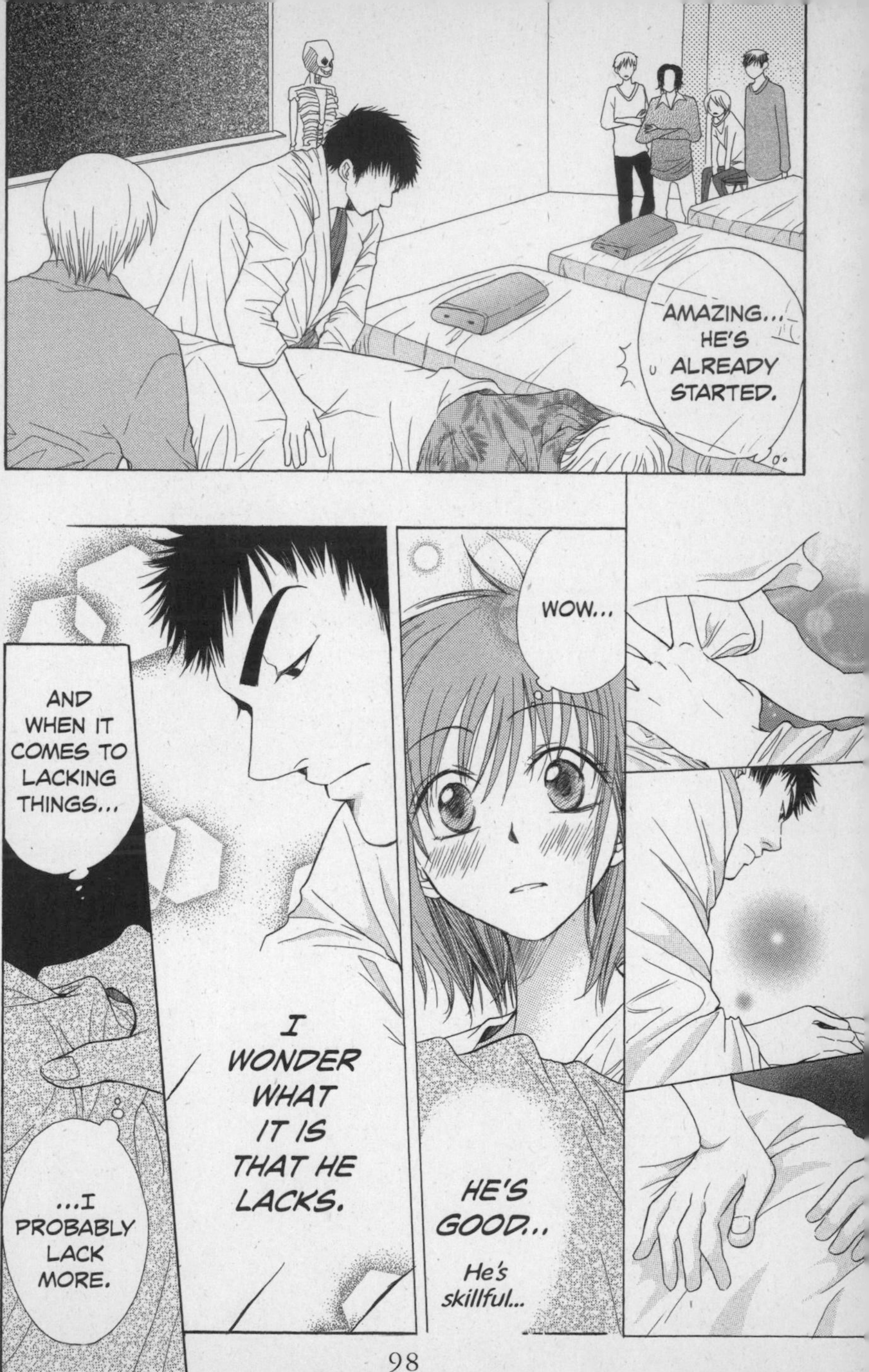
AMAZING... HE'S ALREADY STARTED.
WOW...
HE'S GOOD...
He's skillful...
I WONDER WHAT IT IS THAT HE LACKS.
AND WHEN IT COMES TO LACKING THINGS...
...I PROBABLY LACK MORE.

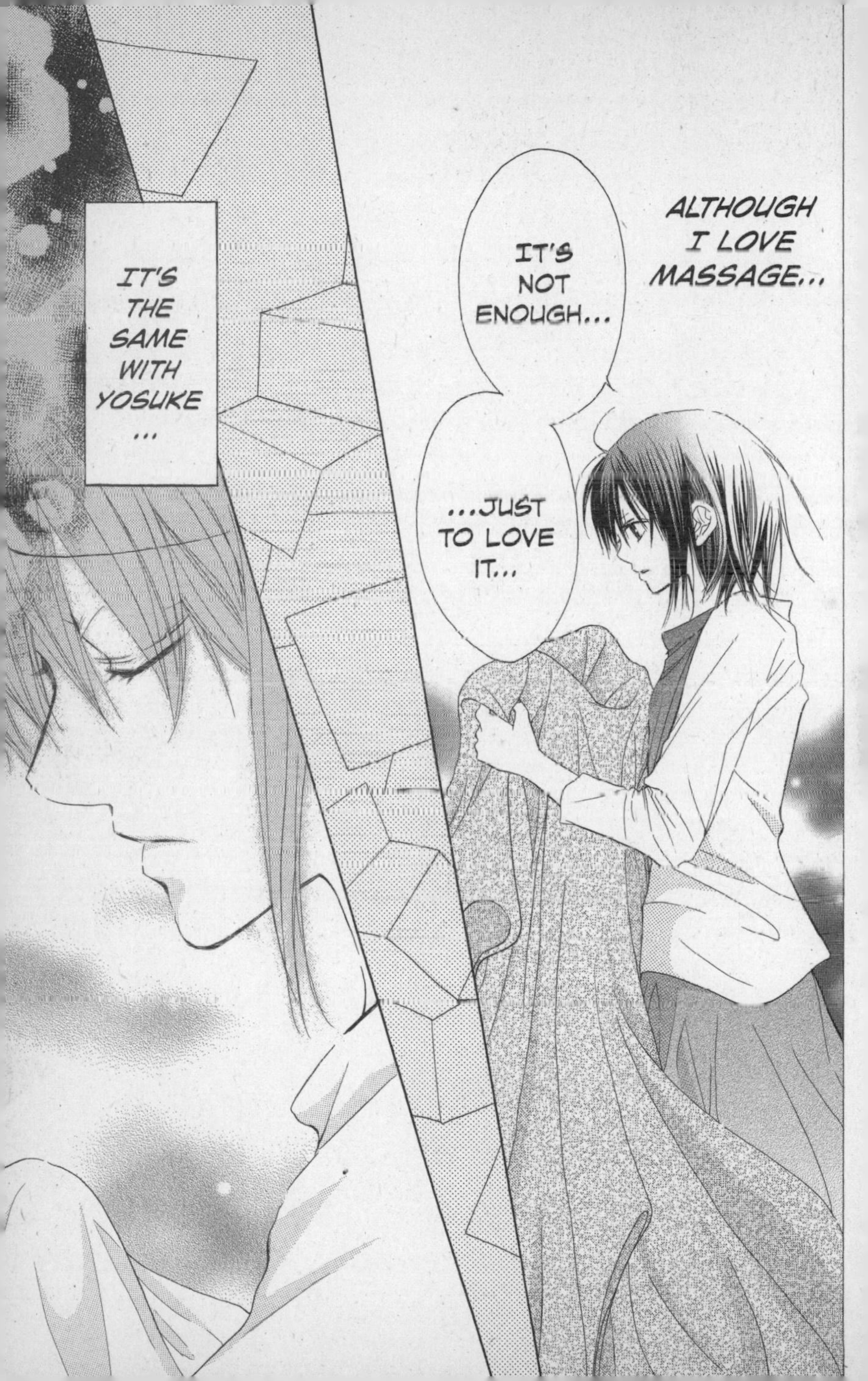
ALTHOUGH I LOVE MASSAGE...
IT'S NOT ENOUGH...
...JUST TO LOVE IT...
IT'S THE SAME WITH YOSUKE ...

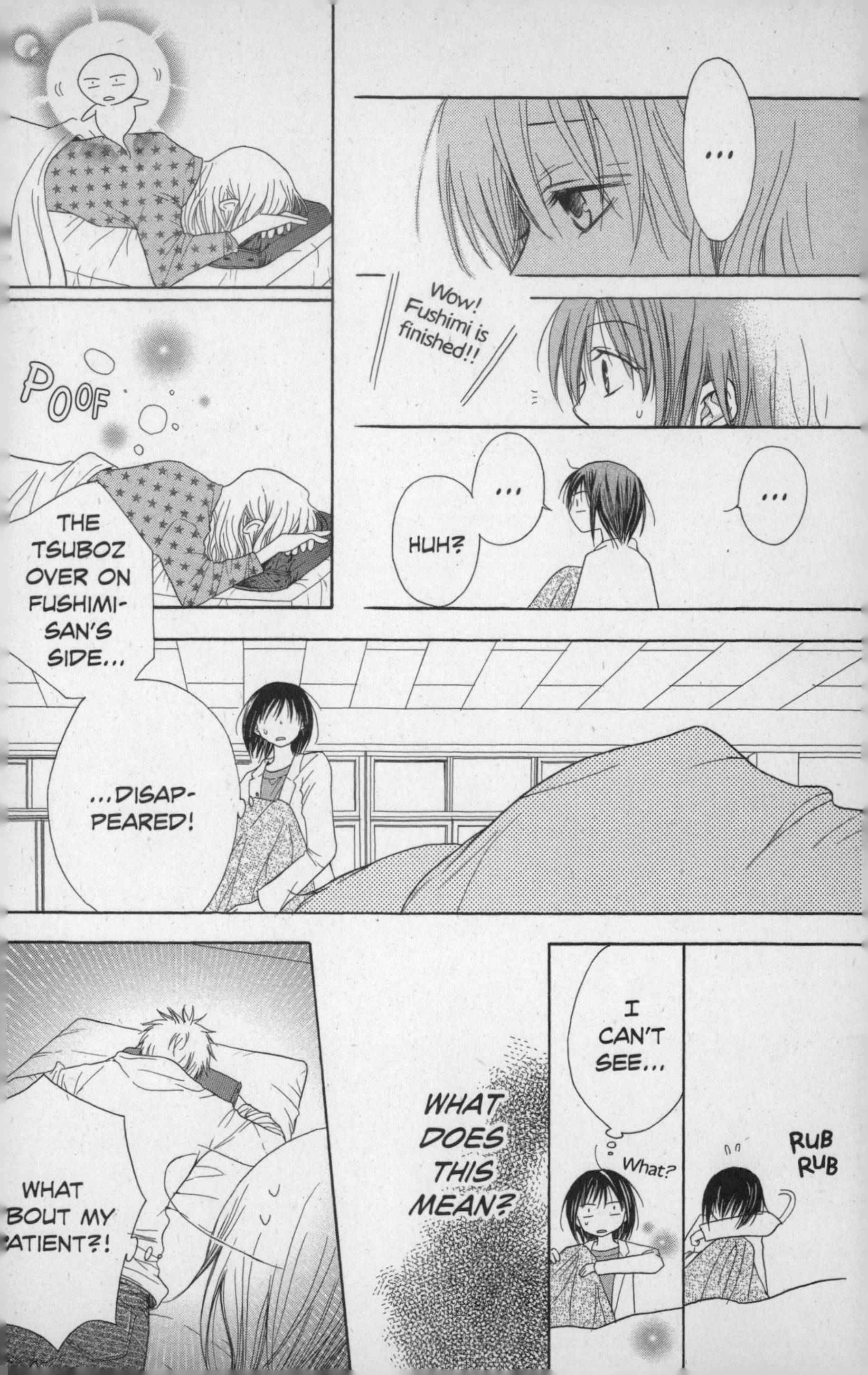
...
Wow! Fushimi is finished!!
...
...
HUH?
POOF
THE TSUBOZ OVER ON FUSHIMI-SAN'S SIDE...
...DISAPPEARED!
RUB RUB
I CAN'T SEE...
What?
WHAT DOES THIS MEAN?
WHAT BOUT MY ATIENT?!

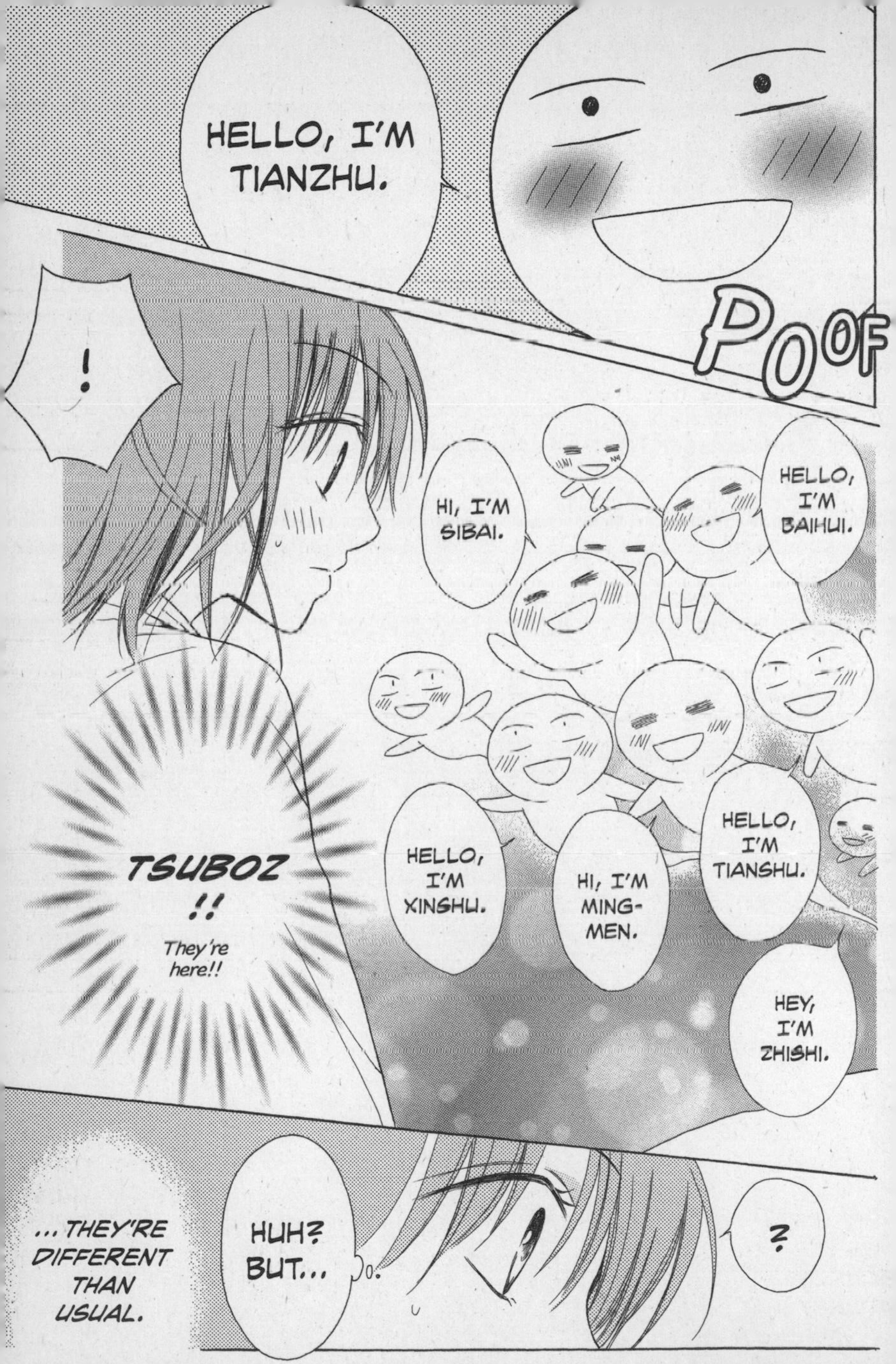
HELLO, I'M TIANZHU.
POOF
HELLO, I'M BAIHUI.
HI, I'M SIBAI.
!
HELLO, I'M TIANSHU.
HEY, I'M ZHISHI.
HI, I'M MING-MEN.
HELLO, I'M XINSHU.
TSUBOZ!!
They're here!!
?
HUH? BUT...
...THEY'RE DIFFERENT THAN USUAL.

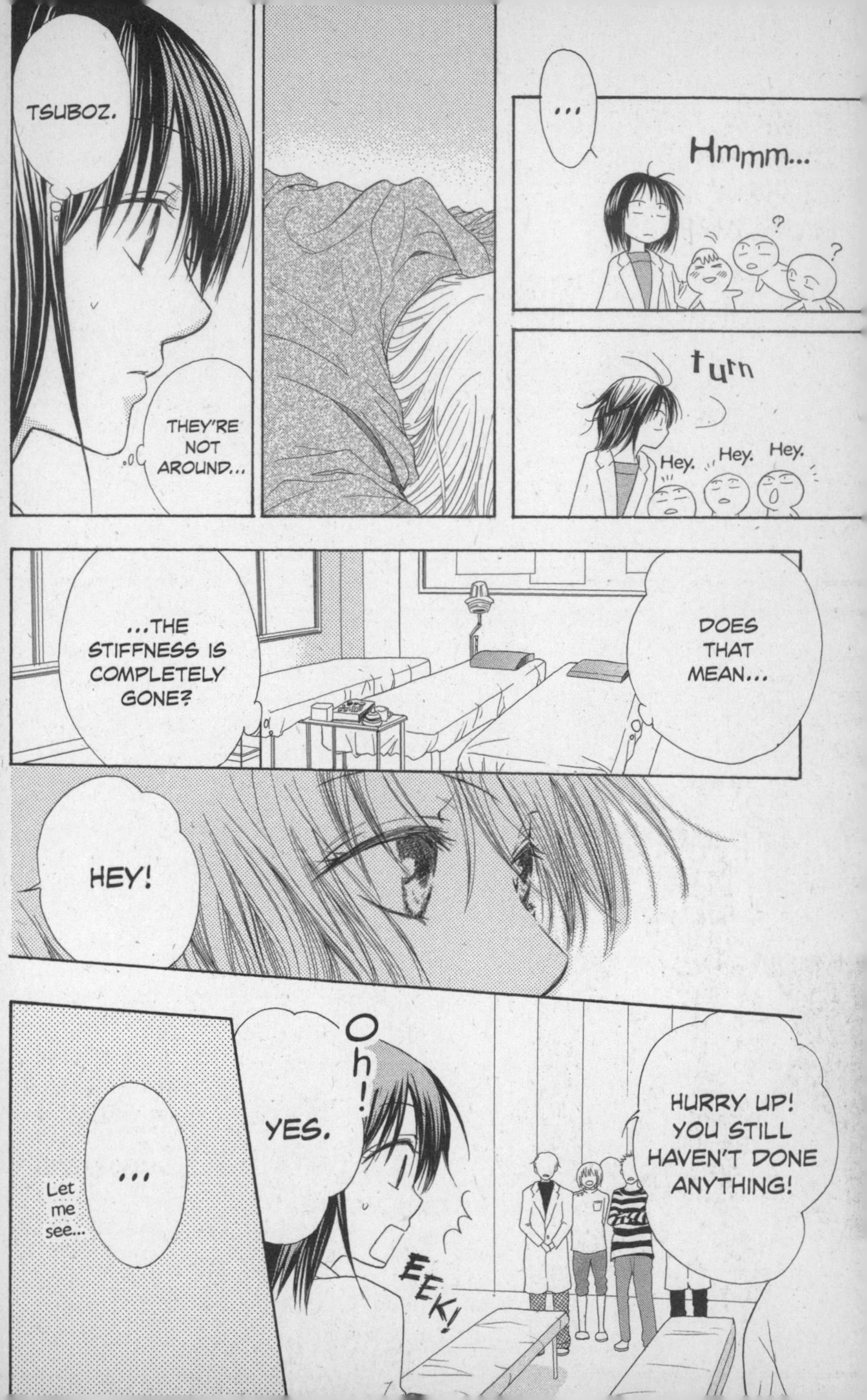
...
Hmmm...
?
?
turn
Hey.
Hey.
Hey.
TSUBOZ.
THEY'RE NOT AROUND...
DOES THAT MEAN...
...THE STIFFNESS IS COMPLETELY GONE?
HEY!
HURRY UP! YOU STILL HAVEN'T DONE ANYTHING!
Oh!
EEK!
YES.
...
Let me see...

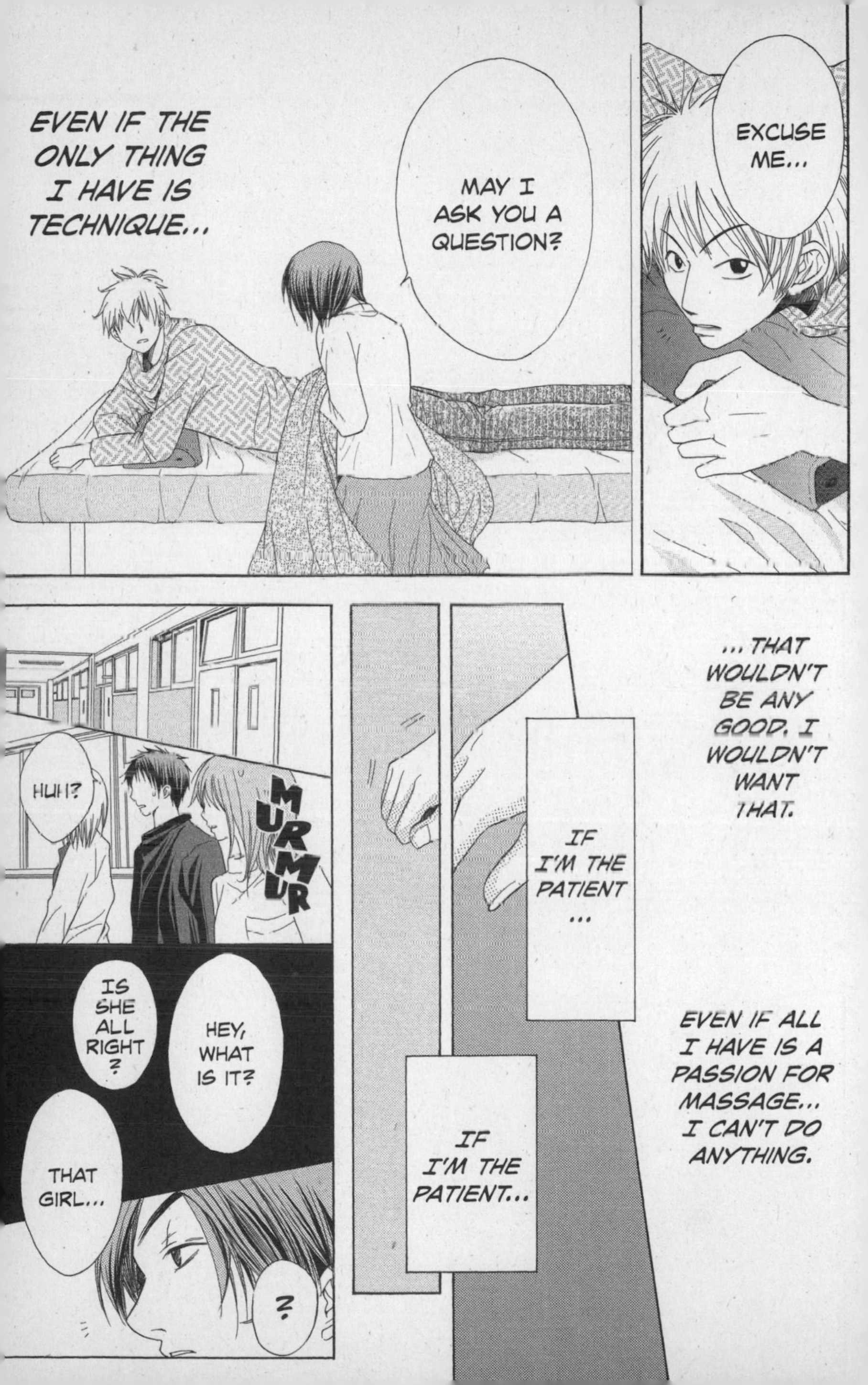
EXCUSE ME...
MAY I ASK YOU A QUESTION?
EVEN IF THE ONLY THING I HAVE IS TECHNIQUE...
...THAT WOULDN'T BE ANY GOOD. I WOULDN'T WANT THAT.
IF I'M THE PATIENT...
IF I'M THE PATIENT...
EVEN IF ALL I HAVE IS A PASSION FOR MASSAGE... I CAN'T DO ANYTHING.
MURMUR
HUH?
HEY, WHAT IS IT?
IS SHE ALL RIGHT?
THAT GIRL...
?

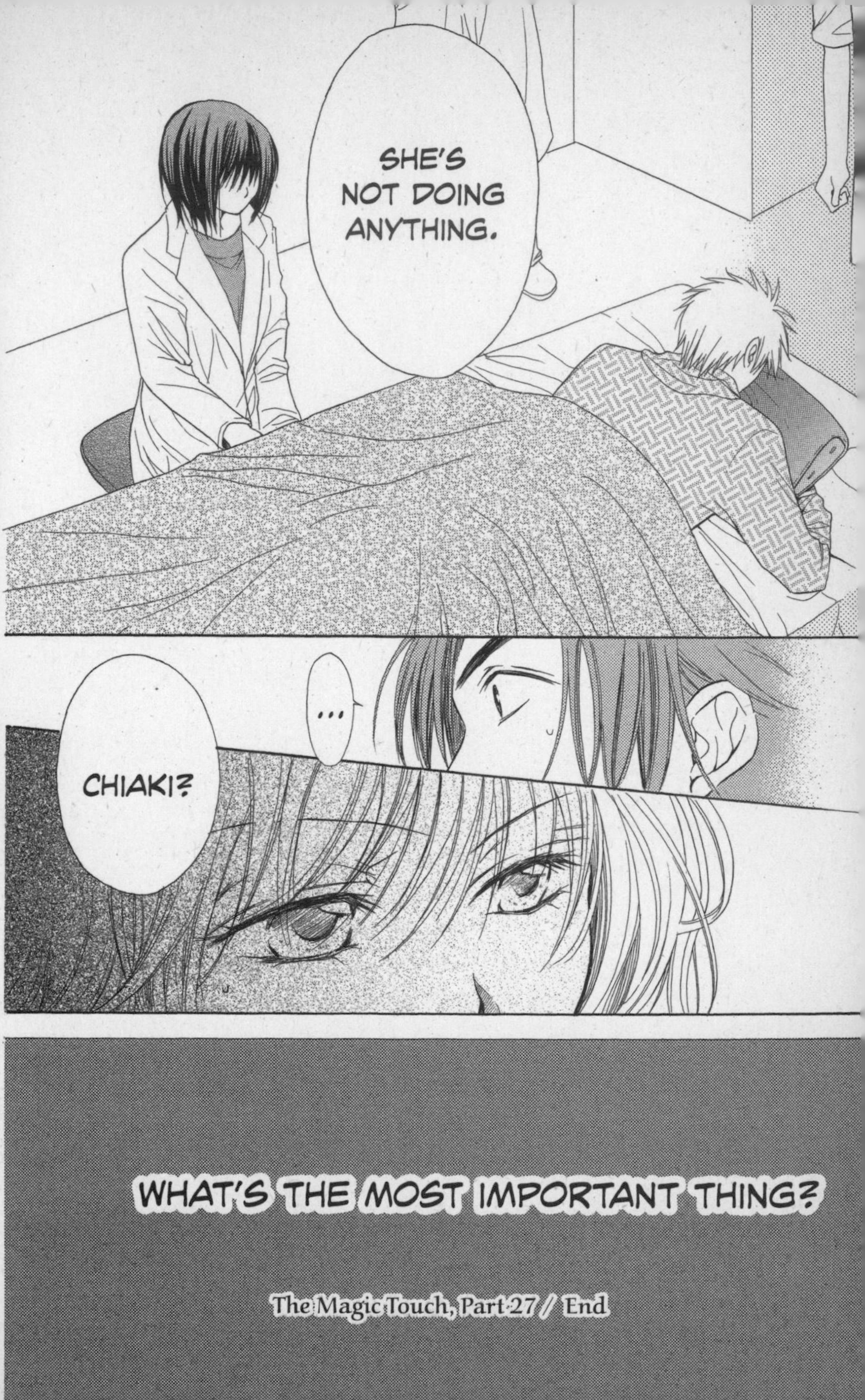
SHE'S NOT DOING ANYTHING.
...
CHIAKI?
WHAT'S THE MOST IMPORTANT THING?
The Magic Touch, Part 27 / End

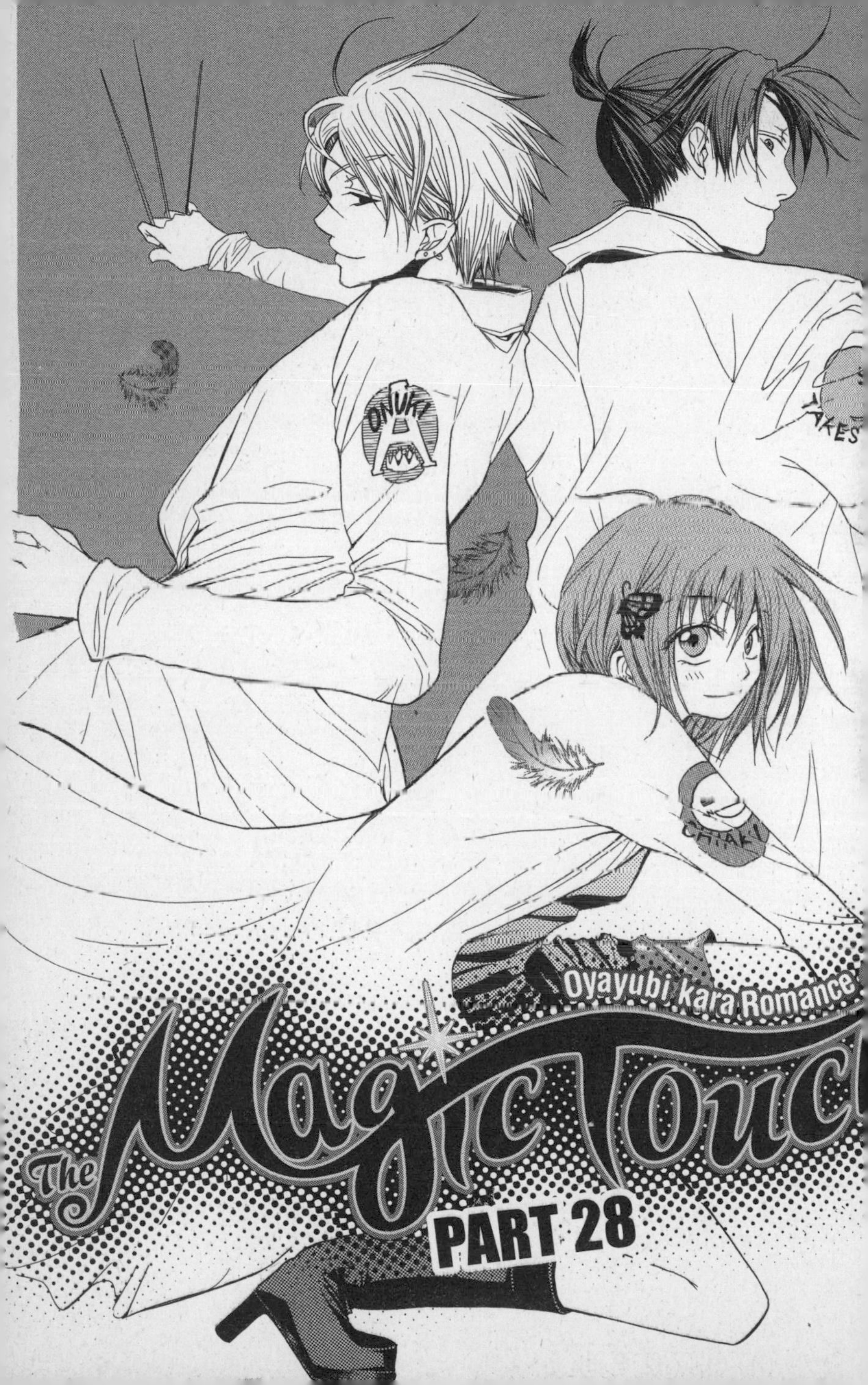
ONUKI
TAKES
CHIAKI
Oyayubi kara Romance
The Magic Touch
PART 28

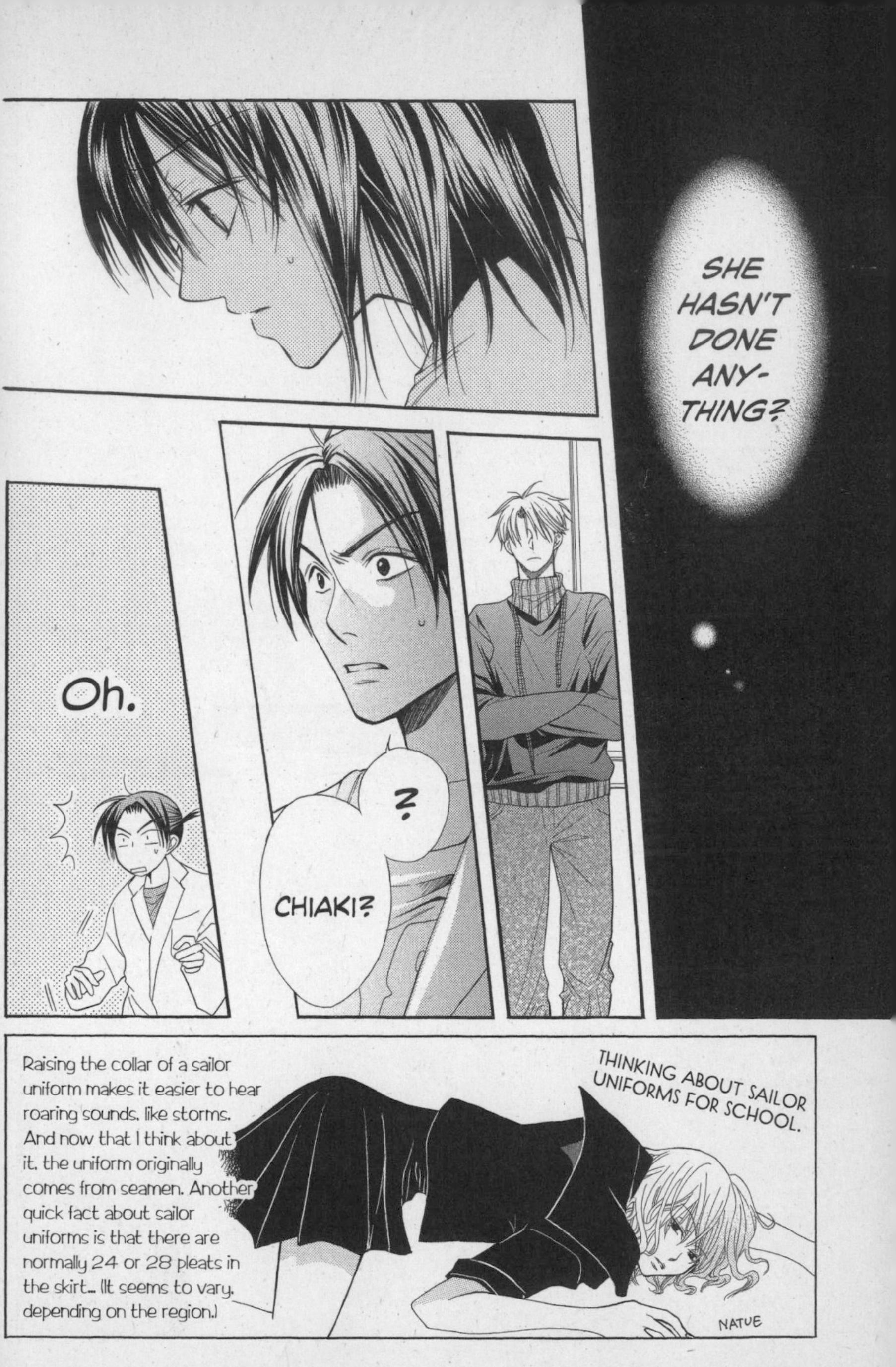
SHE HASN'T DONE ANY-THING?
?
CHIAKI?
Oh.
THINKING ABOUT SAILOR UNIFORMS FOR SCHOOL.
Raising the collar of a sailor uniform makes it easier to hear roaring sounds, like storms. And now that I think about it, the uniform originally comes from seamen. Another quick fact about sailor uniforms is that there are normally 24 or 28 pleats in the skirt... (It seems to vary, depending on the region.)
NATUE

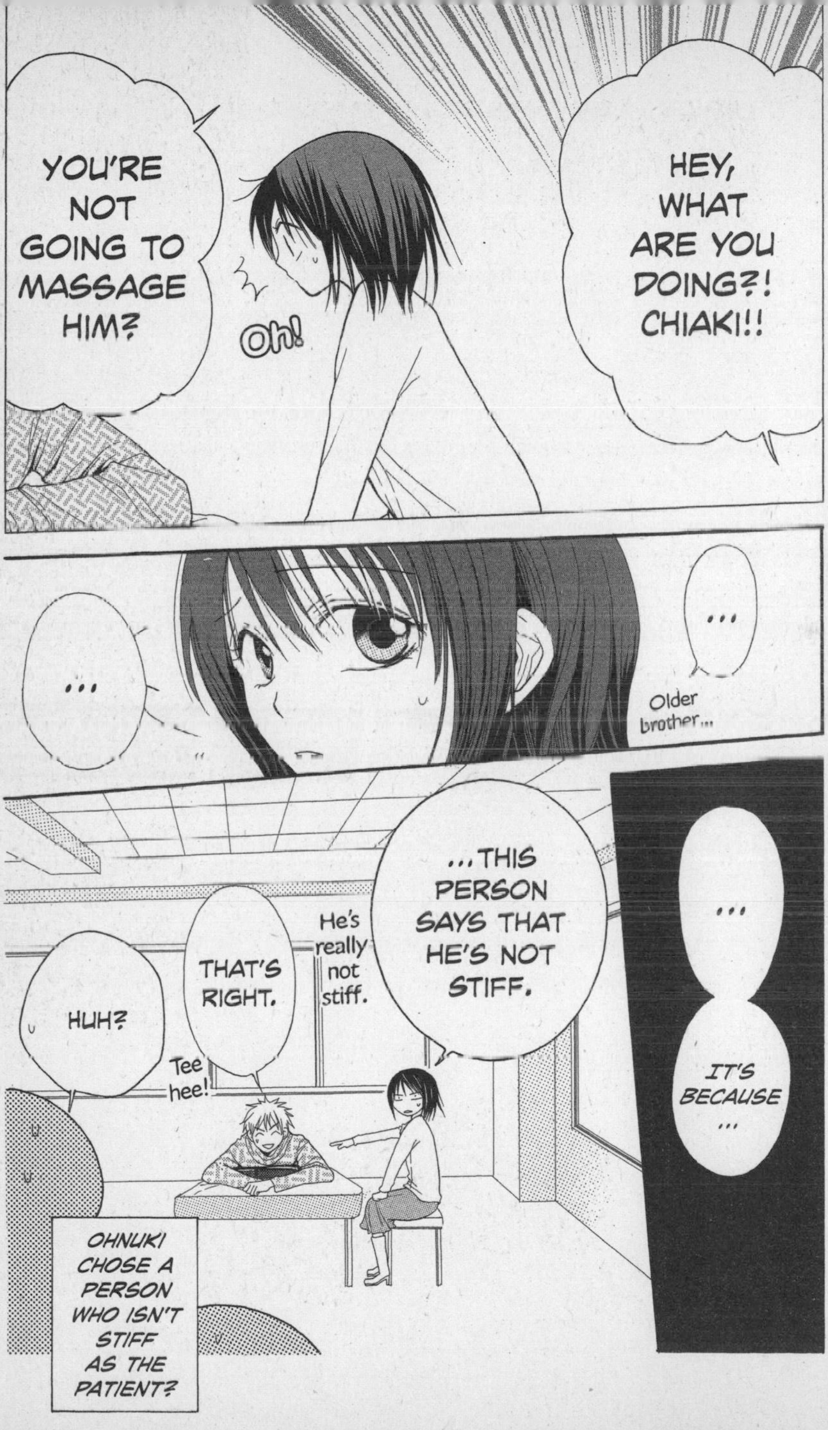
HEY, WHAT ARE YOU DOING?! CHIAKI!!
Oh!
YOU'RE NOT GOING TO MASSAGE HIM?
...
Older brother...
...
...
IT'S BECAUSE ...
...THIS PERSON SAYS THAT HE'S NOT STIFF.
He's really not stiff.
THAT'S RIGHT.
Tee hee!
HUH?
OHNUKI CHOSE A PERSON WHO ISN'T STIFF AS THE PATIENT?

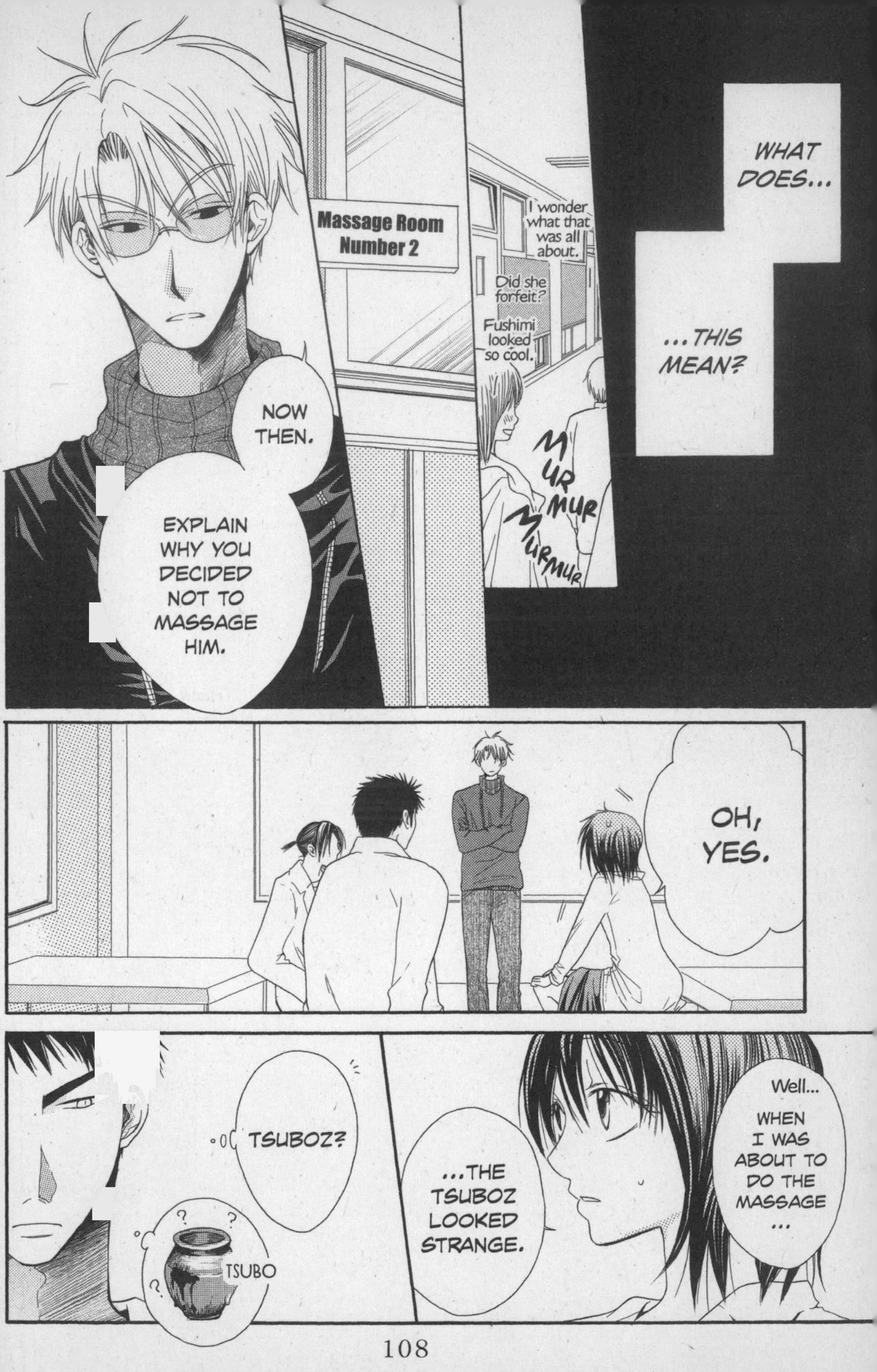
WHAT DOES...
...THIS MEAN?
Massage Room Number 2
I wonder what that was all about.
Did she forfeit?
Fushimi looked so cool.
MUR MUR MURMUR
NOW THEN.
EXPLAIN WHY YOU DECIDED NOT TO MASSAGE HIM.
OH, YES.
Well...
WHEN I WAS ABOUT TO DO THE MASSAGE...
...THE TSUBOZ LOOKED STRANGE.
TSUBOZ?
TSUBO

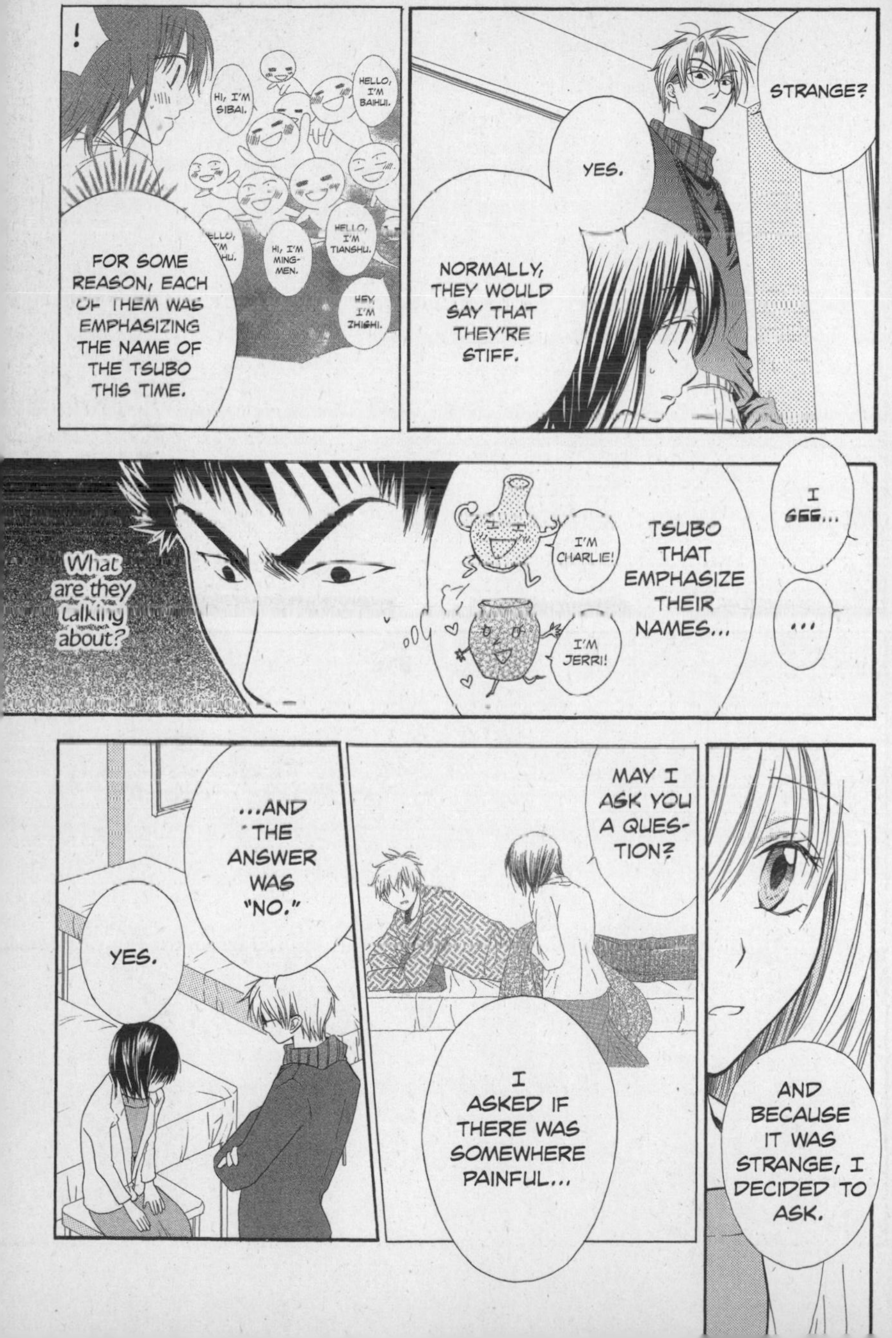
STRANGE?
YES.
NORMALLY, THEY WOULD SAY THAT THEY'RE STIFF.
!
HELLO, I'M BAIHUI.
HI, I'M SIBAI.
HELLO, I'M TIANSHU.
HI, I'M MING-MEN.
HEY, I'M ZHISHI.
FOR SOME REASON, EACH OF THEM WAS EMPHASIZING THE NAME OF THE TSUBO THIS TIME.
I SEE...
...
TSUBO THAT EMPHASIZE THEIR NAMES...
I'M CHARLIE!
I'M JERRI!
What are they talking about?
AND BECAUSE IT WAS STRANGE, I DECIDED TO ASK.
MAY I ASK YOU A QUESTION?
I ASKED IF THERE WAS SOMEWHERE PAINFUL...
...AND THE ANSWER WAS "NO."
YES.

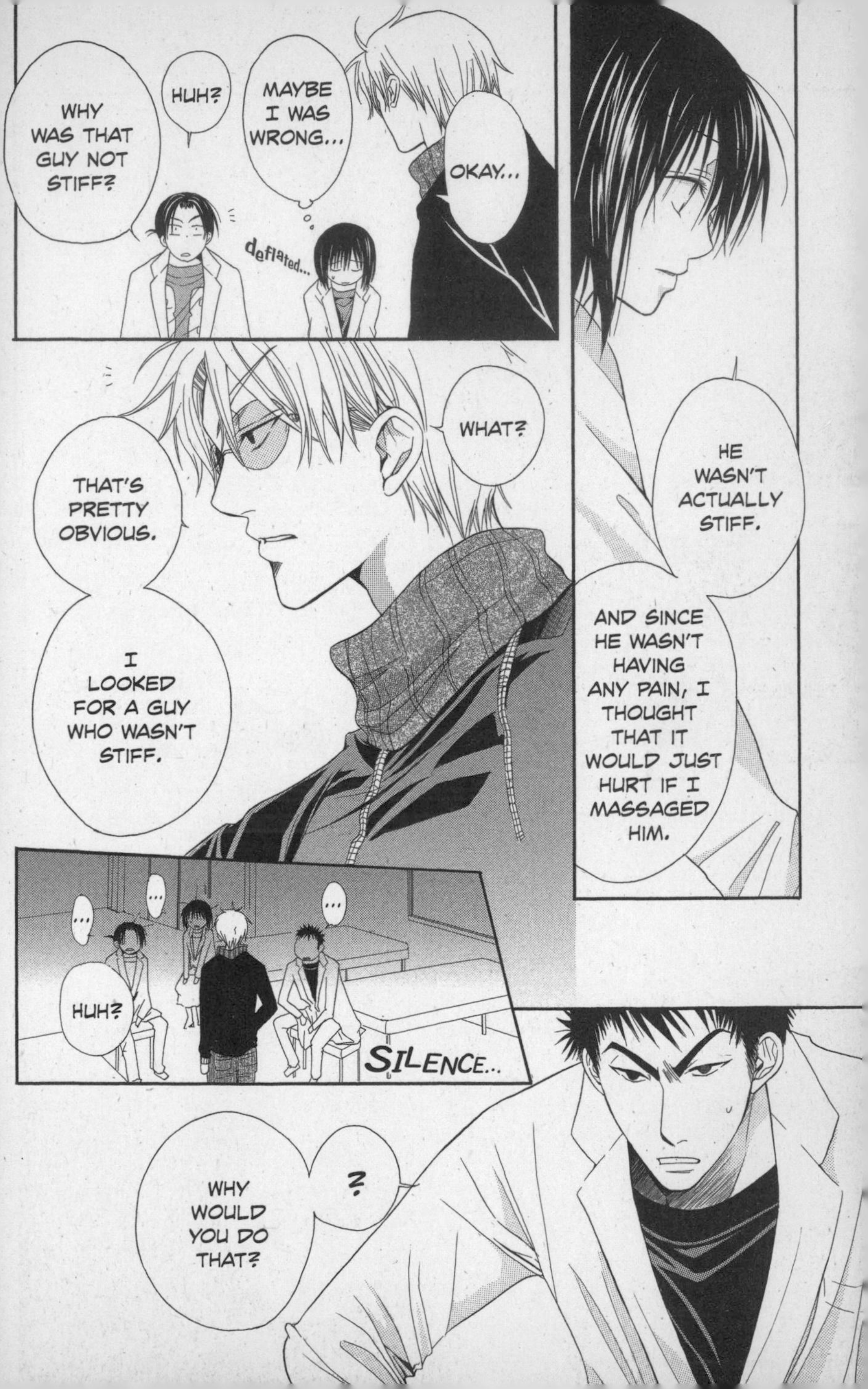
HE WASN'T ACTUALLY STIFF.
AND SINCE HE WASN'T HAVING ANY PAIN, I THOUGHT THAT IT WOULD JUST HURT IF I MASSAGED HIM.
OKAY...
MAYBE I WAS WRONG...
deflated...
HUH?
WHY WAS THAT GUY NOT STIFF?
WHAT?
THAT'S PRETTY OBVIOUS.
I LOOKED FOR A GUY WHO WASN'T STIFF.
...
...
...
HUH?
SILENCE...
?
WHY WOULD YOU DO THAT?

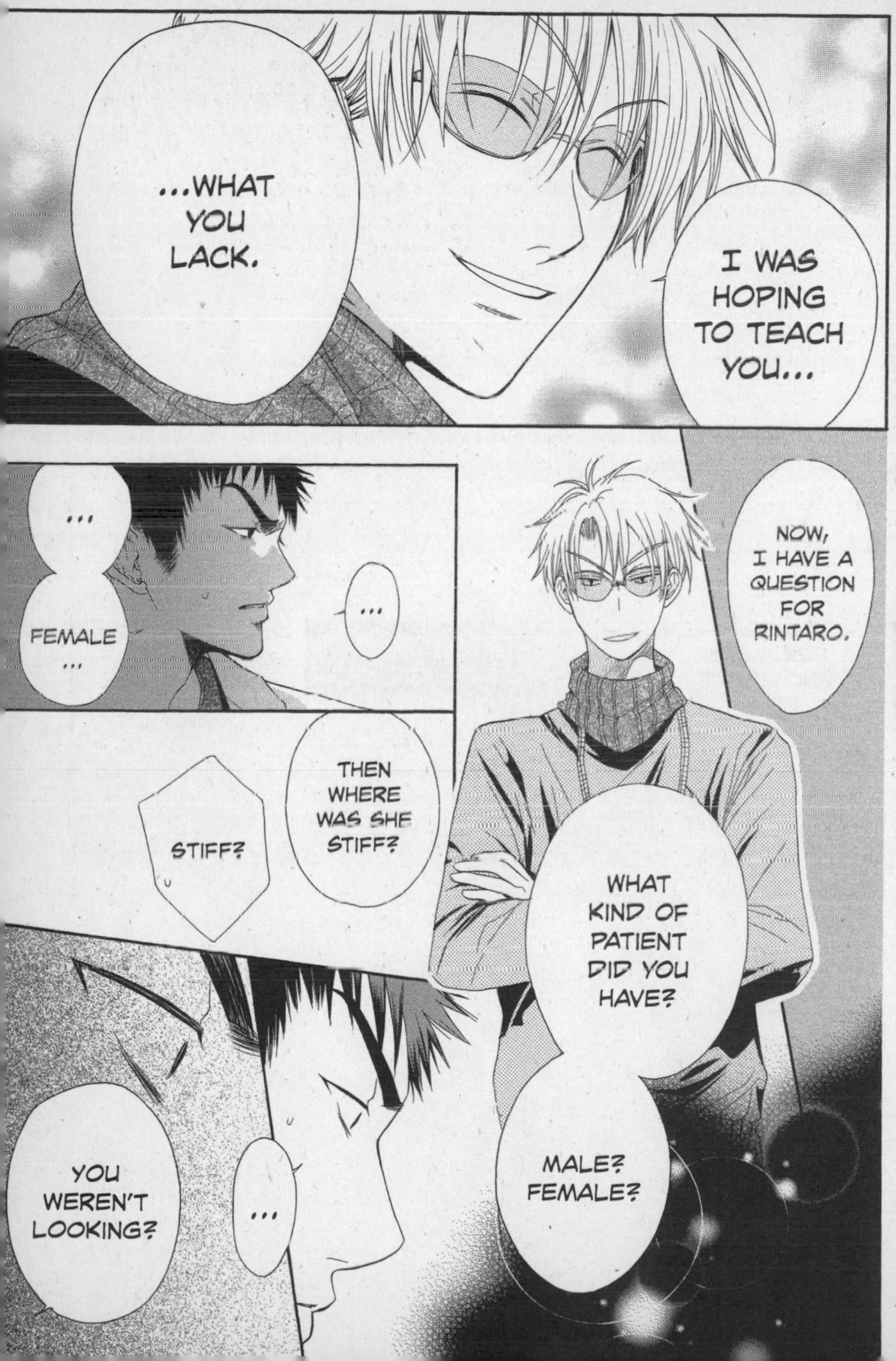
I WAS HOPING TO TEACH YOU...
...WHAT YOU LACK.
NOW, I HAVE A QUESTION FOR RINTARO.
WHAT KIND OF PATIENT DID YOU HAVE?
MALE? FEMALE?
...
...
FEMALE ...
THEN WHERE WAS SHE STIFF?
STIFF?
...
YOU WEREN'T LOOKING?

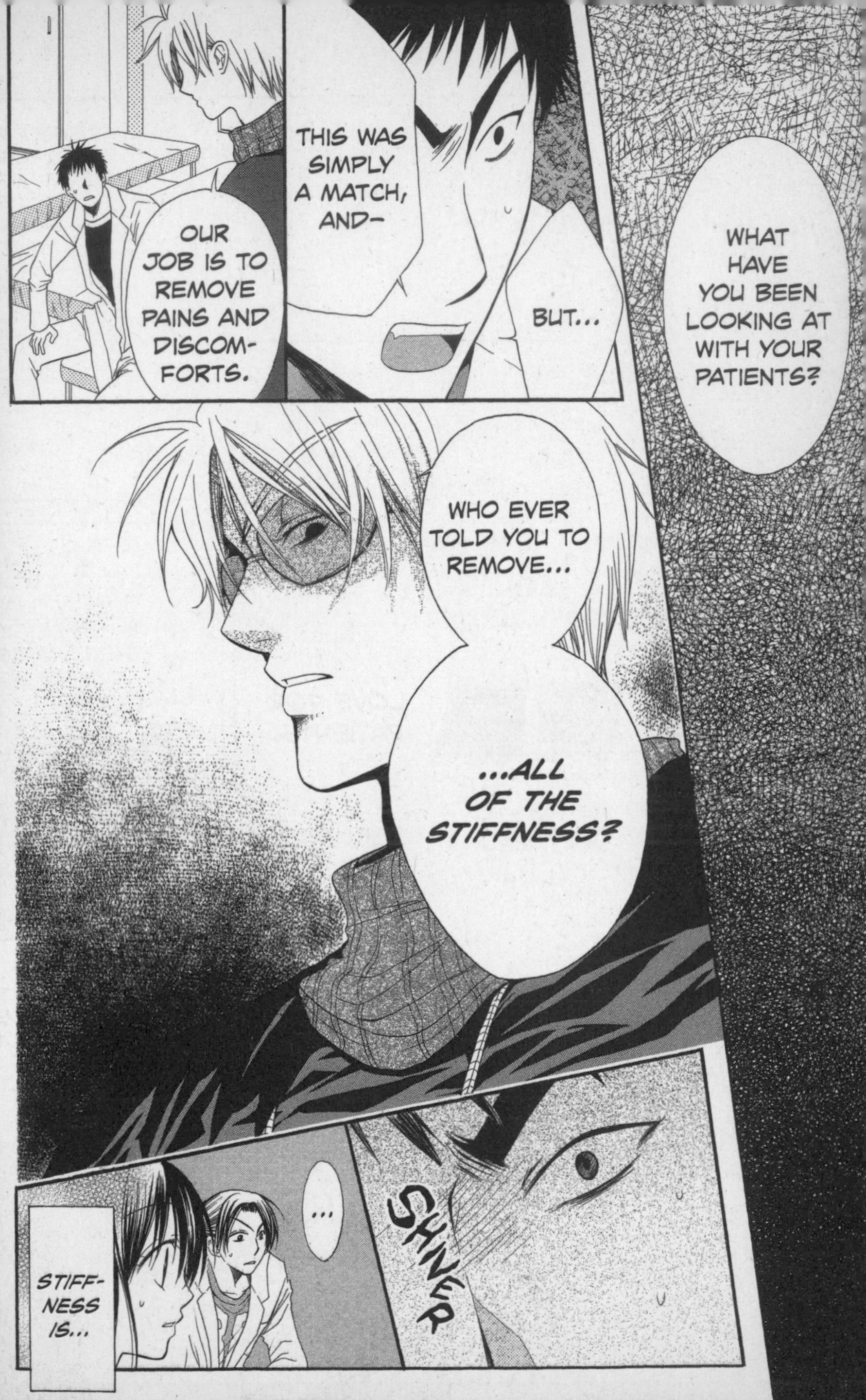
WHAT HAVE YOU BEEN LOOKING AT WITH YOUR PATIENTS?
BUT...
THIS WAS SIMPLY A MATCH, AND-
OUR JOB IS TO REMOVE PAINS AND DISCOM-FORTS.
WHO EVER TOLD YOU TO REMOVE...
...ALL OF THE STIFFNESS?
SHIVER
...
STIFF-NESS IS...

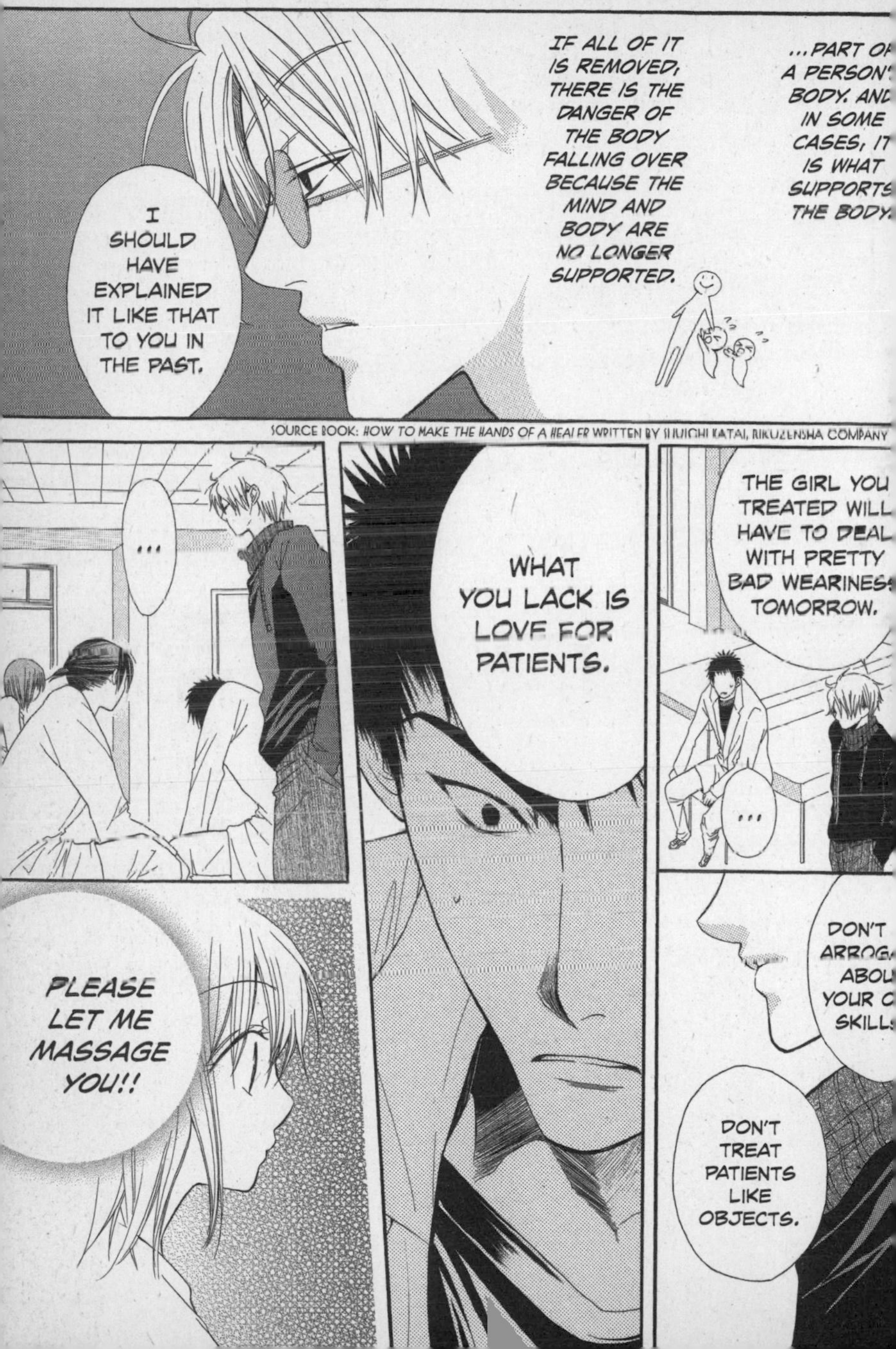
...PART OF A PERSON'S BODY. AND IN SOME CASES, IT IS WHAT SUPPORTS THE BODY.
IF ALL OF IT IS REMOVED, THERE IS THE DANGER OF THE BODY FALLING OVER BECAUSE THE MIND AND BODY ARE NO LONGER SUPPORTED.
I SHOULD HAVE EXPLAINED IT LIKE THAT TO YOU IN THE PAST.
SOURCE BOOK: HOW TO MAKE THE HANDS OF A HEALER WRITTEN BY SHUICHI KATAI, RIKUZENSHA COMPANY
THE GIRL YOU TREATED WILL HAVE TO DEAL WITH PRETTY BAD WEARINESS TOMORROW.
...
DON'T ARROG ABOU YOUR SKILLS
DON'T TREAT PATIENTS LIKE OBJECTS.
WHAT YOU LACK IS LOVE FOR PATIENTS.
...
PLEASE LET ME MASSAGE YOU!!

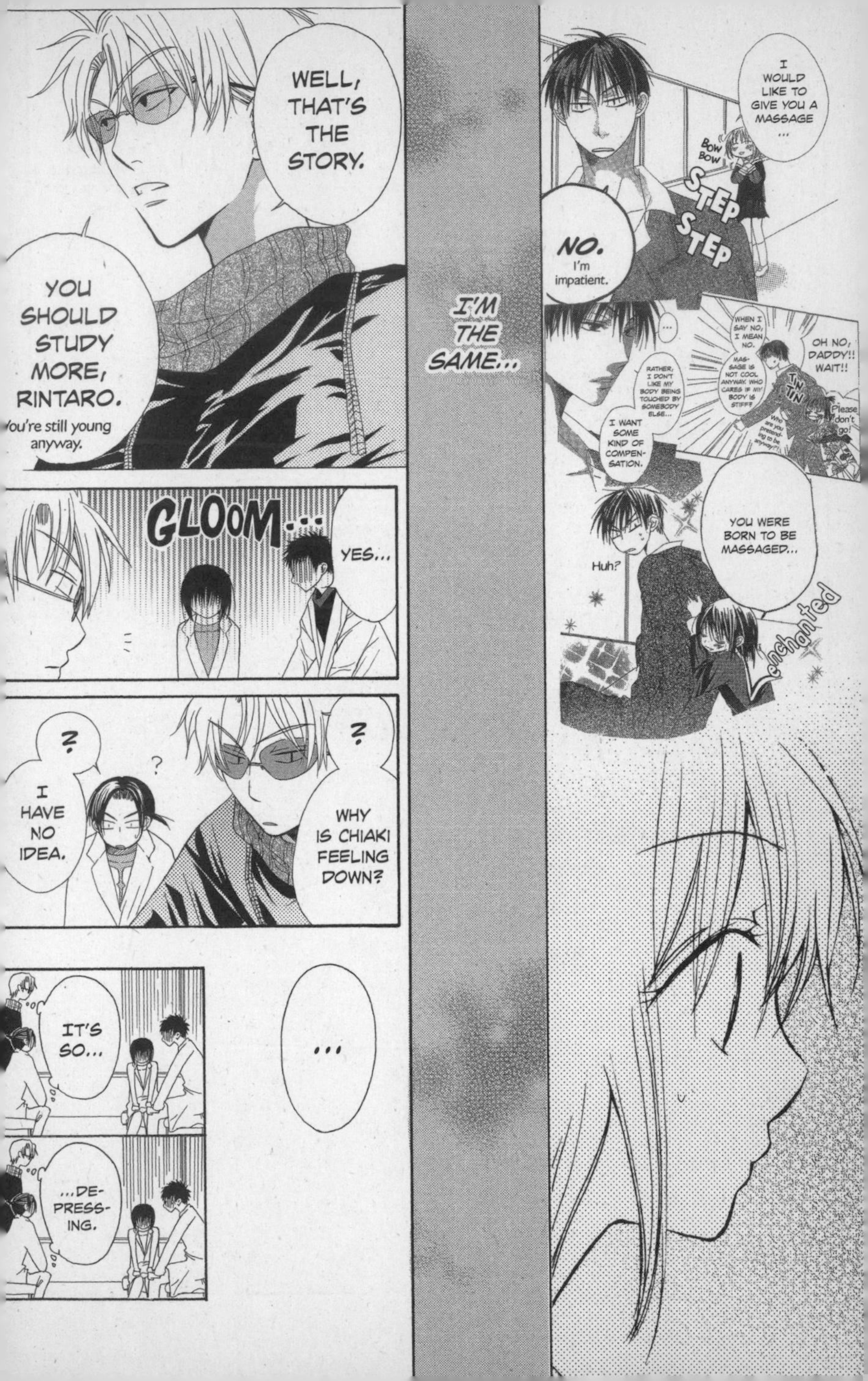
I WOULD LIKE TO GIVE YOU A MASSAGE ...
BOW BOW
STEP STEP
NO. I'm impatient.
OH NO, DADDY!! WAIT!!
Please don't go!
Who are you pretending to be anyway?!
TIN TIN
WHEN I SAY NO, I MEAN NO. MASSAGE IS NOT COOL ANYWAY. WHO CARES IF MY BODY IS STIFF?
RATHER, I DON'T LIKE MY BODY BEING TOUCHED BY SOMEBODY ELSE...
I WANT SOME KIND OF COMPENSATION.
...
YOU WERE BORN TO BE MASSAGED...
enchanted
Huh?
I'M THE SAME...
WELL, THAT'S THE STORY.
YOU SHOULD STUDY MORE, RINTARO. You're still young anyway.
GLOOM...
YES...
? WHY IS CHIAKI FEELING DOWN?
? I HAVE NO IDEA.
?
...
IT'S SO...
...DEPRESSING.

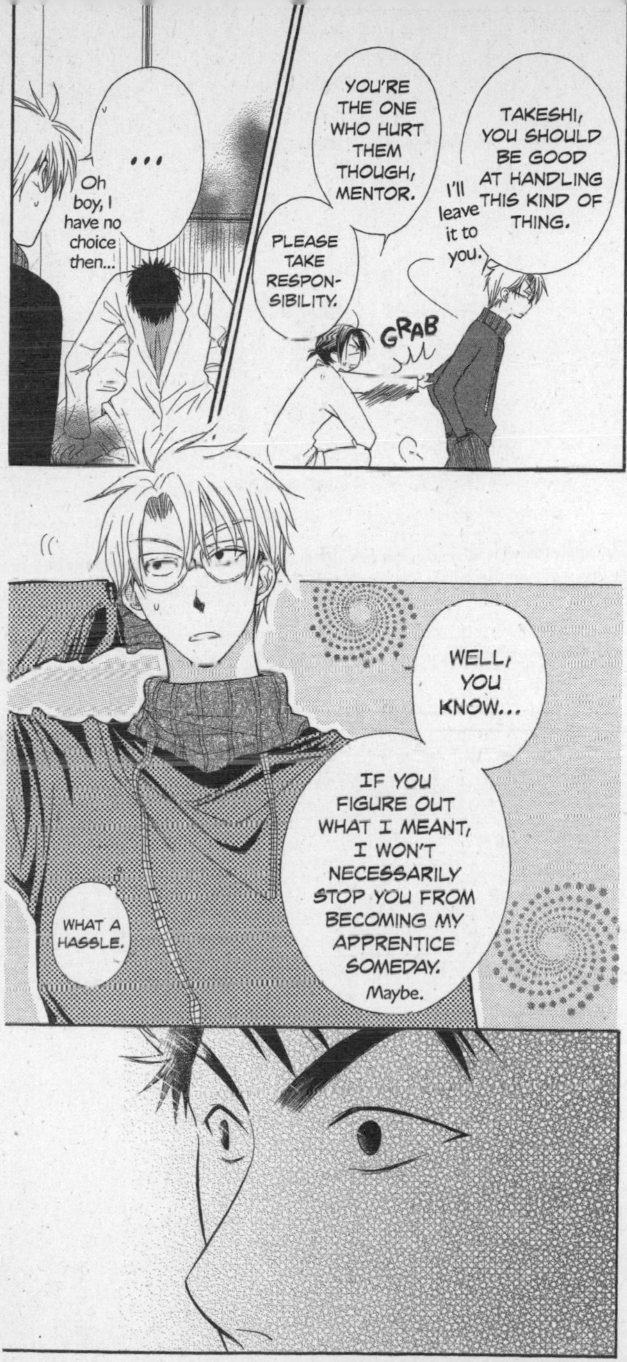
TAKESHI, YOU SHOULD BE GOOD AT HANDLING THIS KIND OF THING.
I'll leave it to you.
YOU'RE THE ONE WHO HURT THEM THOUGH, MENTOR.
PLEASE TAKE RESPON-SIBILITY.
GRAB
...
Oh boy, I have no choice then...
WELL, YOU KNOW...
IF YOU FIGURE OUT WHAT I MEANT, I WON'T NECESSARILY STOP YOU FROM BECOMING MY APPRENTICE SOMEDAY.
Maybe.
WHAT A HASSLE.

Kaji Shiraiwa

I was shown very basic things about acupuncture. Because it was so cool, I thought that being an acupuncturist must be nice.

I assumed that an acupuncture needle would be hard...

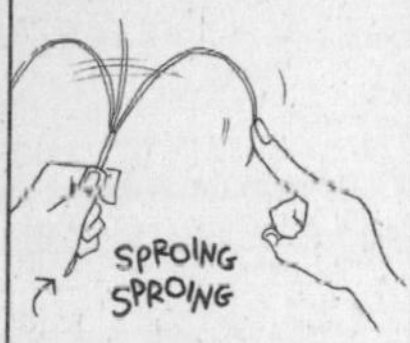
SPROING
SPROING

...but they're really soft, like this. I was a bit surprised!

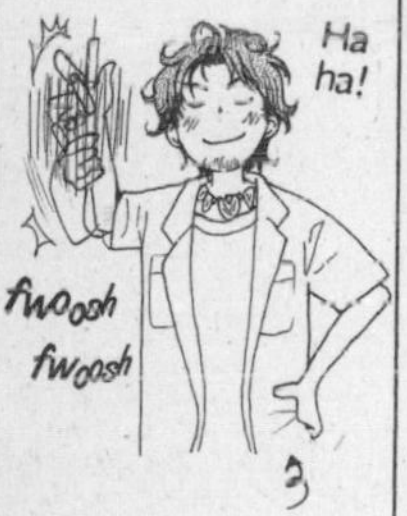
Ha ha!
fwoosh
fwoosh

It was so cool to see how the acupuncturist takes out and puts back in the needle!! Superfast!! It was great to see the acupuncturist do this casually too.

Oh yeah, I didn't talk about the character in the story at all...

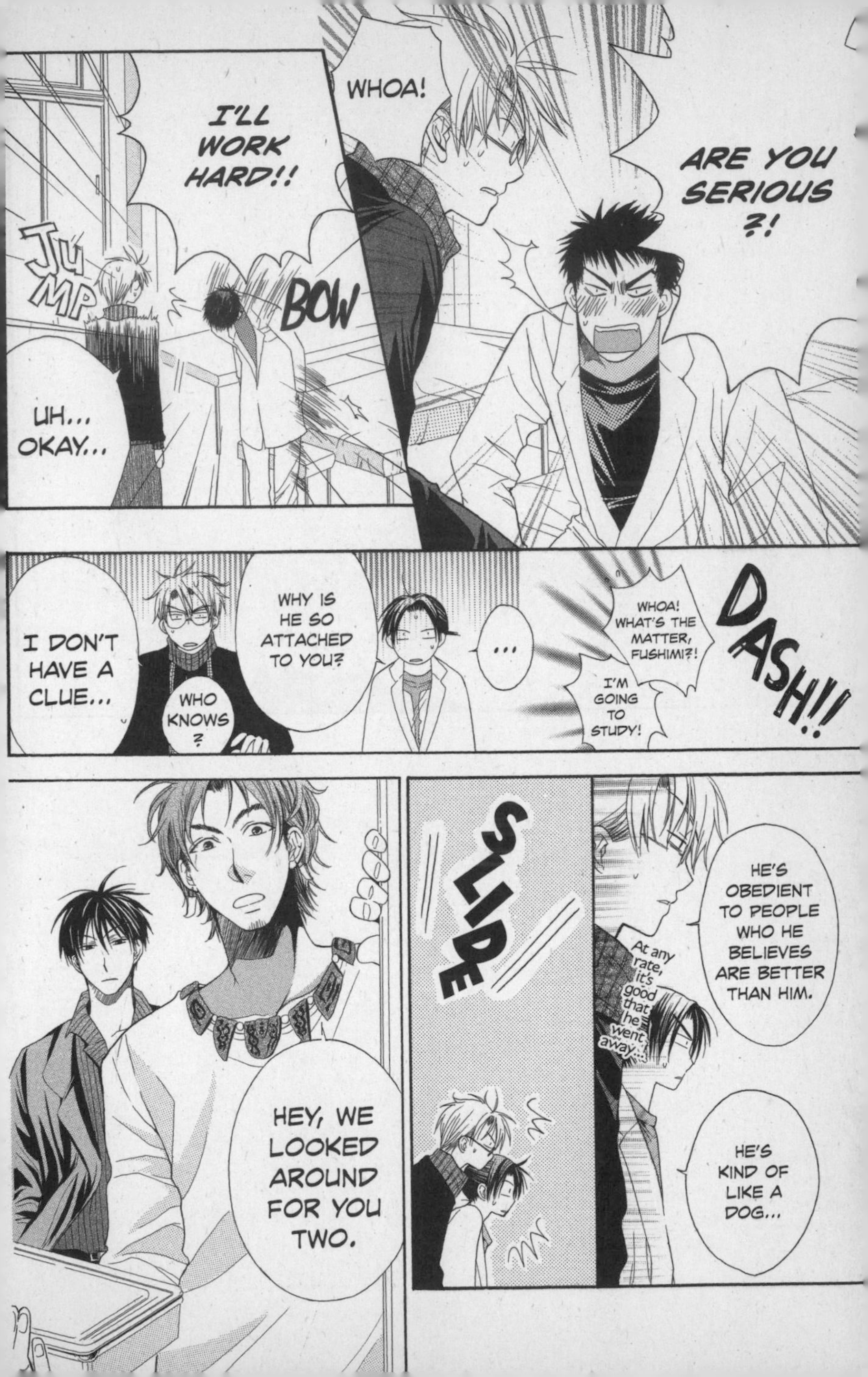
ARE YOU SERIOUS ?!
WHOA!
I'LL WORK HARD!!
BOW
JUMP
UH... OKAY...
DASH!!
WHOA! WHAT'S THE MATTER, FUSHIMI?!
I'M GOING TO STUDY!
...
WHY IS HE SO ATTACHED TO YOU?
WHO KNOWS?
I DON'T HAVE A CLUE...
HE'S OBEDIENT TO PEOPLE WHO HE BELIEVES ARE BETTER THAN HIM.
At any rate, it's good that he went away...
HE'S KIND OF LIKE A DOG...
SLIDE
HEY, WE LOOKED AROUND FOR YOU TWO.

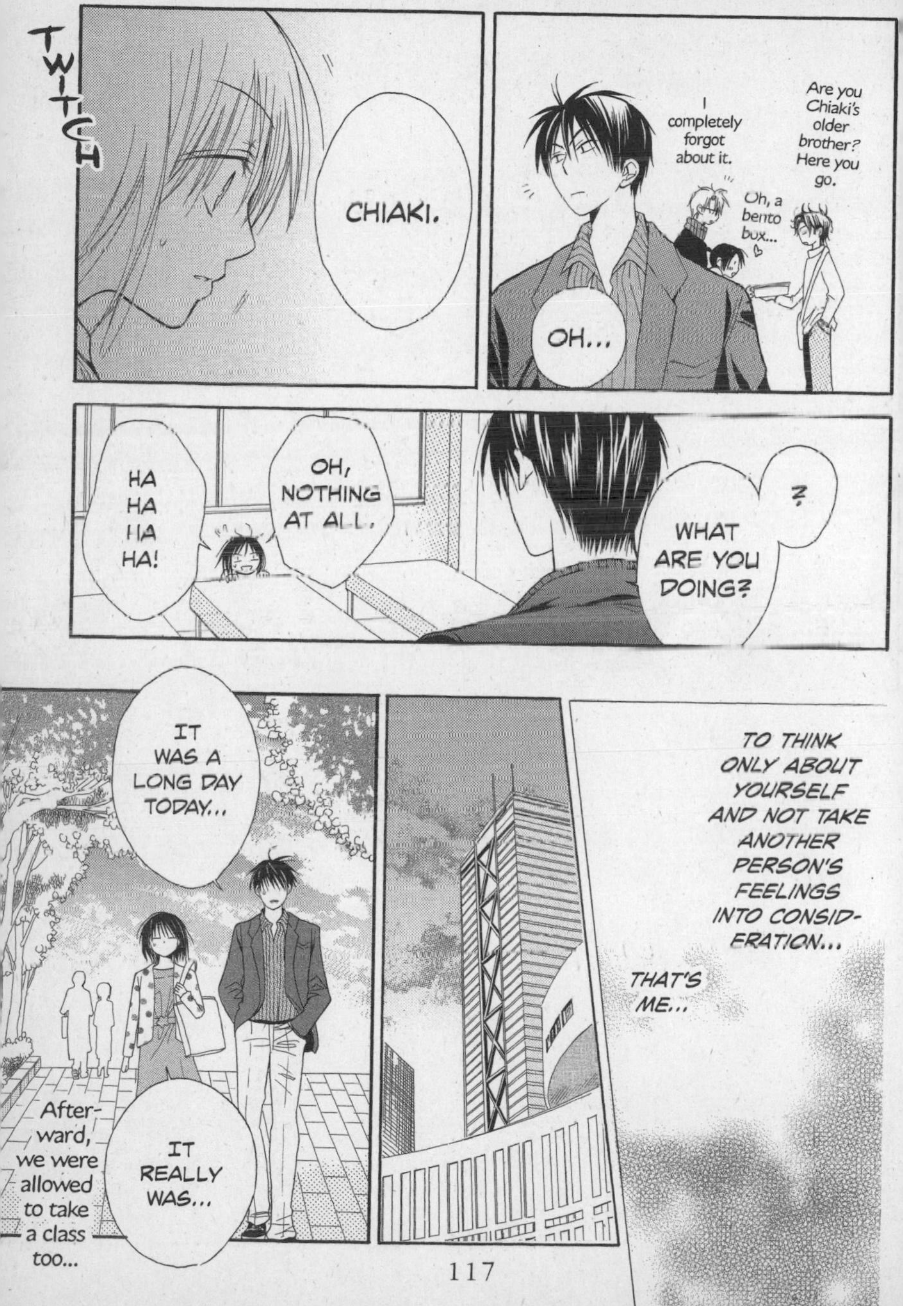
Are you Chiaki's older brother? Here you go.
I completely forgot about it.
Oh, a bento box...
OH...
CHIAKI.
TWITCH
?
WHAT ARE YOU DOING?
OH, NOTHING AT ALL.
HA HA HA HA!
TO THINK ONLY ABOUT YOURSELF AND NOT TAKE ANOTHER PERSON'S FEELINGS INTO CONSID-ERATION...
THAT'S ME...
IT WAS A LONG DAY TODAY...
IT REALLY WAS...
After-ward, we were allowed to take a class too...

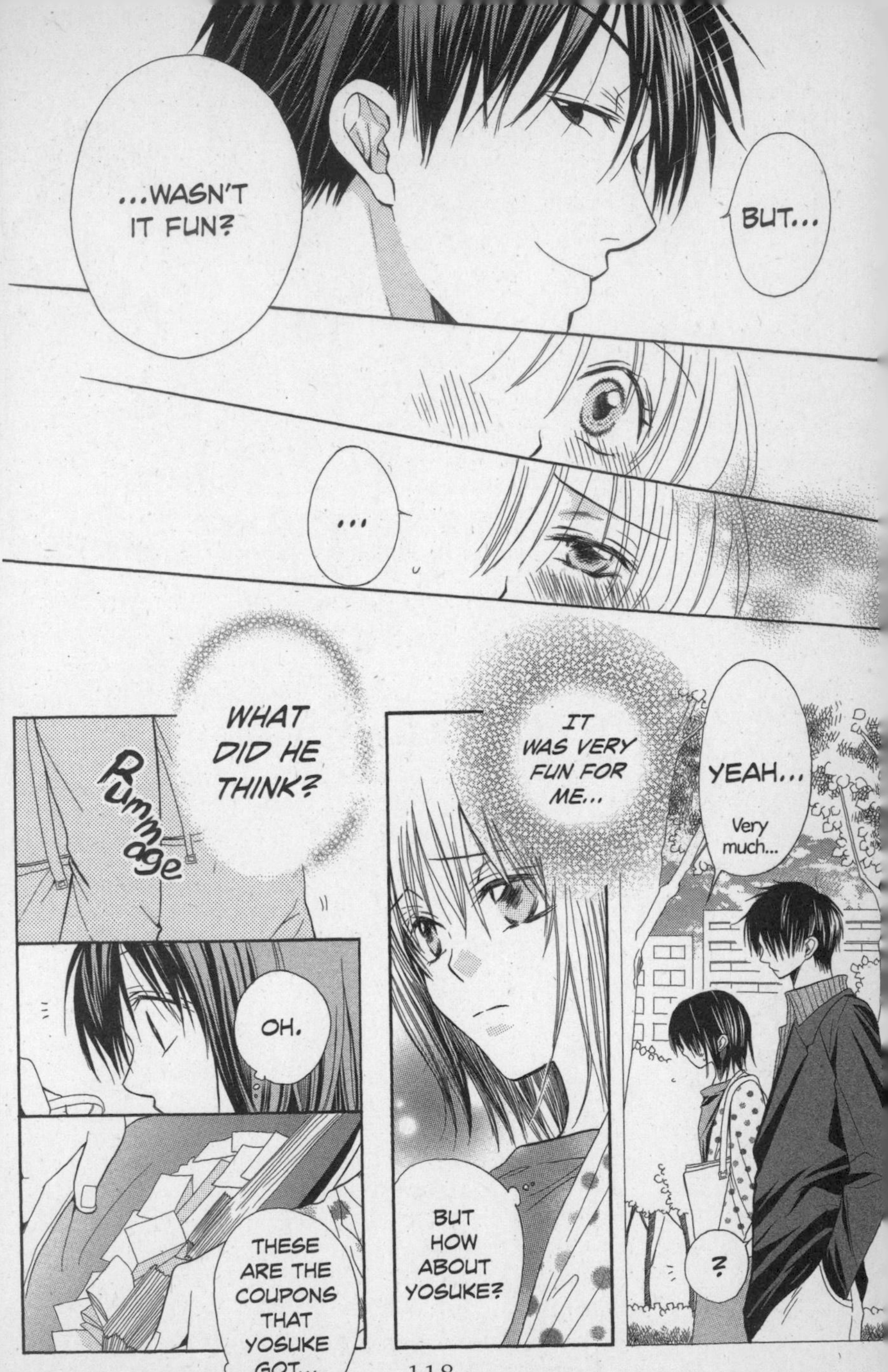
BUT...
...WASN'T IT FUN?
...
YEAH...
Very much...
?
IT WAS VERY FUN FOR ME...
BUT HOW ABOUT YOSUKE?
WHAT DID HE THINK?
Rummage
OH.
THESE ARE THE COUPONS THAT YOSUKE GOT...

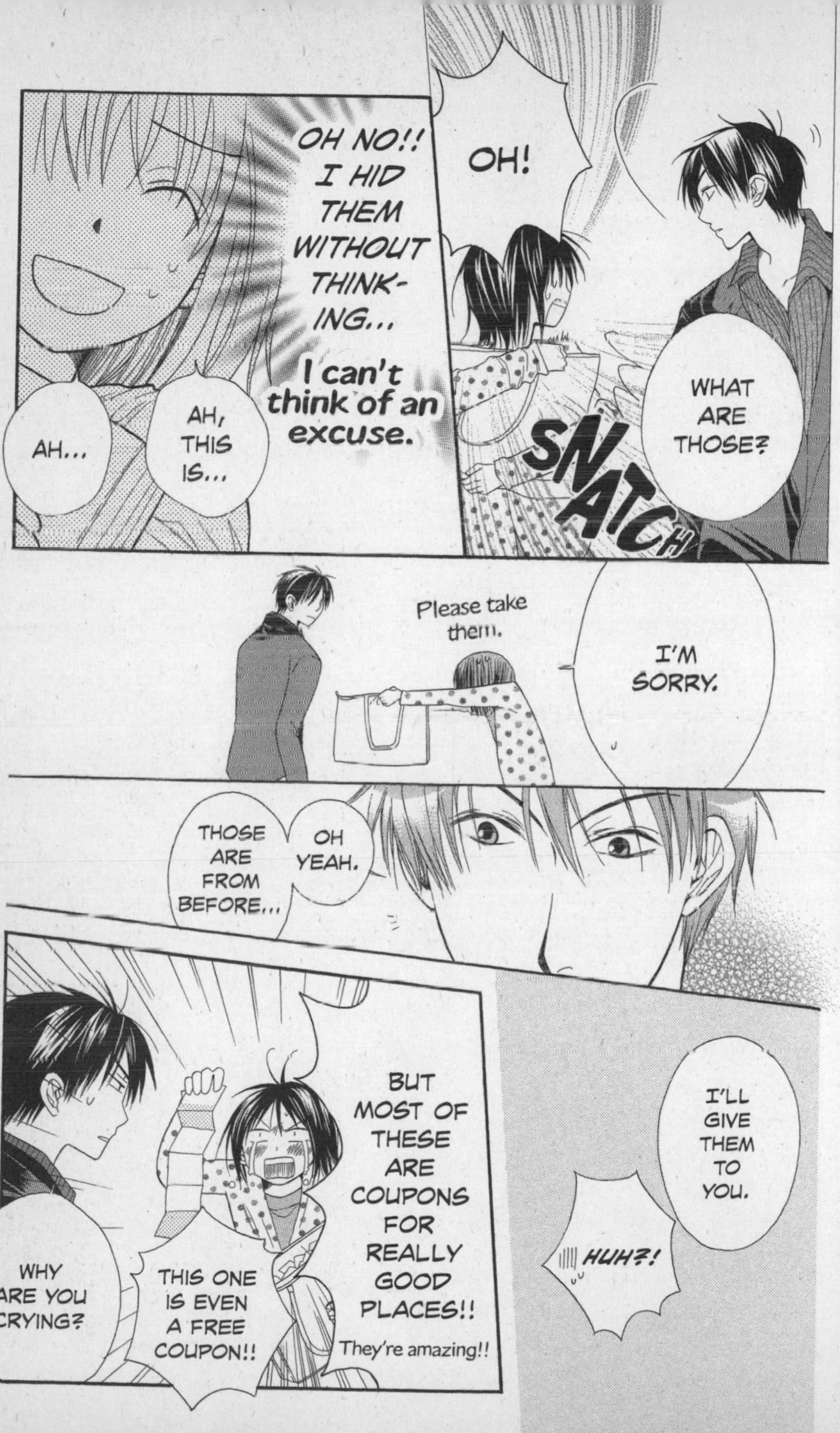
WHAT ARE THOSE?
OH!
SNATCH
OH NO!! I HID THEM WITHOUT THINKING...
I can't think of an excuse.
AH, THIS IS...
AH...
I'M SORRY.
Please take them.
OH YEAH.
THOSE ARE FROM BEFORE...
I'LL GIVE THEM TO YOU.
HUH?!
BUT MOST OF THESE ARE COUPONS FOR REALLY GOOD PLACES!!
They're amazing!!
THIS ONE IS EVEN A FREE COUPON!!
WHY ARE YOU CRYING?

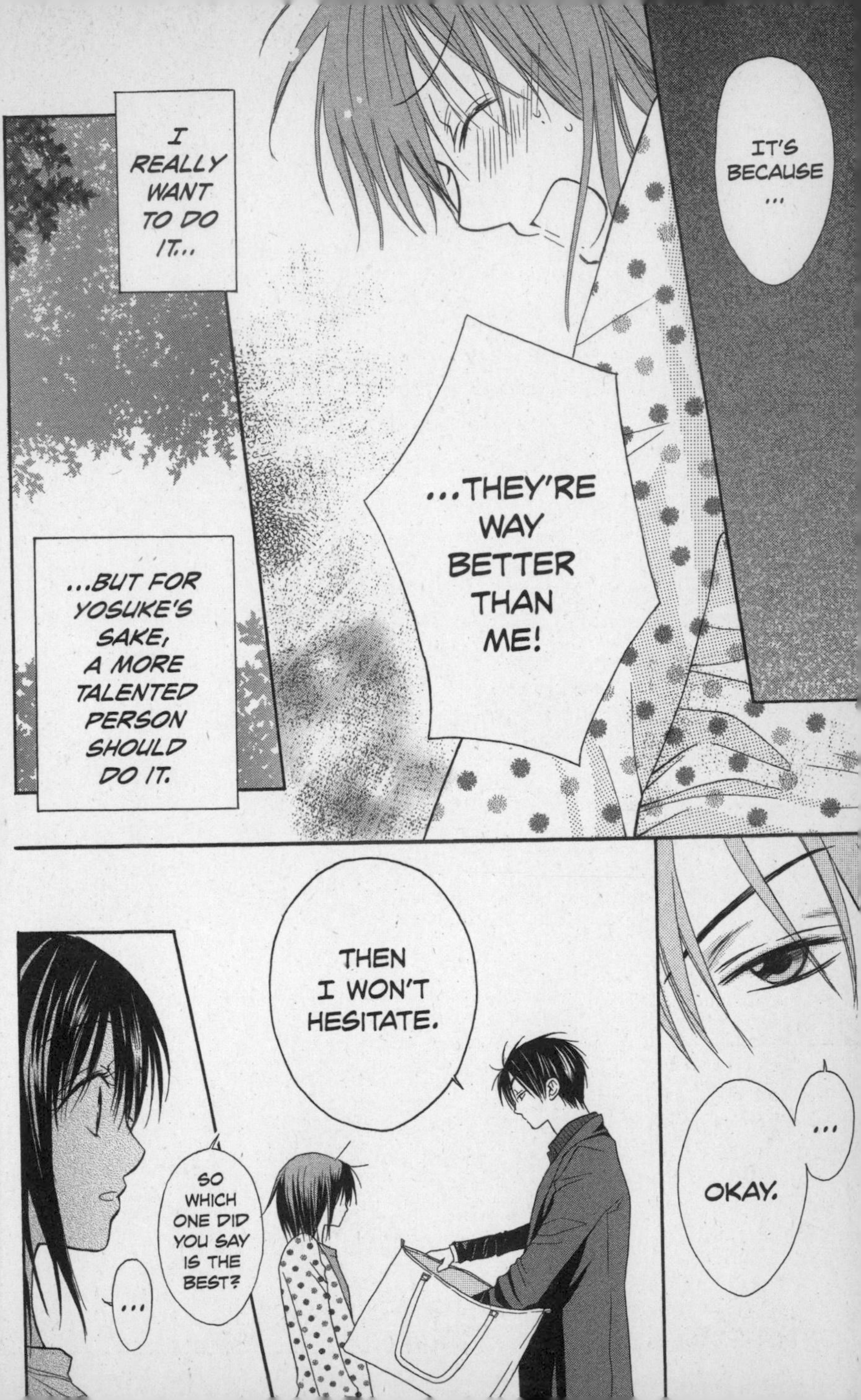
IT'S BECAUSE ...
...THEY'RE WAY BETTER THAN ME!
I REALLY WANT TO DO IT...
...BUT FOR YOSUKE'S SAKE, A MORE TALENTED PERSON SHOULD DO IT.
...
OKAY.
THEN I WON'T HESITATE.
SO WHICH ONE DID YOU SAY IS THE BEST?
...

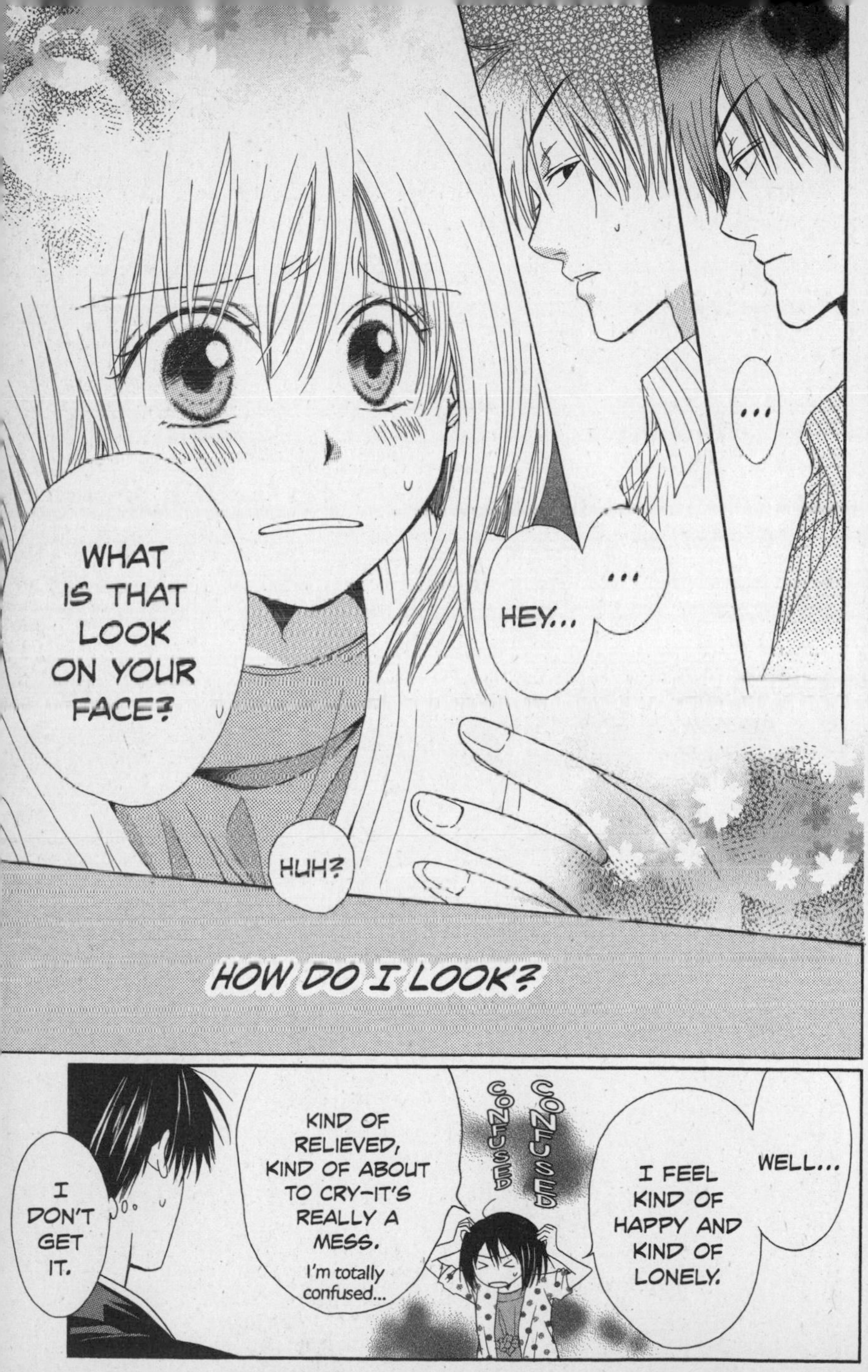
...
... HEY...
WHAT IS THAT LOOK ON YOUR FACE?
HUH?
HOW DO I LOOK?
WELL...
I FEEL KIND OF HAPPY AND KIND OF LONELY.
CONFUSED
CONFUSED
KIND OF RELIEVED, KIND OF ABOUT TO CRY-IT'S REALLY A MESS.
I'm totally confused...
I DON'T GET IT.

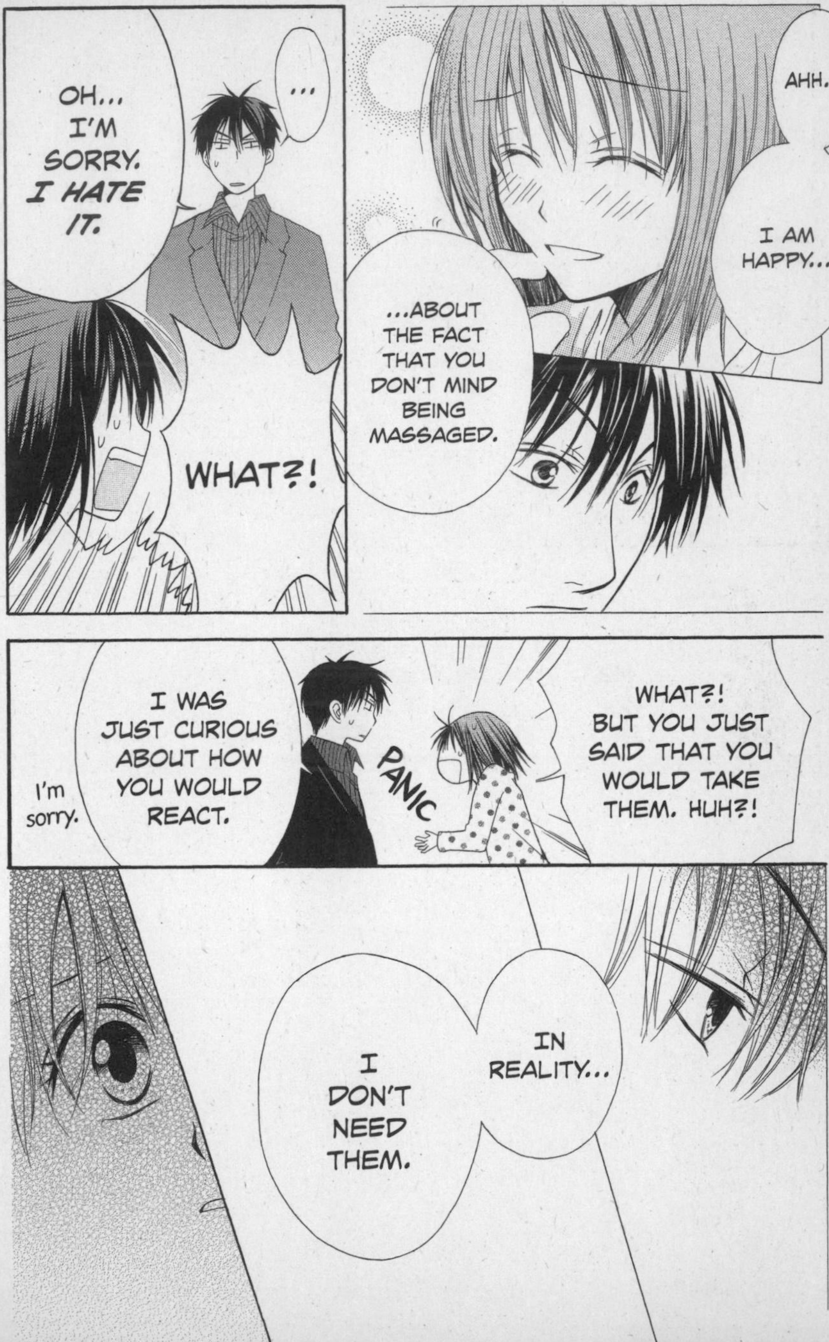
AHH...
I AM HAPPY...
...ABOUT THE FACT THAT YOU DON'T MIND BEING MASSAGED.
...
OH... I'M SORRY. *I HATE IT.*
WHAT?!
WHAT?! BUT YOU JUST SAID THAT YOU WOULD TAKE THEM. HUH?!
PANIC
I WAS JUST CURIOUS ABOUT HOW YOU WOULD REACT.
I'm sorry.
IN REALITY...
I DON'T NEED THEM.

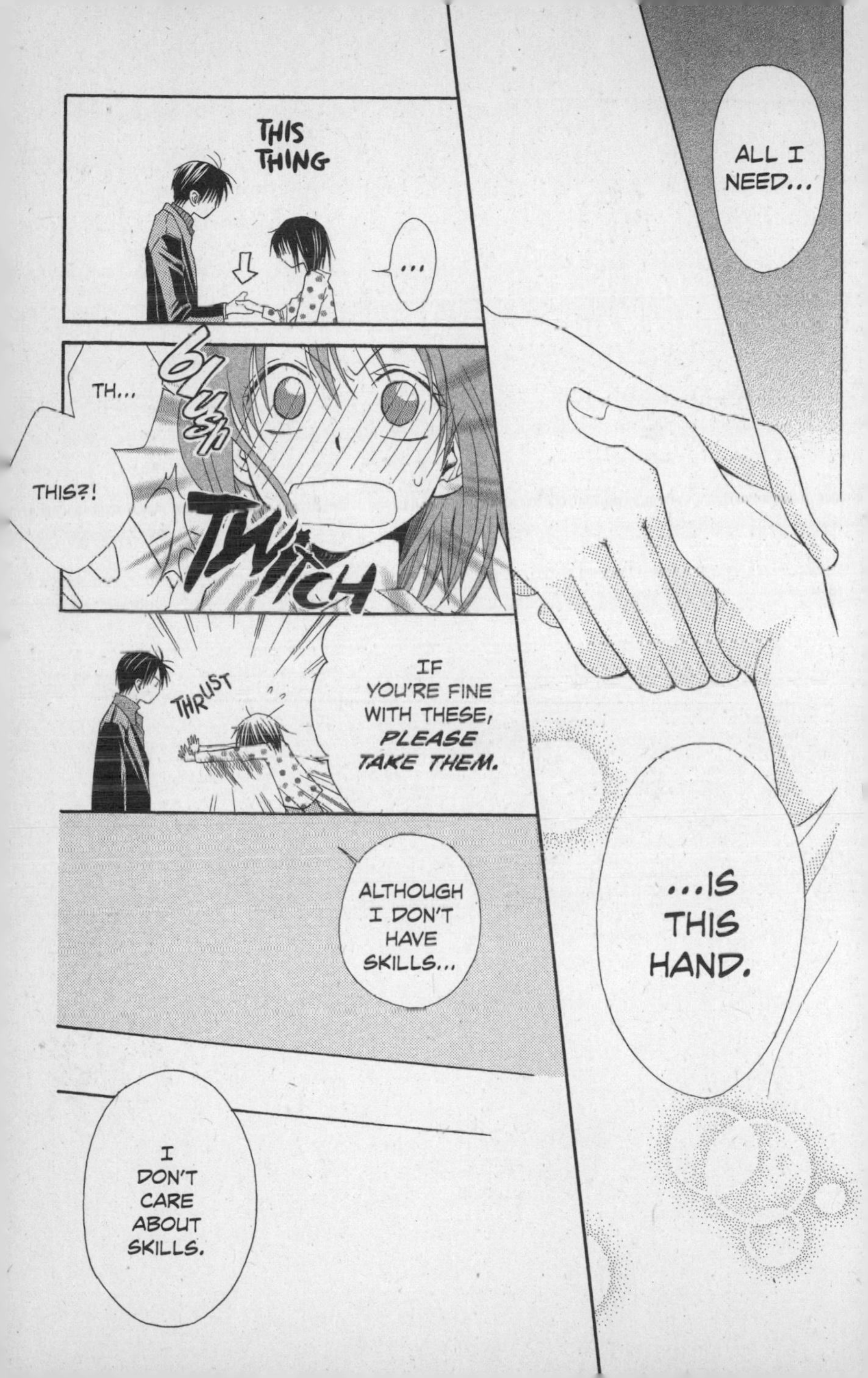
ALL I NEED...
...IS THIS HAND.
THIS THING
...
TH...
THIS?!
blush
TWITCH
THRUST
IF YOU'RE FINE WITH THESE, *PLEASE TAKE THEM.*
ALTHOUGH I DON'T HAVE SKILLS...
I DON'T CARE ABOUT SKILLS.

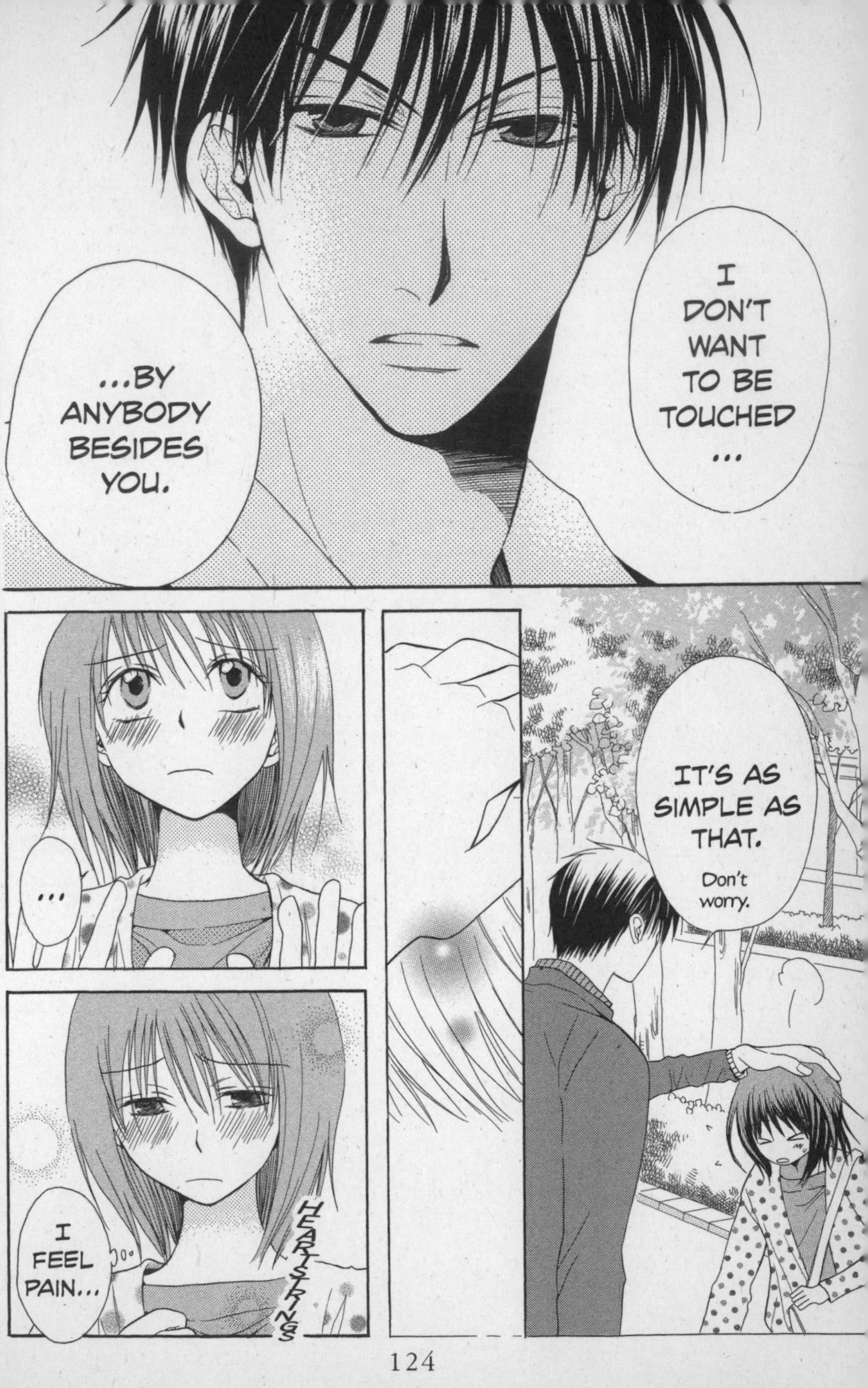
I DON'T WANT TO BE TOUCHED...
...BY ANYBODY BESIDES YOU.
IT'S AS SIMPLE AS THAT.
Don't worry.
...
I FEEL PAIN...
HEARTSTRINGS

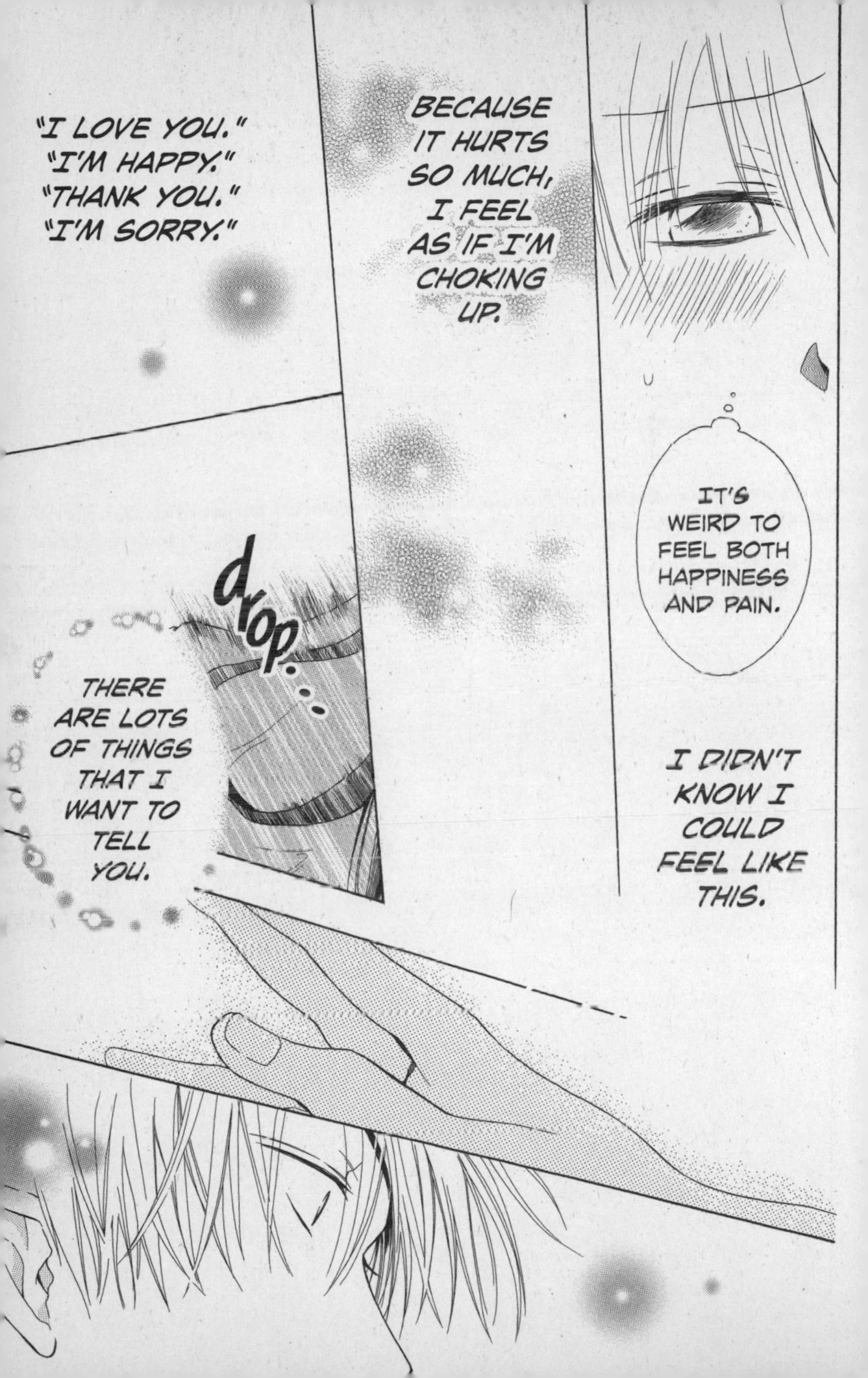
IT'S WEIRD TO FEEL BOTH HAPPINESS AND PAIN.
I DIDN'T KNOW I COULD FEEL LIKE THIS.
BECAUSE IT HURTS SO MUCH, I FEEL AS IF I'M CHOKING UP.
"I LOVE YOU." "I'M HAPPY." "THANK YOU." "I'M SORRY."
drop...
THERE ARE LOTS OF THINGS THAT I WANT TO TELL YOU.

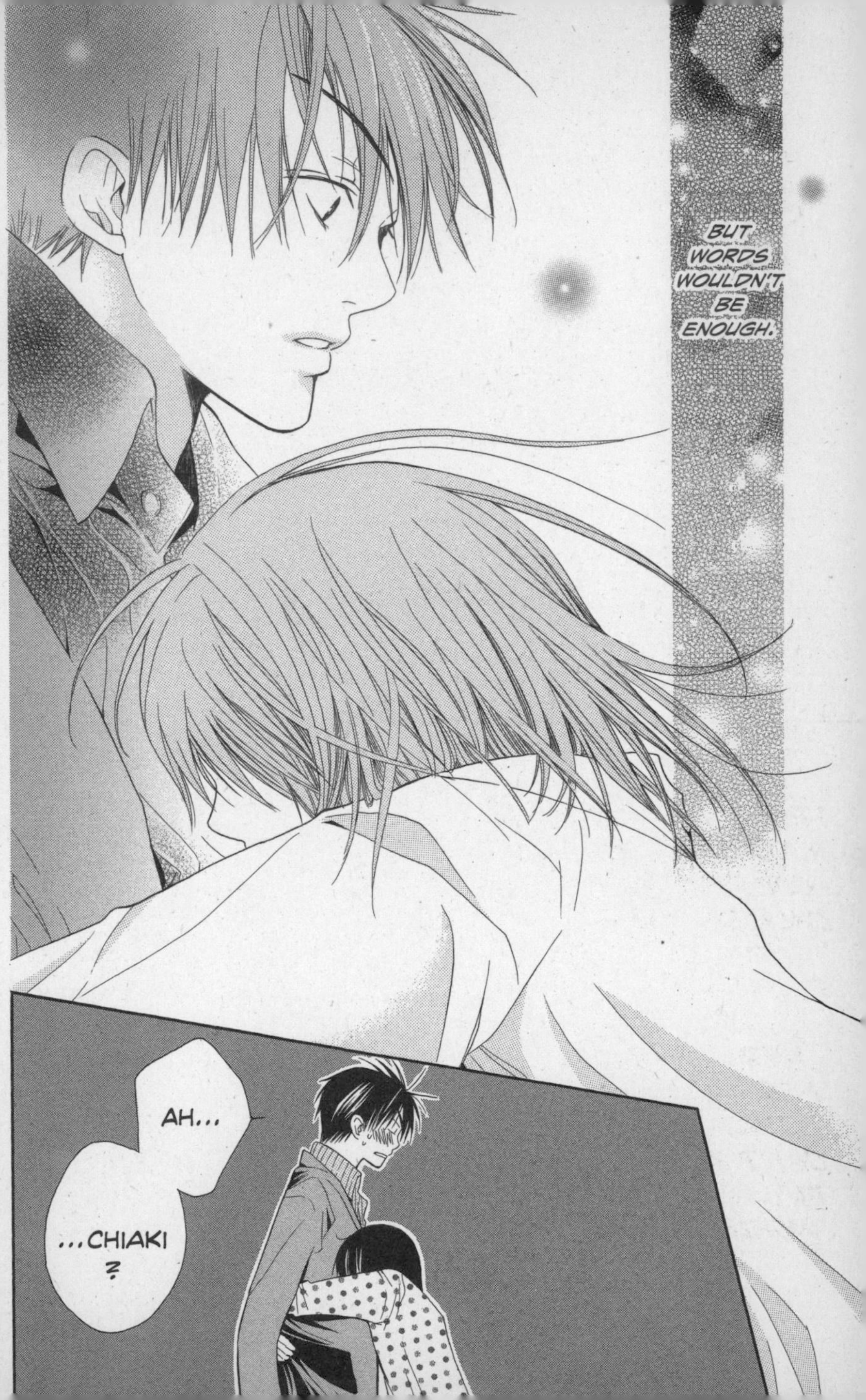
BUT WORDS WOULDN'T BE ENOUGH.
AH...
...CHIAKI?

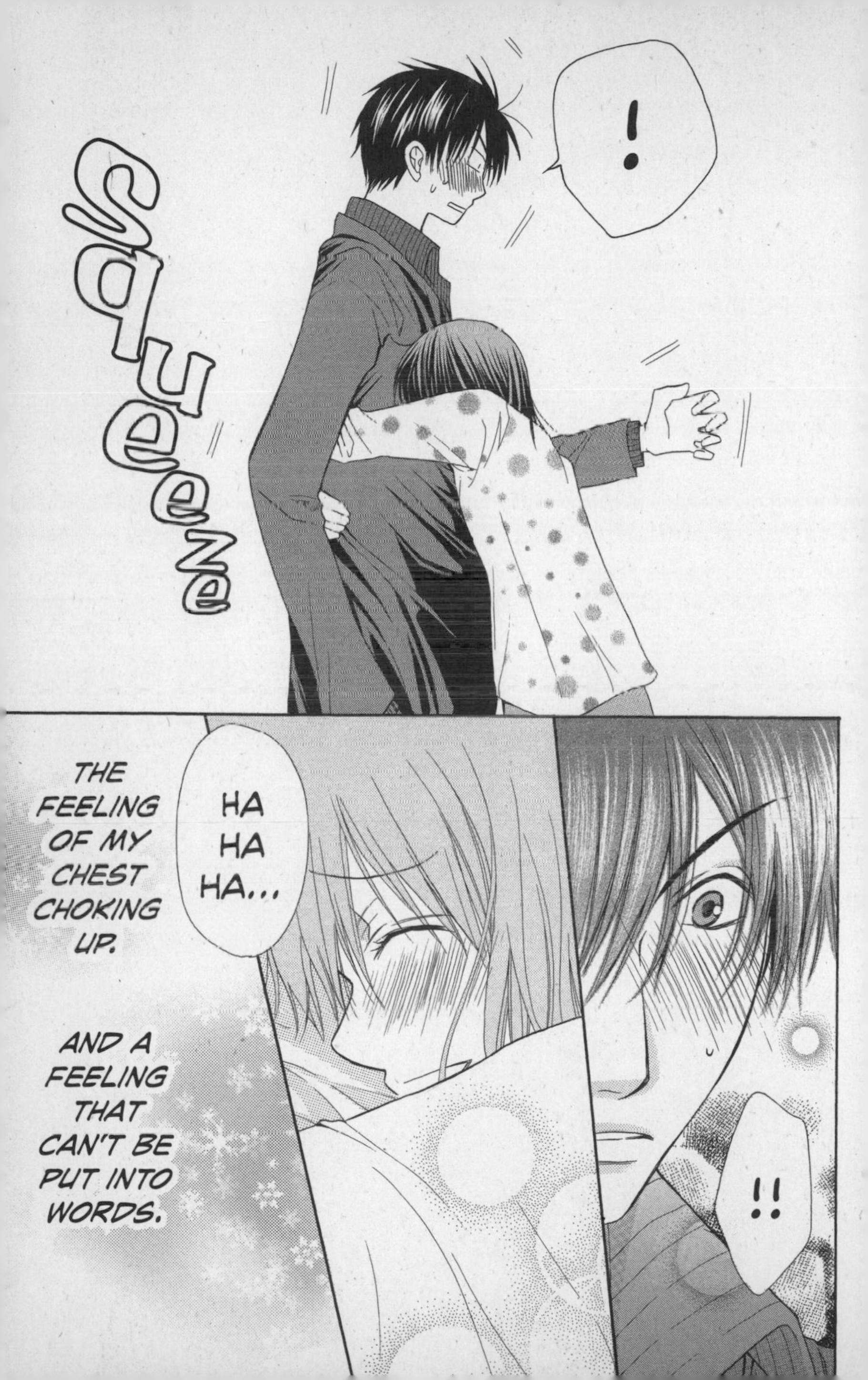

!
SQUEEZE
!!
HA HA HA...
THE FEELING OF MY CHEST CHOKING UP.
AND A FEELING THAT CAN'T BE PUT INTO WORDS.

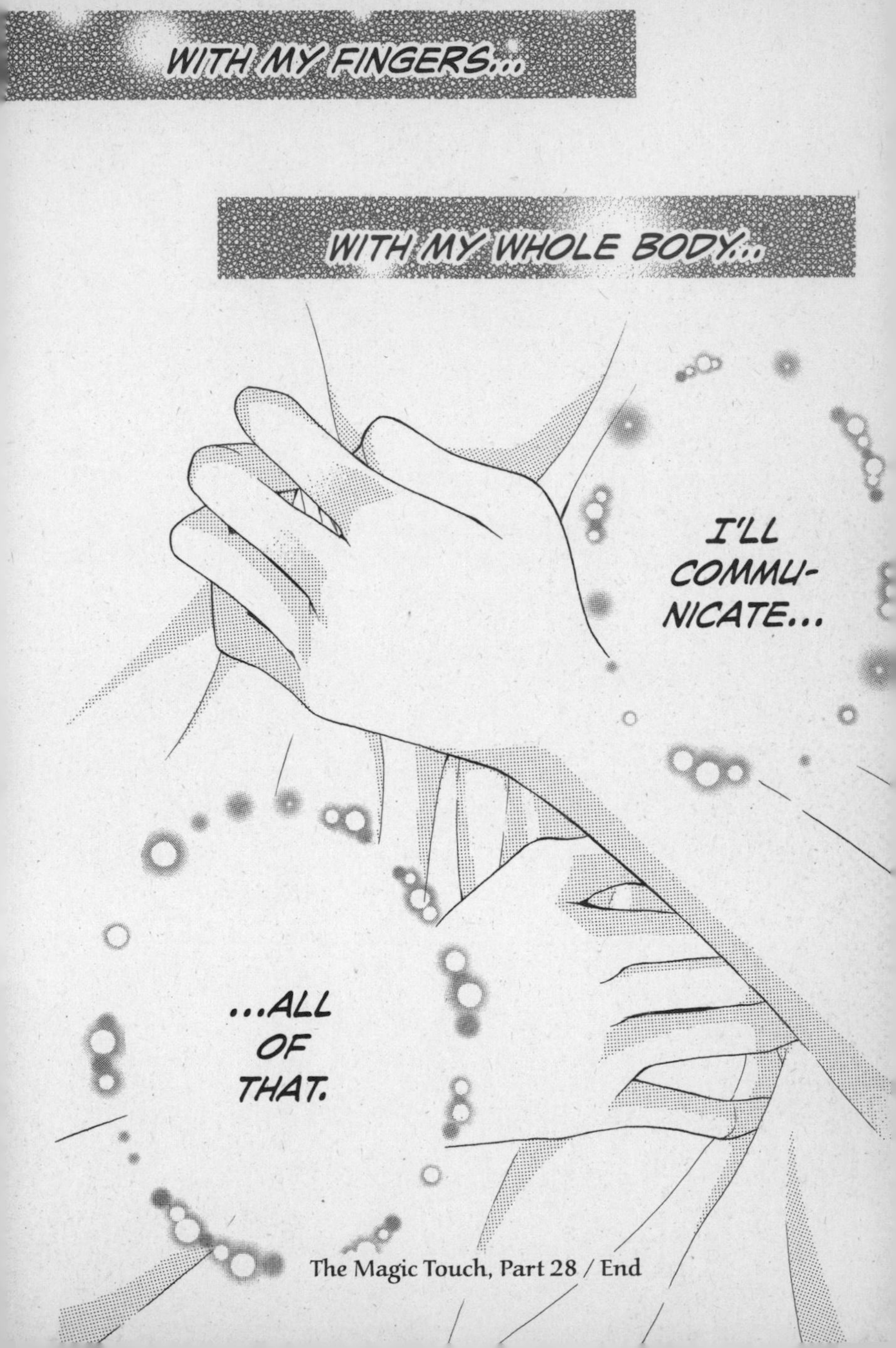
WITH MY FINGERS...
WITH MY WHOLE BODY...
I'LL COMMUNICATE...
...ALL OF THAT.

The Magic Touch, Part 28 / End

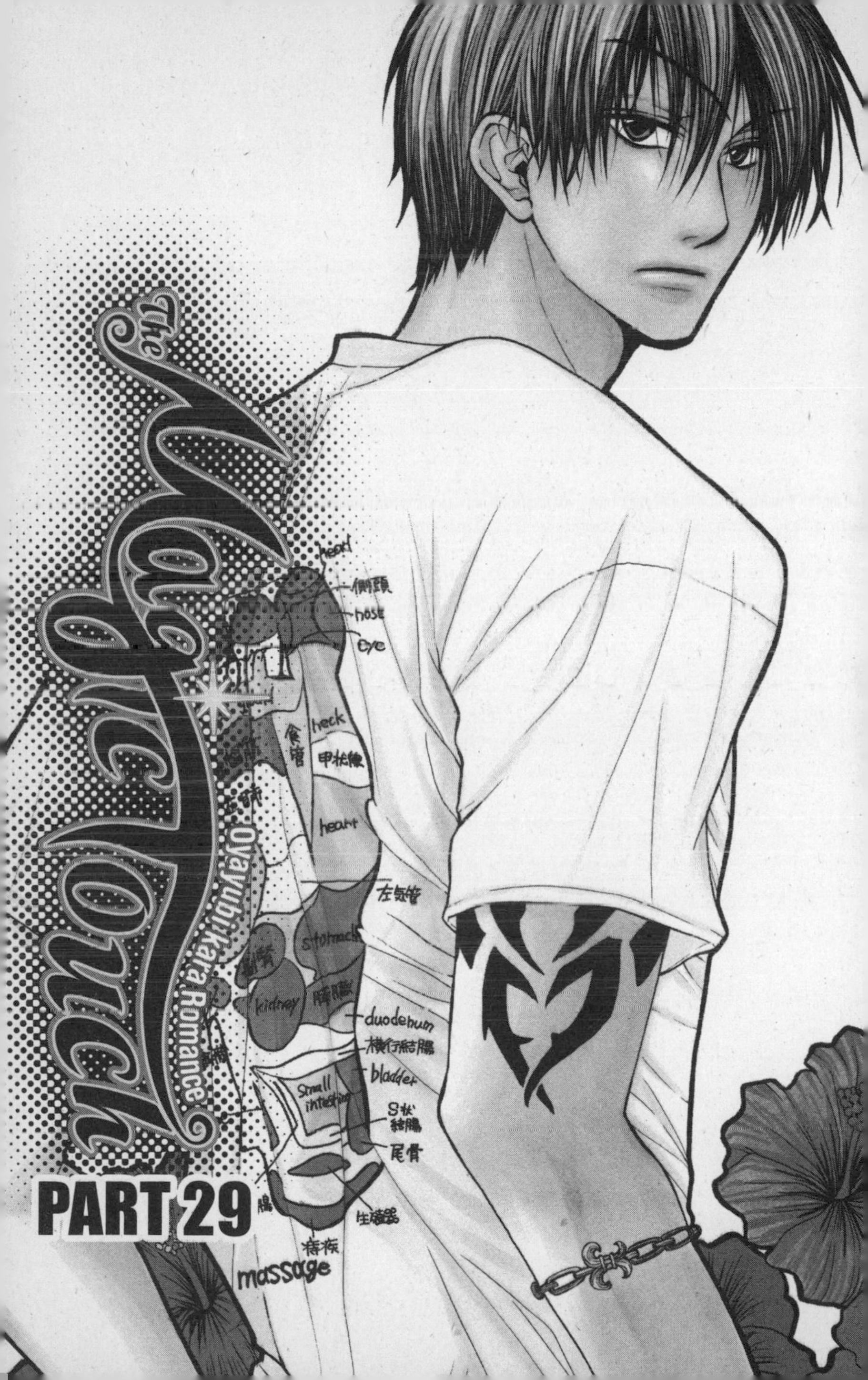
The Magic Touch
Oyayubi kara Romance
PART 29
eye
heart
stomach
kidney
duodenum
bladder
Small intestine
massage
甲状腺
左気管
横行結腸
S状結腸
尾骨
生殖器

SENPAI AND ME 3

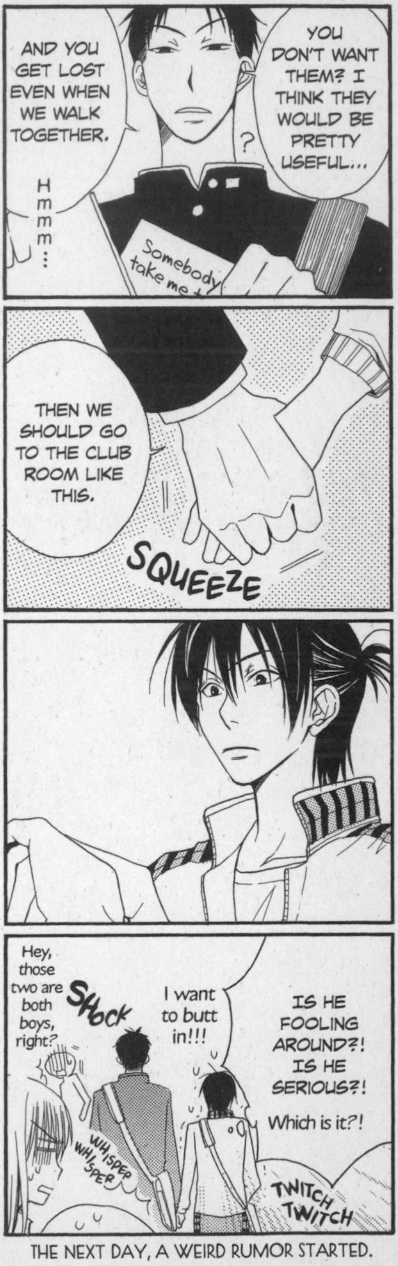
YOU DON'T WANT THEM? I THINK THEY WOULD BE PRETTY USEFUL...
?
AND YOU GET LOST EVEN WHEN WE WALK TOGETHER.
Hmmm...
Somebody take me t
THEN WE SHOULD GO TO THE CLUB ROOM LIKE THIS.
SQUEEZE
IS HE FOOLING AROUND?! IS HE SERIOUS?!
Which is it?!
I want to butt in!!!
SHOCK
Hey, those two are both boys, right?
WHISPER WHISPER
TWITCH TWITCH

THE NEXT DAY, A WEIRD RUMOR STARTED.

SENPAI AND ME 4

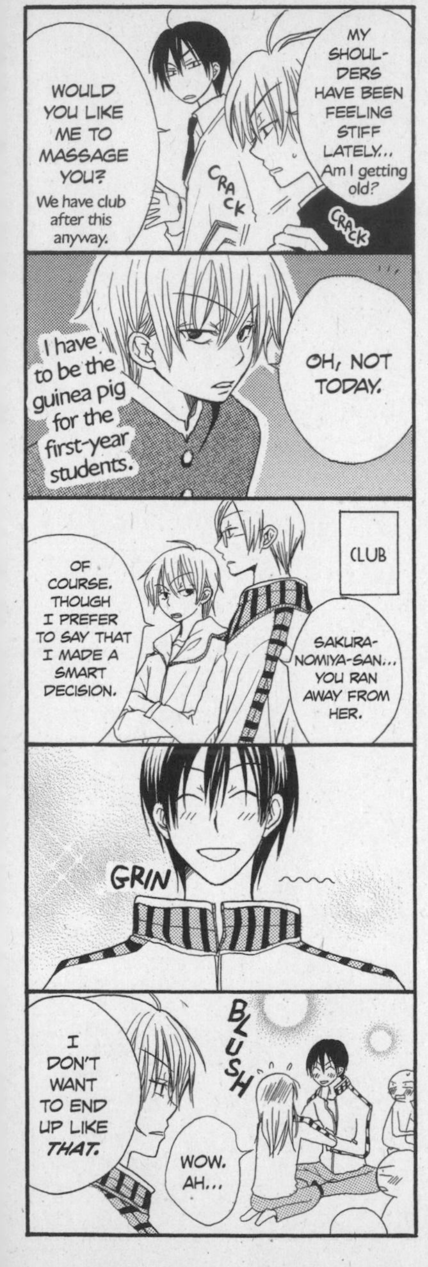
MY SHOUL-DERS HAVE BEEN FEELING STIFF LATELY... Am I getting old?
CRACK
CRACK
WOULD YOU LIKE ME TO MASSAGE YOU?
We have club after this anyway.
OH, NOT TODAY.
I have to be the guinea pig for the first-year students.
CLUB
SAKURA-NOMIYA-SAN... YOU RAN AWAY FROM HER.
OF COURSE. THOUGH I PREFER TO SAY THAT I MADE A SMART DECISION.
GRIN
BLUSH
WOW. AH...
I DON'T WANT TO END UP LIKE THAT.

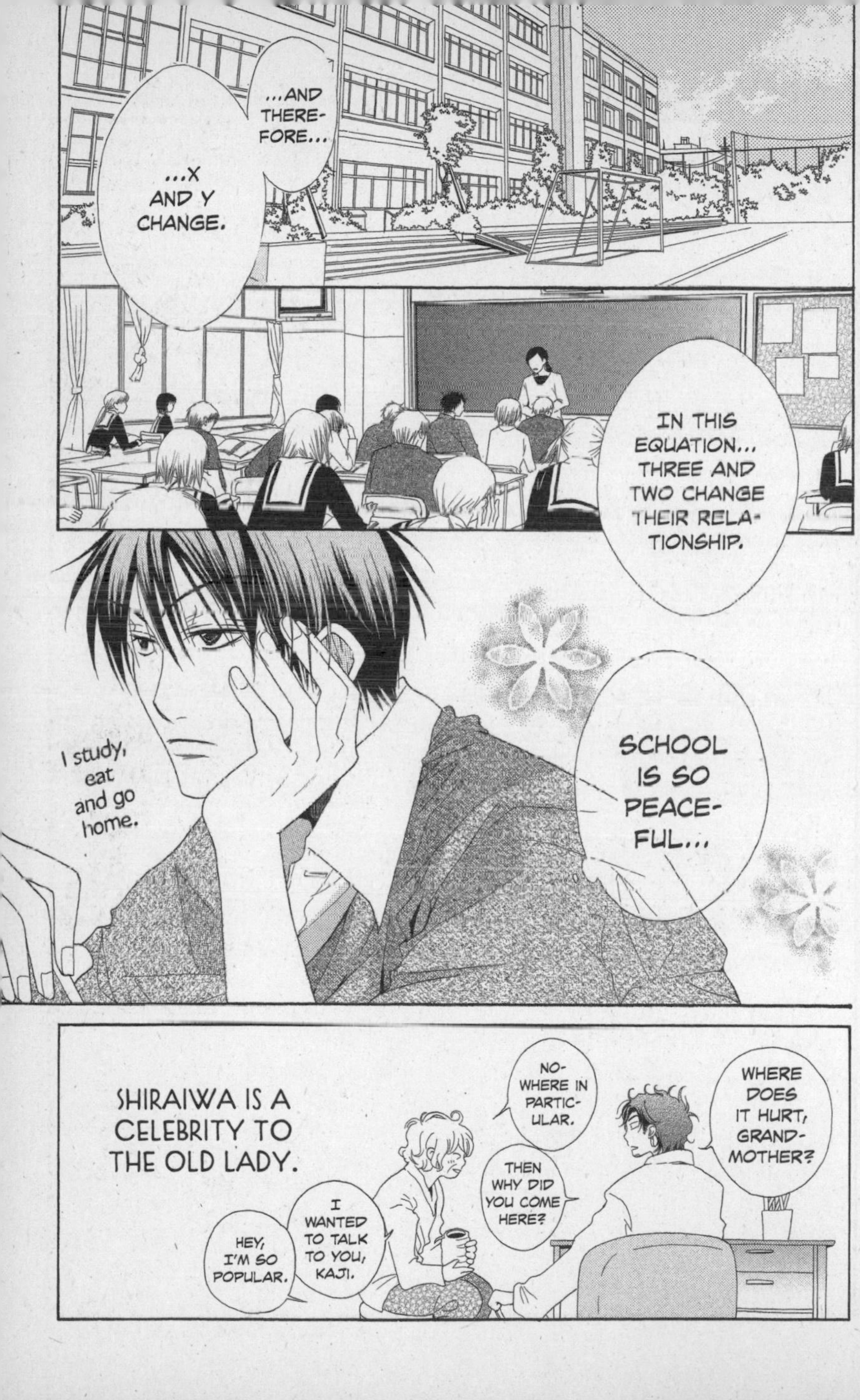
...AND THERE-FORE...
...X AND Y CHANGE.
IN THIS EQUATION... THREE AND TWO CHANGE THEIR RELA-TIONSHIP.
SCHOOL IS SO PEACE-FUL...
I study, eat and go home.
WHERE DOES IT HURT, GRAND-MOTHER?
NO-WHERE IN PARTIC-ULAR.
THEN WHY DID YOU COME HERE?
I WANTED TO TALK TO YOU, KAJI.
HEY, I'M SO POPULAR.
SHIRAIWA IS A CELEBRITY TO THE OLD LADY.

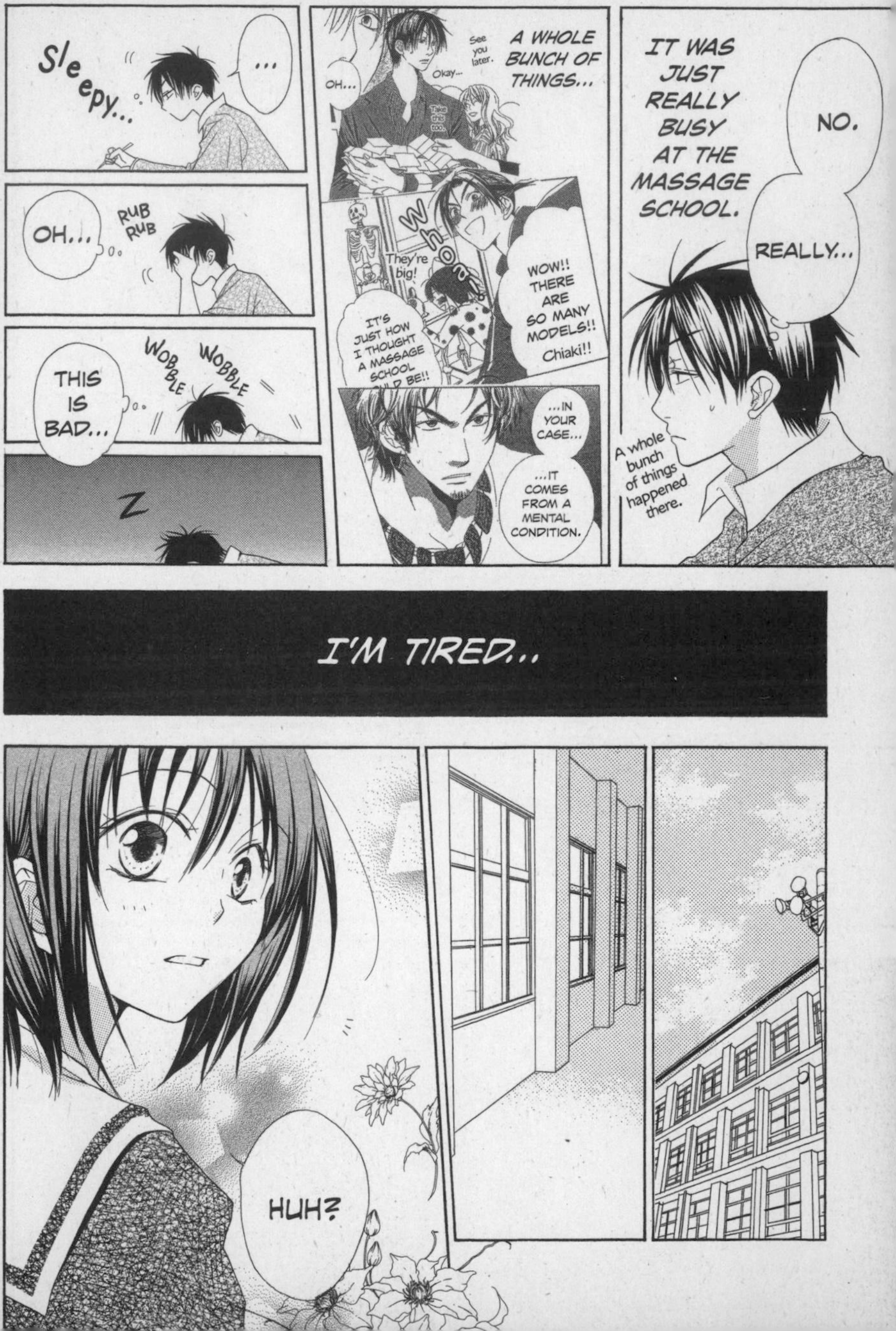
NO.
IT WAS JUST REALLY BUSY AT THE MASSAGE SCHOOL.
REALLY...
A whole bunch of things happened there.
A WHOLE BUNCH OF THINGS...
See you later.
Okay...
Take this too.
OH...
WOW!! THERE ARE SO MANY MODELS!! Chiaki!!
They're big!
IT'S JUST HOW I THOUGHT A MASSAGE SCHOOL
...IN YOUR CASE...
...IT COMES FROM A MENTAL CONDITION.
...
Sleepy...
RUB RUB
OH...
WOBBLE WOBBLE
THIS IS BAD...
Z
I'M TIRED...
HUH?

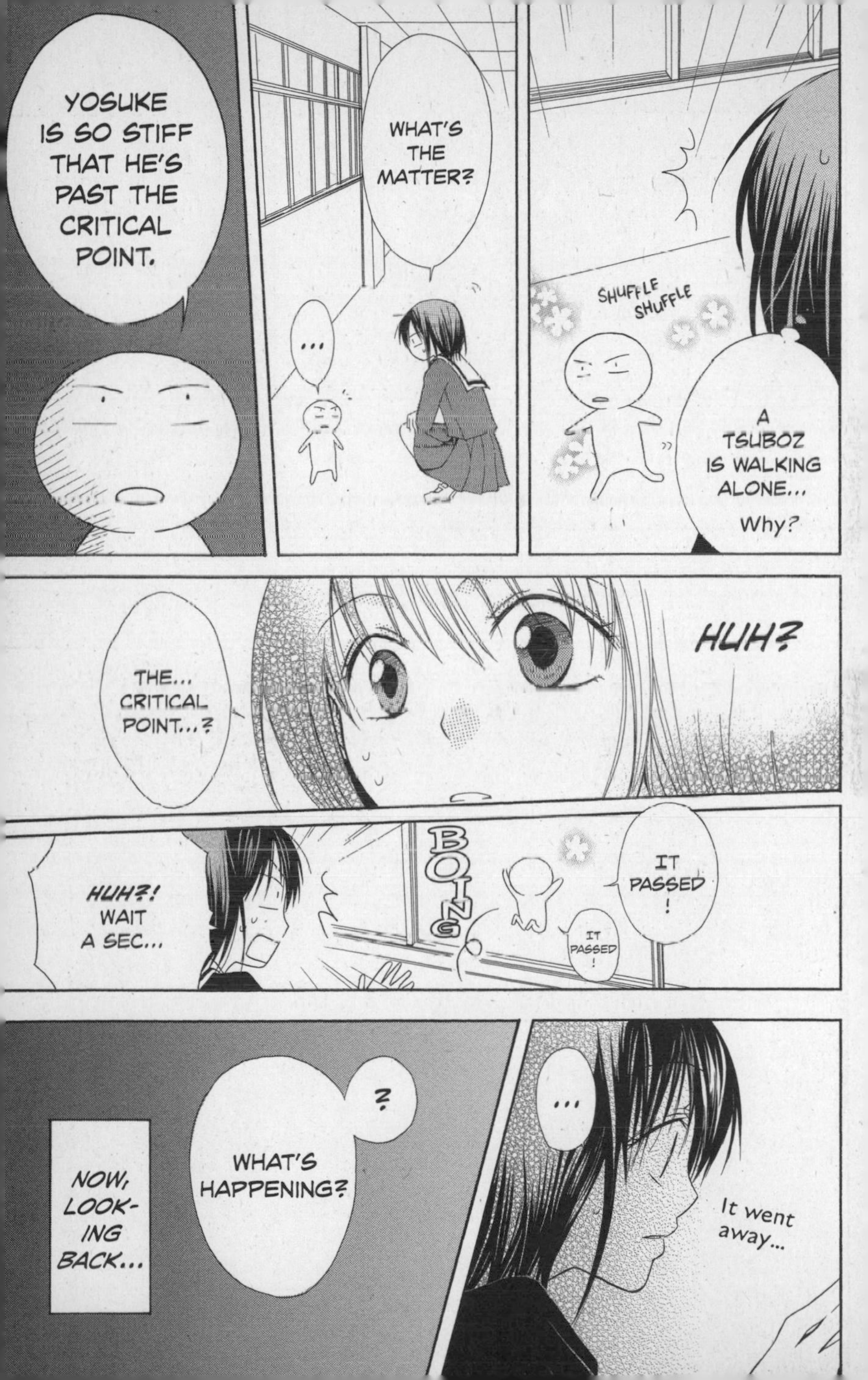
A TSUBOZ IS WALKING ALONE... Why?
SHUFFLE SHUFFLE
WHAT'S THE MATTER?
...
YOSUKE IS SO STIFF THAT HE'S PAST THE CRITICAL POINT.
HUH?
THE... CRITICAL POINT...?
IT PASSED!
IT PASSED!
BOING
HUH?! WAIT A SEC...
...
It went away...
?
WHAT'S HAPPENING?
NOW, LOOKING BACK...

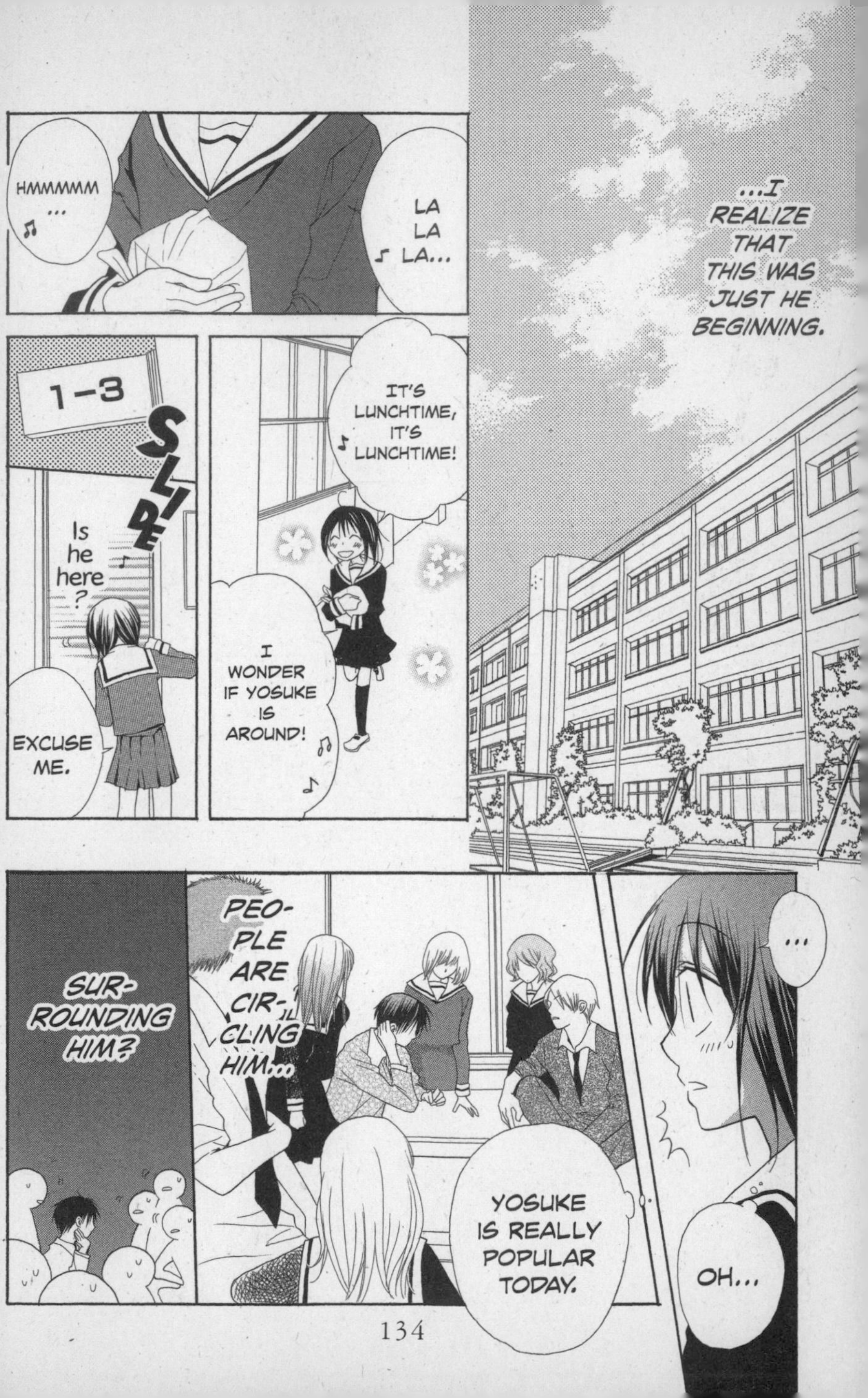
...I REALIZE THAT THIS WAS JUST HE BEGINNING.
LA LA LA...
HMMMMM...
IT'S LUNCHTIME, IT'S LUNCHTIME!
I WONDER IF YOSUKE IS AROUND!
1-3
SLIDE
Is he here?
EXCUSE ME.
...
OH...
YOSUKE IS REALLY POPULAR TODAY.
PEO-PLE ARE CIR-CLING HIM...
SUR-ROUNDING HIM?

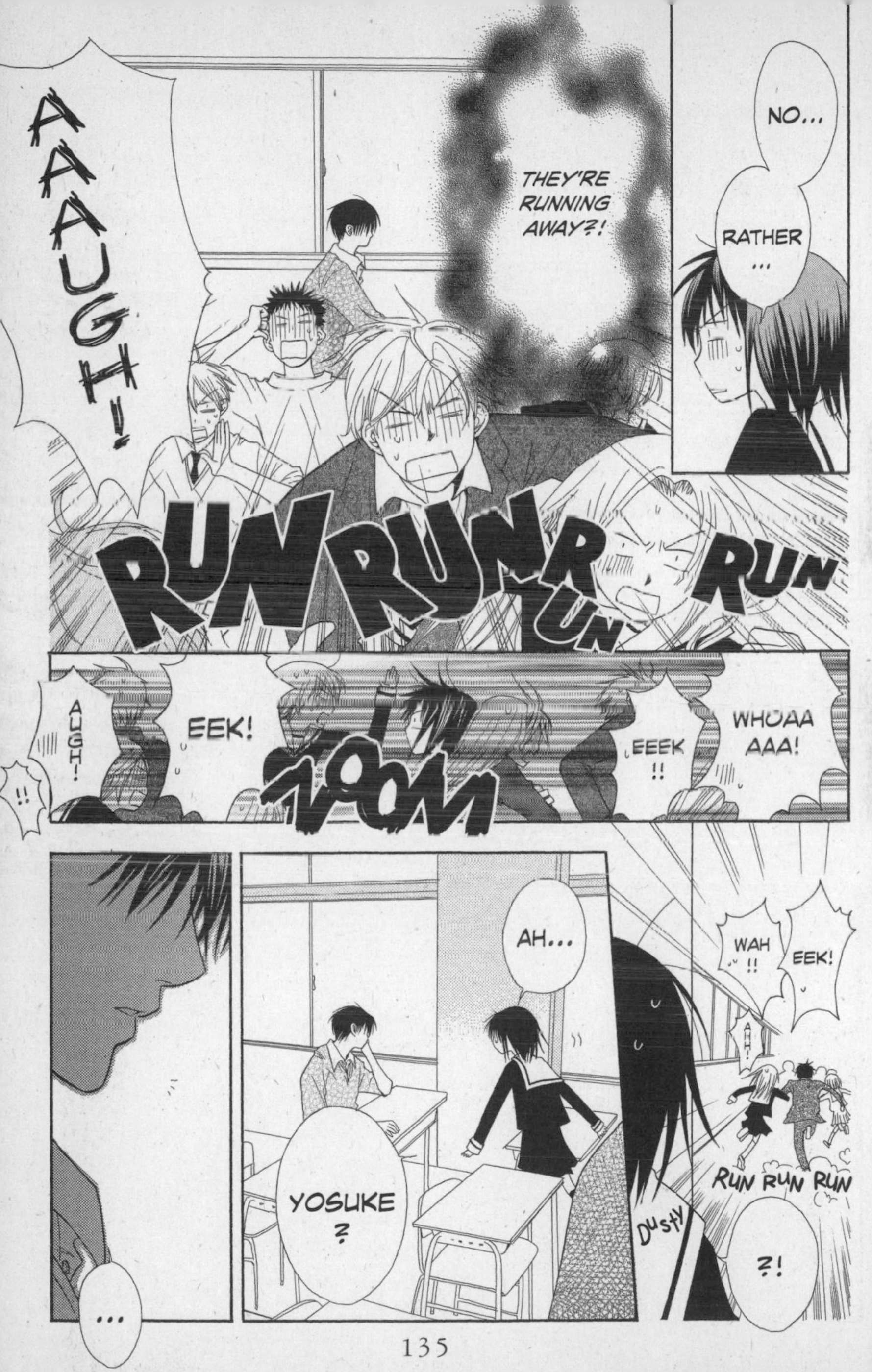
NO...
RATHER...
THEY'RE RUNNING AWAY?!
AAAUGH!
RUN RUN RUN RUN
WHOAA AAA!
EEEK!!
VOOM
EEK!
AUGH!
!!
EEK!
WAH!!
AHH!
RUN RUN RUN
Dusty
?!
AH...
YOSUKE?
...

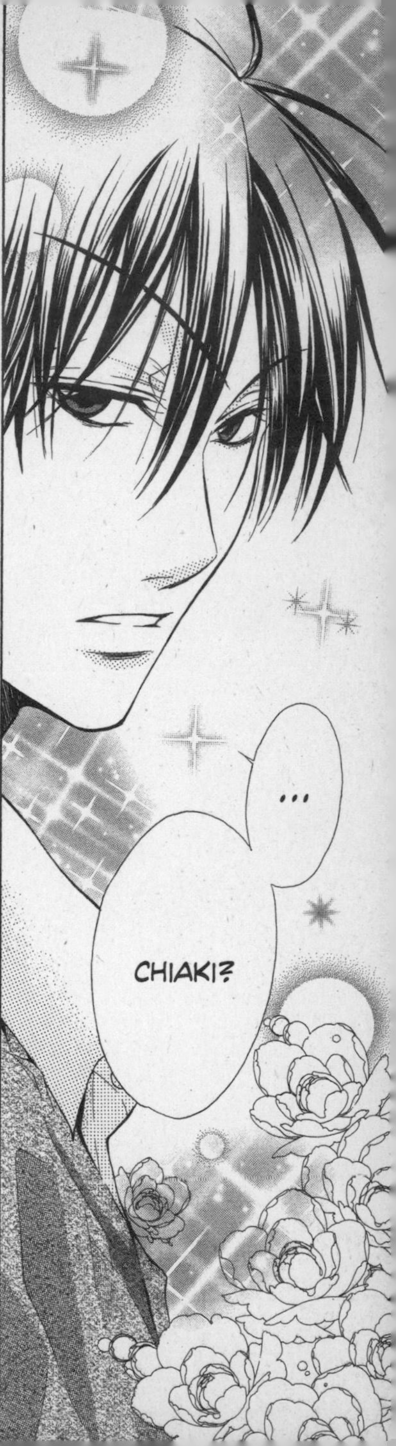
...
CHIAKI?

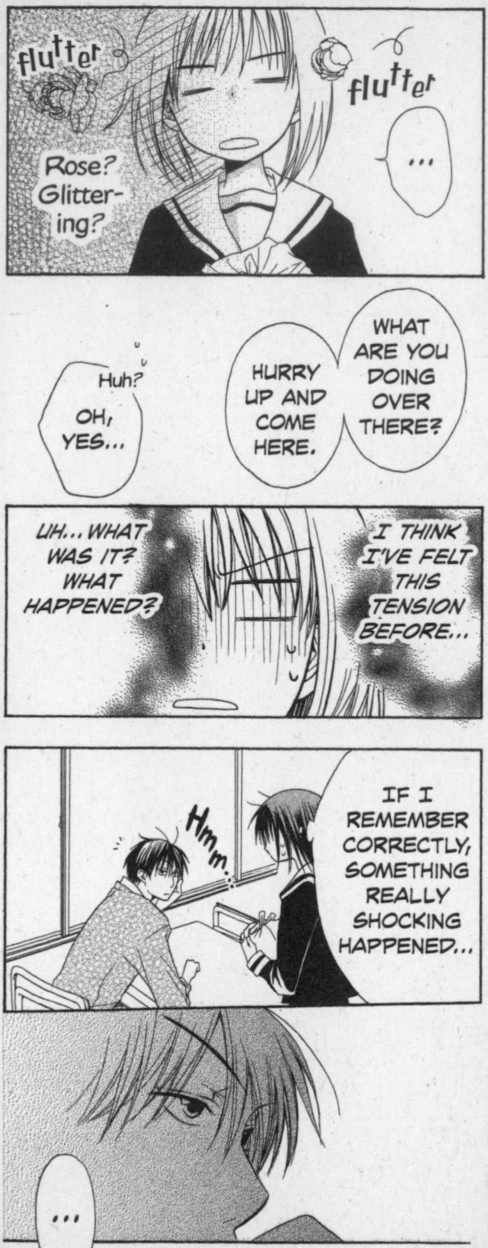
flutter
...
flutter
Rose? Glitter-ing?
WHAT ARE YOU DOING OVER THERE?
HURRY UP AND COME HERE.
Huh?
OH, YES...
I THINK I'VE FELT THIS TENSION BEFORE...
UH... WHAT WAS IT? WHAT HAPPENED?
IF I REMEMBER CORRECTLY, SOMETHING REALLY SHOCKING HAPPENED...
Hmm
...

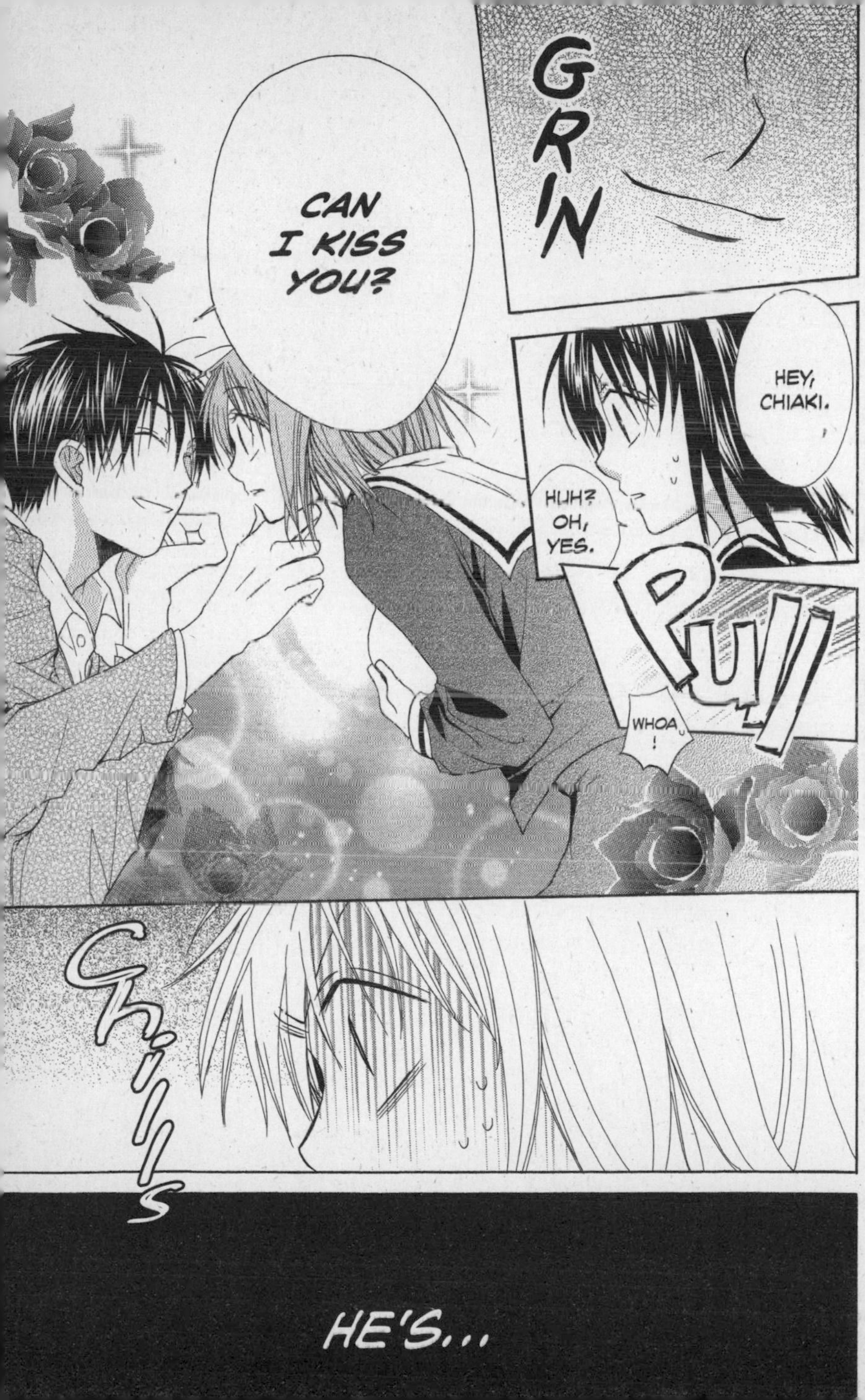
GRIN
HEY, CHIAKI.
HUH? OH, YES.
PULL
WHOA!
CAN I KISS YOU?
CHILLS
HE'S...

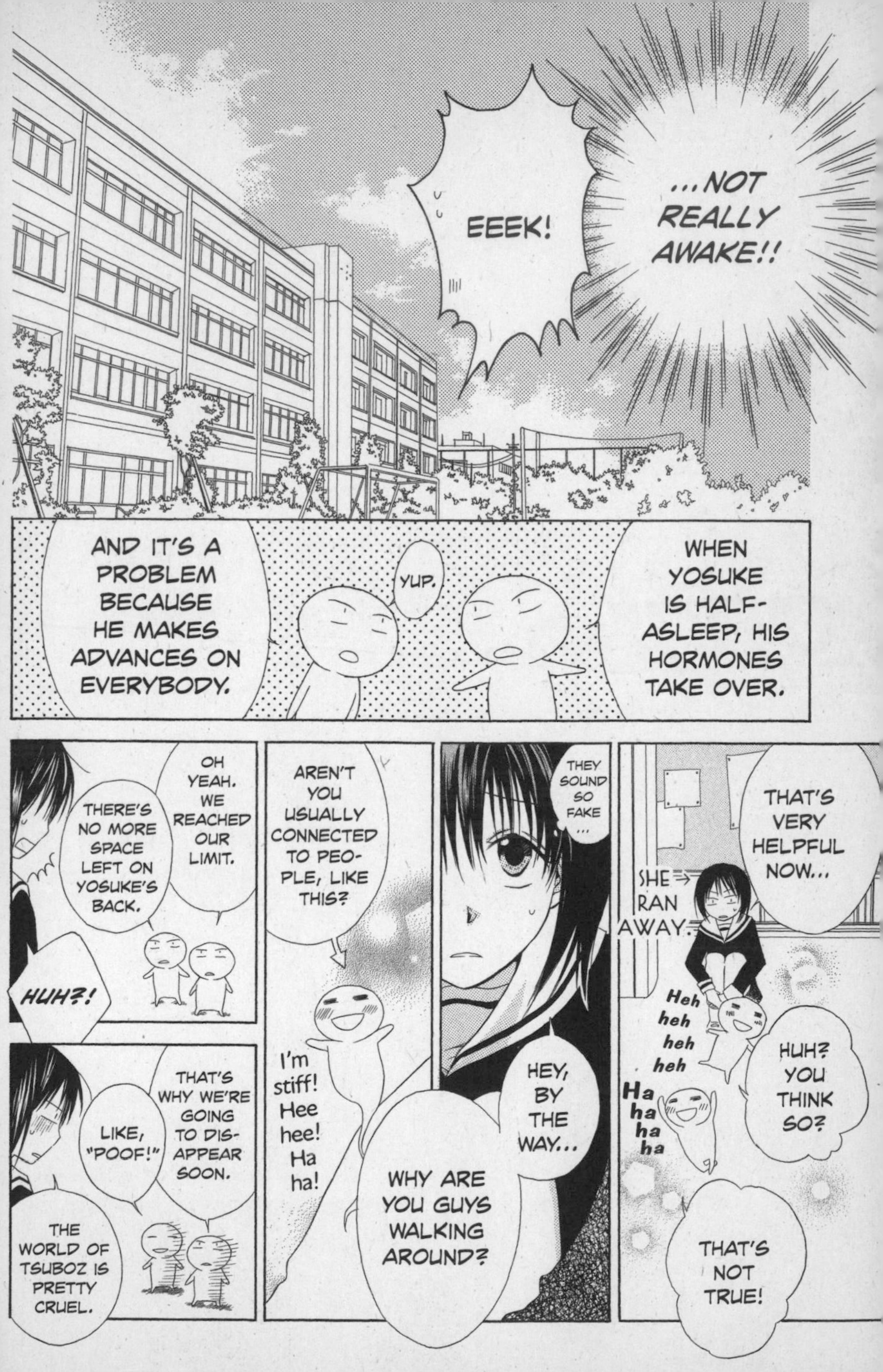
...NOT REALLY AWAKE!!
EEEK!
WHEN YOSUKE IS HALF-ASLEEP, HIS HORMONES TAKE OVER.
YUP.
AND IT'S A PROBLEM BECAUSE HE MAKES ADVANCES ON EVERYBODY.
THAT'S VERY HELPFUL NOW...
SHE RAN AWAY.
Heh heh heh heh
Ha ha ha ha ha
HUH? YOU THINK SO?
THAT'S NOT TRUE!
THEY SOUND SO FAKE...
HEY, BY THE WAY...
WHY ARE YOU GUYS WALKING AROUND?
AREN'T YOU USUALLY CONNECTED TO PEO-PLE, LIKE THIS?
I'm stiff! Hee hee! Ha ha!
OH YEAH. WE REACHED OUR LIMIT.
THERE'S NO MORE SPACE LEFT ON YOSUKE'S BACK.
HUH?!
THAT'S WHY WE'RE GOING TO DIS-APPEAR SOON.
LIKE, "POOF!"
THE WORLD OF TSUBOZ IS PRETTY CRUEL.

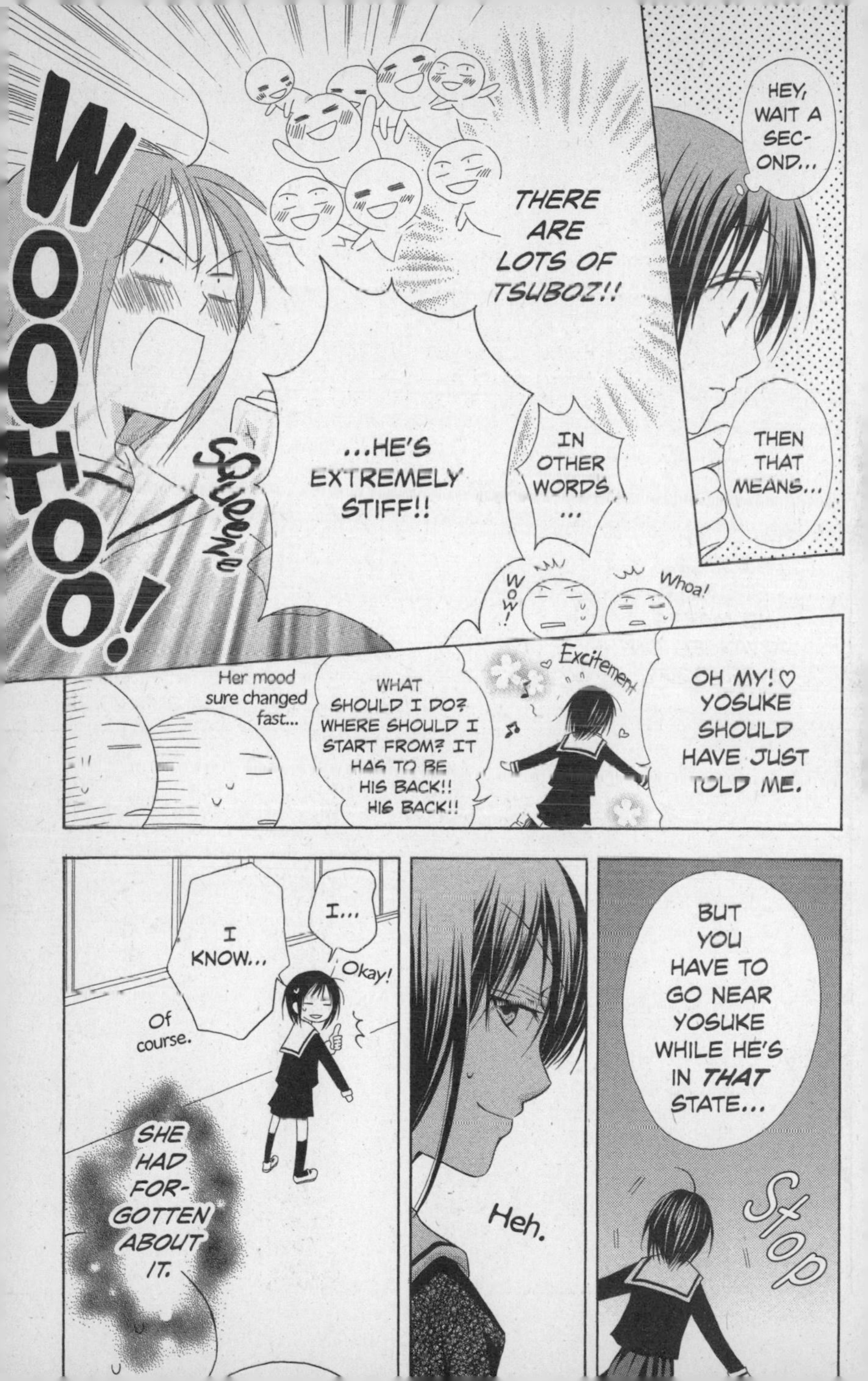
HEY, WAIT A SEC-OND...
THEN THAT MEANS...
IN OTHER WORDS ...
...HE'S EXTREMELY STIFF!!
THERE ARE LOTS OF TSUBOZ!!
Wow!
Whoa!
Squeeze
WOOHOO!
OH MY! ♡ YOSUKE SHOULD HAVE JUST TOLD ME.
Excitement
WHAT SHOULD I DO? WHERE SHOULD I START FROM? IT HAS TO BE HIS BACK!! HIS BACK!!
Her mood sure changed fast...
BUT YOU HAVE TO GO NEAR YOSUKE WHILE HE'S IN *THAT* STATE...
Stop
Heh.
I...
Okay!
I KNOW...
Of course.
SHE HAD FOR-GOTTEN ABOUT IT.

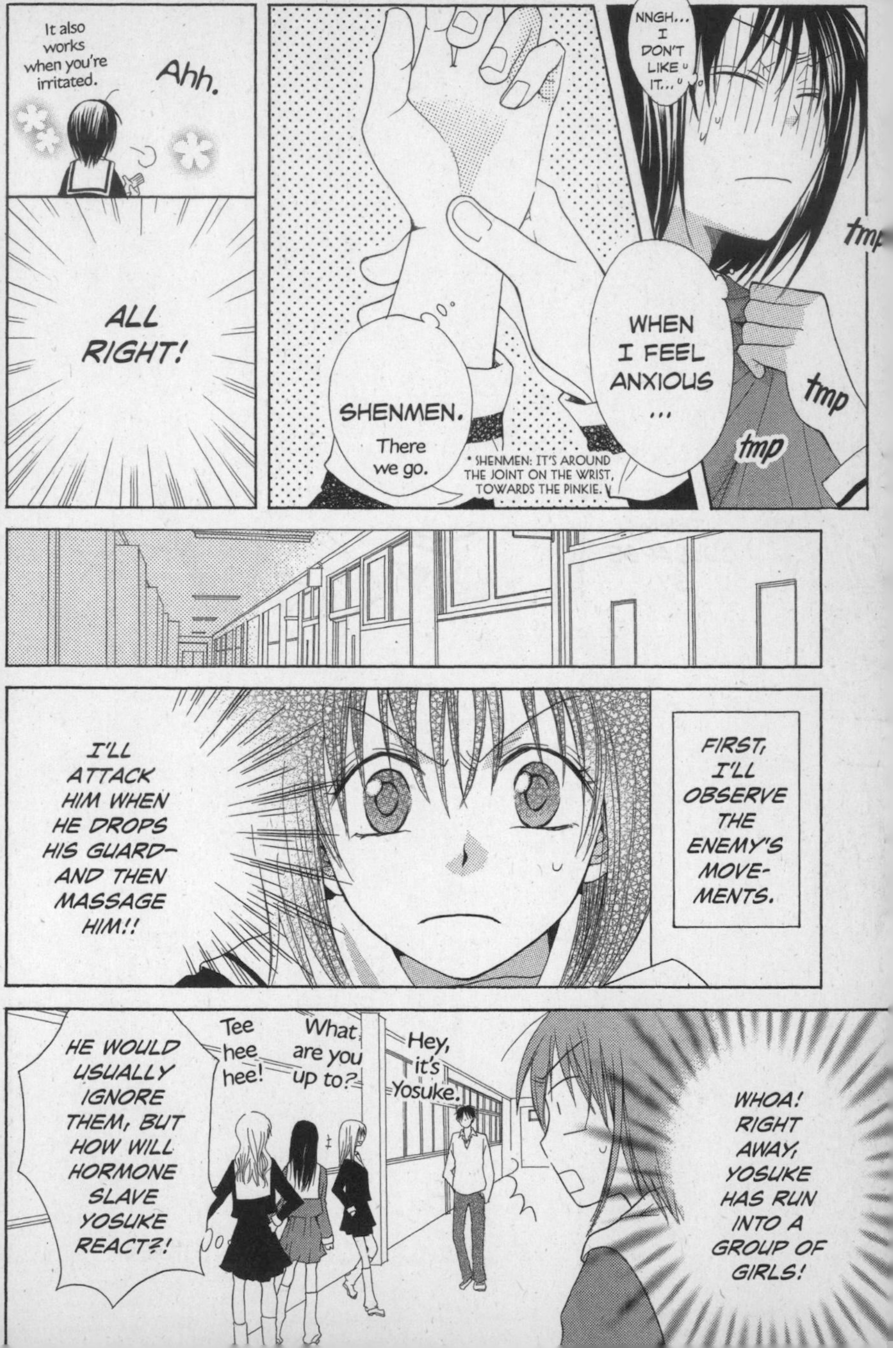
NNGH... I DON'T LIKE IT...
WHEN I FEEL ANXIOUS...
tmp
tmp
tmp
SHENMEN.
There we go.
* SHENMEN: IT'S AROUND THE JOINT ON THE WRIST, TOWARDS THE PINKIE.
It also works when you're irritated.
Ahh.
ALL RIGHT!
FIRST, I'LL OBSERVE THE ENEMY'S MOVEMENTS.
I'LL ATTACK HIM WHEN HE DROPS HIS GUARD—AND THEN MASSAGE HIM!!
WHOA! RIGHT AWAY, YOSUKE HAS RUN INTO A GROUP OF GIRLS!
Hey, it's Yosuke.
What are you up to?
Tee hee hee!
HE WOULD USUALLY IGNORE THEM, BUT HOW WILL HORMONE SLAVE YOSUKE REACT?!

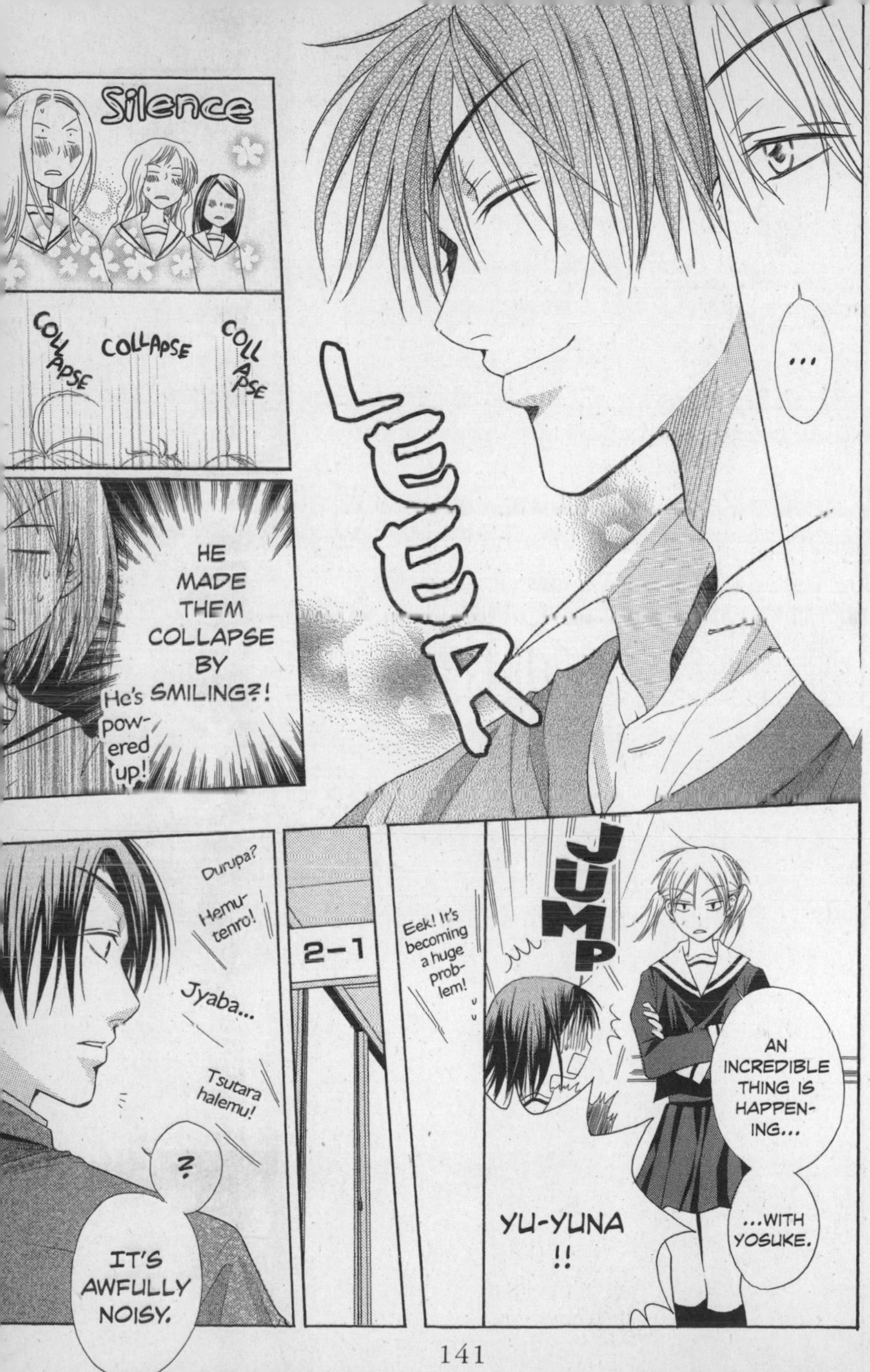
...
LEER
Silence
COLLAPSE
COLLAPSE
COLLAPSE
HE MADE THEM COLLAPSE BY SMILING?!
He's powered up!
JUMP
Eek! It's becoming a huge problem!
AN INCREDIBLE THING IS HAPPENING...
...WITH YOSUKE.
YU-YUNA!!
2-1
Durupa?
Hemu-tenro!
Jyaba...
Tsutara halemu!
?
IT'S AWFULLY NOISY.

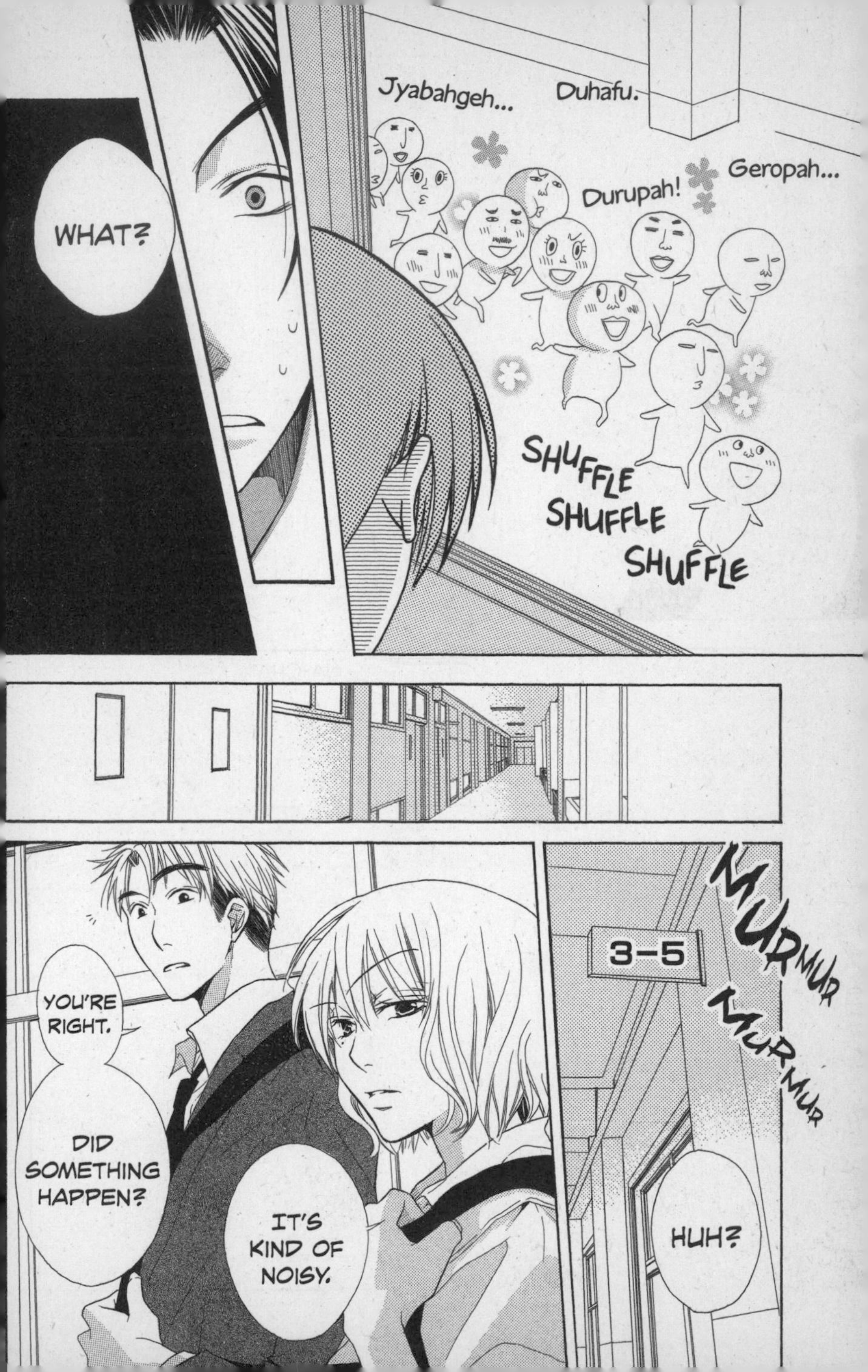
Geropah...
Durupah!
Duhafu.
Jyabahgeh...
SHUFFLE
SHUFFLE
SHUFFLE
WHAT?
3-5
MURMUR
MURMUR
HUH?
IT'S KIND OF NOISY.
YOU'RE RIGHT.
DID SOMETHING HAPPEN?

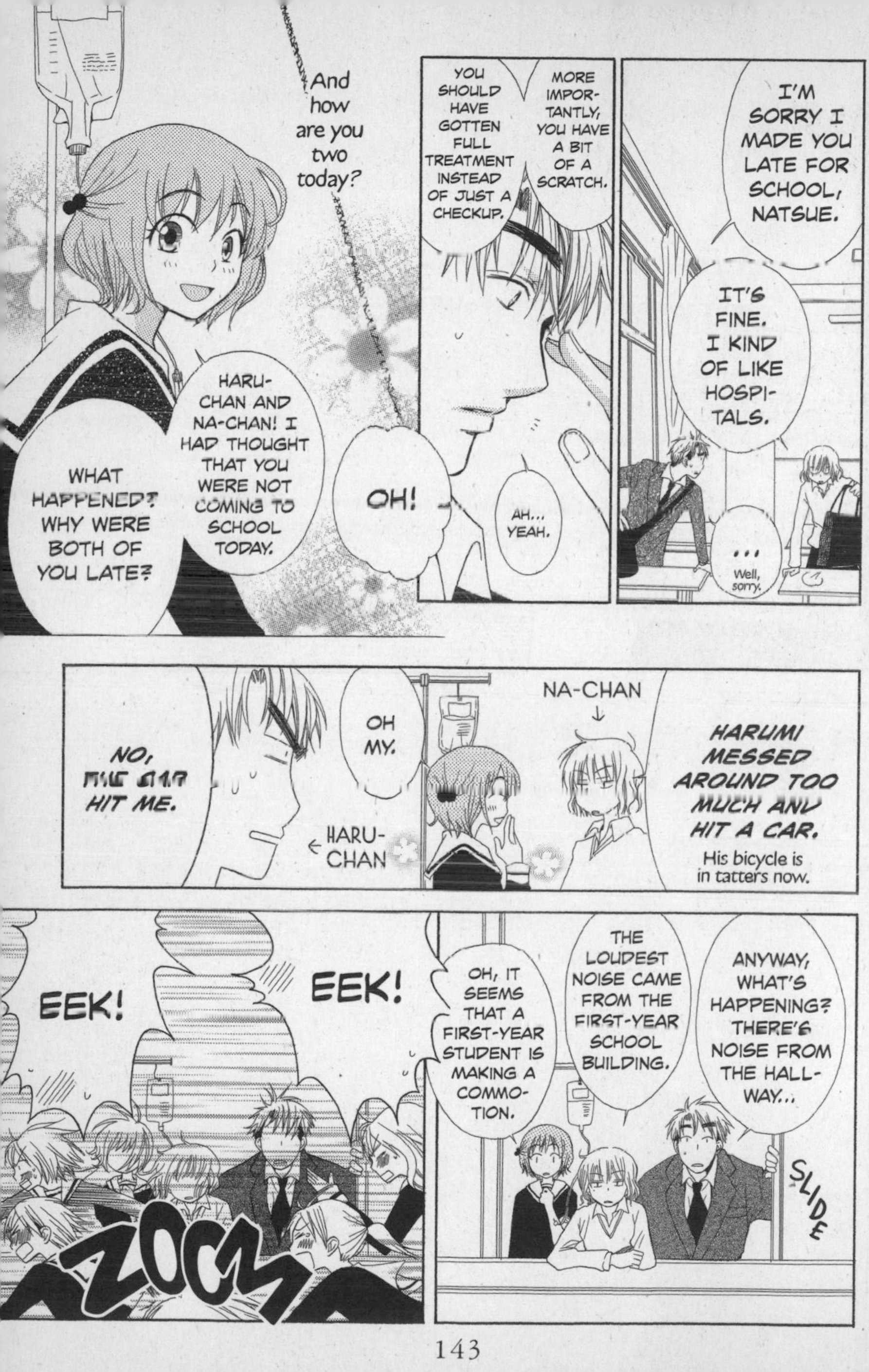
I'M SORRY I MADE YOU LATE FOR SCHOOL, NATSUE.
IT'S FINE. I KIND OF LIKE HOSPITALS.
... Well, sorry.
MORE IMPORTANTLY, YOU HAVE A BIT OF A SCRATCH.
YOU SHOULD HAVE GOTTEN FULL TREATMENT INSTEAD OF JUST A CHECKUP.
AH... YEAH.
OH!
HARU-CHAN AND NA-CHAN! I HAD THOUGHT THAT YOU WERE NOT COMING TO SCHOOL TODAY.
WHAT HAPPENED? WHY WERE BOTH OF YOU LATE?
And how are you two today?
HARUMI MESSED AROUND TOO MUCH AND HIT A CAR.
His bicycle is in tatters now.
NA-CHAN
OH MY.
HARU-CHAN
NO, THE CAR HIT ME.
SLIDE
ANYWAY, WHAT'S HAPPENING? THERE'S NOISE FROM THE HALLWAY...
THE LOUDEST NOISE CAME FROM THE FIRST-YEAR SCHOOL BUILDING.
OH, IT SEEMS THAT A FIRST-YEAR STUDENT IS MAKING A COMMOTION.
EEK!
EEK!

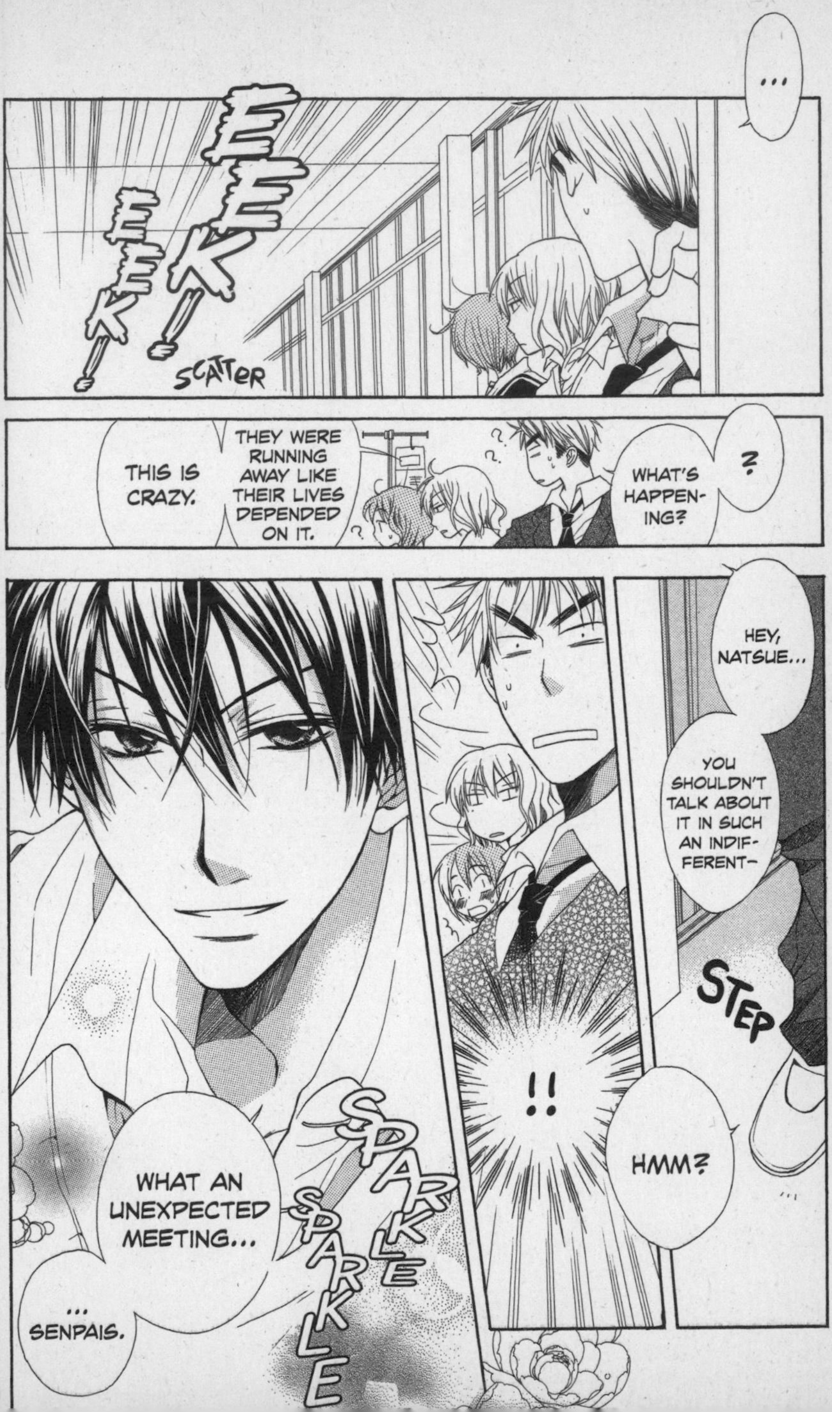
...
EEEK!
EEEK!
SCATTER
?
WHAT'S HAPPENING?
THEY WERE RUNNING AWAY LIKE THEIR LIVES DEPENDED ON IT.
THIS IS CRAZY.
HEY, NATSUE...
YOU SHOULDN'T TALK ABOUT IT IN SUCH AN INDIF-FERENT-
STEP
HMM?
!!
WHAT AN UNEXPECTED MEETING...
... SENPAIS.
SPARKLE
SPARKLE

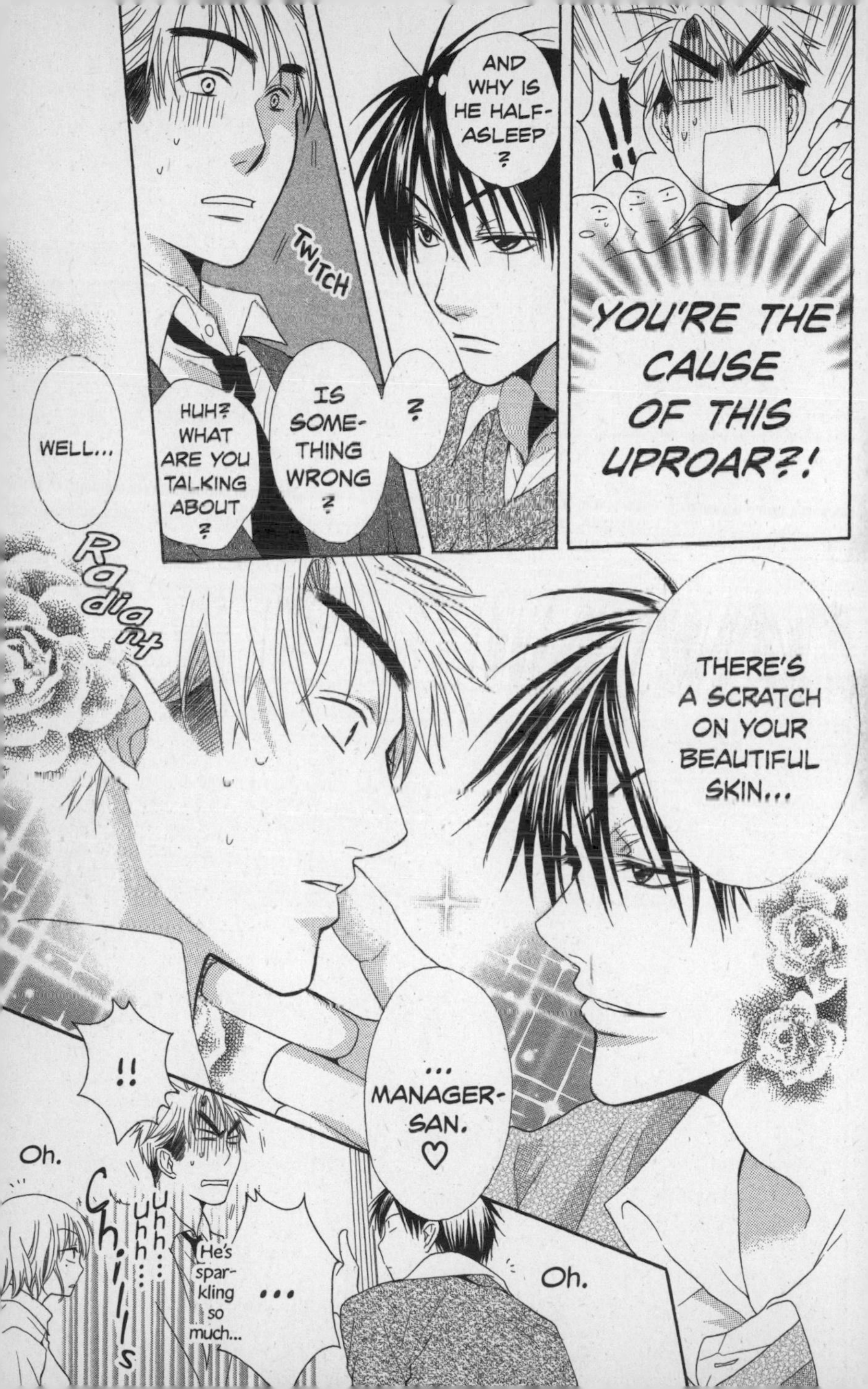
!!
YOU'RE THE CAUSE OF THIS UPROAR?!
AND WHY IS HE HALF-ASLEEP?
?
TWITCH
IS SOMETHING WRONG?
HUH? WHAT ARE YOU TALKING ABOUT?
WELL...
THERE'S A SCRATCH ON YOUR BEAUTIFUL SKIN...
Radiant
... MANAGER-SAN. ♡
Oh.
!!
Uhh... Uhh...
He's sparkling so much...
...
Chills
Oh.

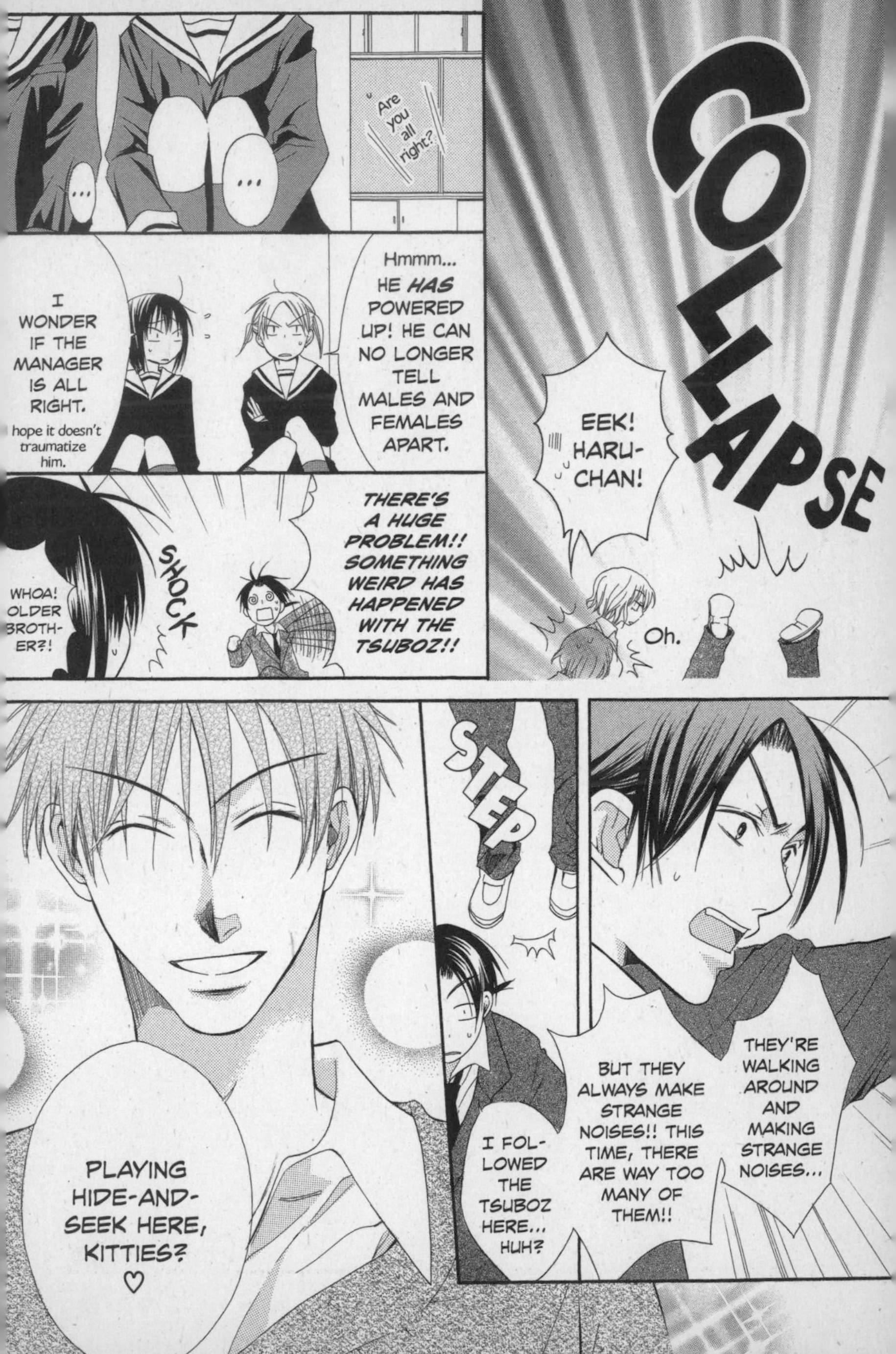
COLLAPSE
EEK! HARU-CHAN!
Oh.
Are you all right?
...
...
Hmmm... HE HAS POWERED UP! HE CAN NO LONGER TELL MALES AND FEMALES APART.
I WONDER IF THE MANAGER IS ALL RIGHT.
hope it doesn't traumatize him.
THERE'S A HUGE PROBLEM!! SOMETHING WEIRD HAS HAPPENED WITH THE TSUBOZ!!
SHOCK
WHOA! OLDER BROTHER?!
THEY'RE WALKING AROUND AND MAKING STRANGE NOISES...
BUT THEY ALWAYS MAKE STRANGE NOISES!! THIS TIME, THERE ARE WAY TOO MANY OF THEM!!
STEP
I FOL-LOWED THE TSUBOZ HERE... HUH?
PLAYING HIDE-AND-SEEK HERE, KITTIES? ♡

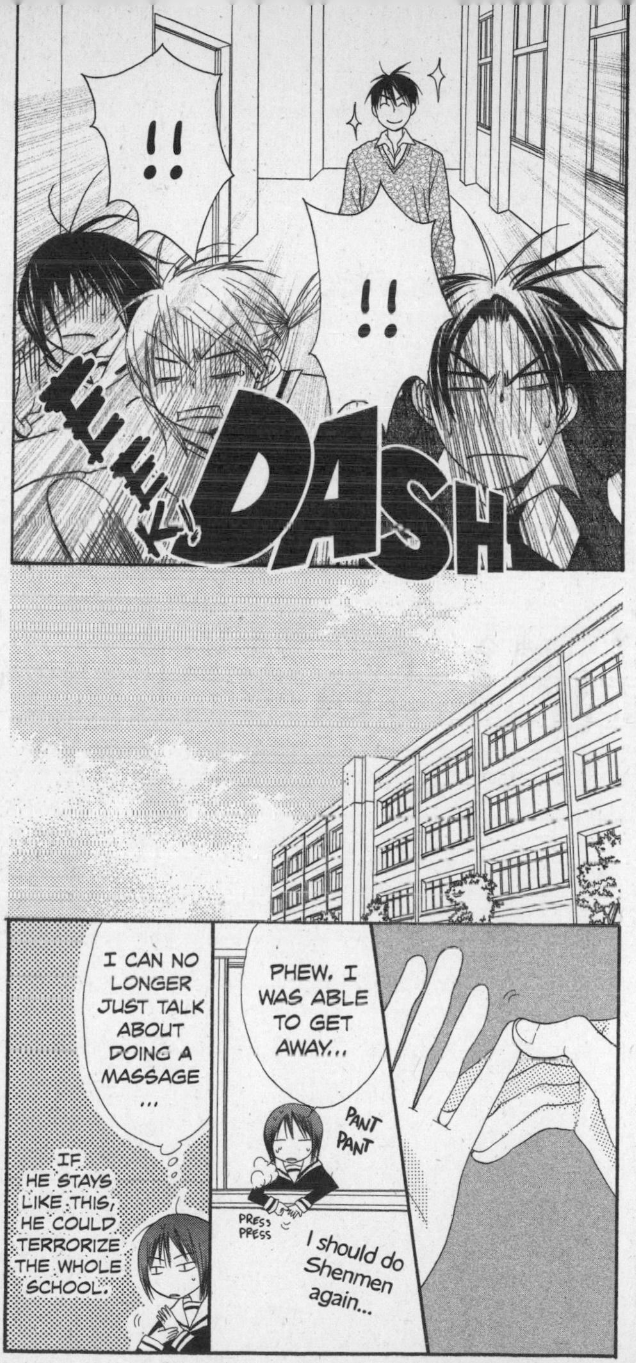
!!
!!
DASH
I should do Shenmen again...
PHEW. I WAS ABLE TO GET AWAY...
PANT PANT
PRESS PRESS
I CAN NO LONGER JUST TALK ABOUT DOING A MASSAGE ...
IF HE STAYS LIKE THIS, HE COULD TERRORIZE THE WHOLE SCHOOL.

Rintaro Fushimi

He's a character who appeared as not a very good type of masseur. He's mentally childish.

He's like a duckling because he's willing to follow somebody he admires anywhere...

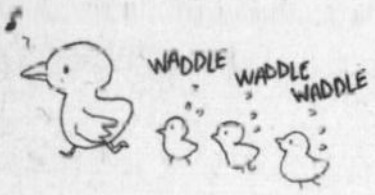
WADDLE
WADDLE
WADDLE

It's too late, since I already drew it, but I wonder why I said he was attractive. I should have thought about drawing him as good looking... I was asked a couple of times, "Hey... is this character supposed to be handsome?" I don't know myself whether he is.

If he admired a dog, he would probably get attached to the dog too.

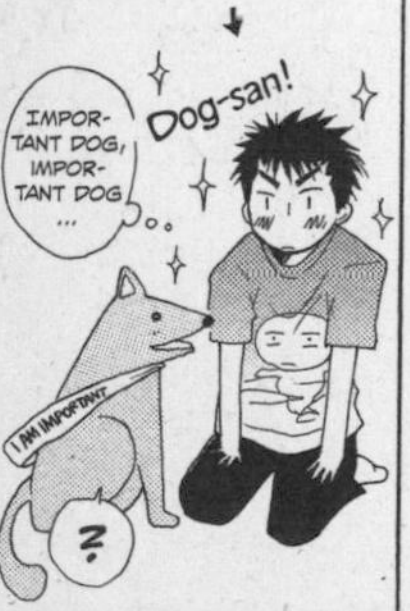
Dog-san!
IMPORTANT DOG, IMPORTANT DOG ...
I AM IMPORTANT
?

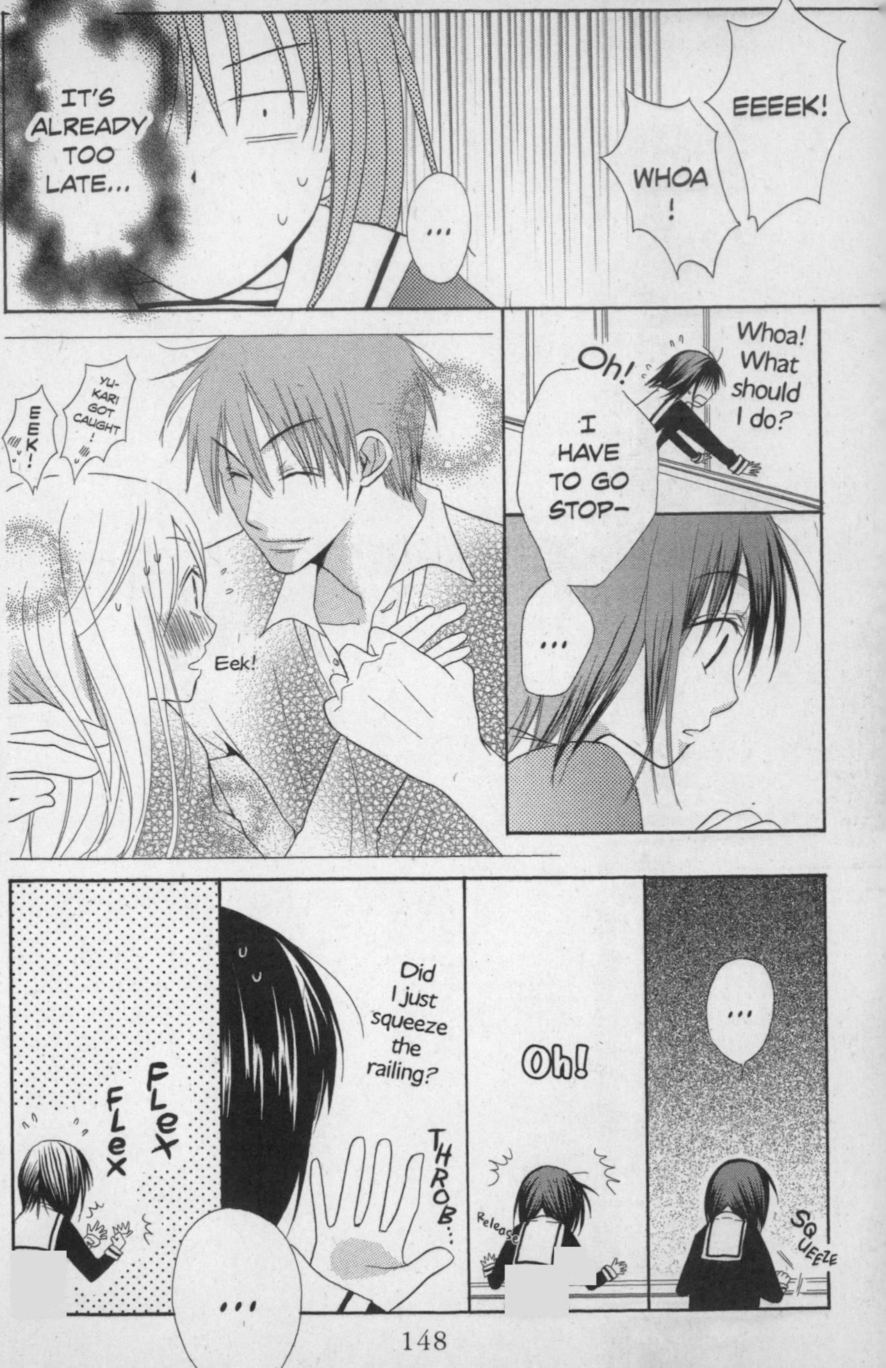
EEEEK!
WHOA !
...
IT'S ALREADY TOO LATE...
Whoa! What should I do?
Oh!
I HAVE TO GO STOP–
...
YU-KARI GOT CAUGHT!
EEK!
Eek!
...
SQUEEZE
Oh!
Release
Did I just squeeze the railing?
THROB...
...
FLEX
FLEX

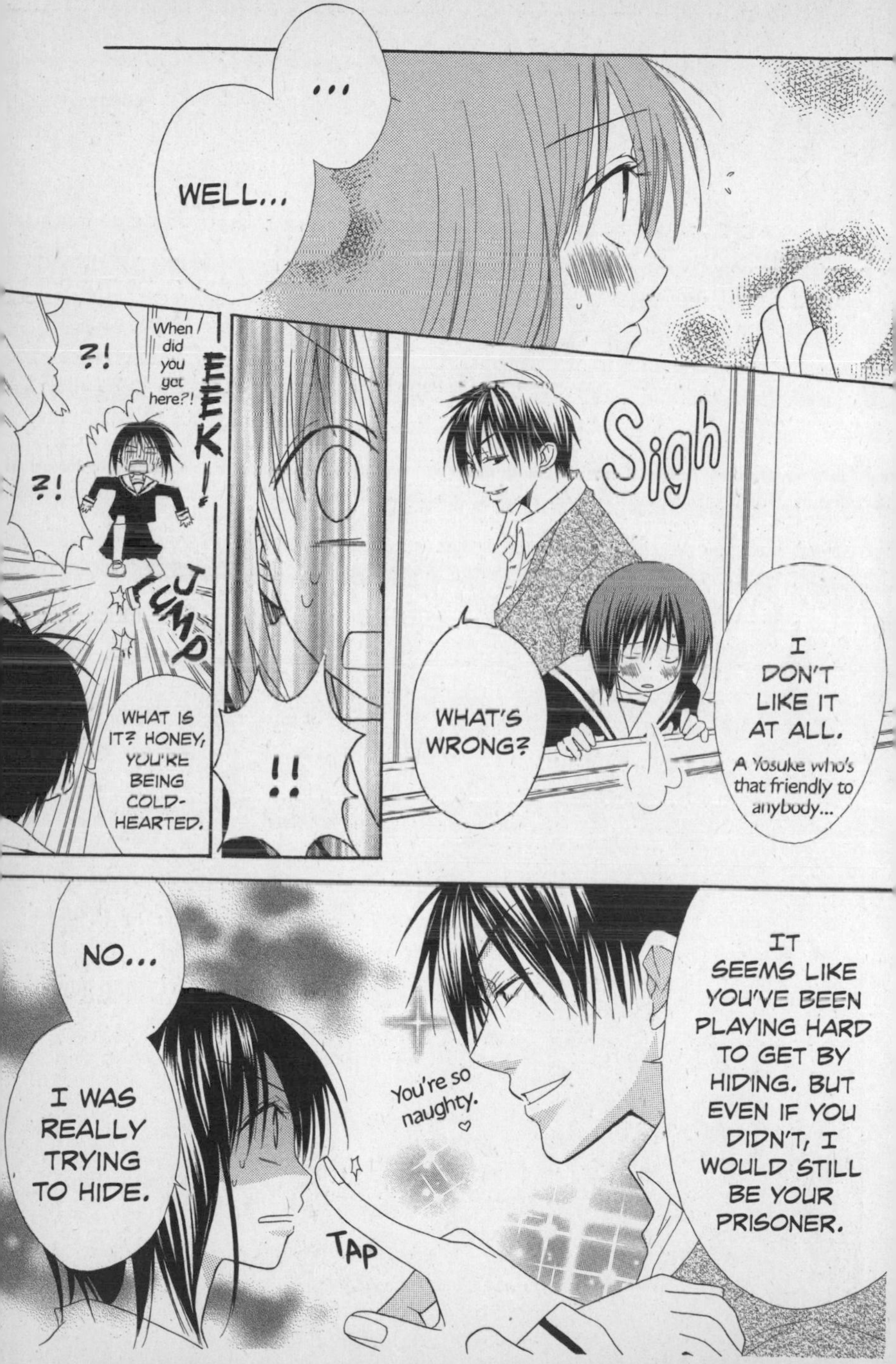
...
WELL...
Sigh
I DON'T LIKE IT AT ALL.
A Yosuke who's that friendly to anybody...
WHAT'S WRONG?
!!
EEEK!
When did you get here?!
?!
?!
JUMP
WHAT IS IT? HONEY, YOU'RE BEING COLD-HEARTED.
IT SEEMS LIKE YOU'VE BEEN PLAYING HARD TO GET BY HIDING. BUT EVEN IF YOU DIDN'T, I WOULD STILL BE YOUR PRISONER.
You're so naughty. ♡
TAP
NO...
I WAS REALLY TRYING TO HIDE.

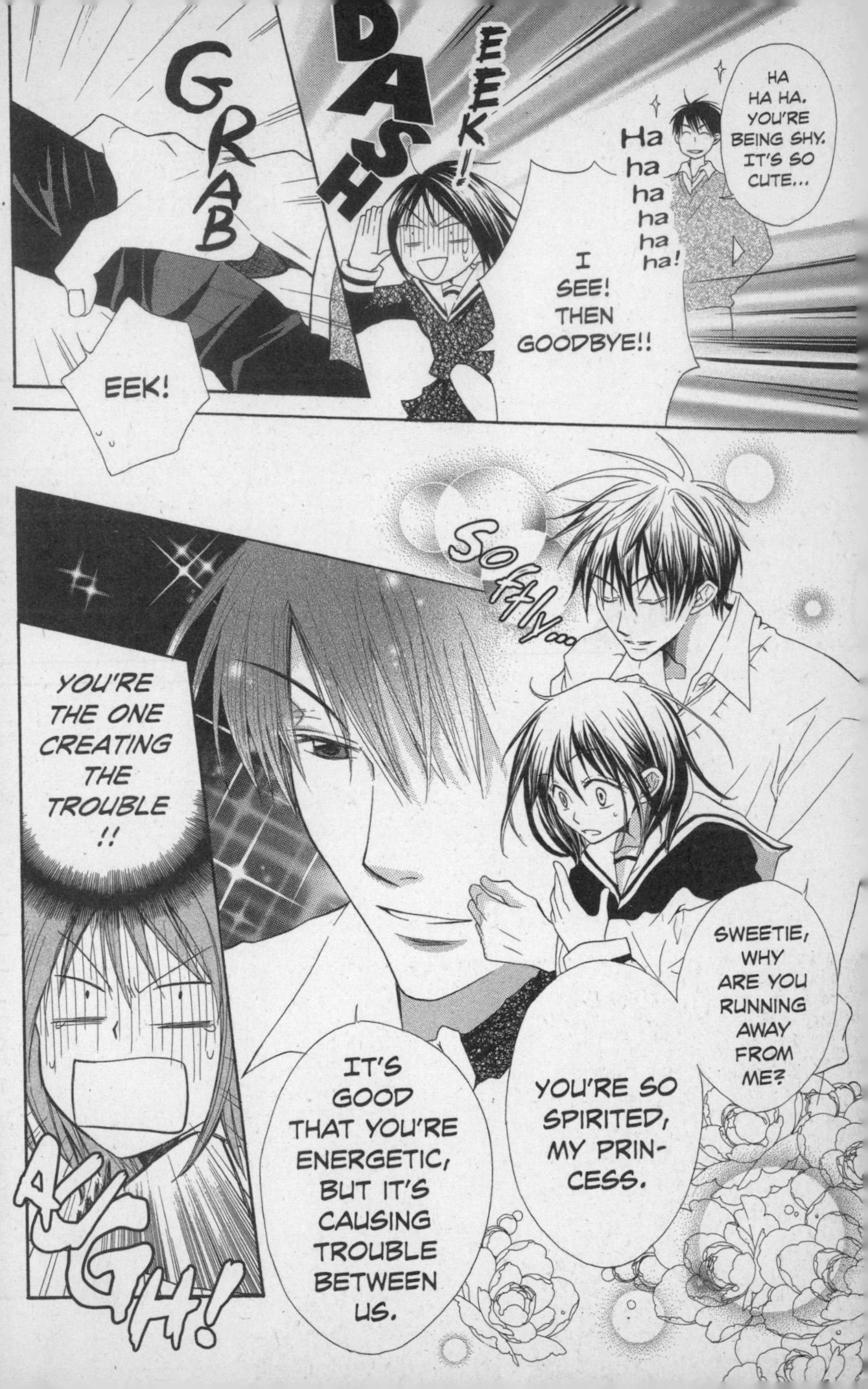
HA HA HA. YOU'RE BEING SHY. IT'S SO CUTE...
Ha ha ha ha ha ha ha!
I SEE! THEN GOODBYE!!
EEEK!
DASH
GRAB
EEK!
Softly...
SWEETIE, WHY ARE YOU RUNNING AWAY FROM ME?
YOU'RE SO SPIRITED, MY PRIN-CESS.
IT'S GOOD THAT YOU'RE ENERGETIC, BUT IT'S CAUSING TROUBLE BETWEEN US.
YOU'RE THE ONE CREATING THE TROUBLE!!
AUGH!

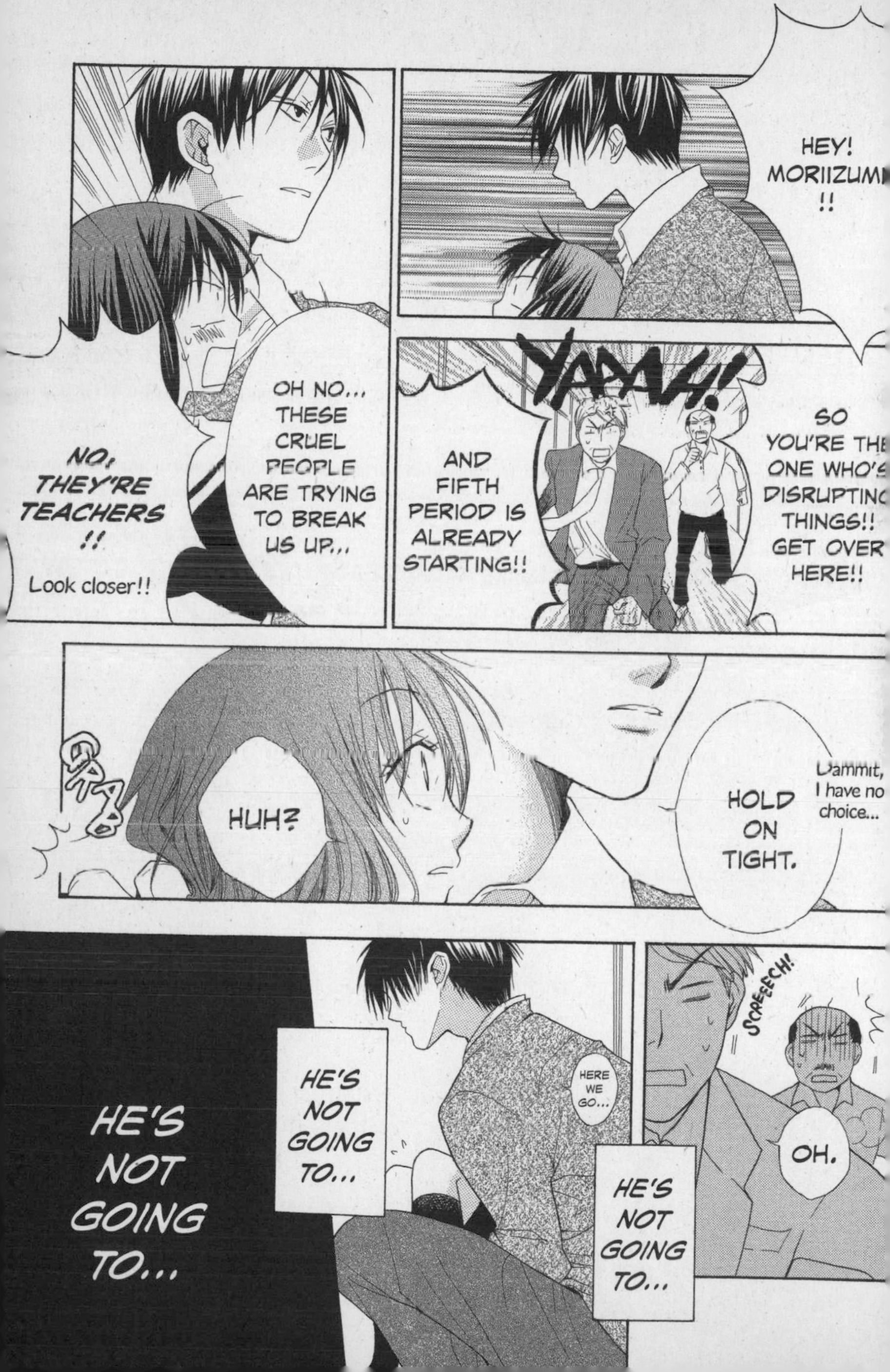
HEY! MORIIZUMI!!
YAAAH!
SO YOU'RE THE ONE WHO'S DISRUPTING THINGS!! GET OVER HERE!!
AND FIFTH PERIOD IS ALREADY STARTING!!
OH NO... THESE CRUEL PEOPLE ARE TRYING TO BREAK US UP...
NO, THEY'RE TEACHERS!!
Look closer!!
Dammit, I have no choice...
HOLD ON TIGHT.
HUH?
GRAB
SCREEECH!
OH.
HE'S NOT GOING TO...
HERE WE GO...
HE'S NOT GOING TO...
HE'S NOT GOING TO...

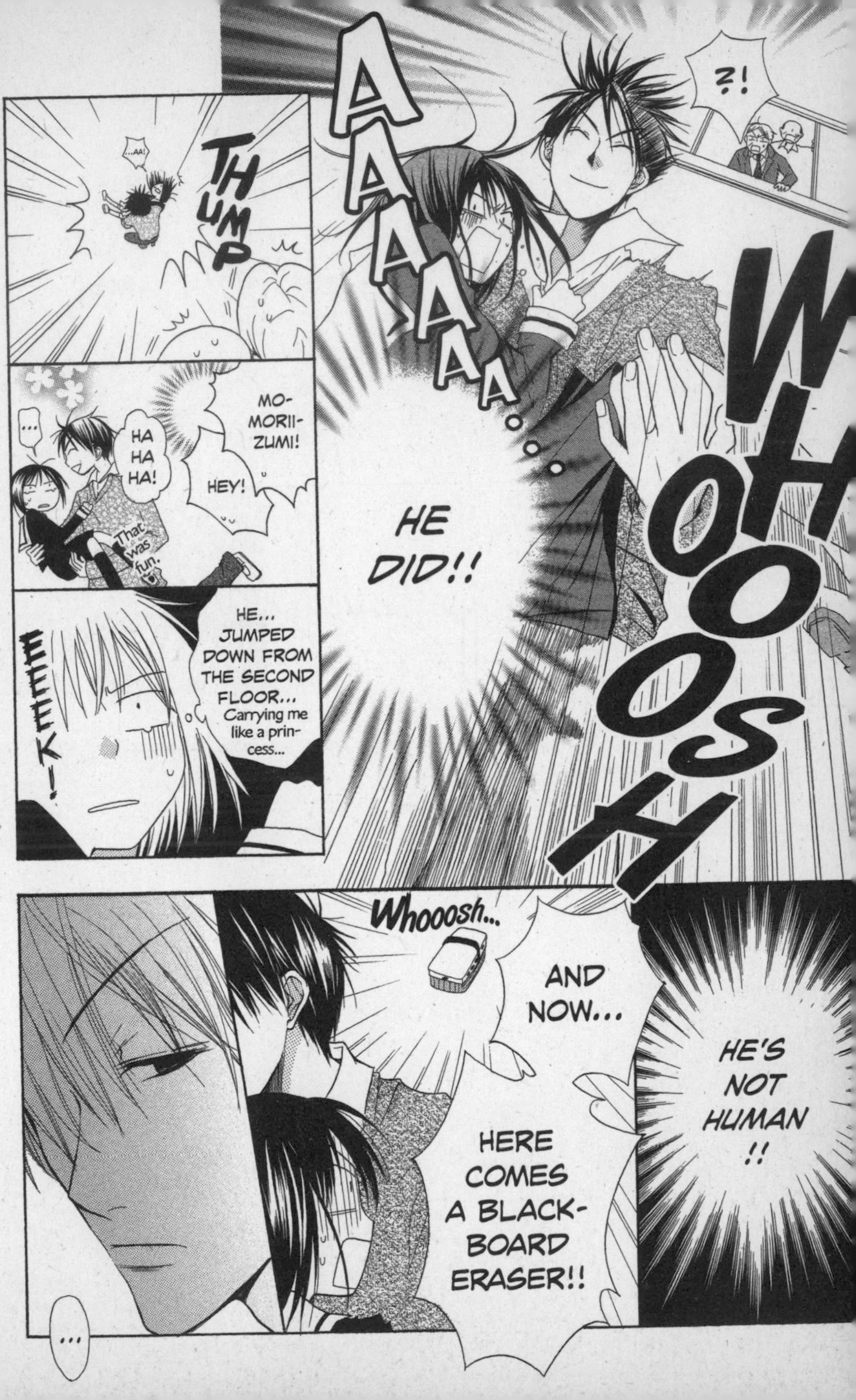
?!
AAAAAA...
WHOOOSH
HE DID!!
...AA!
THUMP
MO-MORIIZUMI!
HEY!
HA HA HA!
...
That was fun.
HE... JUMPED DOWN FROM THE SECOND FLOOR...
Carrying me like a princess...
EEEEK!
HE'S NOT HUMAN!!
Whooosh...
AND NOW...
HERE COMES A BLACKBOARD ERASER!!
...

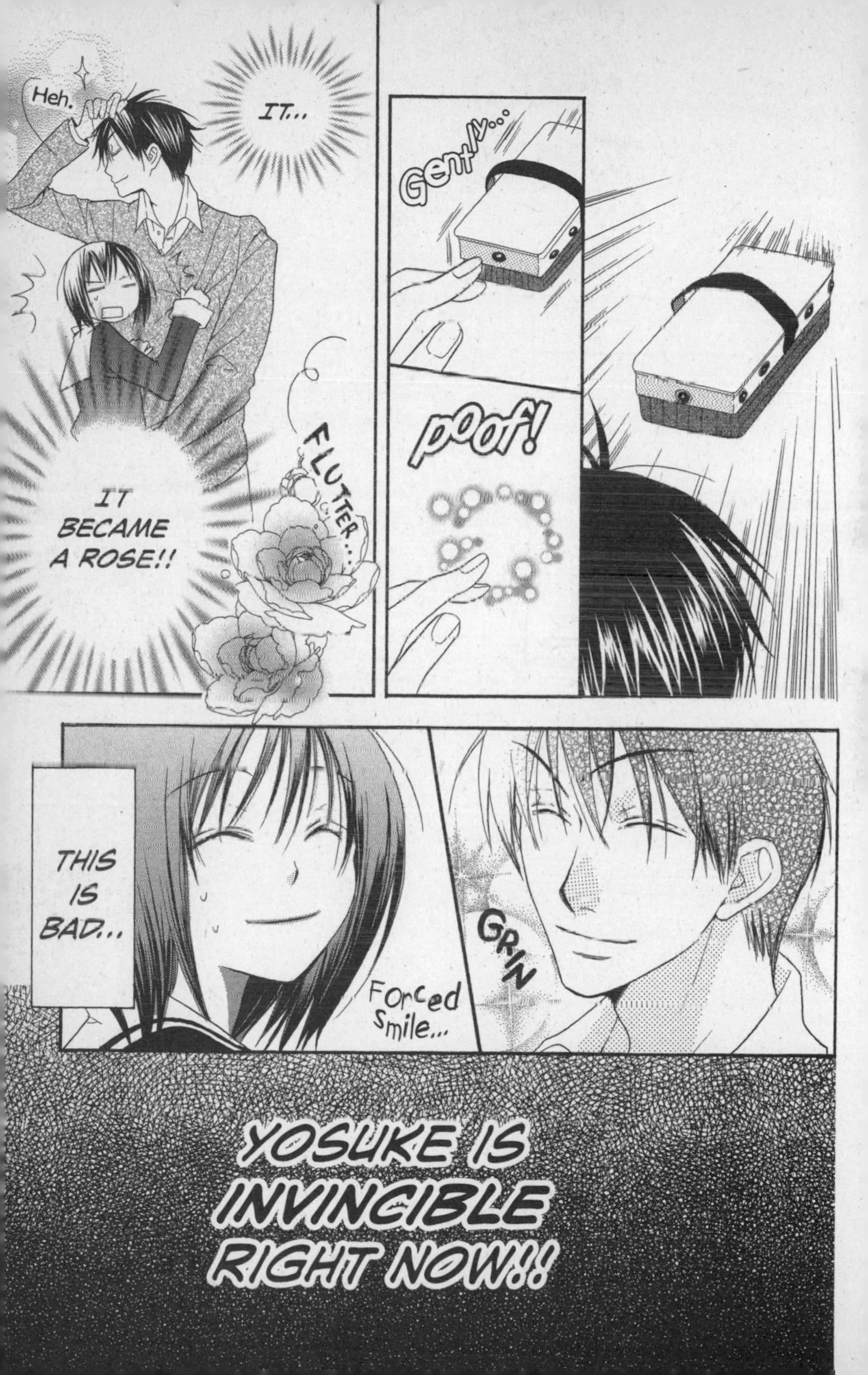
Gently...
poof!
Heh.
IT...
IT BECAME A ROSE!!
FLUTTER...
GRIN
THIS IS BAD...
Forced smile...
YOSUKE IS INVINCIBLE RIGHT NOW!!

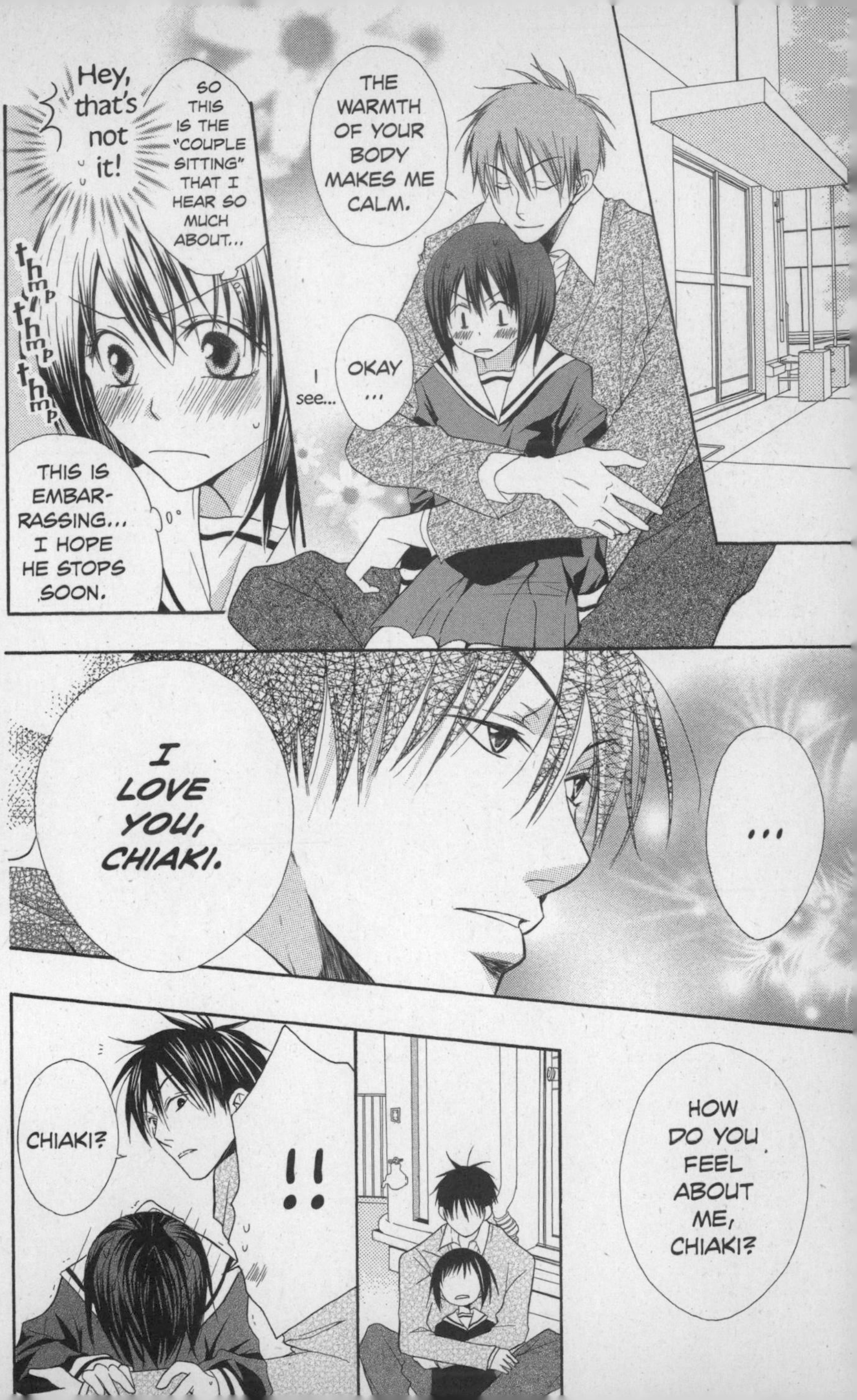
THE WARMTH OF YOUR BODY MAKES ME CALM.
OKAY ...
I see...
SO THIS IS THE "COUPLE SITTING" THAT I HEAR SO MUCH ABOUT...
Hey, that's not it!
thmp thmp thmp
THIS IS EMBARRASSING... I HOPE HE STOPS SOON.
I LOVE YOU, CHIAKI.
...
HOW DO YOU FEEL ABOUT ME, CHIAKI?
!!
CHIAKI?

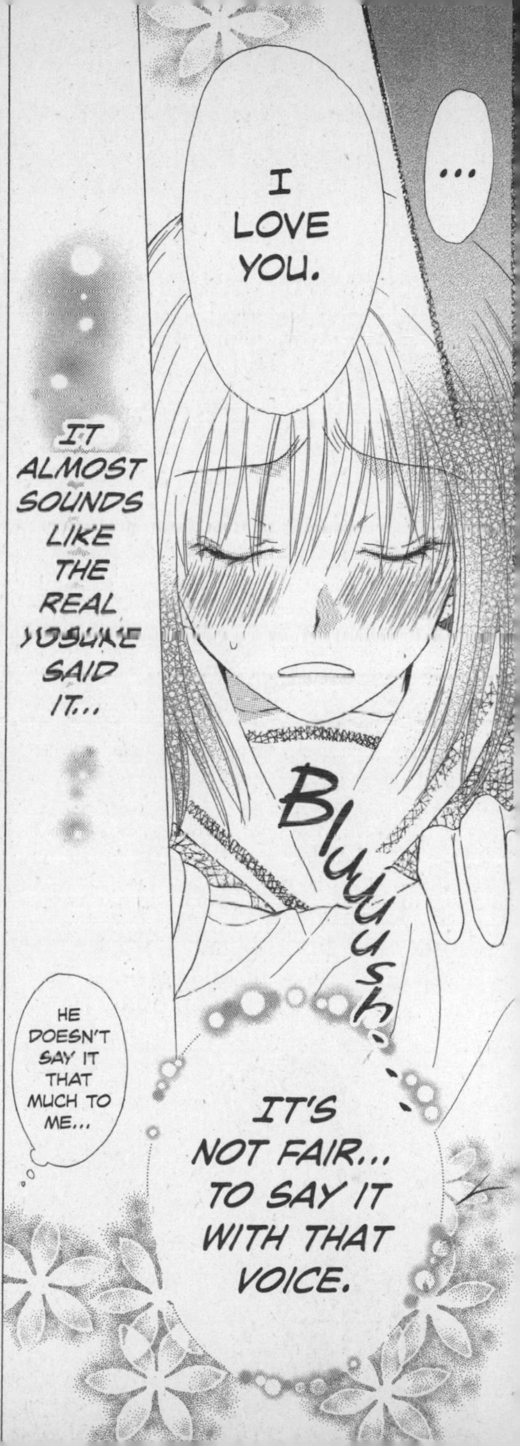
...
I LOVE YOU.
IT ALMOST SOUNDS LIKE THE REAL YOSUKE SAID IT...
Bluuush
IT'S NOT FAIR... TO SAY IT WITH THAT VOICE.
HE DOESN'T SAY IT THAT MUCH TO ME...
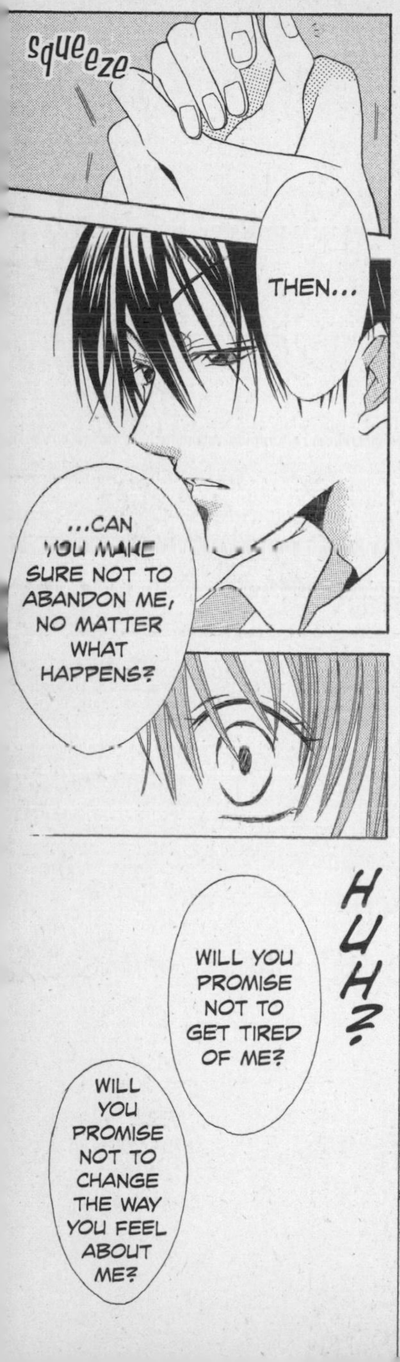
squeeze
THEN...
...CAN YOU MAKE SURE NOT TO ABANDON ME, NO MATTER WHAT HAPPENS?
HUH?
WILL YOU PROMISE NOT TO GET TIRED OF ME?
WILL YOU PROMISE NOT TO CHANGE THE WAY YOU FEEL ABOUT ME?

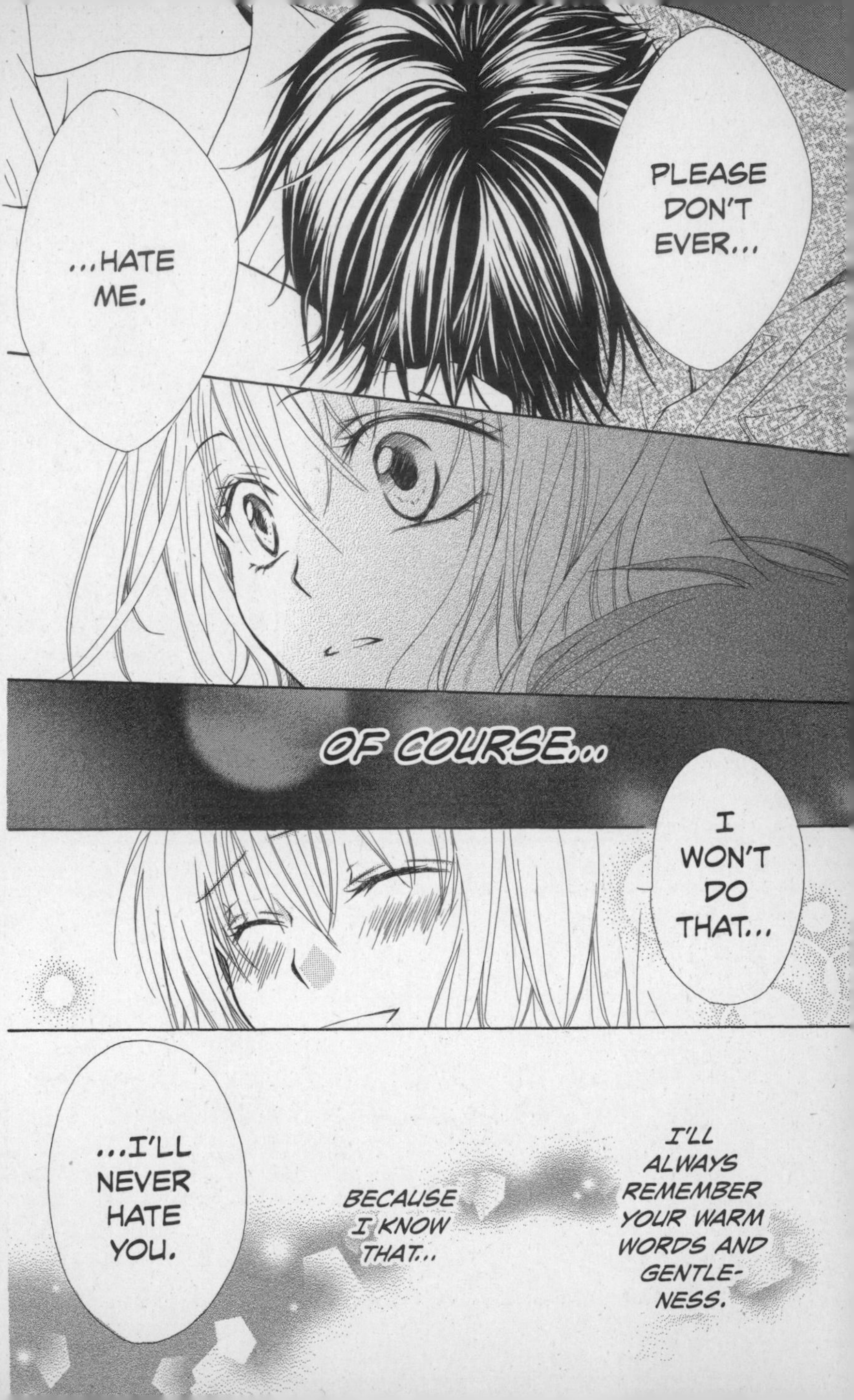
PLEASE DON'T EVER...
...HATE ME.
OF COURSE...
I WON'T DO THAT...
I'LL ALWAYS REMEMBER YOUR WARM WORDS AND GENTLE-NESS.
BECAUSE I KNOW THAT...
...I'LL NEVER HATE YOU.

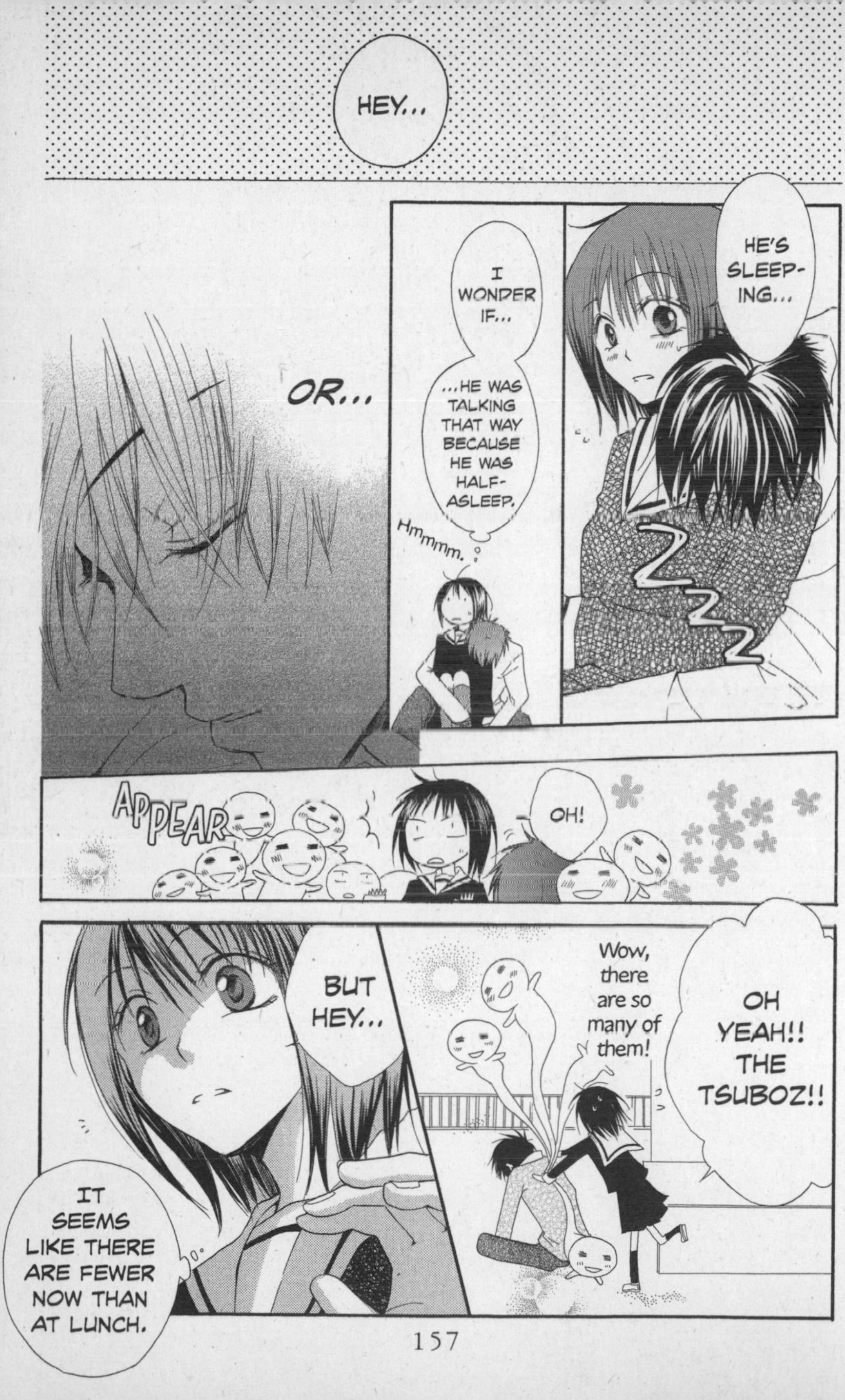
HEY...
HE'S SLEEPING...
I WONDER IF...
...HE WAS TALKING THAT WAY BECAUSE HE WAS HALF-ASLEEP.
Hmmmm.
OR...
OH!
APPEAR
OH YEAH!! THE TSUBOZ!!
Wow, there are so many of them!
BUT HEY...
IT SEEMS LIKE THERE ARE FEWER NOW THAN AT LUNCH.

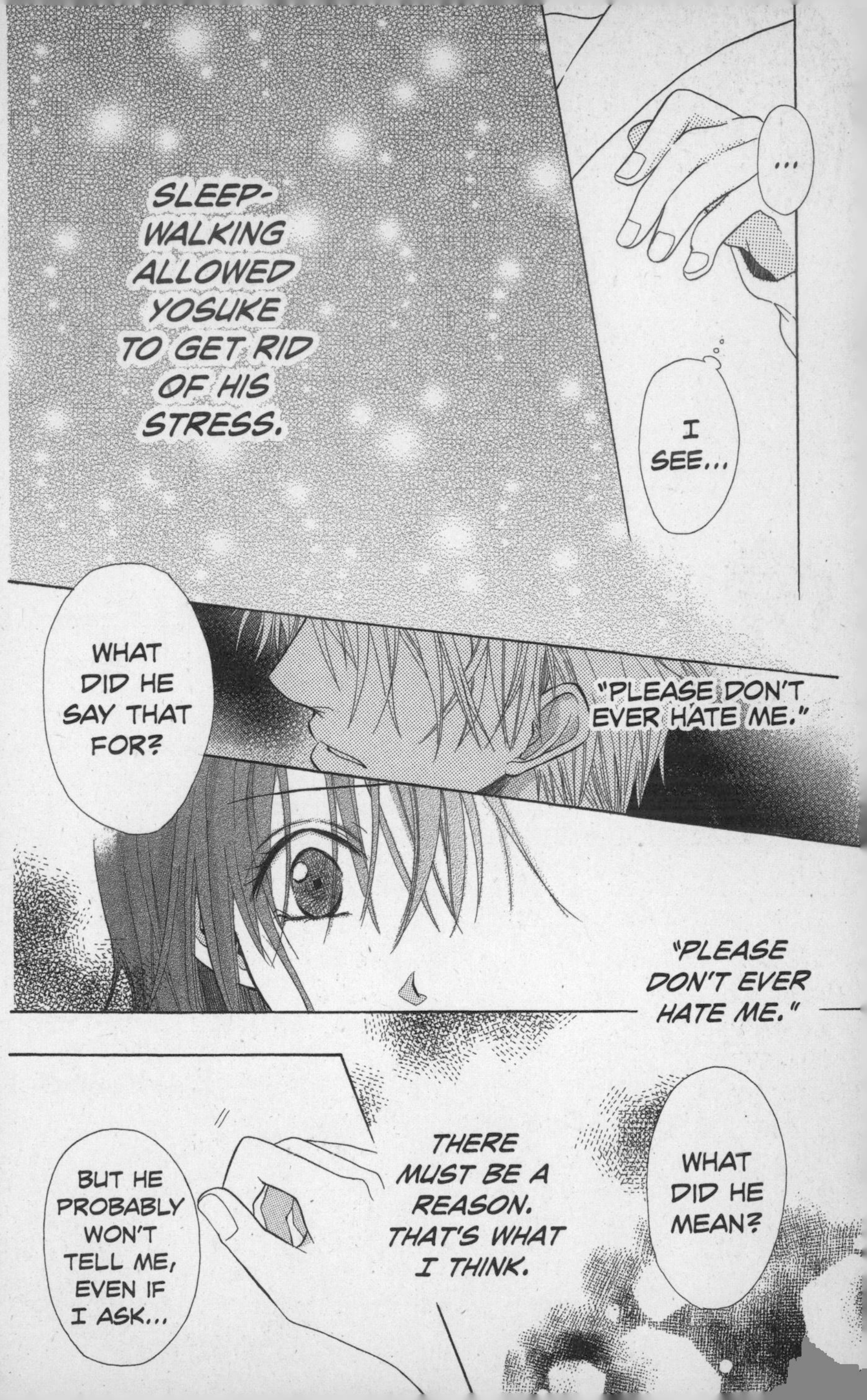
...
I SEE...
SLEEP-WALKING ALLOWED YOSUKE TO GET RID OF HIS STRESS.
"PLEASE DON'T EVER HATE ME."
WHAT DID HE SAY THAT FOR?
"PLEASE DON'T EVER HATE ME."
WHAT DID HE MEAN?
THERE MUST BE A REASON. THAT'S WHAT I THINK.
BUT HE PROBABLY WON'T TELL ME, EVEN IF I ASK...

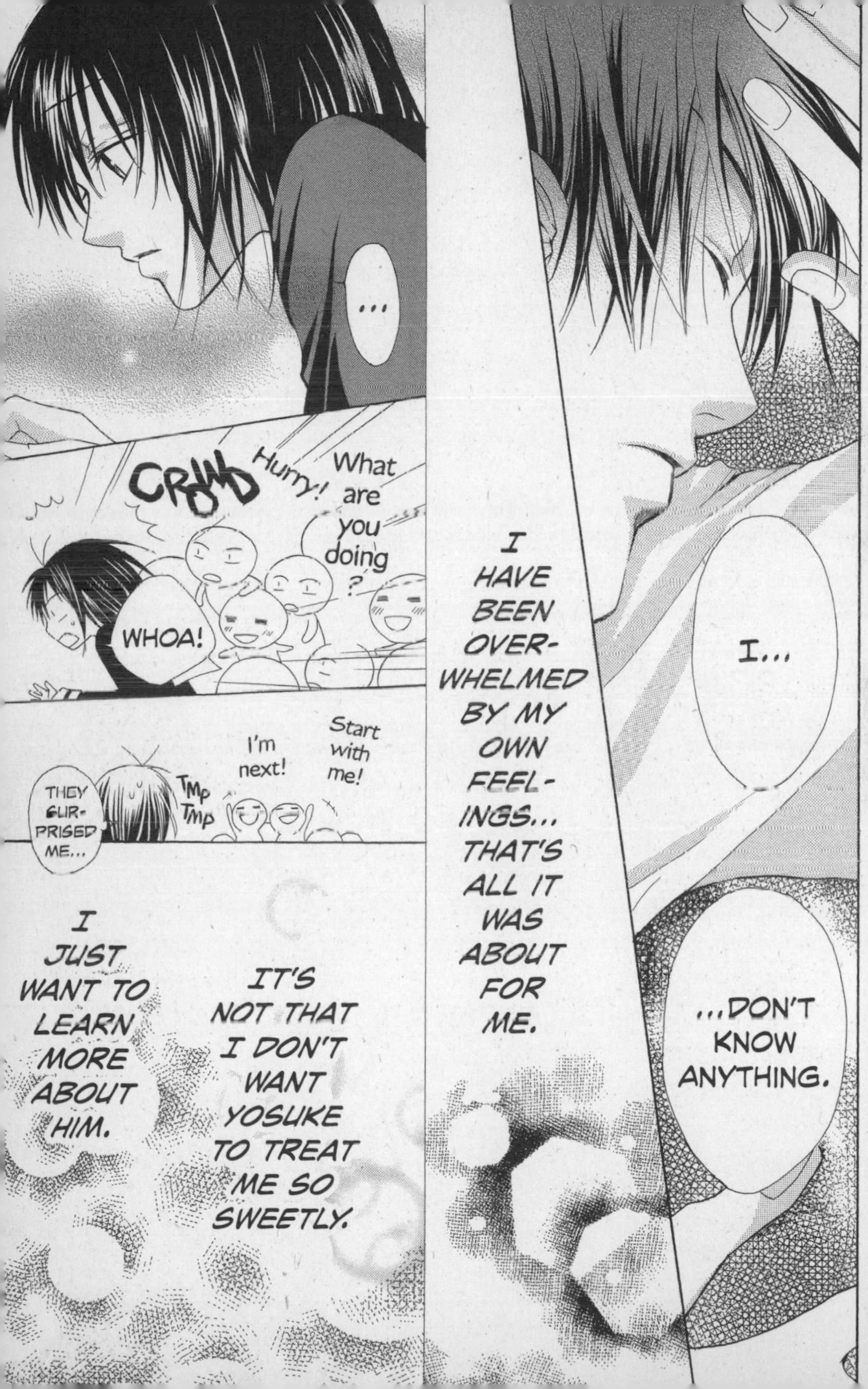
I...
...DON'T KNOW ANYTHING.
I HAVE BEEN OVER-WHELMED BY MY OWN FEEL-INGS... THAT'S ALL IT WAS ABOUT FOR ME.
...
What are you doing?
Hurry!
CROWD
WHOA!
Start with me!
I'm next!
TMP TMP
THEY SUR-PRISED ME...
IT'S NOT THAT I DON'T WANT YOSUKE TO TREAT ME SO SWEETLY.
I JUST WANT TO LEARN MORE ABOUT HIM.

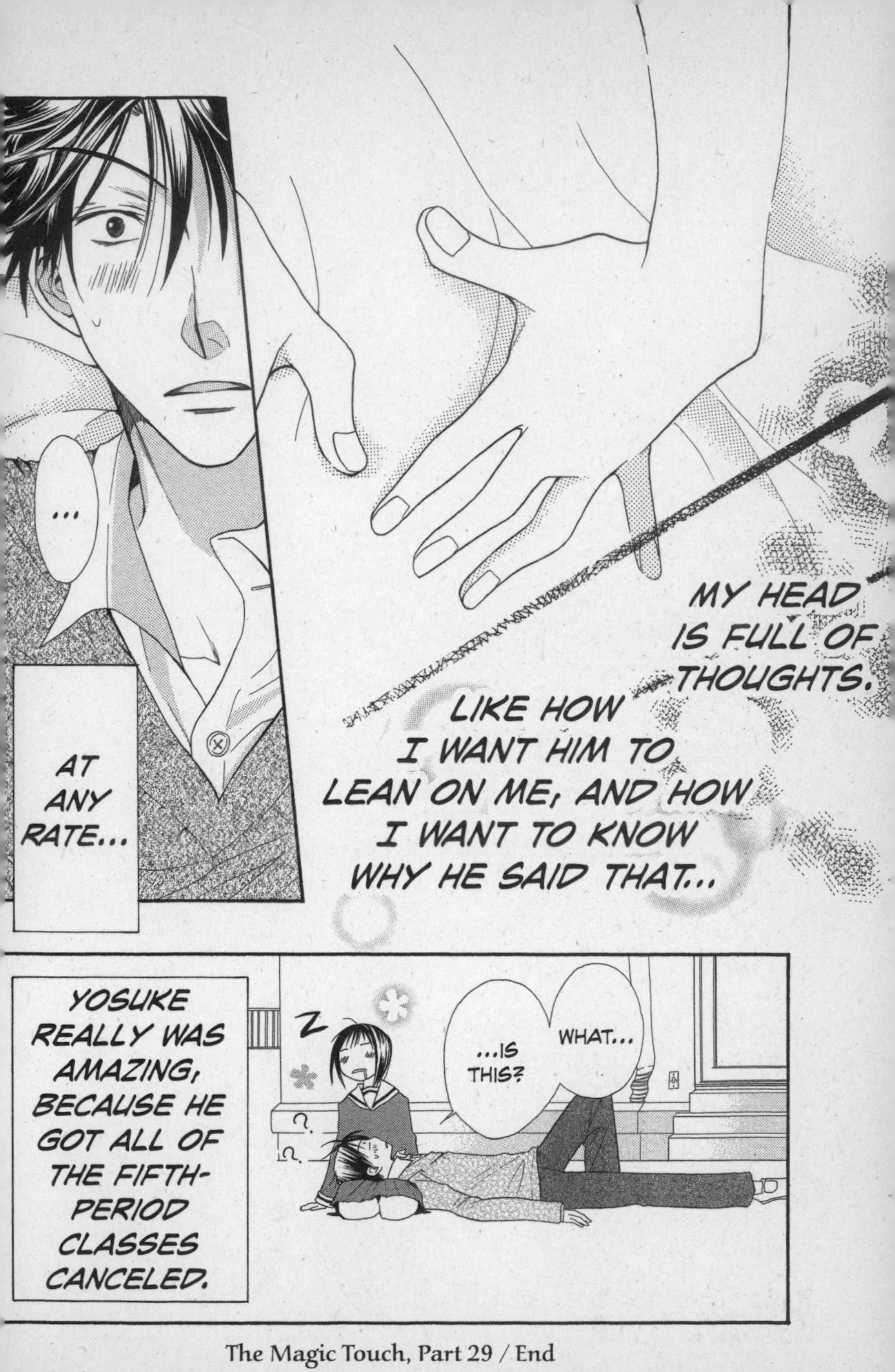
MY HEAD IS FULL OF THOUGHTS.
LIKE HOW I WANT HIM TO LEAN ON ME, AND HOW I WANT TO KNOW WHY HE SAID THAT...
...
AT ANY RATE...
WHAT... ...IS THIS?
Z
YOSUKE REALLY WAS AMAZING, BECAUSE HE GOT ALL OF THE FIFTH-PERIOD CLASSES CANCELED.

The Magic Touch, Part 29 / End

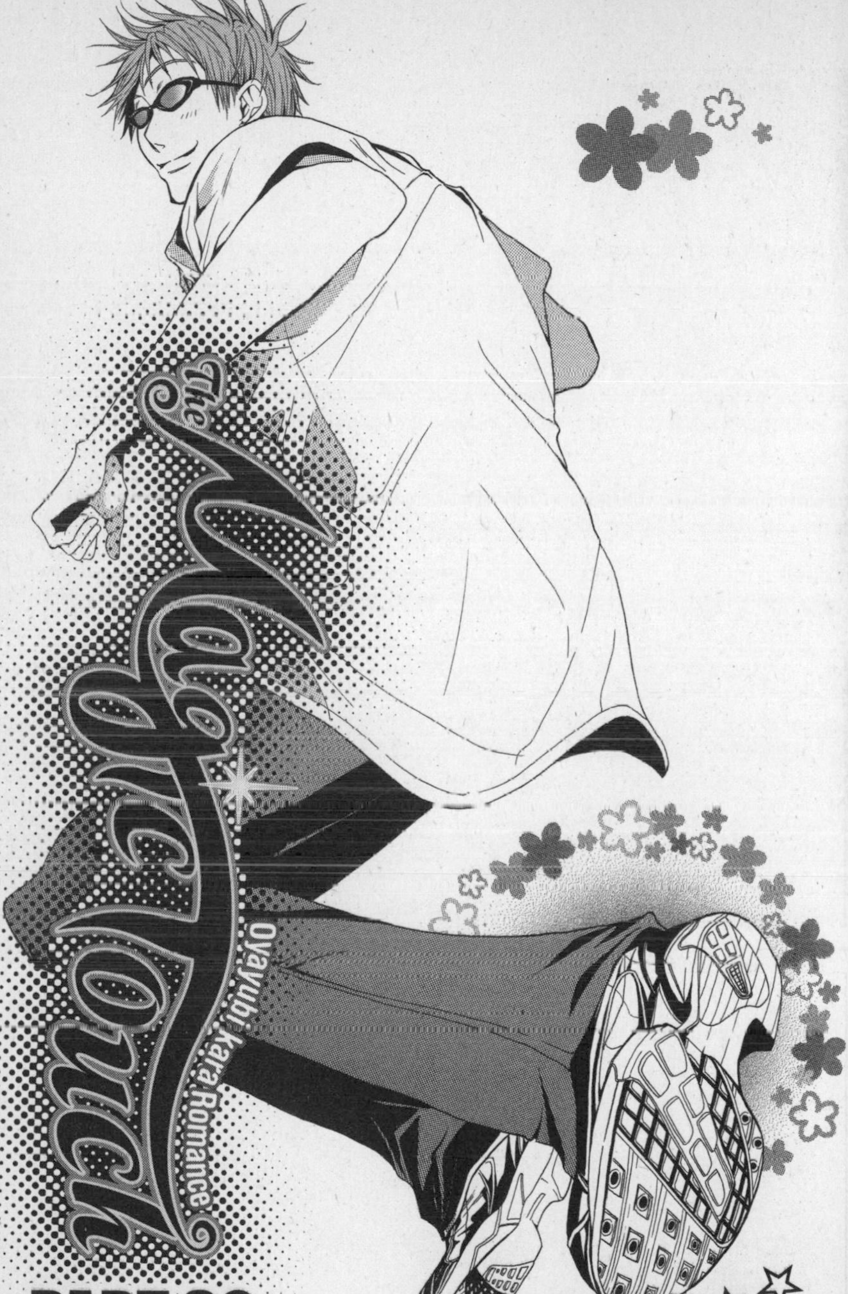
The Magic Touch
Oyayubi kara Romance
PART 30

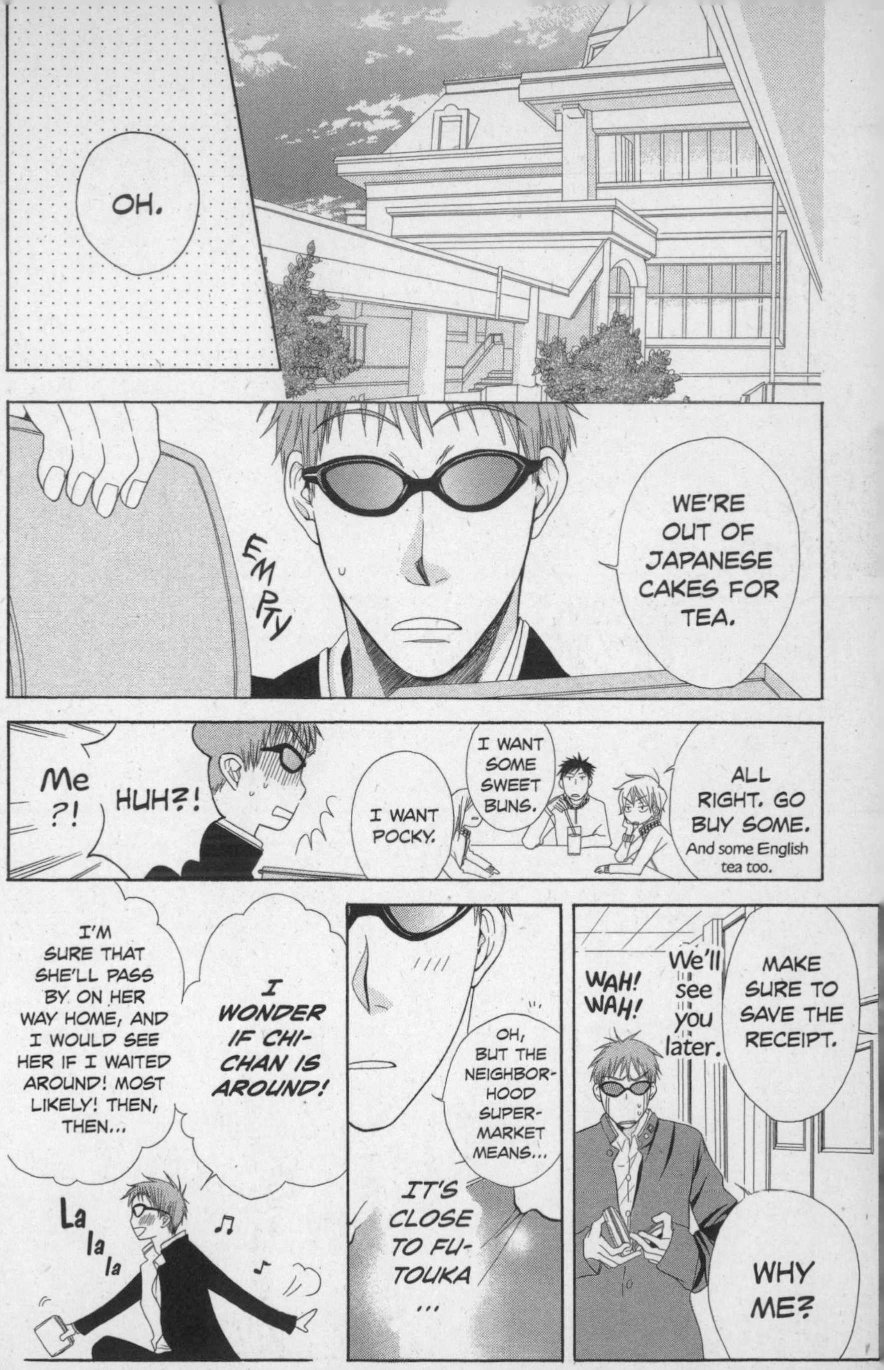
OH.
WE'RE OUT OF JAPANESE CAKES FOR TEA.
EMPTY
ALL RIGHT. GO BUY SOME.
And some English tea too.
I WANT SOME SWEET BUNS.
I WANT POCKY.
HUH?!
Me ?!
MAKE SURE TO SAVE THE RECEIPT.
We'll see you later.
WAH! WAH!
WHY ME?
OH, BUT THE NEIGHBORHOOD SUPERMARKET MEANS...
IT'S CLOSE TO FUTOUKA...
I WONDER IF CHI-CHAN IS AROUND!
I'M SURE THAT SHE'LL PASS BY ON HER WAY HOME, AND I WOULD SEE HER IF I WAITED AROUND! MOST LIKELY! THEN, THEN...
La la la

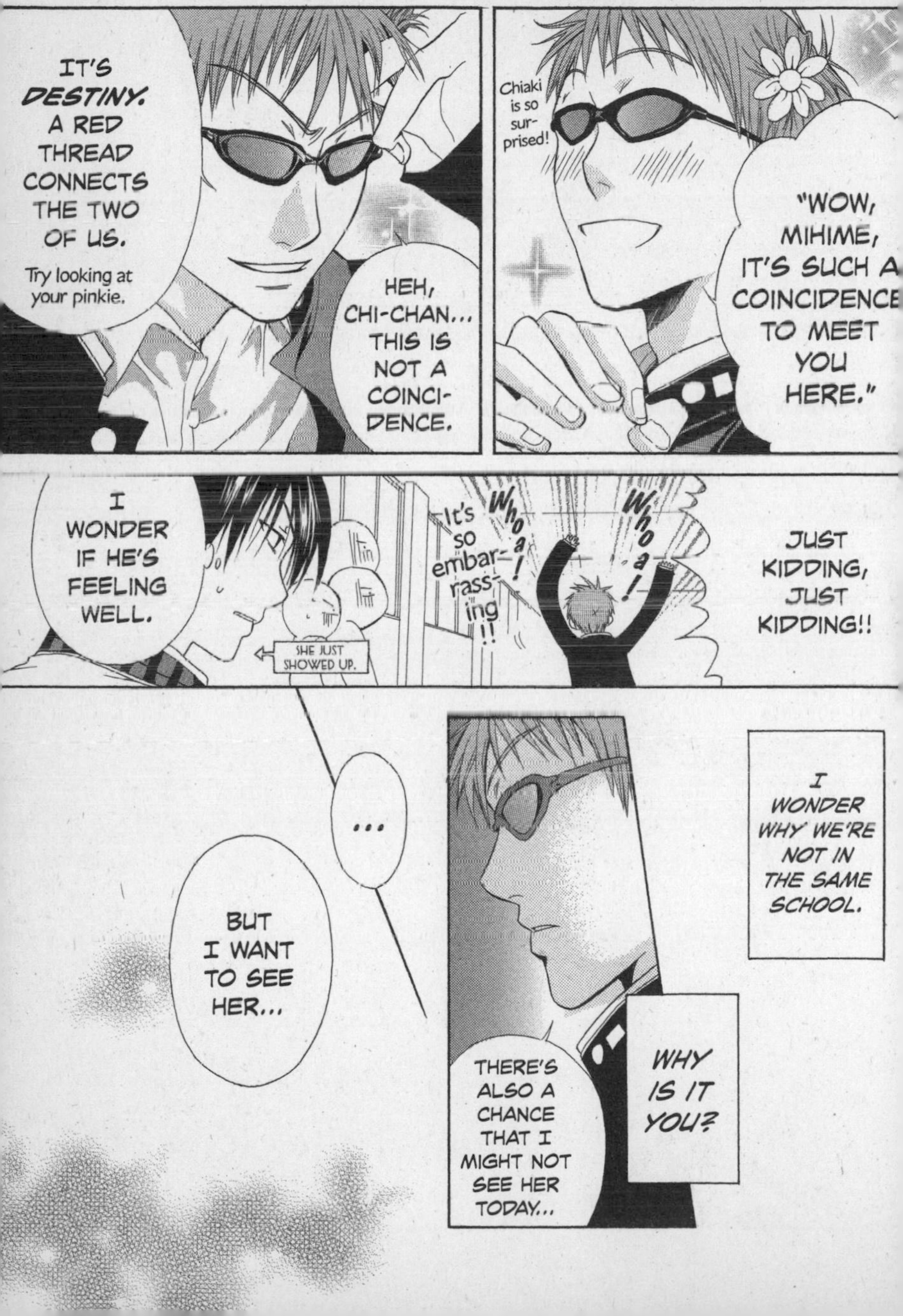
Chiaki is so surprised!
"WOW, MIHIME, IT'S SUCH A COINCIDENCE TO MEET YOU HERE."
HEH, CHI-CHAN... THIS IS NOT A COINCIDENCE.
IT'S DESTINY. A RED THREAD CONNECTS THE TWO OF US.
Try looking at your pinkie.
JUST KIDDING, JUST KIDDING!!
Whoa!
Whoa!
It's so embarrassing!!
SHE JUST SHOWED UP.
I WONDER IF HE'S FEELING WELL.
I WONDER WHY WE'RE NOT IN THE SAME SCHOOL.
WHY IS IT YOU?
THERE'S ALSO A CHANCE THAT I MIGHT NOT SEE HER TODAY...
...
BUT I WANT TO SEE HER...

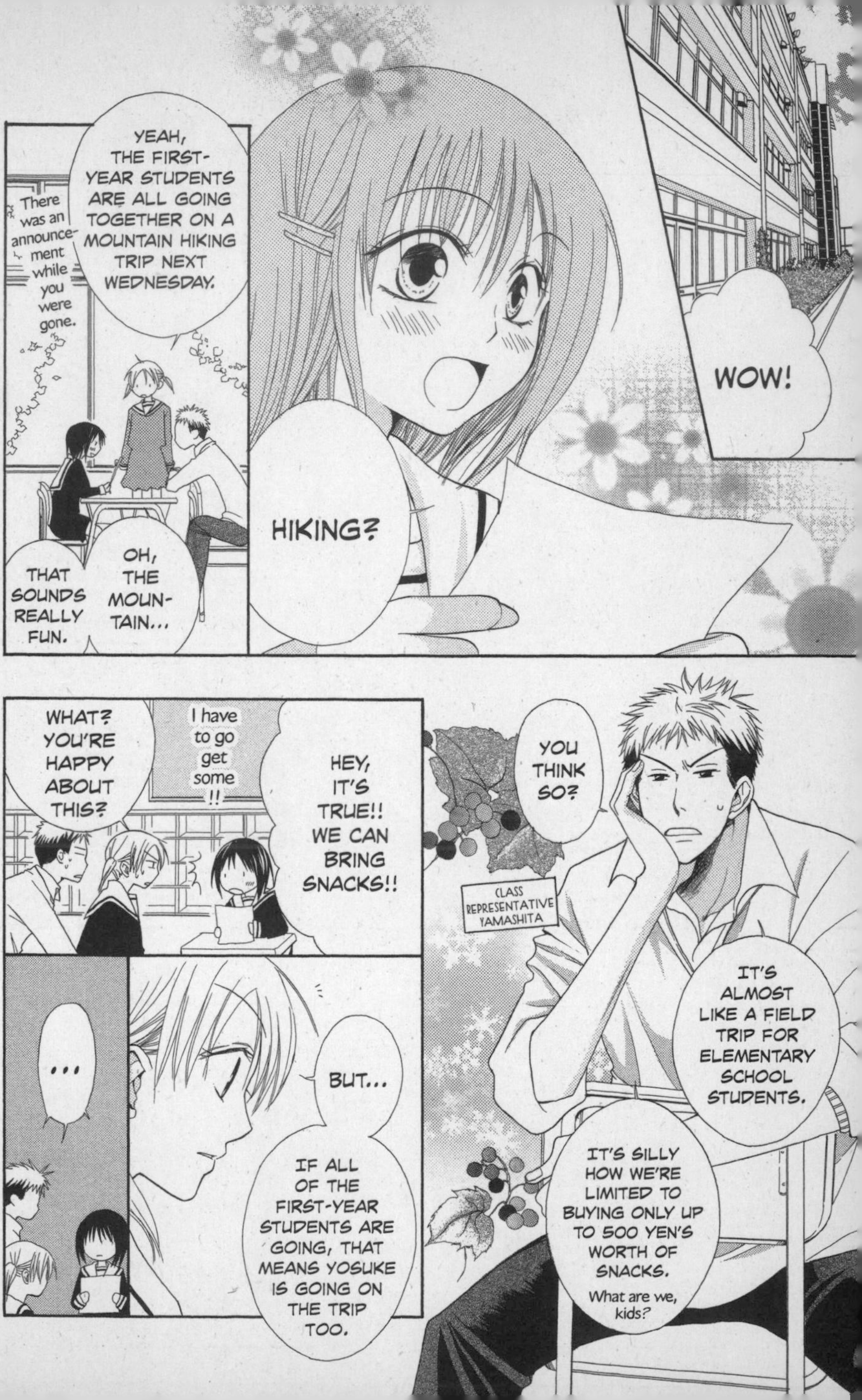
WOW!
HIKING?
YEAH, THE FIRST-YEAR STUDENTS ARE ALL GOING TOGETHER ON A MOUNTAIN HIKING TRIP NEXT WEDNESDAY.
There was an announcement while you were gone.
OH, THE MOUNTAIN...
THAT SOUNDS REALLY FUN.
YOU THINK SO?
CLASS REPRESENTATIVE YAMASHITA
IT'S ALMOST LIKE A FIELD TRIP FOR ELEMENTARY SCHOOL STUDENTS.
IT'S SILLY HOW WE'RE LIMITED TO BUYING ONLY UP TO 500 YEN'S WORTH OF SNACKS.
What are we, kids?
HEY, IT'S TRUE!! WE CAN BRING SNACKS!!
I have to go get some!!
WHAT? YOU'RE HAPPY ABOUT THIS?
BUT...
IF ALL OF THE FIRST-YEAR STUDENTS ARE GOING, THAT MEANS YOSUKE IS GOING ON THE TRIP TOO.
...

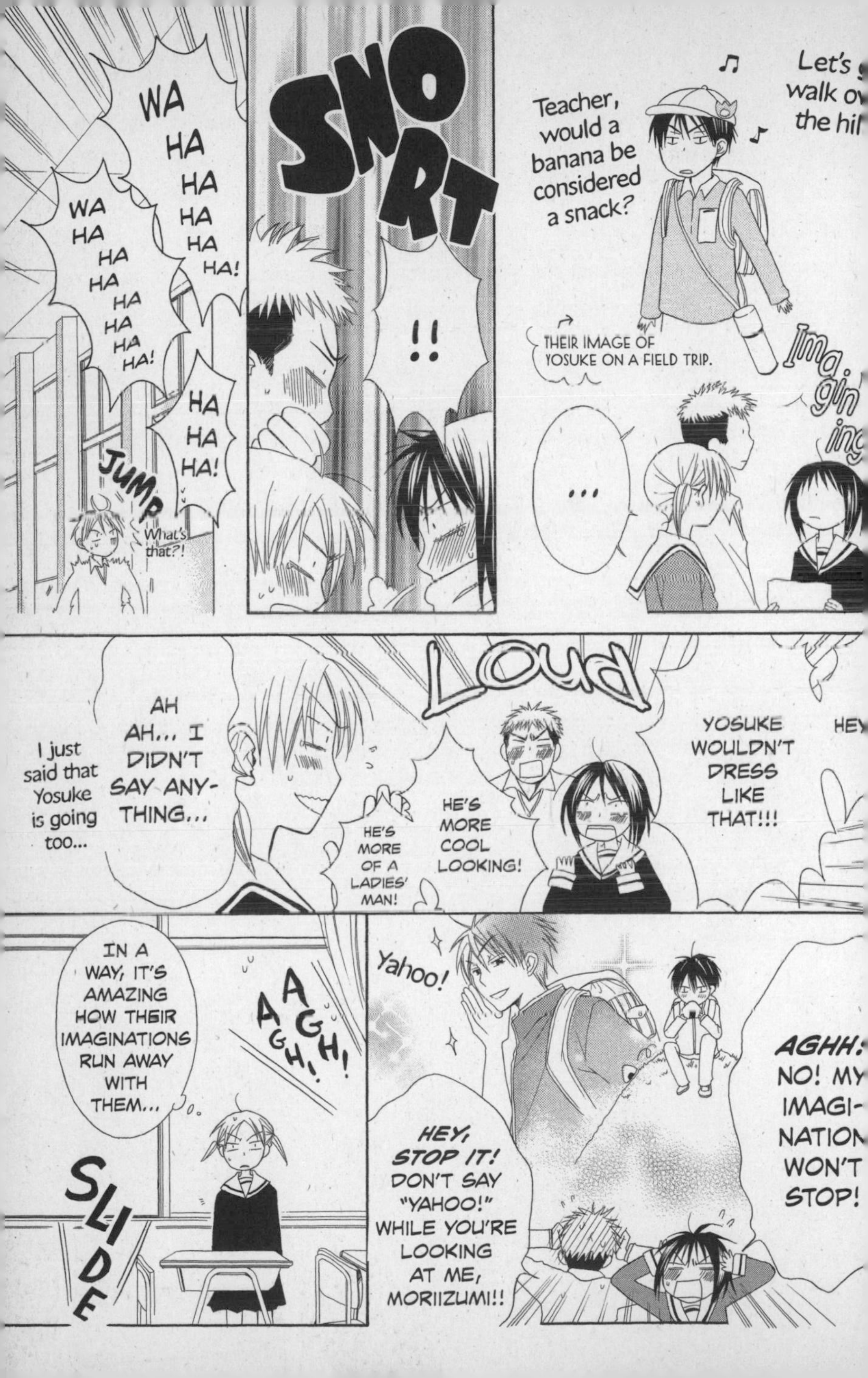

Let's walk ov the hil
Teacher, would a banana be considered a snack?
THEIR IMAGE OF YOSUKE ON A FIELD TRIP.
Imagining
...
SNORT
!!
WA HA HA HA HA HA!
WA HA HA HA HA HA HA HA!
HA HA HA!
JUMP
What's that?!
HE
YOSUKE WOULDN'T DRESS LIKE THAT!!!
Loud
HE'S MORE COOL LOOKING!
HE'S MORE OF A LADIES' MAN!
AH AH... I DIDN'T SAY ANY-THING...
I just said that Yosuke is going too...
AGHH! NO! MY IMAGI-NATION WON'T STOP!
Yahoo!
HEY, STOP IT! DON'T SAY "YAHOO!" WHILE YOU'RE LOOKING AT ME, MORIIZUMI!!
AAGHH!
IN A WAY, IT'S AMAZING HOW THEIR IMAGINATIONS RUN AWAY WITH THEM...
SLIDE

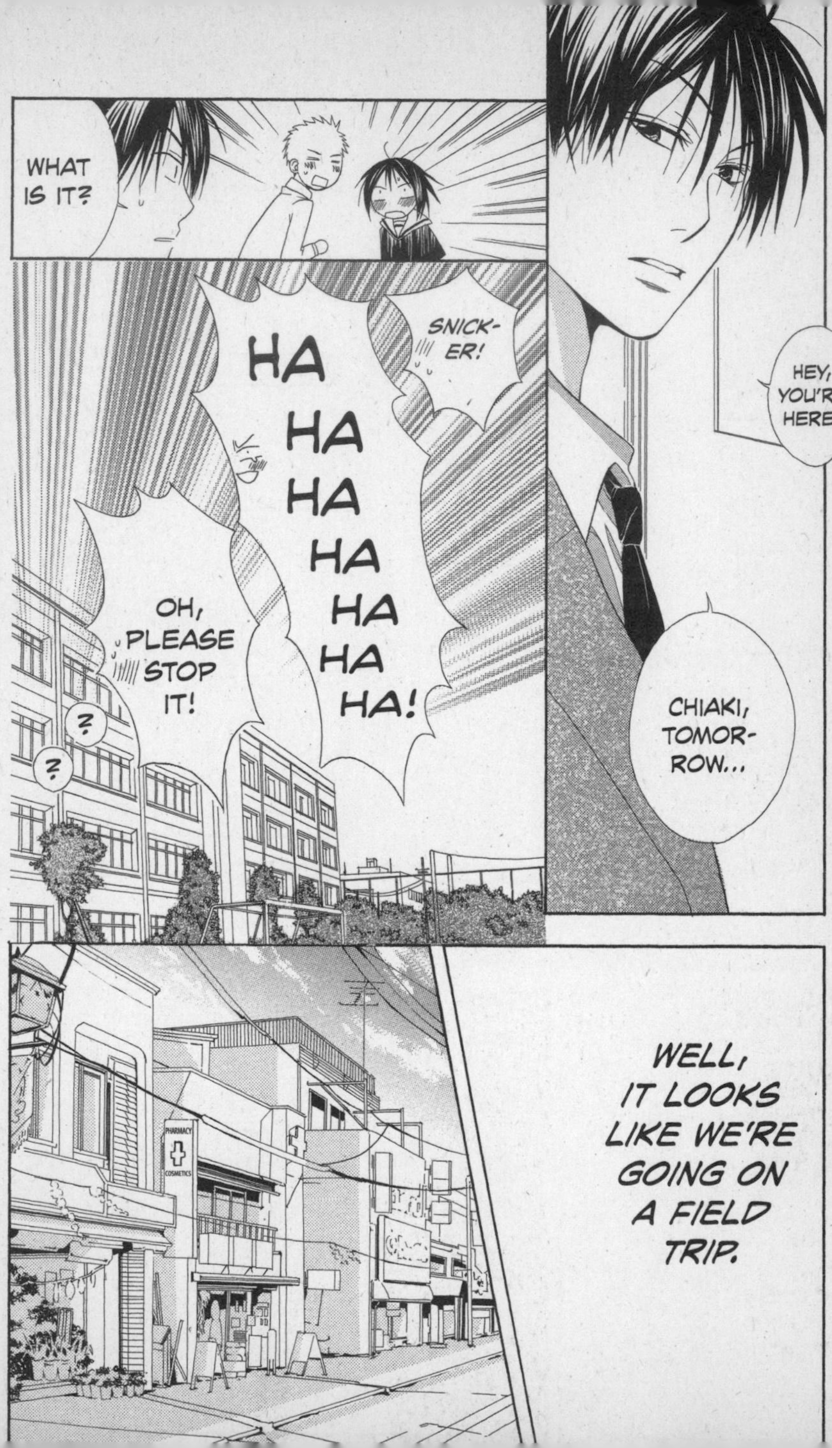
HEY, YOU'RE HERE.
CHIAKI, TOMORROW...
WHAT IS IT?
SNICKER!
HA HA HA HA HA HA HA!
OH, PLEASE STOP IT!
?
?
WELL, IT LOOKS LIKE WE'RE GOING ON A FIELD TRIP.
PHARMACY
COSMETICS

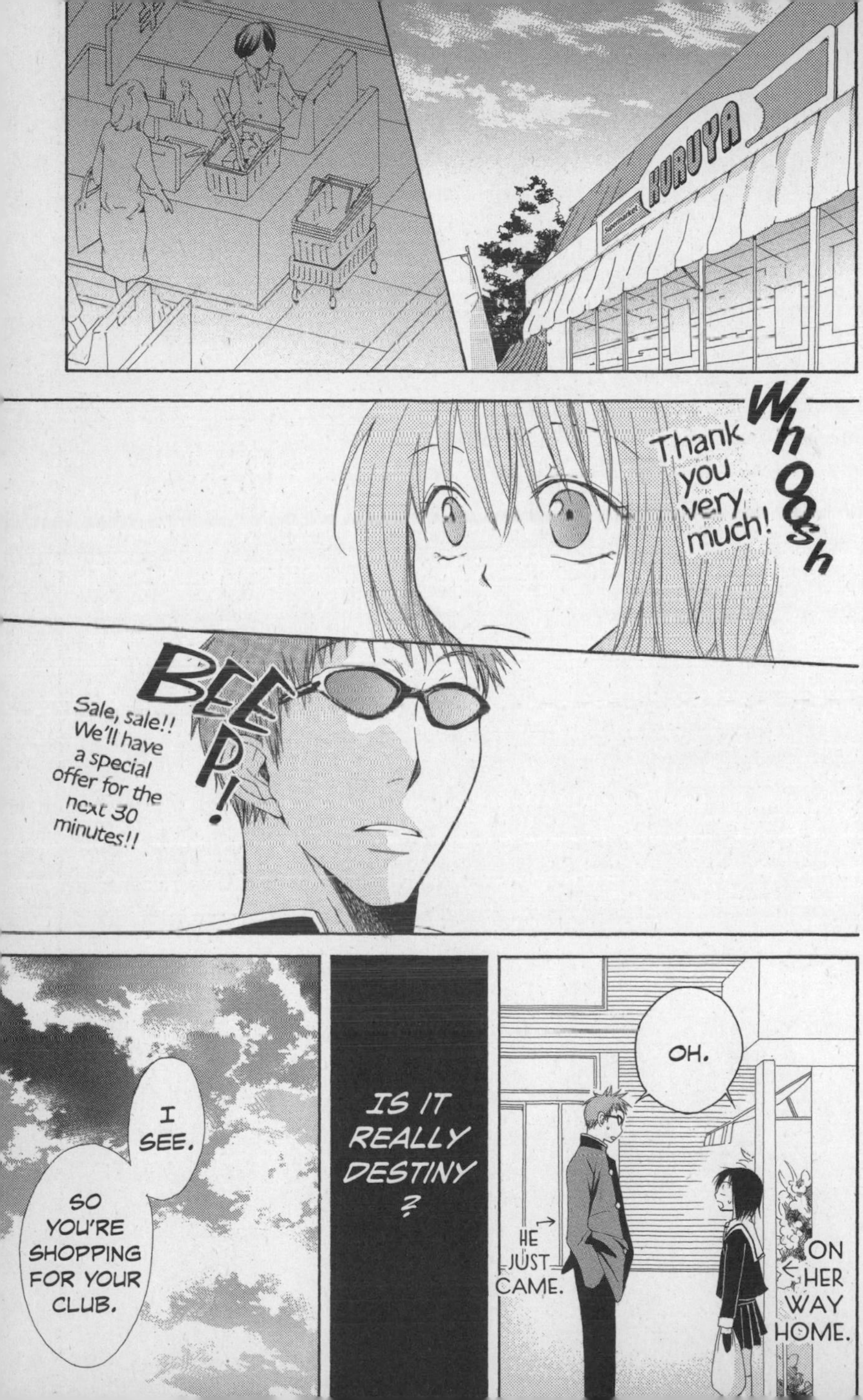
Supermarket
HURUYA
Whoosh
Thank you very much!
BEEP!
Sale, sale!! We'll have a special offer for the ncxt 30 minutes!!
OH.
ON HER WAY HOME.
HE JUST CAME.
IS IT REALLY DESTINY?
I SEE.
SO YOU'RE SHOPPING FOR YOUR CLUB.

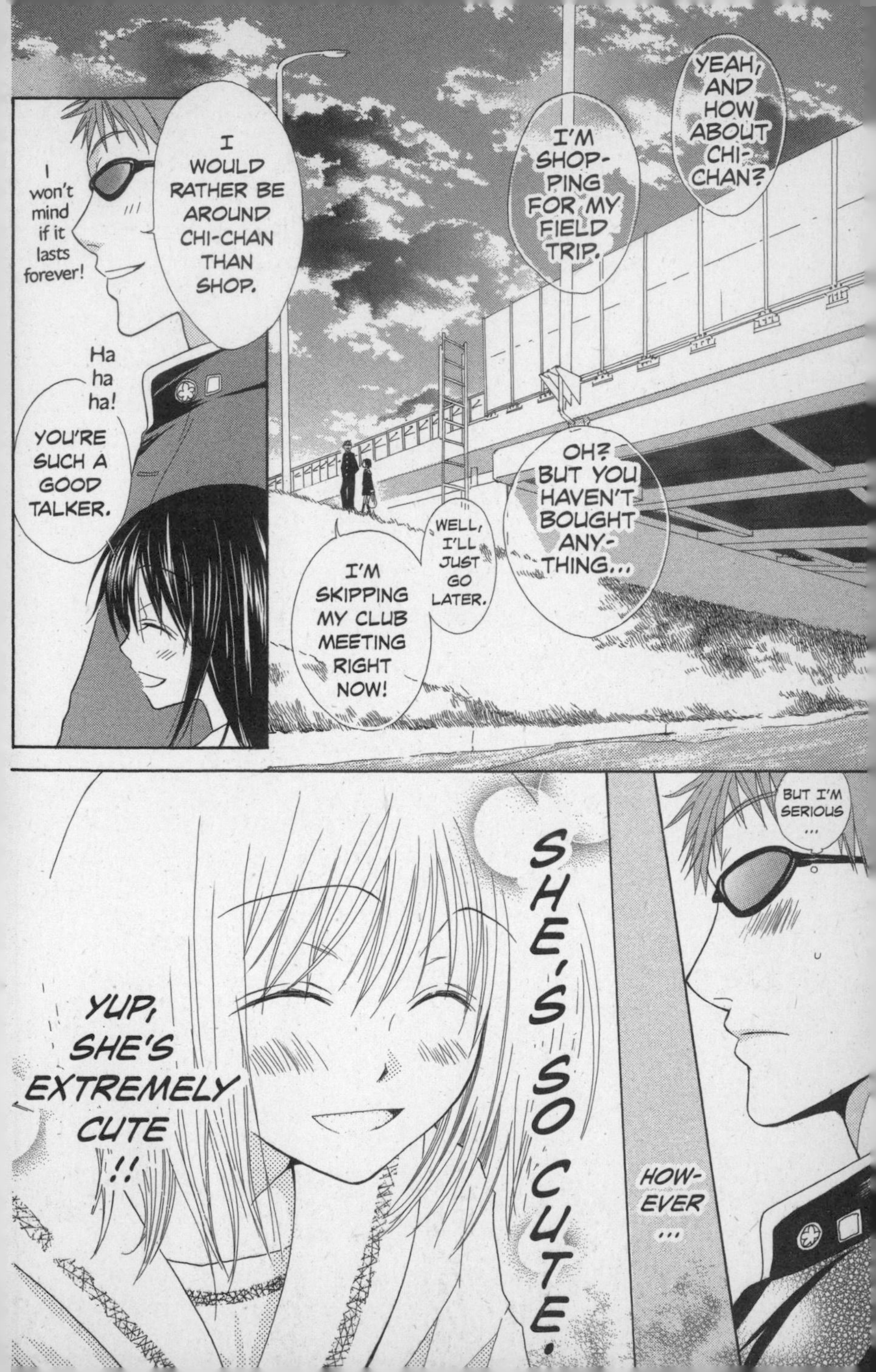
YEAH, AND HOW ABOUT CHI-CHAN?
I'M SHOP-PING FOR MY FIELD TRIP.
OH? BUT YOU HAVEN'T BOUGHT ANY-THING...
WELL, I'LL JUST GO LATER.
I'M SKIPPING MY CLUB MEETING RIGHT NOW!
I WOULD RATHER BE AROUND CHI-CHAN THAN SHOP.
I won't mind if it lasts forever!
Ha ha ha!
YOU'RE SUCH A GOOD TALKER.
BUT I'M SERIOUS...
HOW-EVER...
SHE'S SO CUTE.
YUP, SHE'S EXTREMELY CUTE!!

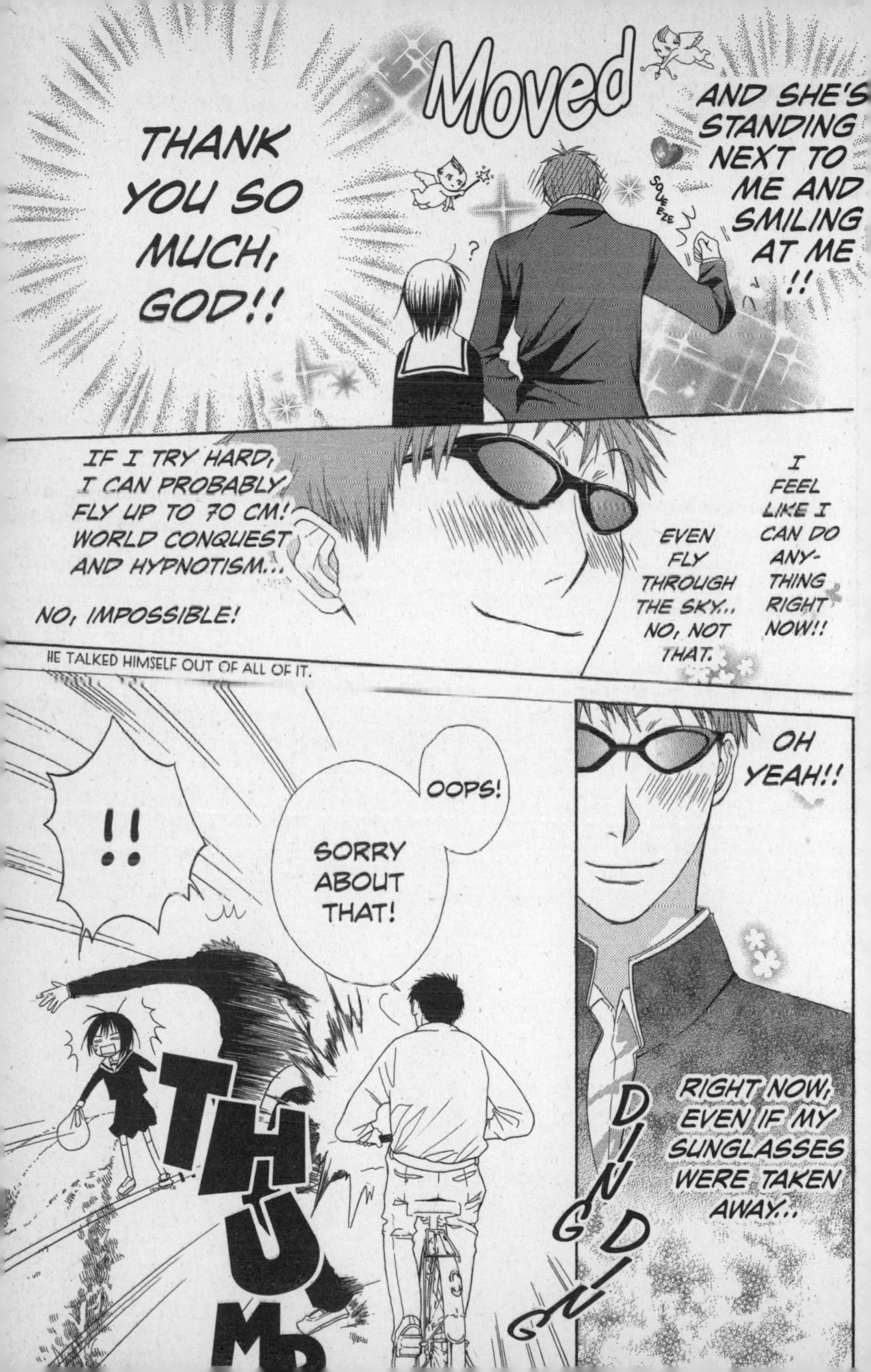
AND SHE'S STANDING NEXT TO ME AND SMILING AT ME!!
Moved
SQUEEZE
THANK YOU SO MUCH, GOD!!
I FEEL LIKE I CAN DO ANYTHING RIGHT NOW!!
EVEN FLY THROUGH THE SKY... NO, NOT THAT.
IF I TRY HARD, I CAN PROBABLY FLY UP TO 70 CM! WORLD CONQUEST AND HYPNOTISM...
NO, IMPOSSIBLE!
HE TALKED HIMSELF OUT OF ALL OF IT.
OH YEAH!!
RIGHT NOW, EVEN IF MY SUNGLASSES WERE TAKEN AWAY...
DING DING
OOPS!
SORRY ABOUT THAT!
!!
THUMP

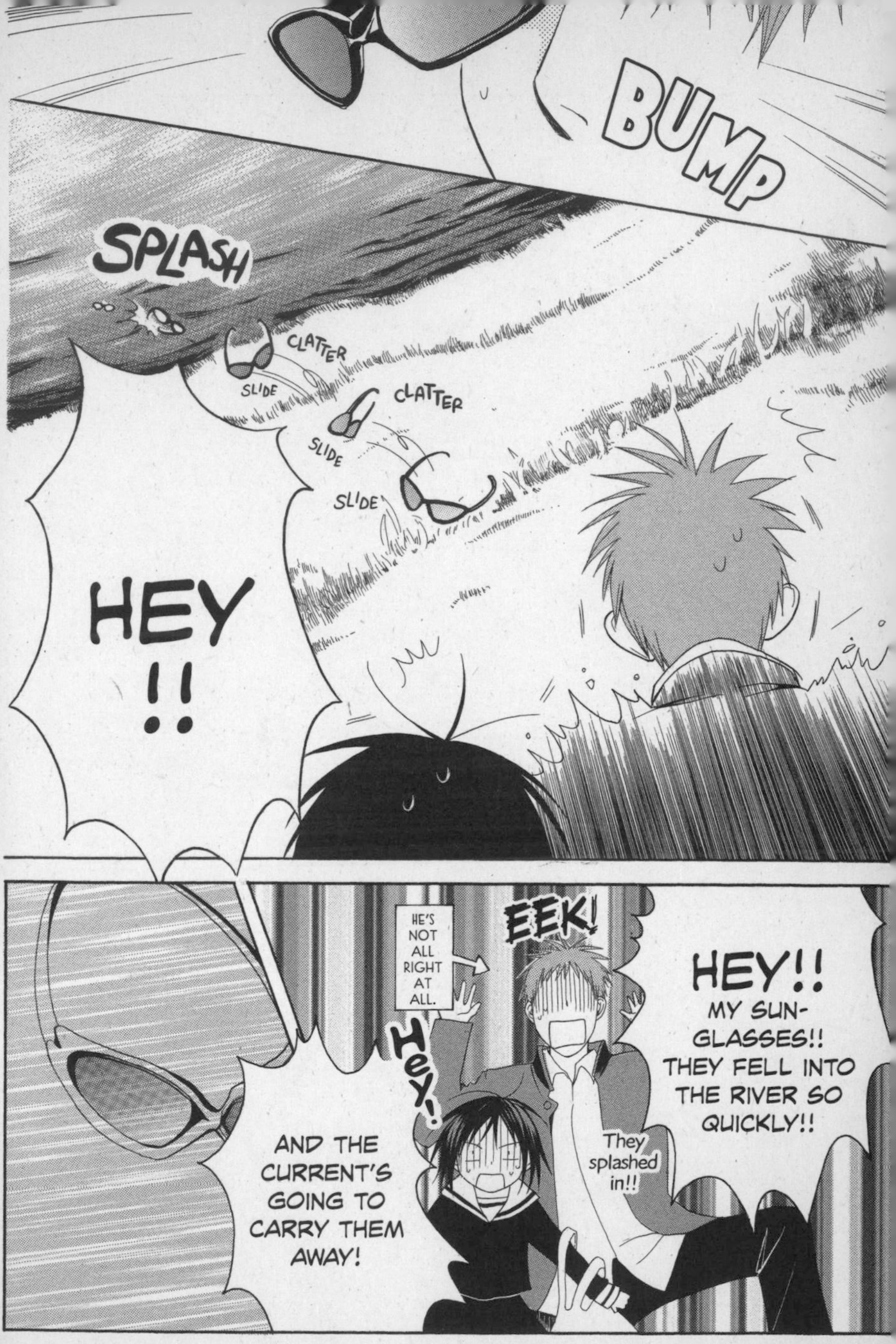
BUMP
SPLASH
CLATTER
SLIDE
CLATTER
SLIDE
SLIDE
HEY!!
HEY!! MY SUN-GLASSES!! THEY FELL INTO THE RIVER SO QUICKLY!!
They splashed in!!
EEK!
HE'S NOT ALL RIGHT AT ALL.
Hey!
AND THE CURRENT'S GOING TO CARRY THEM AWAY!

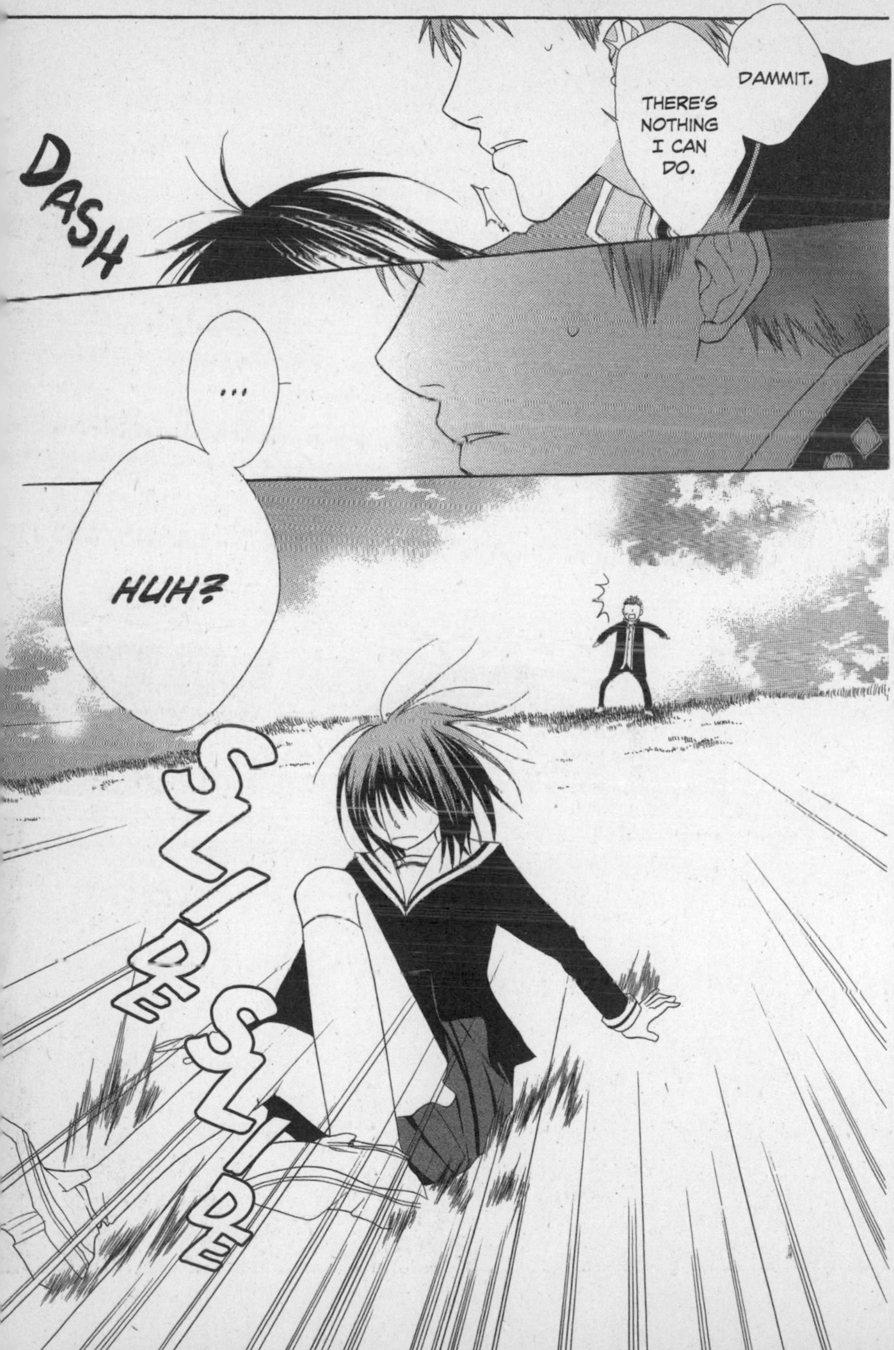
DAMMIT.
THERE'S NOTHING I CAN DO.
DASH
...
HUH?
SLIDE SLIDE

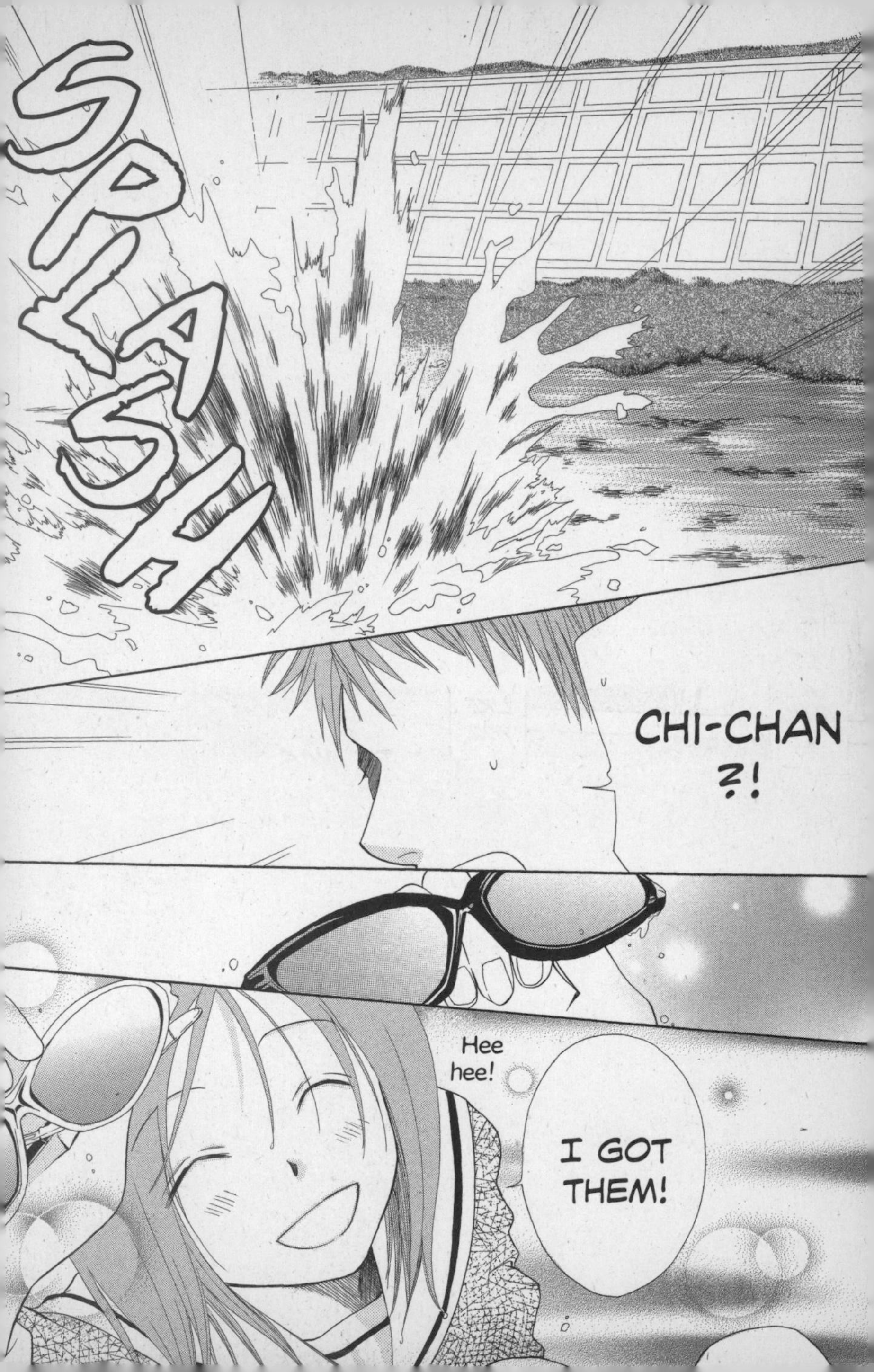
SPLASH
CHI-CHAN ?!
Hee hee!
I GOT THEM!

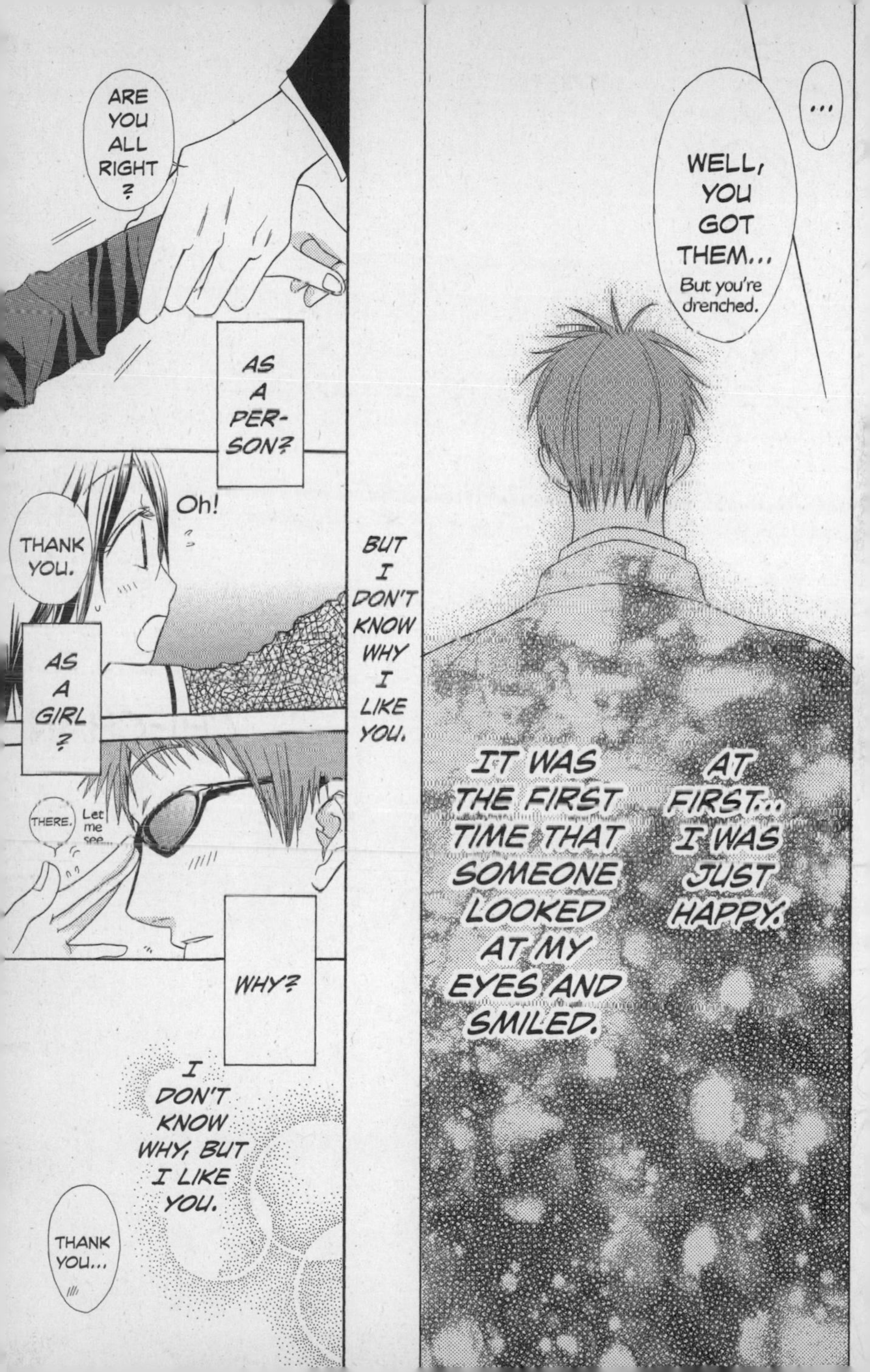
...
WELL, YOU GOT THEM... But you're drenched.
AT FIRST... I WAS JUST HAPPY.
IT WAS THE FIRST TIME THAT SOMEONE LOOKED AT MY EYES AND SMILED.
BUT I DON'T KNOW WHY I LIKE YOU.
ARE YOU ALL RIGHT?
AS A PERSON?
Oh!
THANK YOU.
AS A GIRL?
Let me see...
THERE.
WHY?
I DON'T KNOW WHY, BUT I LIKE YOU.
THANK YOU...

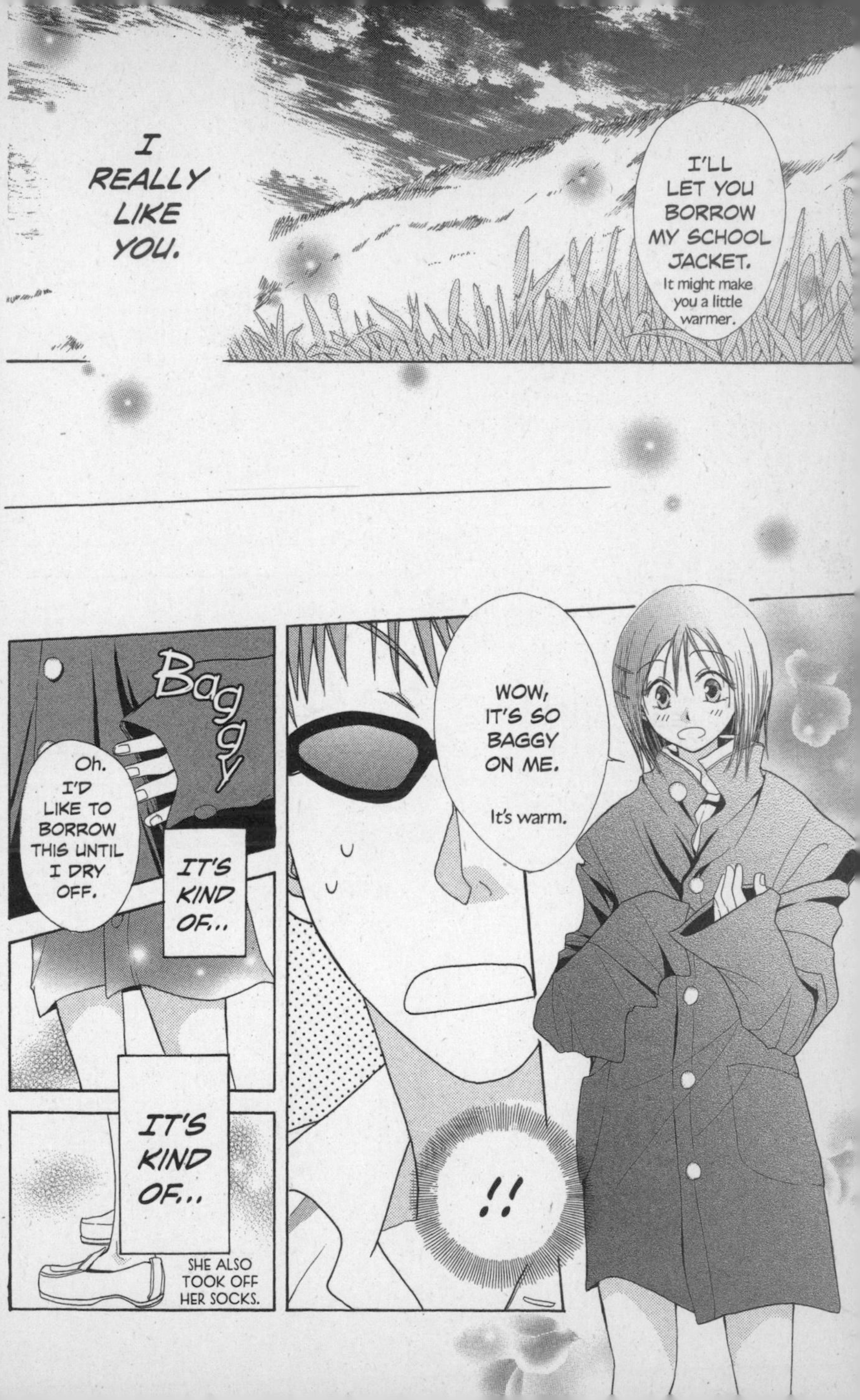
I'LL LET YOU BORROW MY SCHOOL JACKET.
It might make you a little warmer.
I REALLY LIKE YOU.
WOW, IT'S SO BAGGY ON ME.
It's warm.
!!
Baggy
Oh. I'D LIKE TO BORROW THIS UNTIL I DRY OFF.
IT'S KIND OF...
IT'S KIND OF...
SHE ALSO TOOK OFF HER SOCKS.

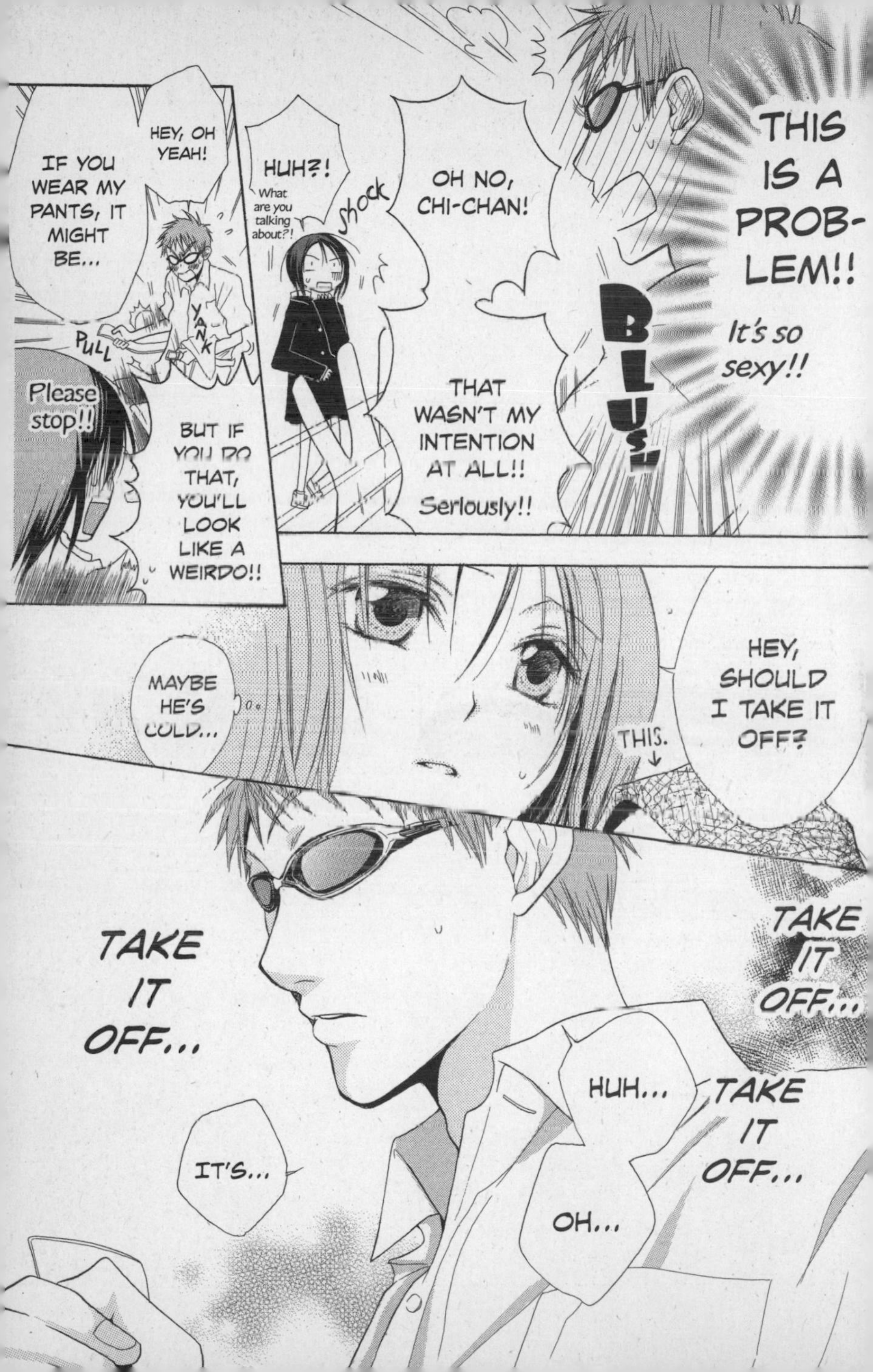
THIS IS A PROBLEM!!
It's so sexy!!
BLUSH
OH NO, CHI-CHAN!
THAT WASN'T MY INTENTION AT ALL!!
Seriously!!
HUH?!
What are you talking about?!
shock
HEY, OH YEAH!
IF YOU WEAR MY PANTS, IT MIGHT BE...
YANK
PULL
Please stop!!
BUT IF YOU DO THAT, YOU'LL LOOK LIKE A WEIRDO!!
HEY, SHOULD I TAKE IT OFF?
THIS.
MAYBE HE'S COLD...
TAKE IT OFF...
TAKE IT OFF...
HUH...
OH...
IT'S...
TAKE IT OFF...

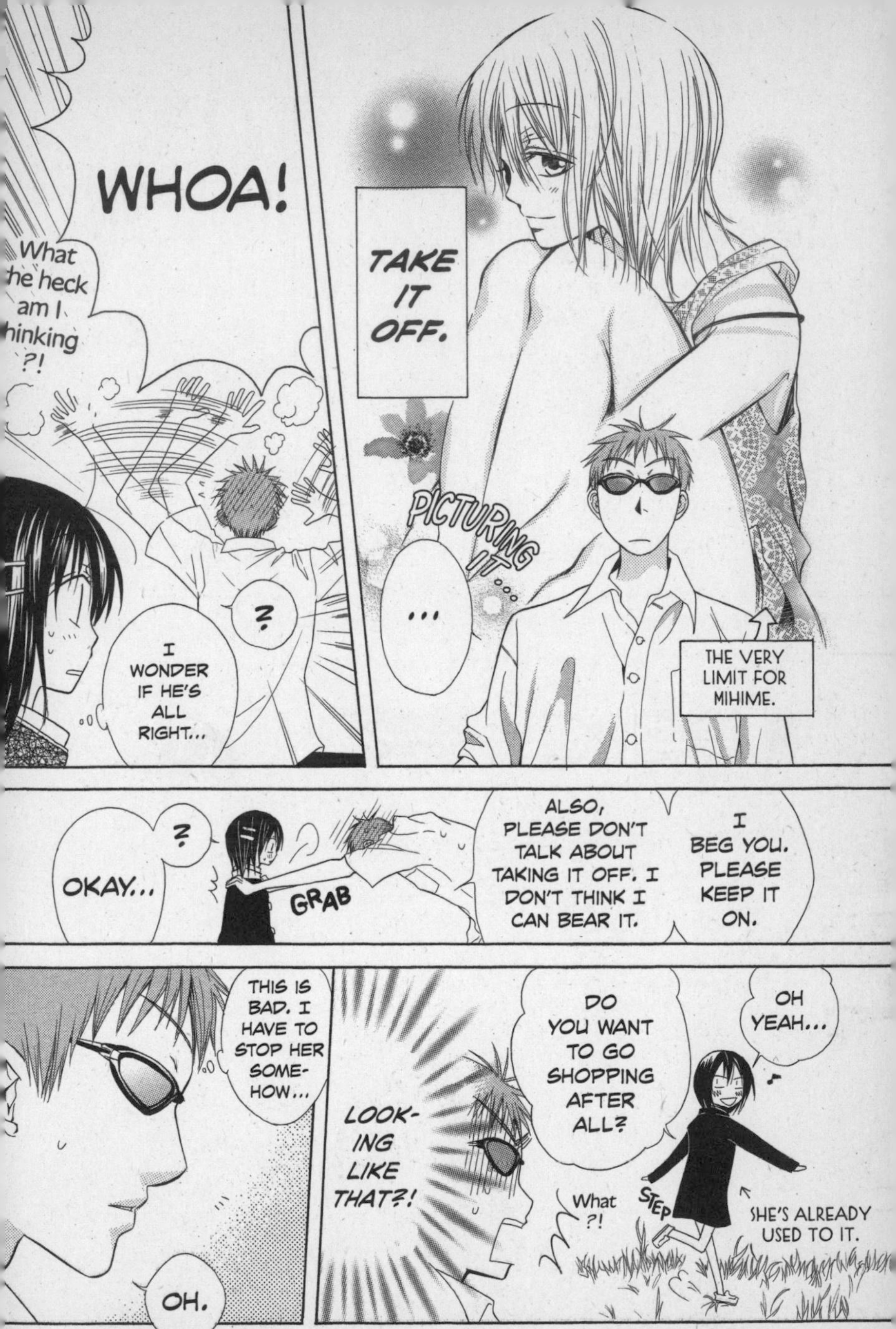
TAKE IT OFF.
PICTURING IT...
...
THE VERY LIMIT FOR MIHIME.
WHOA!
What he heck am I hinking ?!
?
I WONDER IF HE'S ALL RIGHT...
I BEG YOU. PLEASE KEEP IT ON.
ALSO, PLEASE DON'T TALK ABOUT TAKING IT OFF. I DON'T THINK I CAN BEAR IT.
GRAB
?
OKAY...
OH YEAH...
DO YOU WANT TO GO SHOPPING AFTER ALL?
SHE'S ALREADY USED TO IT.
STEP
What ?!
LOOKING LIKE THAT?!
THIS IS BAD. I HAVE TO STOP HER SOMEHOW...
OH.

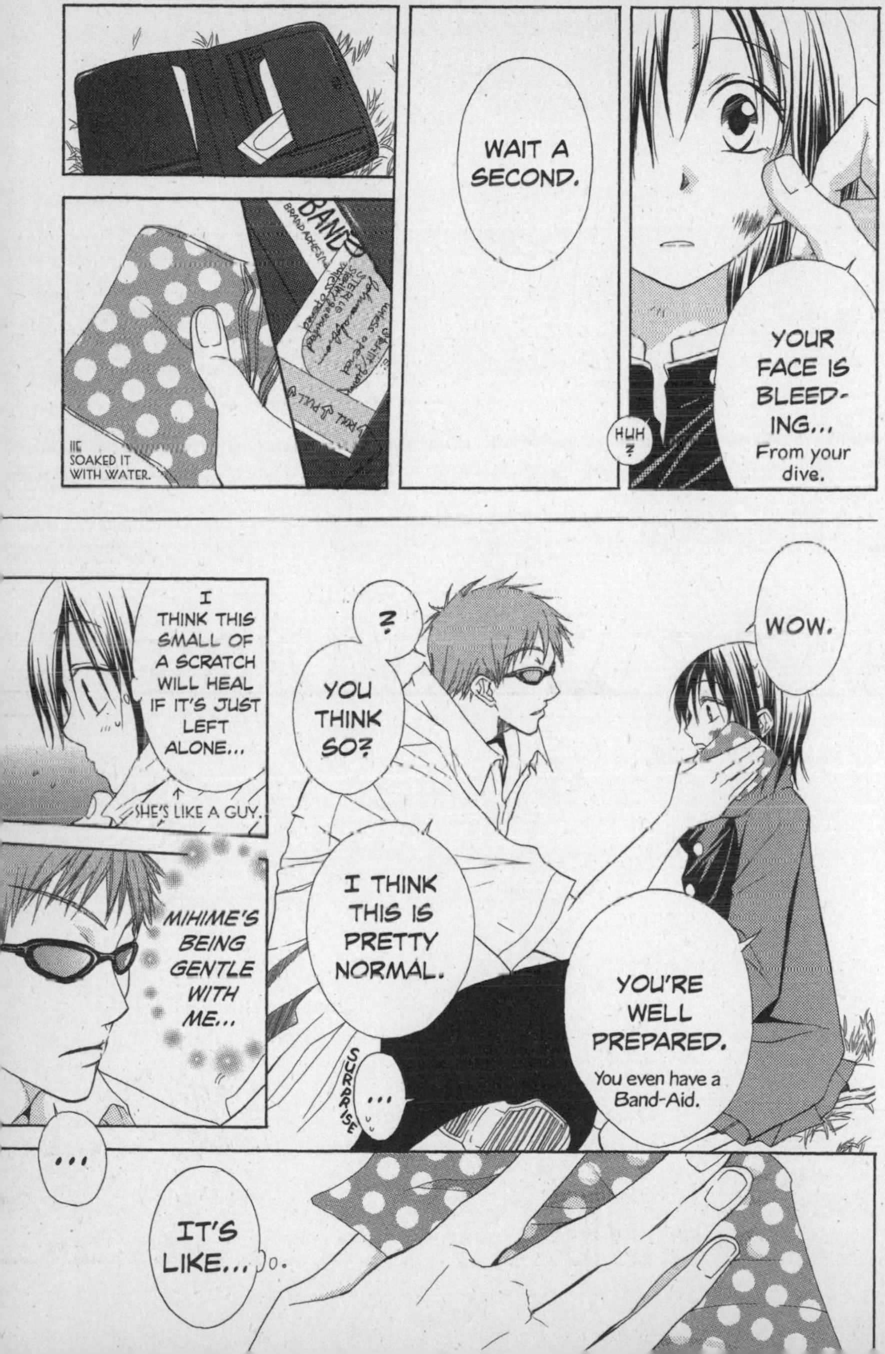
YOUR FACE IS BLEEDING... From your dive.
HUH?
WAIT A SECOND.
HE SOAKED IT WITH WATER.
WOW.
YOU'RE WELL PREPARED. You even have a Band-Aid.
?
YOU THINK SO?
I THINK THIS IS PRETTY NORMAL.
SURPRISE
...
I THINK THIS SMALL OF A SCRATCH WILL HEAL IF IT'S JUST LEFT ALONE...
SHE'S LIKE A GUY.
MIHIME'S BEING GENTLE WITH ME...
...
IT'S LIKE...

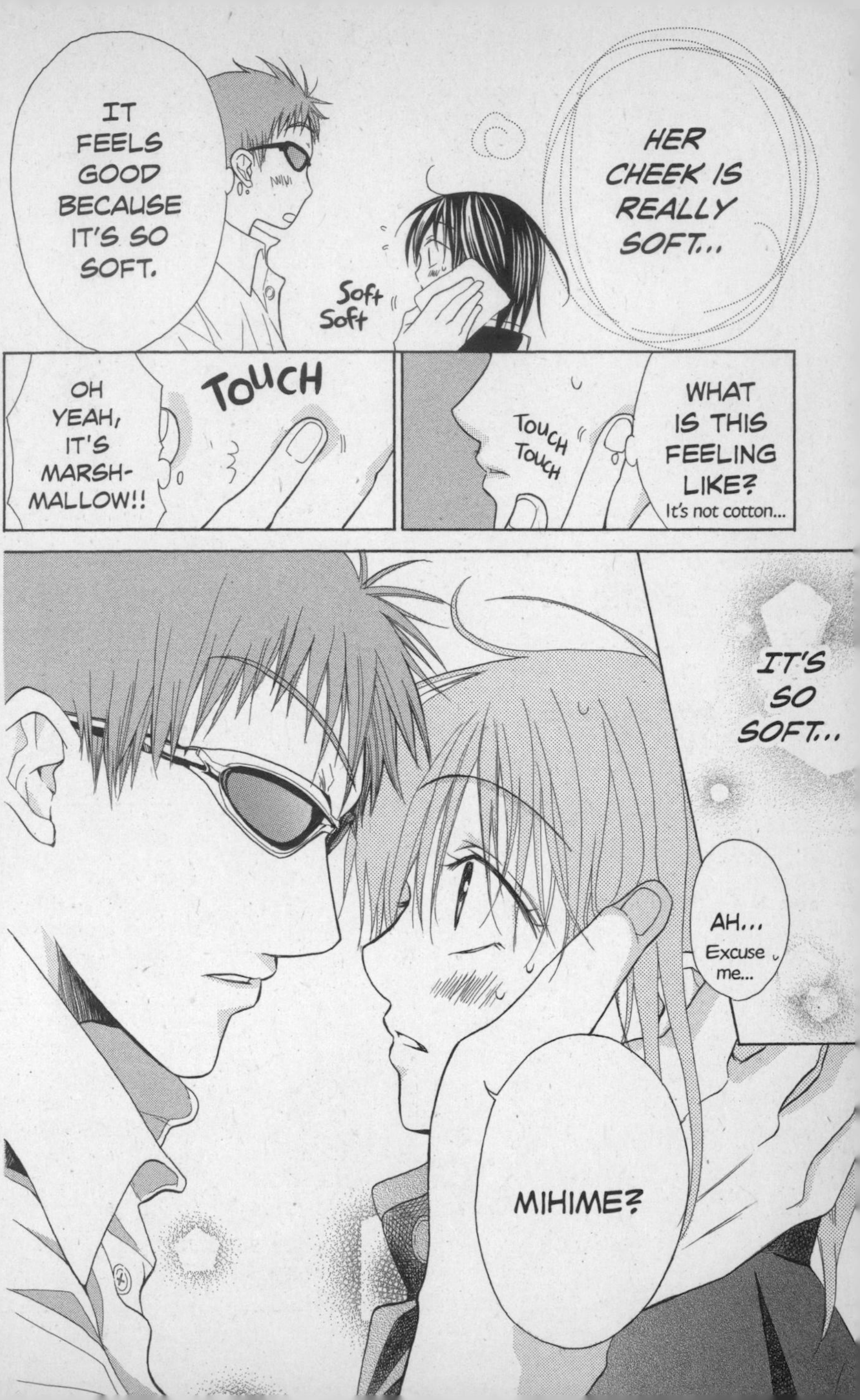
HER CHEEK IS REALLY SOFT...
IT FEELS GOOD BECAUSE IT'S SO SOFT.
Soft Soft
WHAT IS THIS FEELING LIKE? It's not cotton...
TOUCH TOUCH
TOUCH
OH YEAH, IT'S MARSH-MALLOW!!
IT'S SO SOFT...
AH... Excuse me...
MIHIME?

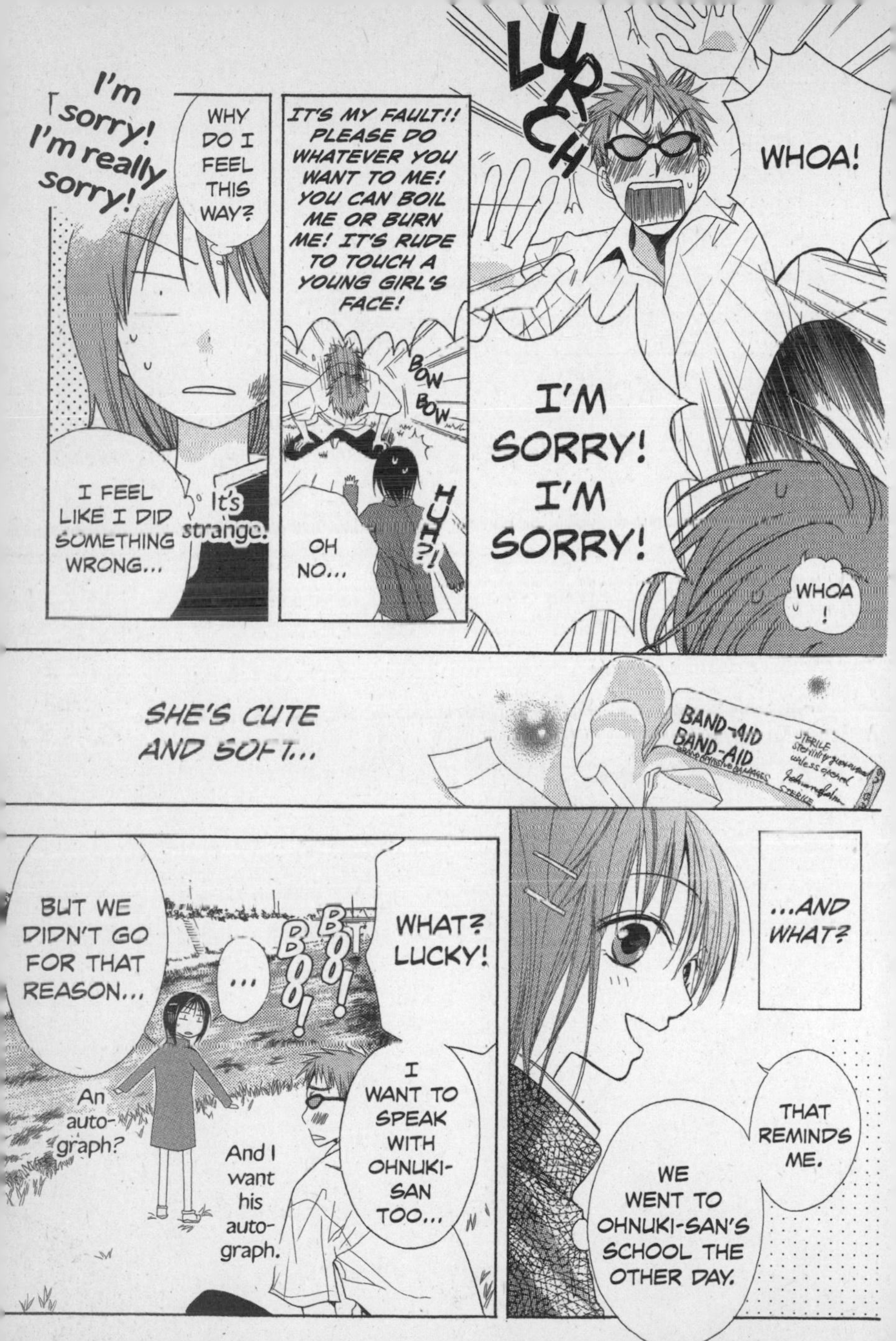
LURCH
WHOA!
I'M SORRY! I'M SORRY!
WHOA!
IT'S MY FAULT!! PLEASE DO WHATEVER YOU WANT TO ME! YOU CAN BOIL ME OR BURN ME! IT'S RUDE TO TOUCH A YOUNG GIRL'S FACE!
BOW BOW
HUH?!
OH NO...
WHY DO I FEEL THIS WAY?
I FEEL LIKE I DID SOMETHING WRONG...
It's strange.
I'm sorry! I'm really sorry!
BAND-AID
BAND-AID
SHE'S CUTE AND SOFT...
...AND WHAT?
THAT REMINDS ME.
WE WENT TO OHNUKI-SAN'S SCHOOL THE OTHER DAY.
WHAT? LUCKY!
I WANT TO SPEAK WITH OHNUKI-SAN TOO...
...
BUT WE DIDN'T GO FOR THAT REASON...
And I want his autograph.
An autograph?

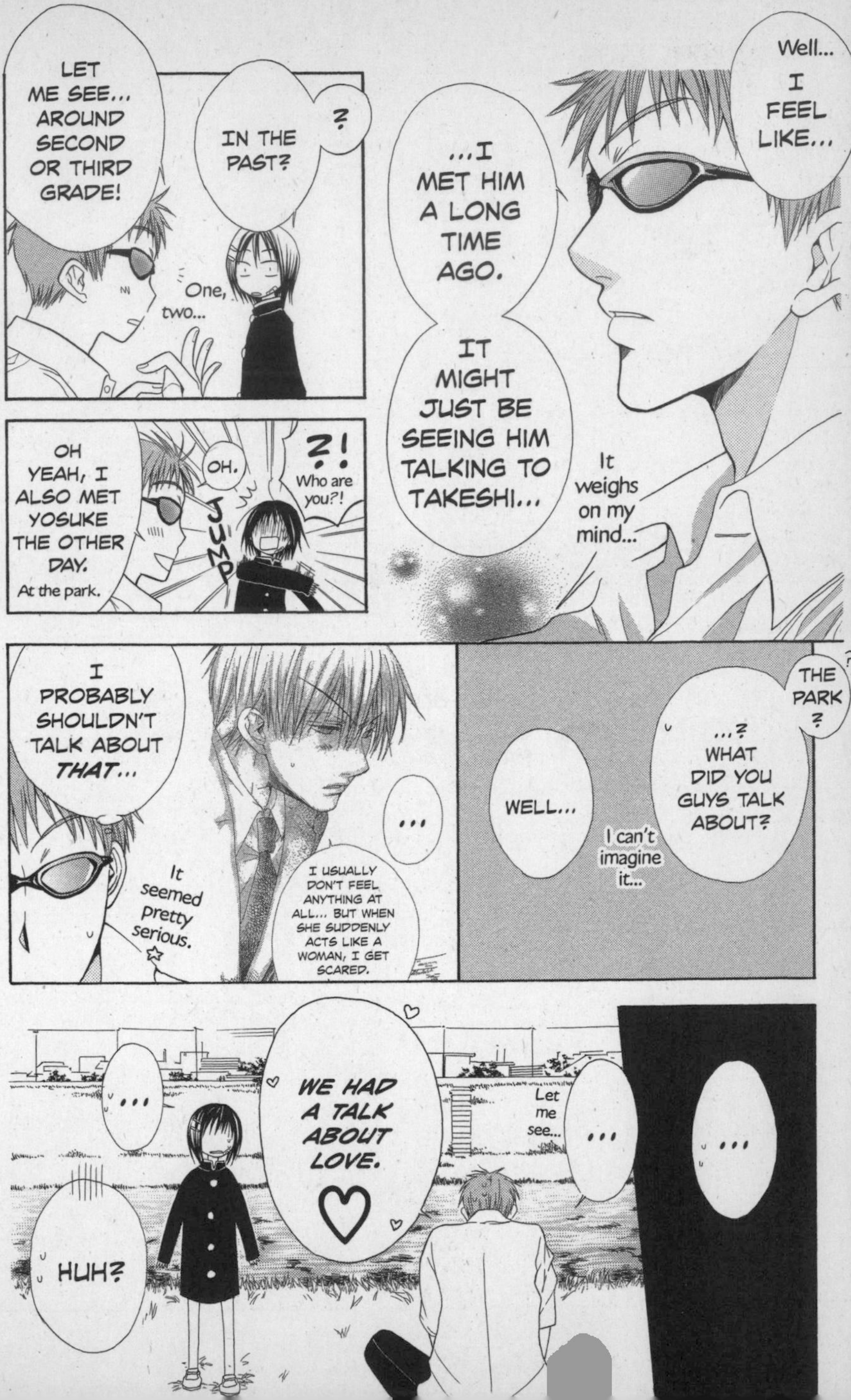
Well... I FEEL LIKE...
...I MET HIM A LONG TIME AGO.
IT MIGHT JUST BE SEEING HIM TALKING TO TAKESHI...
It weighs on my mind...
?
IN THE PAST?
LET ME SEE... AROUND SECOND OR THIRD GRADE!
One, two...
?!
Who are you?!
OH.
JUMP
OH YEAH, I ALSO MET YOSUKE THE OTHER DAY.
At the park.
?
THE PARK?
...? WHAT DID YOU GUYS TALK ABOUT?
I can't imagine it...
WELL...
...
I USUALLY DON'T FEEL ANYTHING AT ALL... BUT WHEN SHE SUDDENLY ACTS LIKE A WOMAN, I GET SCARED.
I PROBABLY SHOULDN'T TALK ABOUT *THAT*...
It seemed pretty serious.
...
...
Let me see...
WE HAD A TALK ABOUT LOVE.
...
HUH?

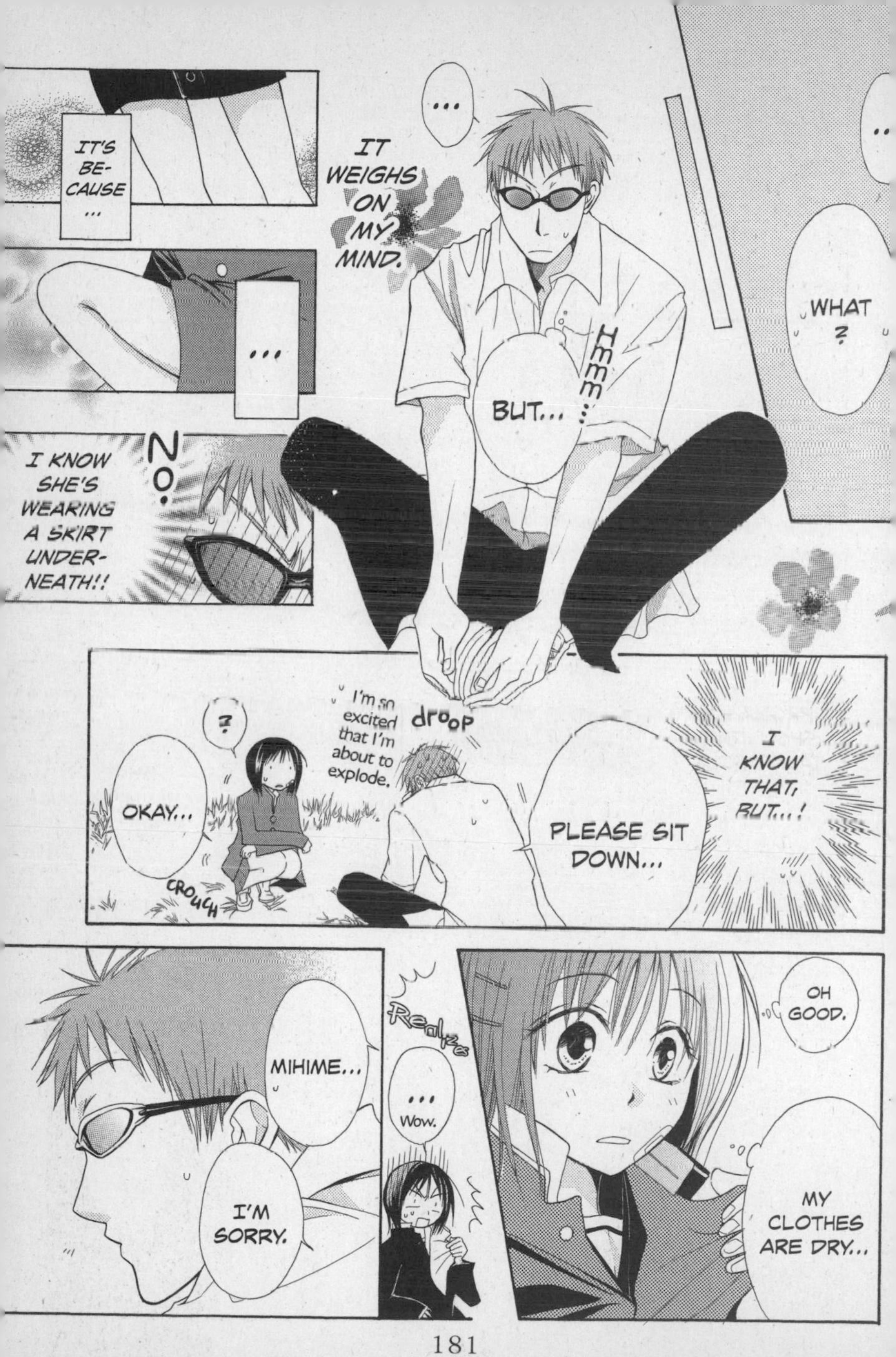
..
WHAT?
...
IT WEIGHS ON MY MIND.
BUT...
Hmmm...
IT'S BE-CAUSE ...
...
NO!
I KNOW SHE'S WEARING A SKIRT UNDER-NEATH!!
I KNOW THAT, BUT...!
PLEASE SIT DOWN...
droop
I'm so excited that I'm about to explode.
?
OKAY...
CROUCH
OH GOOD.
MY CLOTHES ARE DRY...
Realize
... Wow.
MIHIME...
I'M SORRY.

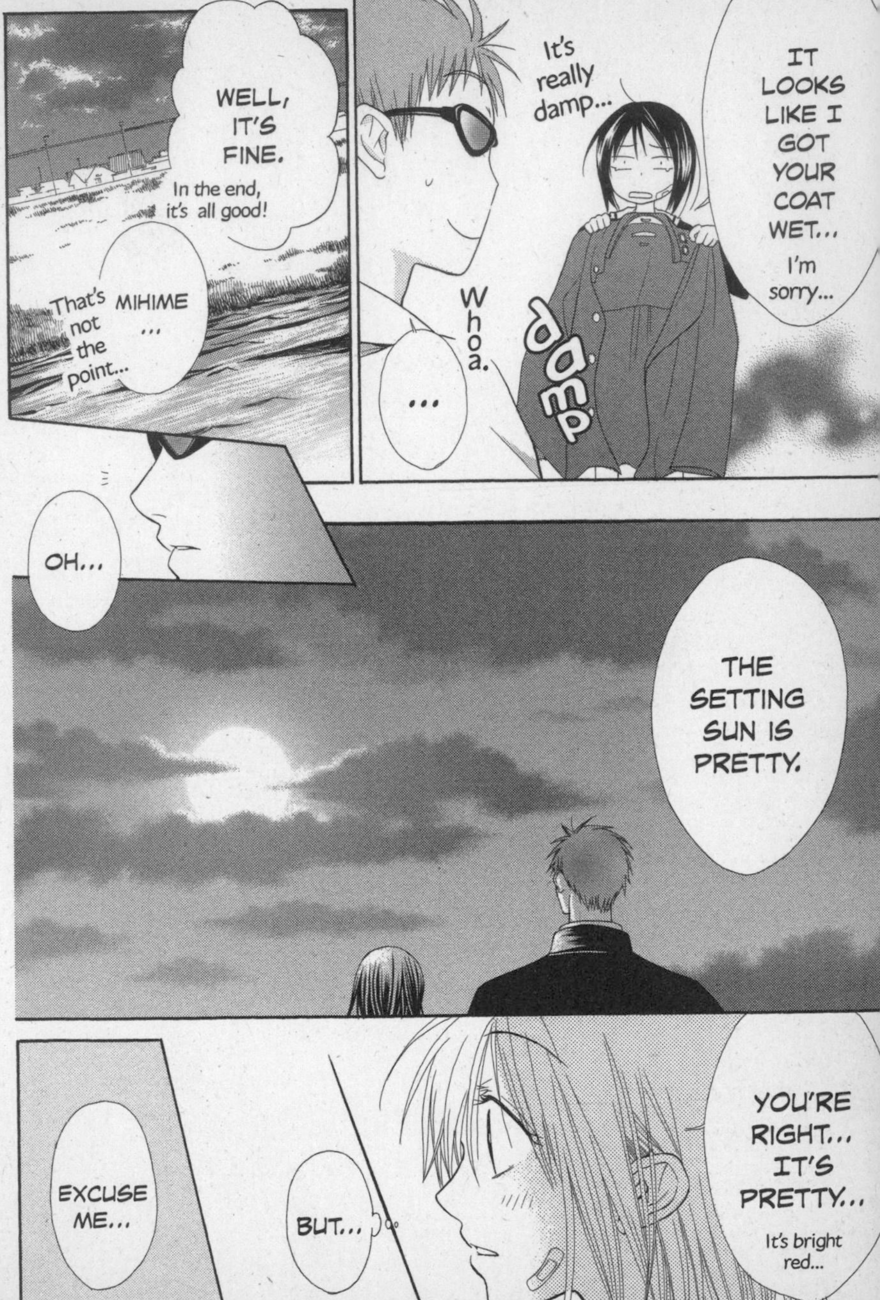
IT LOOKS LIKE I GOT YOUR COAT WET...
I'm sorry...
It's really damp...
DAMP
Whoa.
...
WELL, IT'S FINE.
In the end, it's all good!
MIHIME...
That's not the point...
OH...
THE SETTING SUN IS PRETTY.
YOU'RE RIGHT... IT'S PRETTY...
It's bright red...
BUT...
EXCUSE ME...

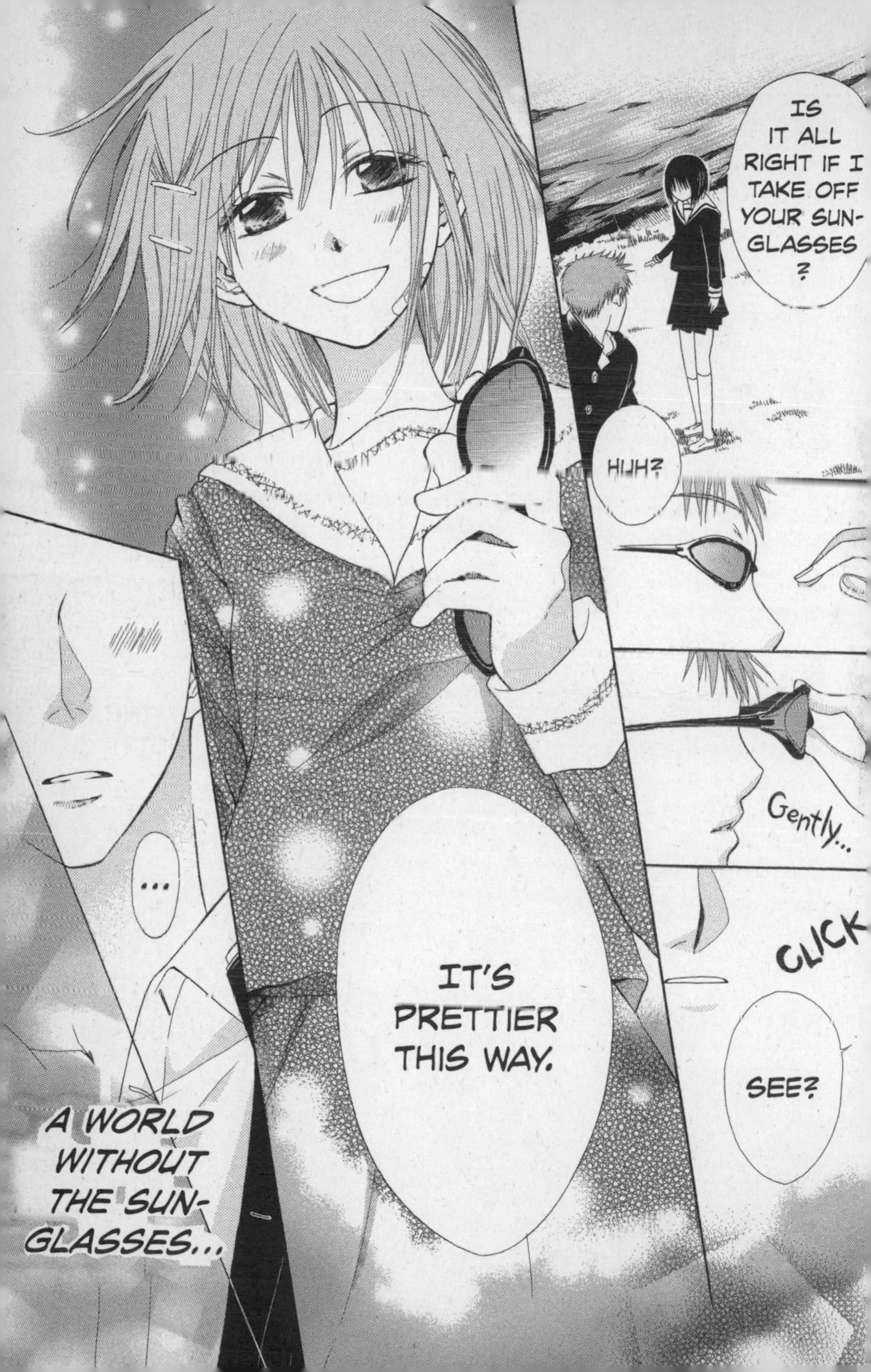
IS IT ALL RIGHT IF I TAKE OFF YOUR SUN-GLASSES?
HUH?
Gently...
CLICK
SEE?
IT'S PRETTIER THIS WAY.
...
A WORLD WITHOUT THE SUN-GLASSES...

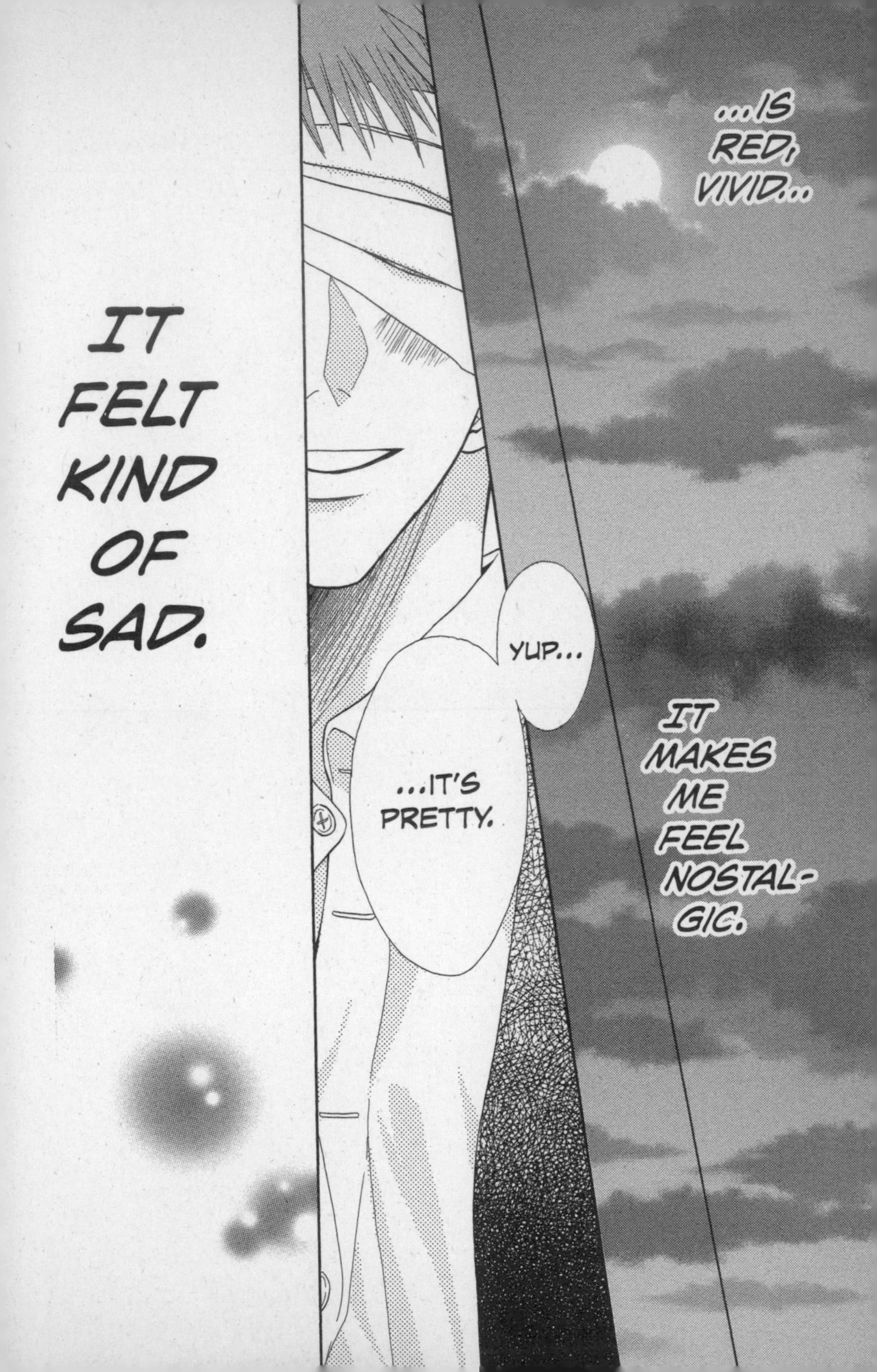
...IS RED, VIVID...
IT MAKES ME FEEL NOSTAL-GIC.
YUP...
...IT'S PRETTY.
IT FELT KIND OF SAD.

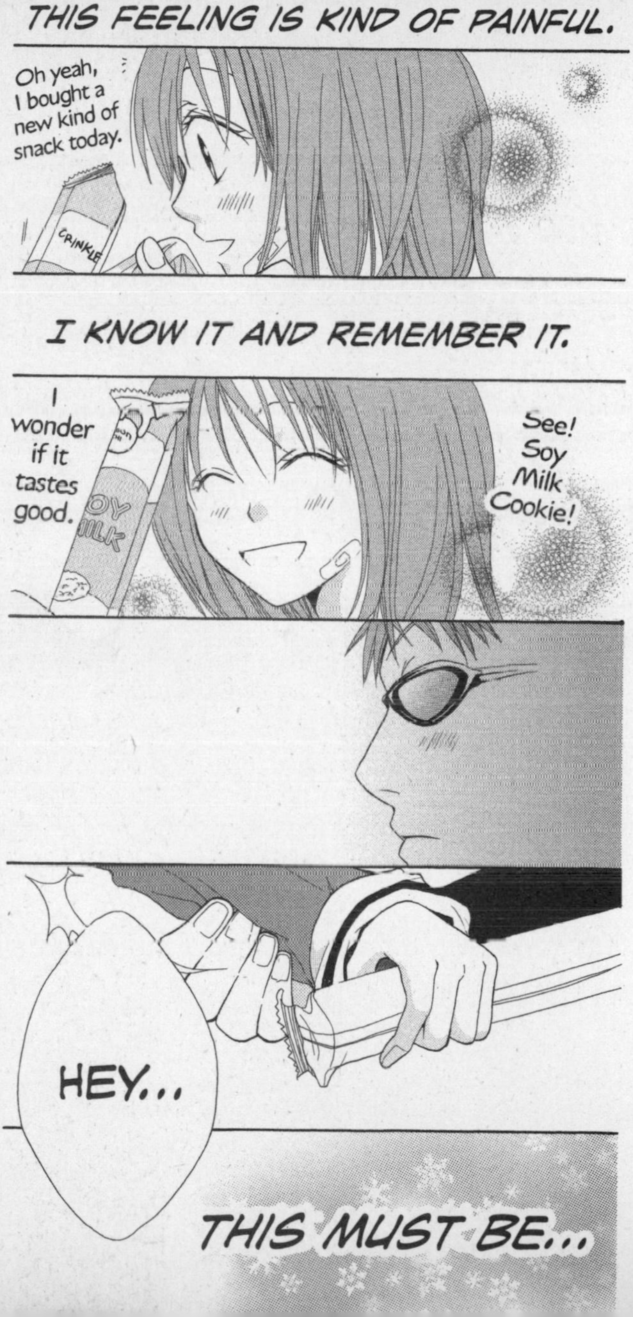
THIS FEELING IS KIND OF PAINFUL.
Oh yeah, I bought a new kind of snack today.
CRINKLE
I KNOW IT AND REMEMBER IT.
See! Soy Milk Cookie!
I wonder if it tastes good.
HEY...
THIS MUST BE...

Last

This is the last column in this volume. In volume 6, the story will center on a character that hasn't been that active recently.

A plot that has only appeared occasionally will finally see the light! I think. (Most likely...)

Now then, thank you for reading up to this point. It would be great if we could meet again in the next volume.

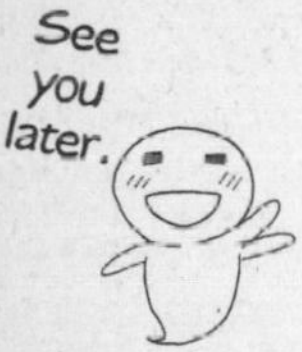
See you later.

I apologize for not being able to send replies back to the letters. I make sure to read each of the letters I get. I want to thank everybody for all of their support!!

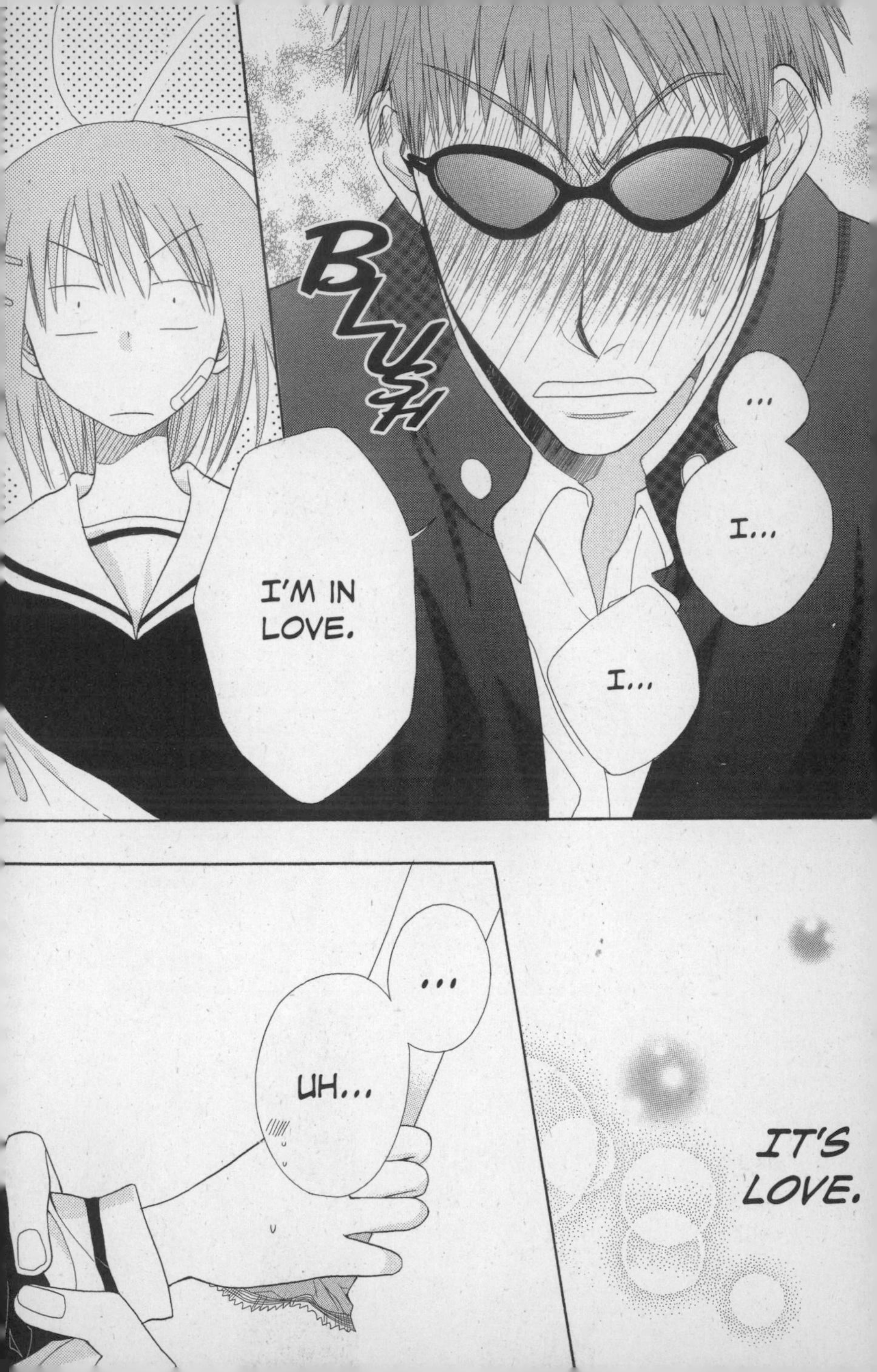
BLUSH
...
I...
I...
I'M IN LOVE.
IT'S LOVE.
...
UH...

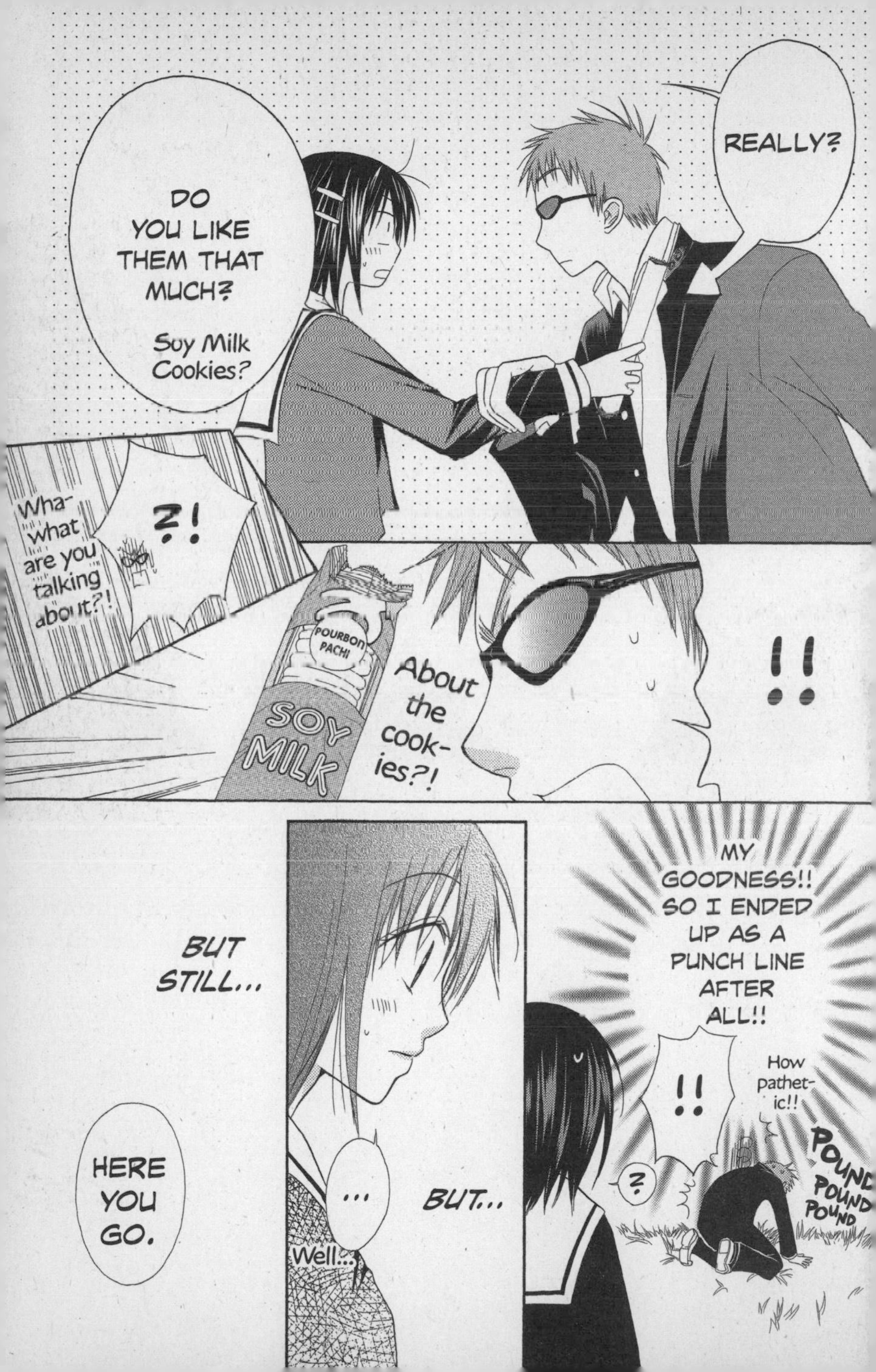
REALLY?
DO YOU LIKE THEM THAT MUCH?
Soy Milk Cookies?
!!
About the cook-ies?!
POURBON PACHI
SOY MILK
?!
Wha-what are you talking about?!
MY GOODNESS!! SO I ENDED UP AS A PUNCH LINE AFTER ALL!!
!!
?
How pathet-ic!!
POUND POUND POUND
BUT STILL...
...
BUT...
Well...
HERE YOU GO.

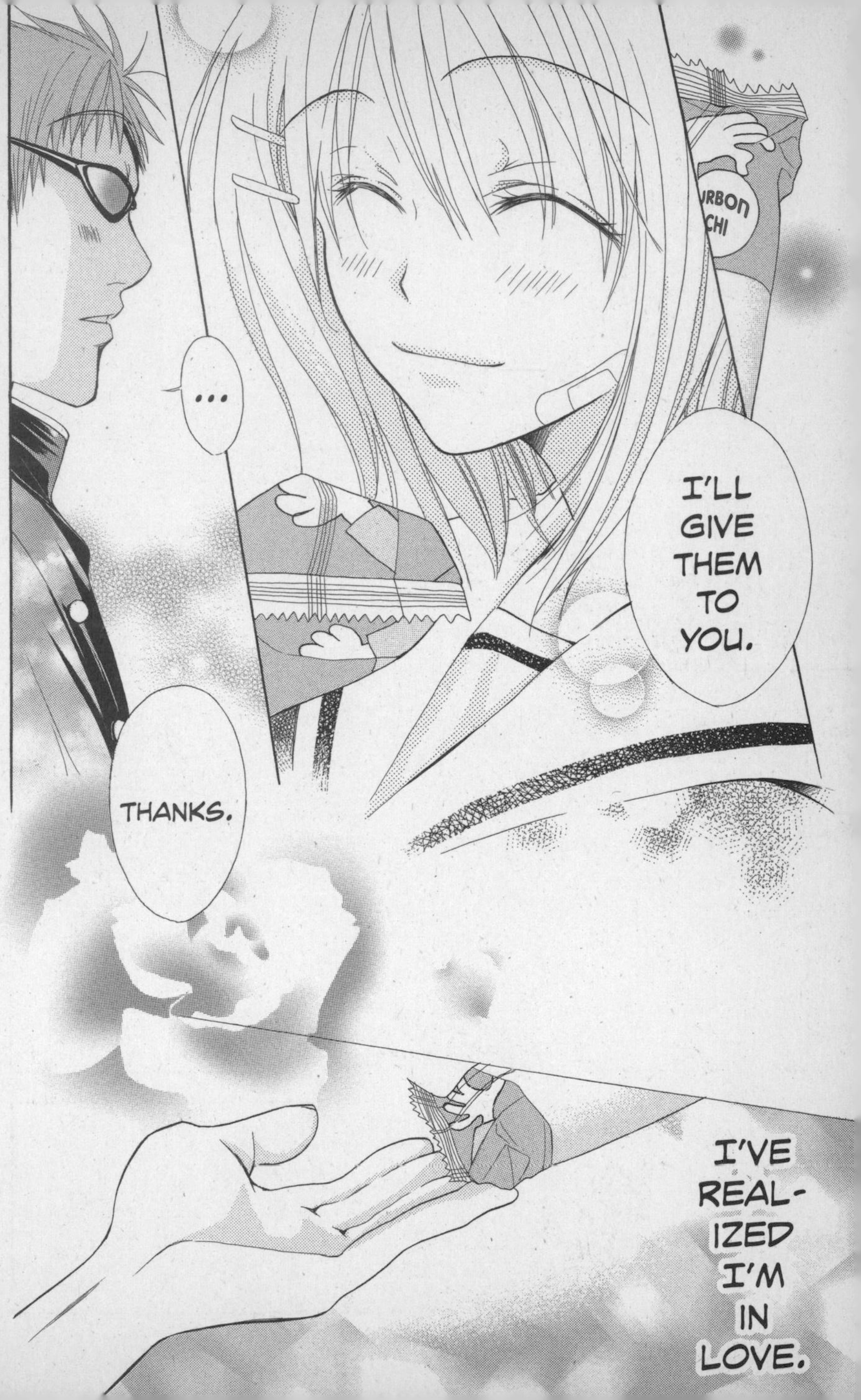
URBON
CHI
I'LL GIVE THEM TO YOU.
...
THANKS.
I'VE REALIZED I'M IN LOVE.

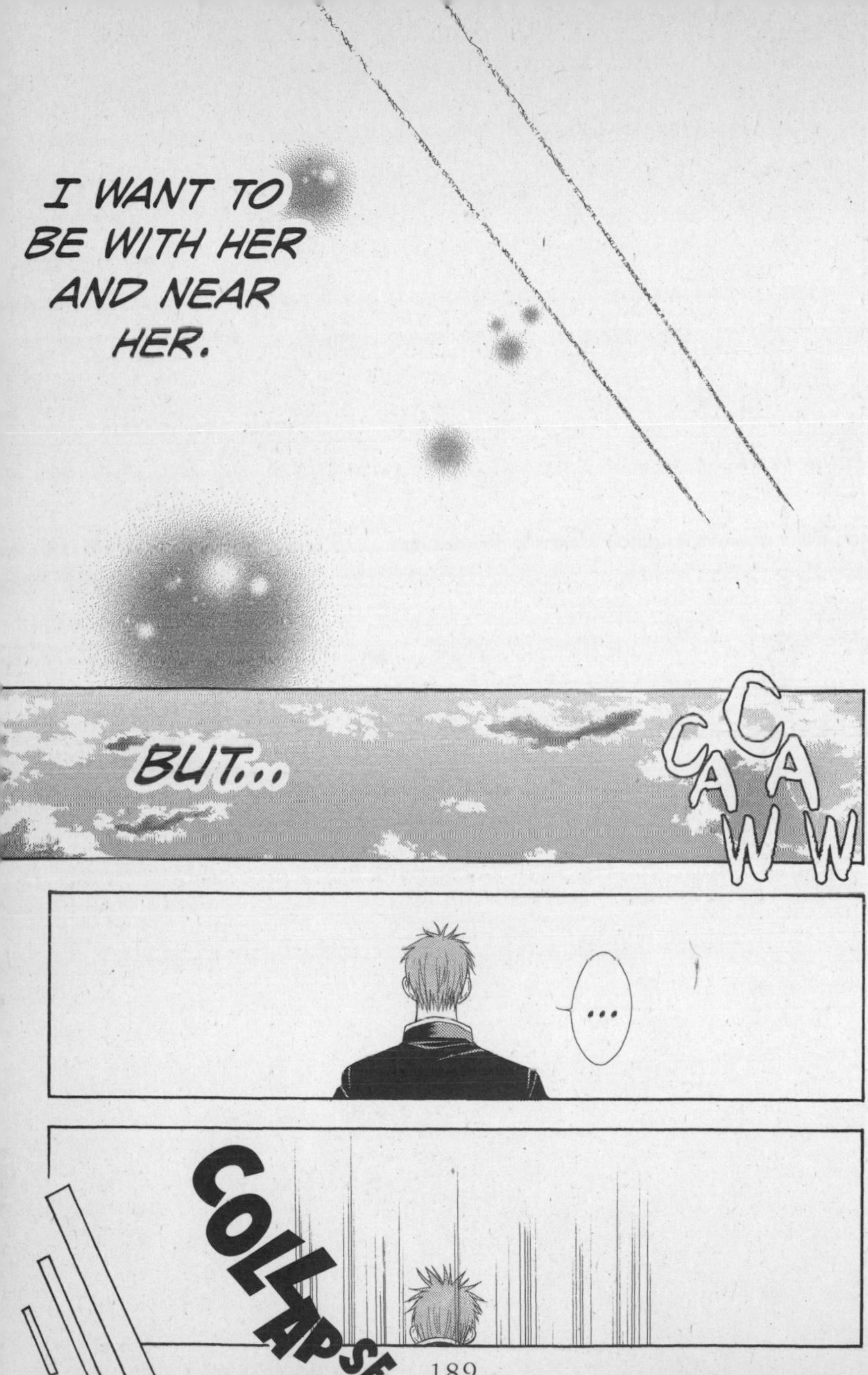
I WANT TO BE WITH HER AND NEAR HER.
CA CAWW
BUT...
...
COLLAPSE

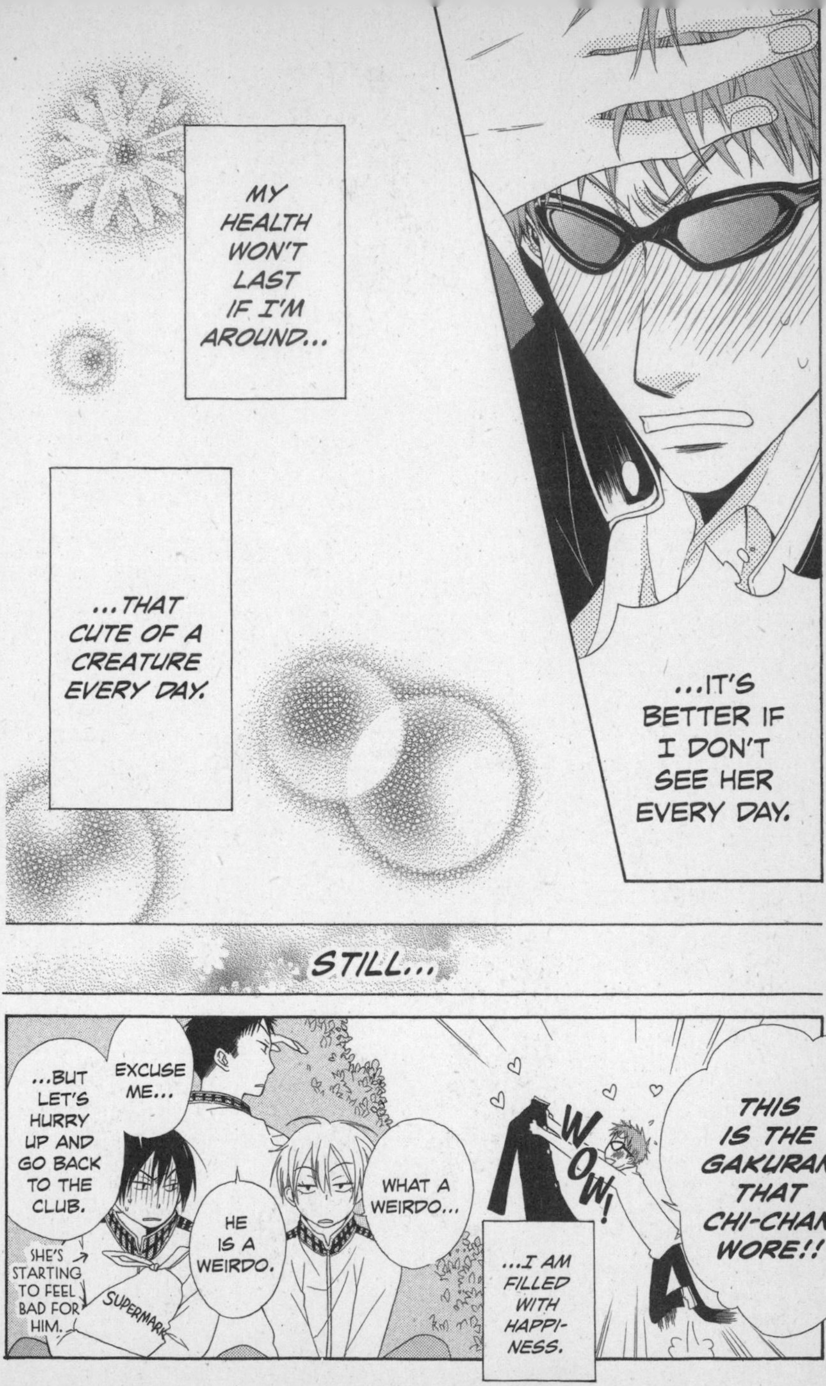
...IT'S BETTER IF I DON'T SEE HER EVERY DAY.
MY HEALTH WON'T LAST IF I'M AROUND...
...THAT CUTE OF A CREATURE EVERY DAY.
STILL...
THIS IS THE GAKURAN THAT CHI-CHAN WORE!!
WOW!
...I AM FILLED WITH HAPPI-NESS.
WHAT A WEIRDO...
HE IS A WEIRDO.
EXCUSE ME...
...BUT LET'S HURRY UP AND GO BACK TO THE CLUB.
SHE'S STARTING TO FEEL BAD FOR HIM.
SUPERMARK

The Magic Touch, Part 30 / End

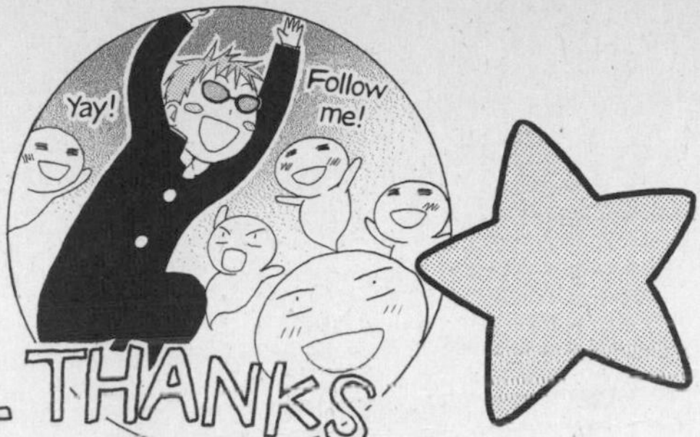
Follow me!
Yay!

SPECIAL THANKS

Younger Sister, My Family
Previous Editor (Thank you for all of your help from the beginning!!)
New Editor (Thank you for working hard with me.)
Dai Shiina
Kaname Hirama
Yuzuru Morinaga (I'm sorry that I'm always working until the deadline, and thanks so much!!)

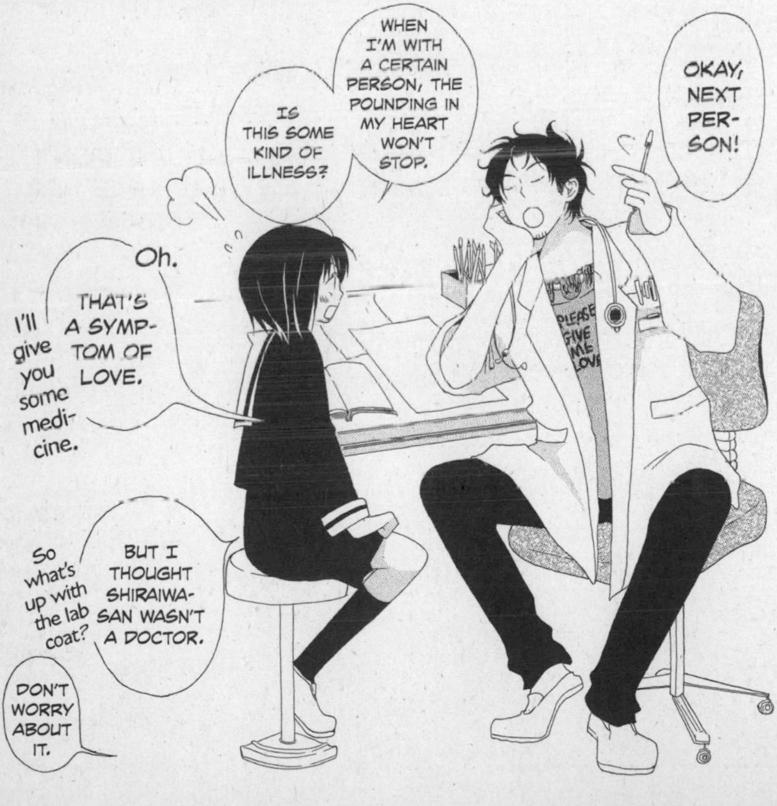
OKAY, NEXT PERSON!
WHEN I'M WITH A CERTAIN PERSON, THE POUNDING IN MY HEART WON'T STOP.
IS THIS SOME KIND OF ILLNESS?
Oh.
THAT'S A SYMPTOM OF LOVE.
I'll give you some medicine.
BUT I THOUGHT SHIRAIWA-SAN WASN'T A DOCTOR.
So what's up with the lab coat?
DON'T WORRY ABOUT IT.

Izumi Tsubaki began drawing manga in her first year of high school. She was soon selected to be in the top ten of *Hana to Yume*'s HMC (Hana to Yume Mangaka Course) and subsequently won *Hana to Yume*'s Big Challenge contest. Her debut title, *Chijimete Distance* (Shrink the Distance), ran in 2002 in *Hana to Yume* magazine, issue 17. In addition to *The Magic Touch* (originally published in Japan as *Oyayubi kara Romance*, or "Romance from the Thumbs"), she is currently working on the manga series *Oresama Teacher* (I'm the Teacher).

Tsubaki-sensei hails from Saitama Prefecture, her birthday is December 11, and she confesses that she enjoys receiving massages more than she enjoys giving them.

THE MAGIC TOUCH
Vol. 5
Shojo Beat Manga Edition

STORY AND ART BY
IZUMI TSUBAKI

English Adaptation/Lorelei Laird
Translator/Nori Minami
Touch-up Art & Lettering/Ben Costa
Design/Sean Lee
Editor/Eric Searleman

VP, Production/Alvin Lu
VP, Publishing Licensing/Rika Inouye
VP, Sales & Product Marketing/Gonzalo Ferreyra
VP, Creative/Linda Espinosa
Publisher/Hyoe Narita

Oyayubi kara Romance by Izumi Tsubaki © Izumi Tsubaki 2005
All rights reserved. First published in Japan in 2005 by HAKUSENSHA, Inc., Tokyo.
English language translation rights arranged with HAKUSENSHA, Inc., Tokyo.

Printed in Canada

Published by VIZ Media, LLC
P.O. Box 77010
San Francisco, CA 94107

10 9 8 7 6 5 4 3 2 1
First printing, December 2009

PARENTAL ADVISORY
THE MAGIC TOUCH is rated T+ for
Older Teen and is recommended
for ages 13 and up.
ratings.viz.com

www.viz.com

www.shojobeat.com

Wild Ones

アラクレ

By Kiyo Fujiwara

Wild Ones

アラクレ

Shojo Beat Manga

1

Kiyo Fujiwara

Only $8.⁹⁹

Sachie Wakamura just lost her mother, and her estranged grandfather has shown up to take care of her. The only problem is that Grandpa is the head of a yakuza gang!

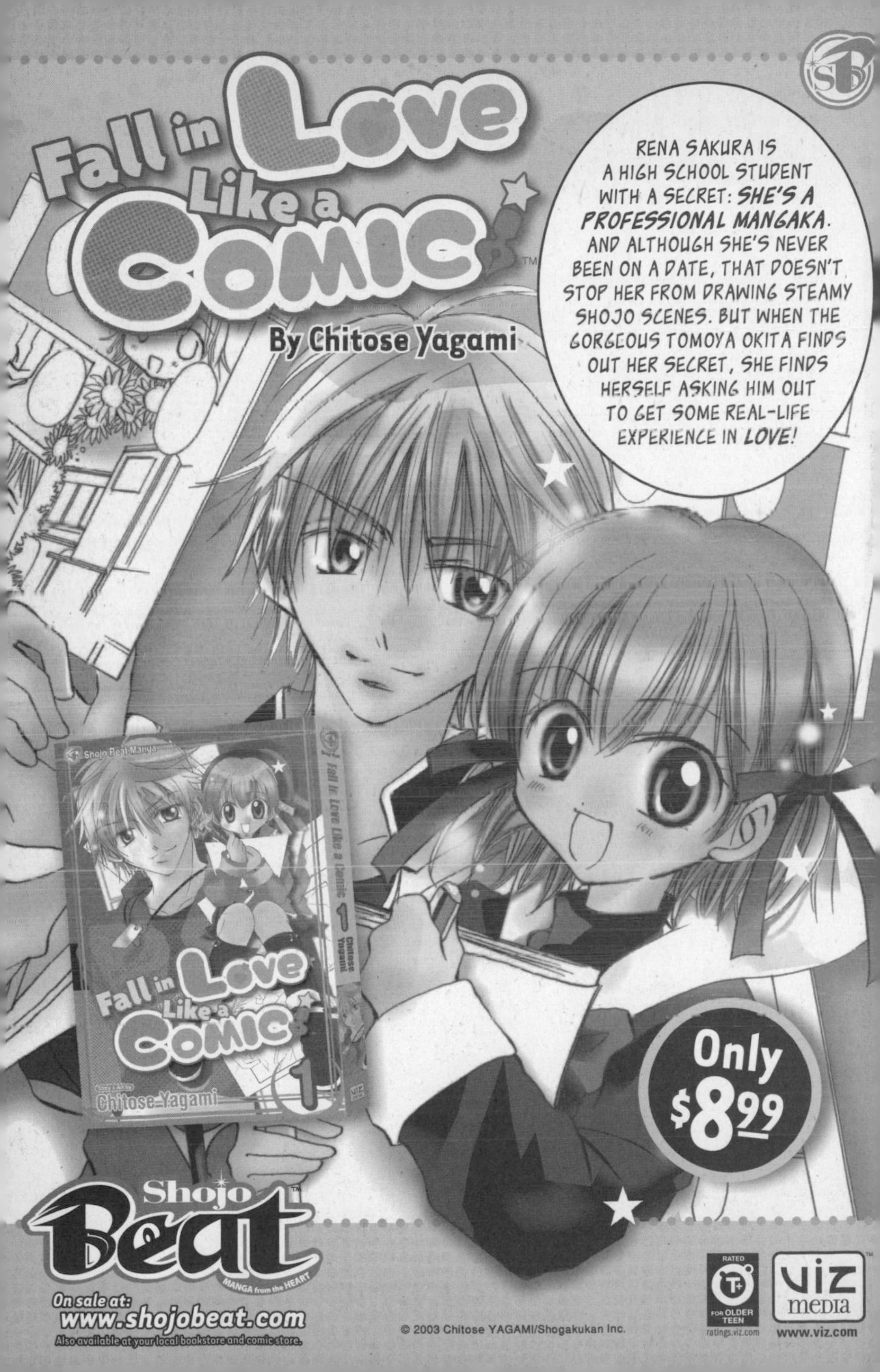

Fall in Love Like a Comic™
By Chitose Yagami
RENA SAKURA IS A HIGH SCHOOL STUDENT WITH A SECRET: SHE'S A PROFESSIONAL MANGAKA. AND ALTHOUGH SHE'S NEVER BEEN ON A DATE, THAT DOESN'T STOP HER FROM DRAWING STEAMY SHOJO SCENES. BUT WHEN THE GORGEOUS TOMOYA OKITA FINDS OUT HER SECRET, SHE FINDS HERSELF ASKING HIM OUT TO GET SOME REAL-LIFE EXPERIENCE IN LOVE!
Shojo Beat Manga
Fall in Love Like a Comic
1
Chitose Yagami
Only $8.99
Shojo Beat™
MANGA from the HEART
On sale at:
www.shojobeat.com
Also available at your local bookstore and comic store.
© 2003 Chitose YAGAMI/Shogakukan Inc.
RATED T+ FOR OLDER TEEN
ratings.viz.com
viz media
www.viz.com